The Hamble—River Britain's principal 'marina' estuary

(*Southern Newspapers Ltd.*)

Books are to be returned on or before
the last date below.

*Marinas and
Small Craft Harbours*

Marinas and Small Craft Harbours

Proceedings of a Symposium held at the University of Southampton on 19-21 April 1972

Edited by

N. B. Webber

University of Southampton

Southampton University Press

Printed in Great Britain by
Unwin Brothers Limited,
Old Woking, Surrey

Foreword

The past few years have witnessed what has been aptly described as 'an explosion of interest' in all forms of watersport, and especially in boating and sailing. More and more people have the desire and the means to spend part of their leisure time afloat—in our estuaries and off our coastline, as well as inland on our lakes, reservoirs and water-ways—and it seems inevitable that the trend will continue. This has created a demand for sheltered berthage and supporting facilities, which, in the more accessible and attractive areas, can only be met adequately by marina-type development.

In planning such a project, consideration needs to be given to a number of aspects, including location in the environment, civil engineering, architecture, operational requirements, and economic viability. It is, therefore, important that there should be mutual understanding and close co-operation between those representing the various interests.

This then was the aim of the Symposium (the first on this topic in Britain)—to provide the opportunity to discuss the recent experiences, current problems and future developments in the field of marinas and small craft harbours.

The response to the Symposium exceeded the most optimistic predictions of the organisers. More than 300 persons (the capacity of the lecture theatre) attended and these were fully representative of the wide cross-section of people with professional or recreational interest in the problems of boat harbours. It is also worthy of note that quite a large number came from distant places, including overseas.

The Symposium was conducted by way of formal presentation and discussion of papers in appropriate groupings, and the Rt. Hon. Eldon Griffiths, M.P., Joint Parliamentary Under-Secretary of State, Department of the Environment, with special responsibility for sport, honoured us by presenting the opening address. An exhibition of models, plans, photographs, etc., relevant to marinas was held concurrently. After the Symposium there was a visit, in excellent weather for the time of the year, to a number of marinas in the Solent area.

In view of the obvious need for information on the subject, the Proceedings have been edited in a way that is rather more detailed than usual. Also, some additional material has been included with the aim of providing a more balanced and useful reference work. Of course, there is much more that could and needs to be written, and no doubt will be in the years ahead. Already, indeed, there are further conferences in the offing.

Since the Symposium, the Government has announced its commitment to making the widest possible use of all our water space as an environmental and recreational asset. It is proposed, in particular, that the new Regional Water Authorities should be charged with the statutory responsibility of making the best possible amenity use of all the waters under their control, and it seems likely that there will also be appropriate provision for the estuaries and coastal waters. The Sports Council is certainly alive to the need for coastal yachting facilities and has initiated a working party to investigate this topic.

No-one knows the precise number and categories of leisure craft in Britain at the present time, but it is probably of the order of 100, 000 on our inland waterways with about four times as many again around our coasts. The annual growth rate is around 10 per cent per annum, and when one bears in mind that the first sizeable marina appeared on the scene less than 10 years ago and that there are now 60 or so in this category, one can appreciate the impressive developments that have taken place in the past few years. Nevertheless, there is still a tremendous potential—we have a very long way to go in this country to reach the 1 boat per 25 head of population which is reported in the United States, and yet here we have, for the most part, a more readily accessibility to boating waters.

If boating is to become popularised to the extent that now appears possible, then one conclusion that may be drawn from the Proceedings is that the greatest challenge which faces developers, designers and contractors is not just the creation of additional boating harbours—important though of course this is—but still more the provision of satisfactory berthing at an economical price, aided perhaps with a subsidy from government or local authority sources for the essential infra-structure, such as quays and breakwaters. The same qualities of ingenuity and resourcefulness, which already have achieved so much, will no doubt be brought to bear increasingly on this problem

Finally, I would like to express my appreciation to all those who have assisted with the planning and conduct of the Symposium and in the compilation of the Proceedings—to the National Yacht Harbour Association and G. Wimpey Laboratories Ltd., and in particular to Rear-Admiral P. D. Gick, Mr. D. P. Bertlin and Mr. N. H. Searle for their invaluable advice, encouragement and enthusiastic support—to the authors, contributors and exhibitors for providing such informative material—and, lastly, but not least to my colleagues, and especially to Mr. M. A. McSweeney, who have given so willingly of their time and effort in our endeavour to make this a worthwhile and successful venture.

Department of Civil Engineering,   N. B. WEBBER
University of Southampton,
December, 1972.

Contents

SESSION 6

Opening Address

by

The Rt. Hon. Eldon Griffiths, M.P.

(Under-Secretary of State for the Environment)

Rt. Hon. Eldon Griffiths, M.P., Under-Secretary of State for the Environment presenting the opening address

The Rt. Hon. Eldon Griffiths:

I am at one considerable disadvantage this morning. The only real experience of sailing that I have had is in a 12-metre. That was during the years I lived in the United States, when I was lucky enough to be asked frequently to go on a 12-metre in the New York regattas. Having done that, and having come back to the impecuniosities of British politics and, at best, to be able to go out only occasionally in a small dinghy, gives one a very grave sense of social inferiority. However, one member of this audience, who has something larger than a dinghy but smaller than a 12-metre, has on one or two occasions given me an opportunity to sample something from the middle.

I have been delighted to be invited to open this Symposium, for it is—at least, in this country—the first that there has ever been on this topic. I hope that it is the first of many which are to come. With you, I would offer my congratulations to the organisers for a constructive and imaginative approach to a subject which is clearly of growing importance but which is, nevertheless, fraught with its problems and frustrations.

I begin with a general proposition. Many countries are experiencing a leisure explosion. This can be measured in two ways: by quantity and by quality. Concerning the quantitative dimension, more people, with more money, more motor cars, and more time off from the office and the work bench, are turning to sport and to physical recreation during the course of a longer period of their lives than ever before. Consequently, the problem of numbers is with us.

There are several aspects of the increase in numbers. One is that children start playing highly organised and highly competitive sports much earlier. It does not surprise me, therefore, that the age of the champion swimmer is coming down to 16, 15, 13 or even 12. Before very long, they may well start swimming in the cradle.

At the other end of the spectrum, there is little doubt that our people feel younger longer. Consequently, they carry on in active physical recreation—whether that takes the form of golf, bowls or sailing—well into their sixties, seventies and beyond. Just as do the young at one end of the spectrum, so do the older people add to the numbers at the other end.

Then there is what I consider the fastest-growing sector of physical recreation of them all: something called middle-aged sport. I do not suppose, on the facts, that there have ever been so many men between the ages of 35 and 55 who get involved, one way or another, with racquets, fishing tackle, golf sticks, boats and the like as there are in Britain today.

On the question of numbers, the women are joining in, too. There was a time, not so long ago, when the last contact with organised sport which the average woman had was when she was 14 years old and was playing in her last school hockey game. Today, I know—and I suspect that you know this, too—that the whole country is jumping with ladies playing badminton or golf, or turning out at 'keep-fit' classes who, in many cases, can put their overweight husbands to shame.

Therefore, strictly in terms of numbers, people are starting younger and carrying on longer. The middle-aged are in there with the pack, and the women are joining in, too. That is the quantitative explosion in the demand for sport and recreation.

The other aspect is the qualitative change in the character of recreation. I discern a switch from watching to participating. There is a generally declining tendency in the numbers attending to watch cricket, horse racing or even—with the exception of the great gladiatorial encounters—anything less than top division football. There is a decline in spectator attendance, and there are many reasons for this. The move to the suburbs, the impact of television, the general availability of the motor-car—all are contributory factors. But, whatever may be the reasons, there is no doubt that this is accompanied by an upsurge which I might even call an outburst in those sports where the tendency is to 'do it yourself'.

Several areas in particular benefit from this switch to participation. One is in the realm of indoor sport—especially handball and racquet games like squash and badminton. There is pressure for facilities to enable busy people to play without interruption from weather or darkness, and at any time of the day or night. The second boom area is in the high-risk sports. By this, I mean the sports which enable people to obtain a sense of elemental elation from taking risks. Here, the remarkable increase is in such high-risk sports as sky diving, skiing, horse riding and mountaineering.

Above all, in assessing the qualitative change, there is water, for which I must admit a passion. One of the most encouraging trends of our times is the way in which the British people are turning to water for their recreation, which brings me squarely to the matter in hand.

I do not need to provide a conference of this kind with the evidence of what I say. Anyone who doubts the move to water sports needs only to look at the suburbs of any major British town. The dinghies and trailers on the lawns make many streets appear to be bristling with masts. Every Saturday morning, a twentieth-century Armada streams out of the towns onto the motorways in such a fashion that one of my colleagues has said that at times it becomes difficult to tell whether one is in the slow lane or in a sea lane. The evidence is there for all to see.

Statistics confirm this story. On an average summer week-end, there are now estimated to be perhaps twice as many people out and about in boats as attend all the professional football matches of an average winter week-end. That is a quite remarkable change. The boat building industry's turnover has risen from £57 million in 1969 to £72 million last year, and it is rising very sharply. Membership of the R.Y.A. has rocketed to over 1,500 clubs and 33,000 members. In the mid-1950s, 'Enterprise' dinghy sales totalled about 10,000 a year. They are now running at about 15,000. The number of 'Mirror' dinghies have risen by 75 per cent over the last two years.

The inevitable result of this is an intense and growing pressure on our water resources, both inland and coastal. The fishermen, the swimmers, the canoeists as well as the sailors are all competing, and sometimes fiercely, for the available water space. Where there is not enough in our inland waters to go around, it is inevitable—and I think that it is right—to turn more and more to what can be described as Britain's greatest national park—namely, the thousands of square miles of sea around our coasts.

What are we—both as a country and as a Government—to do about this? I wish to assure the conference that the Government are responsive. We recognise the demand. We accept that is it good and healthy that this should be so, and we want to help wherever we can. I have great satisfaction in saying those words on behalf of my colleagues and myself.

I hope that you will be aware of two important initiatives concerning inland water space. The first is that we are seeking to open up all reservoirs that are potentially capable of being used for water recreation either to the public or to clubs capable of managing them. When I came into my present post, I was disappointed to discover that, of some 500 or more reservoirs in this country, barely 80 were available for sailing. We expect to change that, and I am very glad that, as a result of some of the initiatives which we have been able to take, many more reservoirs will become available.

Secondly, and much more important, there is the new water policy. As a country, I am afraid we must get used to the fact that we can no longer take our water resources for granted. Water is simply too expensive to collect, transport and distribute to be wasted or to be polluted wantonly. It is, therefore, necessary for us to invest many hundreds of millions of pounds and to reorganise the whole of the water and sewerage industries in order to achieve sufficient water for our people to drink, achieve adequate drainage and sewerage and, above all, good river management. Those three factors—water supply, drainage and river management—constitute the first three dimensions of our new water policy.

For the first time, there now exists a fourth dimension. I was able to announce at the National Water Space Conference in London that we shall lay upon the new regional water authorities a statutory obligation—a legal requirement—that they must, wherever possible, open up and develop all their accessible water space for sport, recreation and amenity. That is new, and I believe that it is important. I believe that, with our policy on reservoirs, it ought greatly to add over the years to the opportunities available for water sports of all kinds—especially, perhaps, sailing—on our rivers, canals and estuaries as well as on our lakes, reservoirs and reclaimed gravel pits.

So much for our inland waters. What do we do about coastal waters? Here, too, we expect to be able to help the development of sailing and other water sports by improving the quality of our estuaries. Many of those present will have read that we intend to control dumping and pollution at sea more effectively and to open up for the benefit of leisure and recreation more of those areas of the coast previously held by the Armed Services or other national bodies.

Turning from some of the things which can be done by Government to the agenda of this conference, I realise that most of those in this large audience are experts in differing aspects of marina and leisure facilities. Therefore, it would be quite wrong of me—as a layman—to attempt to plot for you—the experts—the course which you know better than I. However, I would like to touch upon one or two aspects where our interests overlap.

First, I think we can expect a continuing, rising demand for the land-based facilities which must go with more sailing. Here I think in particular of trailer parks, club houses, berths and moorings and those facilities complementary to the sailing industry. The sailor on his boat is governed largely by natural forces and, in the absence of man-made facilities, he has to enjoy his sport where he can.

Usually, this means where the coast permits. In the past, the bays, the coves or the favourable beaches, together with harbours generally designed for commerical shipping, have met the needs of most recreational sailors. But they meet those needs no longer. In recent years, the pressure on water space and associated land facilities have created what I am bound to describe as an unacceptable situation. In particular, I am thinking of the most popular areas.

I noted with interest the recent statement of Mr. Gerald Smart of the Hampshire County Council that there were 22,000 boats in the Solent area and that 40 per cent might well be out on a fine Sunday. Further, there was an estimate on the only systematic prediction of boat requirements available that, in the Southampton and Portsmouth area, an increase in craft of some 13,000 was expected over a 20-year period.

Against that background, which I think one must welcome and encourage, there is no doubt that many sailors are complaining—and rightly complaining—of the lack of facilities. Where the demands are really acute, a number of marinas have already been built or are in varying stages of planning or construction. You will be discussing

Bradwell, with about 269 berths; Brighton's enormous investment which should produce about 2,000 berths and moorings; Cowes, with 300 or 400; Hamble, with 250; Windsor, and so on.

Clearly, more marinas are to come. I think that you will be interested to learn of the decision which my Department—specifically in the name of the Secretary of State—announced yesterday following an appeal by Poole Harbour Marina Limited against the Poole Borough Council on the development of a marina complex at Baiter Point in Poole.

It is always better to start with the bad news, and it is this. The Inspector reported, and I quote,

'In my opinion, this development would constitute an unacceptable intrusion into views of the harbour from the town quay and the Baiter area, and would have a seriously detrimental effect on the character of the coastal open space which is coming into being. I am not convinced that the spaces open to the public in the development would be an adequate compensation for the loss of the open area of coastline.'

That, in part, was the Inspector's conclusion after the public inquiry.

So much for what you may feel to be the bad news. This is the good news: the decision. The Inspector's conclusions are noted. It is clearly right that a hydrographic survey should be undertaken to establish whether the proposals can be carried out without detriment to Poole Harbour. But, subject to the results of that survey, the Secretary of State sees no sufficient reason to justify disagreement with the Local Authority's view that the site is suitable for a marina. Because of the urgent and growing need for more sailing facilities, he concludes that it would be in the public interest to establish a marina quickly, provided the survey shows the proposals to be acceptable.

I think that that is an important step on the part of my Department and the Secretary of State for the Environment. It is quite clear that, technically, we have rejected the appeal. We have said that, for the reason that a hydrographic survey still needs to be taken, the appeal must be dismissed and, subject only to the hydrographic survey proving to be successful, which all of you would wish, it is our view that, in the national interest and because of the rising demand for marina facilities, there is no reason why this should not go ahead on that proviso.

I have made the point arising from that decision that we here accept the need for more marina development. Demand is running ahead of supply. But, if I may, I want to urge all who will take part in this Symposium to give some thought to the types of users who will want to take advantage of the new marinas. Some will want quite lavish facilities, and can afford to pay for them. Others, of more limited means, have much simpler requirements. I feel that marinas ought to cater for all sections of water sportsmen. It would not be a good thing for marina development in the long run if smaller, light-craft sailors were to be squeezed out of enjoying their hobby and pastime by prohibitive marina tariffs. I hope that there will not be too many 'poor relations' in this—or, indeed, in any other sports. We want to see more marinas, but more marinas for all.

You know as well as I that the need for more sailing amenities will not be met overnight. The job is not an easy one, and facilities are sometimes very difficult to provide. I know, too, that many sailors tend to blame the local planning authorities for the dearth of present-day facilities. I have looked into this in some detail, and I must tell you that no absolute statistics are available to my Department which sufficiently identify marinas and provide the proportions of applications for consent which receive permission and which are refused. The statistics available are not sufficient either to refute or to substantiate the charges made against some local planning authorities.

While I do not say that the fault lies with the local planners, I would like to appeal to them to give extra consideration to marina proposals which are in danger of rejection. I think that planners would do well to realise that it is becoming progressively easier these days to devise solutions to some of the marina problems which, at first sight, look very daunting. Moreover, there is a danger that our European neighbours—from Scandinavia to Portugal, France, Spain and Italy—may be leaving us miles behind in the number and quality of the marinas which they have to offer. These countries, with far less of a maritime tradition than Britain, and with generally fewer boats, have proved in many respects more responsive to the sailing public's demand than we have. They have also shown, in the process, a much better judgment of the commercial possibilities.

In our country, I am pleased to see that a great wealth of knowledge and expertise is being rapidly built up. I think that this Symposium should do much to expand and to disseminate that technical knowledge. The main themes which you will wish to discuss—those of technicalities and finance—will take into consideration the working parties which have been set up by the Sports Council.

All that I wish to say is that we in Government appreciate the rising demand for water sports prevailing around our coasts. We wish you well, and I personally look forward to reading the record of all your deliberations during this Symposium.

Session 1

Chairman: **Prof. P. B. Morice**
*(Department of Civil Engineering,
University of Southampton)*

Requirements of the Yachtsman

J. R. Bryans

Royal Yachting Association

1 Potential Uses of Marinas

There are basically two types of yachtsmen who are potential users of marinas. The first is the 'resident', whose permanent base is the marina. The second is the visitor who may come from anywhere, heralded or unheralded.

Dinghy owners could be described as potential users of a marina, and if provision is going to be made for them, then it must be comprehensive, including facilities for launching and slipping, washing down and parking.

The requirements of the resident yachtsmen can, I think, be taken to cover those of all other categories.

2 Physical Needs

2.1 Shelter

The yachtsman's first requirement is shelter. He must have shelter from wind and sea and from swell and the wash of passing craft. Wave effects on moored vessels have been studied in the United Kingdom and the United States. Accordingly, the marina should be sited on the weather side of a river or harbour and upstream or clear of most of the traffic. Preferably, there should be a substantial area of land behind it, and the higher the better.

2.2 Depth of Water

This should be such that the types of yachts which are going to be moored in the marina can have access and will float freely at all states of the tide. A depth of 2·5 to 3·0 metres (8 to 10 ft) at low water springs should suffice in most cases. Arrangements must be made for periodic dredging to maintain this.

2.3 Bollards

Securing points on the marina pontoons must be substantial and of as great a diameter as possible to save sharp turns and wear and tear on owner's warps. This is a very important point, particularly as yachts are apt to be left for considerable periods without their owners' attention.

2.4 Manoeuvring

Manoeuvring room is an essential requirement and this should be provided at all states of the tide. While it may be desirable to get as many boats as possible into a small space, it ceases to be economic when access to and egress from the berths constitute collision risks. There should be adequate room between each leg of a marina for two boats of the size moored there to pass.

2.5 Fuel

Provision should be made somewhere in the marina or at a nearby yard for all types of yacht engine fuels, lubricants and calor gas to be supplied.

2.6 Water and Electricity

It is a 'must' that both drinking water and electricity be made available to every berth on the marina. The water supply should be at a pressure adequate for washing down. It should be laid on in such a way that it can be readily drained, in the event of frost, and switched off from the main.

Electricity must be supplied with sufficient power on each leg to supply all the boats' demands on that leg. Where large craft are moored, this demand can be very considerable. Where electric cooking is used, 8 kilowatts is not exceptional for one yacht in cold weather.

2.7 Access from the Shore

The marina user must not only have access to the shore; he must have ready access by road from the shore to the marina. Allied to this requirement, there must of course, be adequate parking facilities for cars.

3 Amenity and Discipline

3.1 Security

Security should be provided by the employment of a Dock Master and staff. These people should be ever watchful over what is going on in the marina. They should receive visitors, help to moor their yachts, and keep an eye on them while the owners are away. They should be prepared to convey telephone messages and telegrams and to deliver letters. Telephones should be provided ashore for the marina user.

Arrangements should be made with the local police to patrol the marina during hours of darkness.

3.2 Refuse

Adequate provision should be made for the deposit of refuse and for its collection. This must be done on a scale to cater for the marina at its maximum activity.

3.3 Ablutions and Toilets

Wash basins, showers and lavatories must be provided ashore, and this is particularly important where the smaller boats are concerned. It is true that in a river which has a good ebb and flow of tide there is no reason why the yachts' lavatories should not be used. In a locality where the effect of the tide is inadequate to contain the dangers of pollution, the management must be prepared to provide sewage disposal arrangements. This, of course, necessitates the marina users having suitable lavatories for this purpose. Otherwise, the yachtsman will have to go ashore.

3.4 Children

It is inevitable that boats using a marina should, from time to time, carry children. When the surfaces of pontoons are wet, or when they are icy, or covered with snow, it is the easiest thing in the world to slip. If a child, or even an adult, falls in there must be easy provision for him, or her, to hold onto something and to get up safely out of the water. I hold that any management that fails to provide this facility adequately, is guilty of negligence.

3.5 Noise

Noise is a deterrent to health. This is a well-known medical fact.

In many cases, a yacht is the equivalent of a week-end cottage to her owner. Accordingly, when a lot of week-end cottages find themselves cheek by jowl in a marina, noise abatement becomes a very important requirement. Any marina management must have strictly enforced rules to ensure that people living in their yachts can do so in peace and quiet. It is one thing to have one's friends on board for a drink. It is another to sit in the cockpit and allow raucous laughter to be heard all over the marina. Radios must only be used down below and at such a volume that they cannot be heard outside. Two-way wireless sets and loud hailers must not be used in the marina, except in real emergency.

Last, but by no means least, owners of yachts with masts must be taught and compelled to frap their halliards so that they do not make a noise. Generally, it is only the ignorant few who commit this offence.

Nevertheless, it is sufficient to keep yacht owners and their families awake all night. It is a real menace and must be tackled.

4 Reliability

4.1 *Financial Stability*

It would, I think, be natural to assume that a yachtsman, who is going to depend on the use of a marina for any length of time, would wish to be satisfied that its promoters and management are reputable people, and that they have put up a scheme which has been vetted by competent firms of accountants and lawyers. They should have directors whose names are such that everybody would know that the set-up is going to be viable. It would also be helpful if a yachtsman knew that he could approach one or more of the directors of the marina company, nominated for the purpose, should he have any grievances to air. This is a nice way of doing things and could save a lot of trouble.

4.2 *Security of Tenure*

Arising out of the last heading, and my earlier references to management responsibilities, there should be well advertised rules for the marina, and for all those using it, properly drawn up and capable of enforcement. There should be provision for continuity in the event of the death of major or controlling shareholders. One must not lose sight of the fact that regular residents in a marina have probably given up good moorings elsewhere and, having done that, they cannot afford to lose their berth in a marina. To get other moorings could take several years, for they would start at the bottom of the queue.

5 Provisioning

Going outside the limits of the marina itself, a yachtsman will, of course, expect to be able to reach a shopping centre. If he cannot, this is going to be a real problem for the marina promoter. He is going to be tempted to put up additional buildings in order to provide what the yachtsman wants. He is going to be up against planning permission and all the rest of the red tape. Furthermore, he is going to have to find more money to spend and, in turn, this could make it more expensive for the user of the marina. Accordingly, it is desirable that a marina be sited within reasonable distance from shopping centres so that their customers use the local facilities available and thereby create good will and business in the locality.

6 The Harbour Master

On the assumption that the over-riding local authority is the Harbour Board, it must be in the interests of the yachtsman that the Board appreciates his overall requirements, and takes them fully into consideration before authorising a yacht harbour or marina project.

The Harbour Board, in addition to ensuring it receives adequate remuneration, must take into consideration traffic flow, traffic density, disturbance of traffic flow by yachts crossing the main channel, the yacht mooring situation and waiting list and any effect a concentration of yachts may have on it.

It must always be hoped that the Harbour Master is known by and a friend to all yachtsmen.

7 Conclusions

I hope that in the foregoing I have touched on the main features which a conscientious yachtsman will look for before he is prepared to commit himself to using a marina for any length of time. These main points cover location and physical limitations, services, access, security, hygiene, safety, noise and financial stability.

If I have left out anything important, I feel sure that it will be brought to light during the Symposium. In this respect, I hope that it will be remembered that it is the yachtsman who is doing all the paying. Not only has he bought, or built, his yacht, but he is providing employment and bringing business to the promoters of marinas, designers, construction engineers, dredgers, marine architects and planners. Accordingly, we have a very good case for stating what we want. At the same time, I think we ought to be grateful for the opportunity of saying it, even very briefly, in the presence of these various experts, who, I feel sure, will meet our needs.

The Marina—in the Sailing Scene—and the Environment

D. H. E. Hockley

Deputy County Planning Officer, Hampshire County Council

1 Introduction

As I commence this paper I am sitting in a room overlooking the Solent in late September. The weather is fine and there is a light breeze between force 3 and 4. The shoreline of the Isle of Wight is visible and along that shore is a line of yachts from Gurnard to Bembridge, some sailing for pleasure and some racing.

Nearer to me, the Hamble River Sailing Club have just rounded Cutter Buoy in their Saturday afternoon race – a really mixed lot of dinghies and large craft ranging from Mirrors and Fireballs, Wayfarers and Merlins to Folkboats and Flying Dutchmen.

In mid-Solent, the international offshore powerboat boys have just been exercising themselves and their powerful craft around a collection of very large and luxurious anchored cruisers.

The island ferries, hovercraft and hydrofoil are busy, so are the fishermen, and in every direction sail and power for pleasure is evident and active.

This is, in fact, a typical week-end scene from April to October. Later tomorrow, the more venturesome on larger boats will be returning from far away places on the English or French coasts or the Channel Islands, and, at about 5 p.m., the stream of craft of all descriptions making for the Hamble River must be seen to be believed.

It is a sobering thought that all these craft must land their crews somewhere and park somewhere.

From the same view-point a decade ago much less activity would have been observed, other than in Cowes week, so we are dealing with a leisure pursuit and sport of almost unprecedented growth.

In the following pages I hope to outline the problems as I see them; put forward suggestions to mitigate the worst effects on the environment; stress the need for further study of potential growth; the need for increased facilities; and the degree of use of existing facilities.

In accordance with my term of reference, I shall endeavour to concentrate on the problem of parking boats and giving access for boats, and not on the equally difficult problem of sailing water and places to go, which also merits attention.

My ideas have been conditioned by discussion with many people who are expert in this field, during the studies of the Hamble River and Chichester Harbour, and by my own interest of messing about in boats since well before the Second World War.

2 The Planning Background

It would probably be as well to look first at the involvement of planing authorities with both recreation and coastal preservation.

2.1 *Recreation*

The demands for space for leisure, the increased variety of leisure pursuits and the number of participants have escalated since the Second World War and particularly in the last decade.

Local planning authorities have always had a duty to provide space for recreation, but in recent years they have become increasingly involved in recreation in its widest sense.

Twenty or so years ago, planning authorities were only required to define areas for playing fields, parks, etc., in a 'Development Plan' and to show that the amount of land so defined would be adequate, based on standards recommended by the National Playing Fields Association.

More recently, they have become much more closely concerned with leisure in all its aspects in liaison with other bodies, such as the Countryside Commission, the Regional Sports Councils and the National Playing Fields Association. As time goes on, they are likely to be even more actively engaged in the implementation of schemes for all types of recreation.

2.2 *Coastal Preservation*

It has now become generally accepted that our coastline represents a vital national heritage and that vast areas of this limited commodity have already been spoilt by all types of development. What remains must be cherished, improved and used with the greatest possible care. [1,2,3,4.]

After the submission of the first 'County Development Plan' to the Minister of Housing and Local Government in 1952 (approved in 1955), the next step taken by the Hampshire County Council as Local Planning Authority was to submit a 'Hampshire Coast Green Belt' to the Minister in November 1958.

The joint effect of the 'County Development Plan' and the 'Green Belt' was to curb all but essential development along the coast. These proposals were negative in their approach.

There was a more positive approach in September 1963, when the Ministry of Housing and Local Government issued Circular 56/63[5] which drew attention to pressures for development on the coast and stressed the need for special studies to be undertaken with a view to preserving the coast, increasing its recreational use, enhancing its visual amenity and improving public access.

The Circular required coastal planning authorities in consultation with the National Parks Commission and the Nature Conservancy to:

(a) Ascertain which parts needed safeguarding so that the natural attractions could be enjoyed to the full.
(b) Decide locations where facilities for holiday makers and other development should be concentrated.
(c) Take steps to restore lost amenities as far as possible and create new ones.
(d) Take account of the potential impact of proposals on areas of scientific interest.

This led to the publication, in November 1966, of the 'Coastal Survey from Christchurch to Calshot'[6], which contained a number of policy statements and proposals designed to improve public access and visual aspects, and drew attention to a number of matters requiring further study.

The increasing interest in the environment led to the setting up of a Working Party on Sewage Disposal by the Ministry of Housing and Local Government. Their report 'Taken for Granted'[7] deals particularly with pollution aspects, both on the coast and in tidal rivers. It states yet another case for conservation and improvement.

In December 1967, a strip of coast between Keyhaven and Calshot was designated an 'Area of Outstanding Natural Beauty' by the National Parks Commission (now the Countryside Commission). This designation gives yet more positive protection to this strip of coast and has the additional effect of making some money available, in the form of grants, for improvement.

3 The Planning Appraisal

3.1

Many who sail for recreation are concerned to see that there are still unspoilt places for them to visit and many non-sailors have an

even greater interest in the conservation of the coast. A proportion
of sailors prefer, and are able to pay for, the comfort and convenience
of a marina. What steps should be taken to reconcile the various
interests?

Before action can be taken, information is required – about landscape,
about capacity of waterways, about demand, about other requirements
and, not least, about public opinion. From the information obtained
by survey and soundings, the planner expects a policy to emerge which
will be acceptable to all interests.

3.2 Landscape Studies

Before considering future development of any type, recreational or
otherwise, I am of the opinion that detailed landscape studies should be
undertaken, particularly on the coast and along river valleys.

From these landscape studies should emerge:
  (i)   Areas which should be protected and conserved in their
         natural state.
  (ii)   Intermediate areas which would be worth conservation if at
         all possible, particularly where there is an opportunity to
         improve existing landscape.
  (iii) Areas within which development, such as a yacht harbour
         or a sailing club could be absorbed without detriment.

Both the Hamble River Study[8] and the Chichester Harbour Study[9] are
examples of this approach and the appraisals prepared for each are
examples of how this can be done.

3.3 Capacity of Harbours and Waterways

I feel sure that every waterway has a capacity which should not be
exceeded if yachting is to continue to be a pleasurable recreation and
a safe one.

A great deal of thought has been given to this subject in the prepara-
tion of the River Hamble Policy Plan (see Appendix A) and the Chichester
Harbour Study and indeed similar work has been done in Christchurch
Harbour and for Lymington River. It will be appreciated that such
capacity studies are very difficult exercises and I will use the River
Hamble Study as an example.

At the time of the original Study in 1965, the Planning Authority were
fortunate in having co-operation and advice from all the officers,
(Manager, Engineer, Hydrographic Surveyor and Harbour Master) of
the former Southampton Harbour Board who had been managing the
River as a harbour for many years. After lengthy discussions between
the officers and other persons and authorities having interests in the
River, including the Royal Yachting Association, and a detailed study
of the location and number of boats moored in the River at that time,
the Harbour Board advised that the capacity of the River from Southampton

Figure 1 Hamble River looking seawards, before marina development

(Southern Newspapers Ltd.)

Water to Bursledon Bridge could be 3,000 craft of all descriptions if substantial works were undertaken by them to regulate existing moorings in the river.

Swinging moorings which take up so much space were to be largely eliminated in order to create a clear channel for navigation 46m (150 ft) wide at the mouth of the river reducing to 23m (75 ft) wide at Bursledon Bridge. Manoeuvring areas were to be provided at the narrower points and a separate channel was to be formed for use by the Hamble River Sailing Club so that, from the starting line at Hamble, boats could race out of the River and back again with the minimum interference both to their sport and to yachts in the main channel.

The intensity of use of existing moorings was also studied and it seemed that only about 20 per cent of the total number of boats were away from their moorings on any particular day, and even at the peak of the season, the maximum away did not exceed 40 per cent.

It seems essential for further studies to be carried out, on the widest possible basis, on the frequency and intensity of use of boat and mooring.

The vision of three thousand boats leaving the River Hamble on any one day and trying to get back in that day is a nightmare.

The capacity figure selected must be based on peak periods, and must provide a margin of safety. Consequently it needs to be reviewed, say about every ten years. Once agreed it would rarely be practical or acceptable to review it downwards and reduce numbers.

It is reasonable to count tender dinghies as being one with the boats they serve and consequently discount them in the capacity exercise.

3.4 Sailing Types

While I freely admit that there are very many types of sailor and very many types of boat to be sailed, for practical purposes it is possible to distinguish three broad bands of yachtsmen and, surprisingly enough, each seems to me to take up as much room on the water when sailing. They comprise:

(a) Dinghy sailors, who in the main belong to a recognised sailing club and accept the discipline of that club.

(b) Yachtsmen, owning craft of all types from little more than a dinghy to a miniature liner, who prefer, for many reasons of their own, to be on an open mooring obtained from a harbour authority. A percentage of these comprise people of fixed income who, after investing considerable capital in an expensive boat, are just unable or unwilling to pay yacht harbour prices. They are prepared to put up with the inconvenience, and sometimes discomfort of reaching their boat by dinghy. Even they need to park at least one car and a tender dinghy.

(c) Yachtsmen who prefer and are prepared to pay for the many advantages of yacht harbours and who appreciate the comfort and services provided.

It is necessary for the planning authority to recognise and secure that provision is made for each of these three basic types and to make provision for powerboat owners, water skiers, trail-boat owners and fishermen who may not be associated with any of the three types.

Equally, I believe, the Royal Yachting Association, with whom most local planning authorities keep closely in touch, have similar interests.

Yacht harbour proprietors are primarily interested in my third type, although they must also have a great interest in the other two types, since there is always a tendency for a person to start as a dinghy sailor in a small club and in a few years own a much larger boat in the comfortable surroundings of a yacht harbour.

There must be a broad division of facilities that are available between the three basic types of yachtsman.

4 Marinas and Small Craft Harbours

Having set the scene and given such background as I am able, I feel
that I can now express my own thoughts on the planning aspect of this
Symposium, bearing in mind that there are papers on related topics
such as the design, construction, finance and needs of a yacht harbour.

I will start by quoting Denys Sessions' definition of a marina, included
in his excellent article published in 'The Yachtsman' in 1966. [10]

> 'A marina is a place where boats may be kept afloat whatever the
> state of the tide, where they may be reached without the use of
> a dinghy, where they may be maintained, fitted out, repaired,
> bunkered and provisioned, where their owners and crew may
> obtain all their essential supplies, where cars may be parked
> close to the waterfront and, above all, where order and efficiency
> prevail. The marina is a complex dedicated to boats and boating.
> It may form part of a village or a city waterfront, it may be the
> nucleus of a new community or the modest extension of a boatyard.
> Essentially the marina is intended to make boating more attractive,
> more convenient, and more enjoyable. '

I think I would only suggest, arising from this definition, that we
must not discount the type of service such as is provided at Hamble by
Fairey Marine who, every few minutes in the course of a busy day,
lift quite large boats on to purpose-made trolleys and tow them ashore
with specially designed tractors, into a dry boat park.

From this, I think I would conclude in simple management terms
that the objectives of a yacht harbour are:

(a) To provide all that a boat needs.
(b) To provide facilities for the owner to use his boat (it would
clearly be undesirable for a marina or yacht harbour to
function merely as a floating caravan park).

I would agree with Henry Howard when he was quoted in an article in
'The Yachting World' [11] as saying:

> 'A marina is a community on its own. If you make a brand new
> port of a derelict piece of foreshore or river frontage, and you
> bring into being in that part of the world a community of five
> hundred or a thousand souls, if you like, at any one time over a
> week-end, they need to be sure that their batteries will be ready
> for them when they arrive; that their craft are pumped out and
> safe and sound; that when they get back at six o'clock they can have
> something to eat, if they want it; that they can have somewhere
> to change into dry clothing. '

This leads me to believe that we were right in the Hamble River
proposals of 1965 when we expressed a preference for yacht harbours
to be established wherever practicable in such a position that they
were linked with existing boatyards.

It is well known that a number of schemes for yacht harbours were produced some ten years or so ago where the landward side of the development was the primary objective (i.e. residential development of a type which would not normally have been permitted in that situation by a planning authority). In such cases the yacht harbour part of the development seemed to be a very secondary consideration. This seemed to follow American practice in spite of the fact that it was not particularly relevant to this country where distances between home and the sea are comparatively short.

In more recent years, the schemes produced have been much more practical, much more acceptable and very frequently linked with existing boatyards. A list of marinas serving the Solent (existing and proposed) is presented in Appendix B.

My Authority has attempted to define criteria for the establishment of yacht harbours which are broadly as follows:

(1) Areas of high landscape value should not be chosen.
(2) Priority should be given to sites linked to existing boatyards.
(3) Adequate road access should be available or proposed.
(4) New yacht harbours should provide public access to the water with some car parking and tender dinghy parking for other users.
(5) Ancillary features such as cabins for yachtsmen, hotels or cafés would not seem to be needed unless associated with urban areas.
(6) The prime consideration should be the effect upon navigation and on hydrographic factors, such as the effect of the proposal on river banks, tides, currents, silting, etc.
(7) Vessels should be able to leave their berths at all states of all tides and reach the main channel directly from their berth rather than passing through a locked, or otherwise restricted, approach channel. This would apply particularly to yacht harbours in rivers as distinct from those on open coasts.
(8) Proposals should not encroach upon navigable waters in such a way that they reduce the area available for use by small boats or which would result in the displacement of existing public moorings.

Whilst these criteria are of general application, there would still be scope for more elaborate schemes in special circumstances, but those circumstances would need a great deal of justification.

In dealing with yacht harbour applications, and there have been quite a few in Hampshire over the last ten years, we have been keen to see that wherever possible the yacht harbour developer does provide a service to other yachtsmen besides his berth-holders. Such things as tender dinghy parking and car parking (albeit at a commercial price) can be very helpful to other users. Where yacht harbours are approved, they occupy a prime position to serve other users of the waterway and normally have an outstandingly good access from a main road to the waterway itself which should be exploited to the full.

My Authority has a standard requirement that two car parking spaces be provided for every craft moored in a yacht harbour, together with some additional provision on an agreed scale for other users of the waterway. This standard has been criticised by some yacht harbour managements as being too much, but I am sure that it will remain policy until such time as it can be proved to be over-provision. Car parking space is not wasted, even in a yacht harbour. It can have a dual use, if properly sited and designed, in that many owners require their boats to be lifted ashore during the winter months, and little-used car parks at this time of the year can be used for the winter storage of boats.

5 Discipline

The importance of discipline in all forms of boating activity, both to achieve safety and avoid pollution, cannot be over-stressed. A great deal can be done to promote discipline by yacht harbour management.

The pollution of the waterways has already been commented upon in 'Taken for Granted' and the danger to other yachtsmen of dumping rubbish overboard has been stressed in an excellent article published by the Royal Yachting Association. [12]

The Planning Authority will require the provision of W.C.'s and washing facilities ashore and rubbish receptacles conveniently placed on the pontoons. It is then up to yacht harbour management to keep them clean and in good order, and to enforce their use.

To this end, my Authority have required agreed rules of conduct to be laid down by yacht harbour proprietors when planning permission has been granted. They expect these rules to be strictly observed by the users of the yacht harbour and enforced by the proprietor.

6 Planning Control

It may be helpful if I include a statement on the general mechanics of planning application procedure in Hampshire.

Briefly, all new development – and this includes engineering operations – requires planning permission.

Planning applications have to be submitted to the County Borough or District Council in whose area the development is situated. District Councils transmit the application to the County Council, with recommendations, except where they are able to deal with it under delegated planning functions. This is an over-simplification of the procedure, but is particularly applicable to applications for marinas, since such development would almost certainly be a departure from a statutory Development Plan, which could not be dealt with by a District Council.

Receipt of the application would normally be advertised for public comment, and, if in tidal waters, a number of authorities would be consulted, namely:

(a) Department of Trade and Industry (Coastal Protection and Navigation)*
(b) Harbour Authority (responsible for conservancy)*
(c) Crown Estate Commissioners (responsible for the estuary or sea bed)*
(d) River Authority (drainage and coastal protection)
(e) Highway Authority (access and traffic)
(f) District Councils – who might consult a Parish Council in the area of a Rural District
(g) Police Authority (traffic)†
(h) Adjoining Planning Authority†

There would be a different set of consultations where the marina is sited on inland waters such as a canal, lake, etc.

After the closing date given in the advertisement and receipt of the comments of authorities consulted, the application would, in the case of Hampshire, be considered by:

(i) The District Council Planning Committee who would make a recommendation to:
(ii) The Divisional Planning Committee who would make a recommendation to:
(iii) The County Planning Committee.

The County Planning Committee decide the application unless one of the authorities consulted lodges an objection or there is a considerable body of public opinion against the proposals, in which case the Secretary of State for the Environment would be consulted should the County Planning Committee wish to permit the development. The Secretary of State may decide to call in the application for determination by him after a Public Local Inquiry or decide not to intervene, leaving the Planning Authority to deal with the application.

The application may be in 'Outline' or be fully detailed. In either case it should be well documented, carefully prepared and fully explained by the applicant. It is far better to discuss sketch proposals with planning officers before submission; their advice can be invaluable in securing that the best possible presentation is made – they cannot, however, commit themselves as to the decision likely to be made by the Committee.

---

* Separate consents would also be required from these bodies if planning permission were granted.
† Only consulted in relevant circumstances.

The Planning Authority may not be prepared to grant a permission until arrangements have been made for the roads leading to the site to be improved to serve the development adequately, in which case it may be necessary for the applicant to negotiate with the Highway Authority at an early stage – again the planning officer can advise.

I cannot overstress the desirability of early consultation with the officers involved – it can save a great deal of time and work later on.

7 Further Study – Courses of Action

So far, I have tried to illustrate the type of work already carried out over a limited area to cope with a demand.

With ever increasing pressure it is obvious that much more work needs to be done if recreational sailing is to continue to grow.

Many opportunities exist around our coasts[13], but both the requisite studies and the subsequent provision of facilities are going to cost time and a great deal of money.

Somebody must co-ordinate and monitor the results of local studies and proposals so that a national picture eventually emerges of opportunities and facilities. This might best be done by a governmental agency, under the auspices of a Minister.

The Sports Council and the Countryside Commission requested the Dartington Amenity Research Trust to study Water Recreation, and this body has produced a mass of information (particularly in Volumes 2 and 3 of their report, dealing with the River Hamble and Southampton Water, respectively), which merits careful examination.[14]

The Hampshire County Council have agreed to the recommendation of the County Planning Officer, Mr. A. D. G. Smart, that a conference should be held of all the varying interests in the Solent. A working party representing local and harbour authorities, sailing and allied coastal interests has been set up and the scale and nature of the problem will be debated at a preliminary Solent Sailing Conference in March 1972. This will be followed by a second Conference in the Winter of 1972/73 at which policies, standards, and proposals can be discussed. It should be possible to 'feed in' any ideas emerging from this Symposium.

Meanwhile, it will be seen from Appendix B that a number of approved or agreed projects for yacht harbours have not yet commenced or have only recently been started. Most of these are comparatively easy – if the construction of any yacht harbour can be so described.

Over the last 10 years or so a number of sites in the Hampshire side of the Solent have been thought about, and discarded for one reason or another. Nearly all had direct access open to the Solent, were on a lee shore and required costly protective works, including locked entrances, but had either very poor or no acceptable access by road.

As the 'easy' sites are used up, then the potential of some of the 'open to the Solent' sites will need to be re-assessed – together with any new opportunities which emerge – in relation to other competing development and conservation demands pertaining to the Solent. Examples are:

Gilkicker   A locked basin of small capacity with a difficult entrance.

Titchfield Haven   A locked basin on the site of a nature reserve (described by Bruce Frazer[15]). It would be very difficult to reconcile opposing interests here. Present road access is poor.

Brownwich   No satisfactory road access – a lee shore.

Chilling/Hook   No satisfactory road access – a lee shore.

Southampton Water   A variety of sites might be found within the capacity likely to be permitted by the Docks Board. Possibilities exist at Ower Lake (previously objected to as interfering with shipping in the main channel), Hythe and elsewhere.

8 Conclusion

I can only hope that the effort put into the subject of sailing for recreation by so many authorities and organisations will be adequately co-ordinated and used to provide better and safer facilities for yachtsmen, and satisfy all the competing and complementary interests in the sea.

References

1. Countryside Commission (1970), *The Coastal Heritage – A Conservation Policy for Coasts of High Quality Scenery*, H.M.S.O.
2. Countryside Commission (1970), *The Planning of the Coastline*, H.M.S.O.
3. Countryside Commission (1969), *Coastal Recreation and Holidays*, Special Study Report Vol. 1, H.M.S.O.
4. National Parks Commission (1967), *The Coasts of Hampshire and the Isle of Wight*, H.M.S.O.
5. Ministry of Housing and Local Government (1963), *Coastal Preservation and Development*, Circular 56/63.
6. Hampshire County Council (1966), *Coastal Survey – Christchurch to Calshot*.
7. Ministry of Housing and Local Government (1970), *Taken for Granted*, Report of Working Party on Sewage Disposal, H.M.S.O.
8. Hampshire County Council (1965), *River Hamble Study*.
9. Jefferson, J.G. and Burrows, G.S. (1968), *Chichester Harbour Study*, West Sussex County Council.
10. Sessions, D.H. (May 1966), Yacht Harbours, *The Yachtsman*.
11. ————(June 1966), Marinas, *Yachting World*, **118**, p.258.
12. Cobb, D. (1970), Pollution, *J. Roy, Yachting Assn.*
13. Beazley, E. (1963), Marinas, *Architectural Review*, **134**, pp.34-108.
14. Dartington Amenity Research Trust (1970-71), *Water Recreation Case Studies (vol. 2 – R. Hamble, vol. 3 – Southampton Water)*.
15. Frazer, B. (June 1964), If Marinas there must be ..., *Boats and Sail*.

Appendix A

Hampshire County Council — River Hamble Policy Plan (1971)*

THE OBJECTIVES OF THE PLAN

The plan is concerned primarily with the conservation of landscape and the use of the river and adjacent lands for recreation. The aim of the Hamble River Study (1965) was that the river should be developed in the national interest as a harbour to accommodate pleasure craft to the maximum extent consistent with the maintenance of the essential character of the landscape, satisfactory road access and safe navigation. The objectives of the present plan incorporate this aim and are as follows:-

(i)   To enable full use to be made of the recreational capacity of the river especially for boating and to avoid conflict between different uses.

(ii)   To conserve and enhance the present scenic and natural history value of the valley.

(iii)   To gradually improve and extend public access to the river by means of more detailed plans to be produced in the future.

(iv)   To make proposals and suggest management measures by which these measures might be achieved.

SURVEY AND ANALYSIS

The river valley has been the subject of a wide range of detailed studies concerned with its appearance, use, accessibility and capacity. The studies were undertaken in order to assess the ability of the river to cater for future demands that might be made upon it and to reveal the constraints that will determine the feasibility of any proposals made. The results of these surveys are summarised below.

(i)   The Appearance of the Valley – The attraction of the Hamble River is based largely upon the high quality of its landscape and surveys were made to ascertain those features making a significant contribution to its pleasant appearance; to identify those that detract from the valley's charm and to define visual limits of the valley. The surveys emphasized that the river was in effect contained within an enclosed landscape nowhere wider than 1 mile although longer views along the reaches of the river are common. The appearance varies greatly north and south of Bursledon Bridge; to the north the valley is undeveloped and unspoiled and the wooded

---

* This is an extracted version. The full report can be purchased from the Hampshire County Council Planning Department, price 40p.

slopes run to the water's edge with only narrow and dis-
continuous strips of salting. To the south the saltings
become more extensive and the woodland is more broken,
intermittent urban development occurs on the slopes as
well as intensive concentrations of shipyards and sailing
clubs along the shoreline.

The unspoiled nature of the upper river is unusual in south
east England and merits conservation for this reason alone.
The attractive mixture of scenery of the lower river is
extremely vulnerable particularly if existing woodland were
to be lost. In both stretches the physical condition of most
of the woods, which gives the Hamble much of its special
character, is poor and careful management will be needed
to ensure their continued existence.

(ii)   Use – The uses made of both the water and banks of the two
parts of the river differ considerably. The upper Hamble
is predominantly rural and apart from the Y.M.C.A. International Camping Centre at Fairthorne Manor the banks form
part of agricultural holdings. At Swanwick the existing
brickworks is likely to remain in use for many years. The
river is used for fishing, sailing, canoeing, water-ski-ing
and the banks for walking. There are only about 100
moorings above the bridge.

South of the Bridge the river is largely used as a harbour
catering for the requirements of several types of yachtsmen
and their craft. In most cases dinghies are stored ashore,
particularly in the pounds of the Warsash and Hamble Sailing
Clubs. Larger vessels are either moored in the river itself
on buoys and piles, or have berths at one of the yacht harbours.
There is also the demand for facilities for day visitors who
trail their boats to the Hamble, for childrens' sail training
(River Hamble 'Optimists') and for fishermen. There are
5 sailing Clubs, a number of boat building and repair yards
and other industries mostly connected with yachting.

The activity on the river provides interest at all times of
the year and the villages of Bursledon, Hamble and Warsash
are popular, especially at holiday periods. Each contains
restaurants and inns overlooking the river.

(iii)   Accessibility – Access to the river whether by car or on foot,
is relatively difficult and car parking spaces are limited.
Roads leading to boatyards, public hards and open spaces
are narrow, winding and often congested. Difficulties arise
particularly at the three principal access points to the river,
Bursledon, Hamble and Warsash. Some existing riverside
footpaths are breached. Ample opportunity exists for new
or relocated footpaths and some new car parking provision

may be possible. No major improvements in access can be expected until such time as the future of adjoining areas outside the valley can be determined as part of the South Hampshire Structure Plan. This applies in particular to that part of the river above Bursledon Bridge including the arrangements for access to land at Cricket Camp and Manor Farm, owned by the County Council.

(iv) Capacity – The Hamble River Study (1965) fixed a limit on the number of craft that could be accommodated on the river below Bursledon Bridge. This limit, 3,000 craft of all types (excluding tender dinghies) was put forward by the former Southampton Harbour Board, following a study of potential channel widths and known craft movements, and depending on the execution of certain works, as the maximum number which it appeared could be accommodated in present conditions without dangerous congestion of river borne traffic. It was agreed at that time that this figure should be reviewed following experience of conditions in the river when the limit has been reached.

In 1970 the total number of craft permanently accommodated on the river was about 2,000.

Table 1 shows the distribution of craft in 1970, as well as those schemes to which the County Council has agreed in principle, which would provide for about a further 1,000 craft, provided conditions of access and car parking can be fulfilled.

Table 1

Accommodation for Vessels – River Hamble (1970)

Location and type of mooring		No. of moorings	No. of vessels
(A) Existing			
Above Bursledon Bridge			
Piles and swinging moorings		68	136*
Mud Banks		30	30*
	Total	98	166*

* Estimate

Location and type of mooring			*No. of moorings*	*No. of vessels*
Below Bursledon Bridge				
County Council's	public piles		20	51
"	"	public buoys	21	54
"	"	private piles	504	504
"	"	private buoys	335	335
Fairey Marine				200 (allowance)
Port Hamble Ltd.				194
Moodys Boat Yard				213
Hamble and Warsash Clubs				400 (allowance)
		Total		1,951

(B) Present Commitments (1970)

New Yacht Harbour at Crableck Lane	480
New Yacht Harbour at Badnam Creek	250
Extension to Port Hamble	150
Phase II at Moody's Boat Yard	81
Total	961
Overall Total (Below Bursledon Bridge)	2,912

The County Council has recently become the Harbour Authority and their Management Committee for the River Hamble is considering the replacement of certain buoyed moorings by piles, the placing of additional piles in suitable sections of the River and the re-arrangement of other buoyed moorings which restrict the navigable channel. To facilitate these alterations the remaining 88* moorings, not previously allocated, will be allotted to the County Council.

CONCLUSIONS

(i)   The Hamble River has a special character rare in South East England and, as such, it merits conservation. The fabric of woodlands, open fields and saltings that contribute to this character is vulnerable and positive action is necessary to conserve it.

(ii) The upper river is relatively little used for recreation and there is scope for increased use; nevertheless, the introduction of noisy uses and particularly those likely to attract large crowds could destroy the quiet charm of this stretch.

---

* i.e. the difference between the recommended capacity of 3,000 vessels and the existing figure of 2,912 in Table 1 above.

(iii)   The number of craft that can be permanently accommodated
        on the river should be a maximum of 3,000 until such time
        as a further survey is carried out to ascertain whether any
        increase is possible consistent with amenity and safe naviga-
        tion. Such a survey should be carried out when there are
        3,000 craft in the river or in 1975 whichever is the earlier.

(iv)   There is a need to provide for three types of yachtsmen
        below Bursledon Bridge, i.e.
        (a) dinghy sailors (largely incorporated in two sailing clubs);
        (b) yachtsmen who prefer moorings in the river obtained
             through the Harbour Authority.
        (c) yachtsmen who prefer berths in yacht harbours and are
             prepared to pay rather more for their accommodation.

(v)   There is considerable scope for the gradual improvement of
        public access to the river banks and for picnic sites and
        associated car parking, although in some cases, piecemeal
        provision of facilities may not be appropriate because of
        control and management difficulties, and in these cases a
        more comprehensive approach will have to be sought over a
        longer time scale, through the preparation of more detailed
        plans.

(vi)   No major road improvements can be suggested in advance of
        the Structure Plan for South Hampshire.

GENERAL POLICIES

The Plan is concerned with proposals for the enhancement and
development of the recreational value of the river, and with policies
designed to maintain the present situation pending the preparation of
more detailed plans.

The difference in existing uses and potential between the upper and
lower reaches of the river identified previously affords an opportunity
to cater for a wide range of recreational demands. The policies
adopted and the proposals made are designed to achieve a clear division
of function between the two parts of the valley. It is considered that
the Hamble south of Bursledon Bridge should continue to serve as a
major sailing and boating centre with expansion of existing harbour
facilities up to the estimated limits of its waterborne traffic capacity.
The upper river, from Bursledon Bridge to Botley, should be dedicated
primarily to the quiet enjoyment of the countryside and the river. A
continuing theme for both stretches is the extension of public access to
the river bank, including those areas to be occupied by yacht harbours,
and the conservation of landscape features, particularly woodlands
and unspoiled stretches of foreshore.

In order to ensure satisfactory future development of the river the
following policies are proposed:-

(i)   Use of the River as a Harbour

    (a)   Sites for new and expanded yacht harbours and associated facilities will only be permitted within areas defined on the plan.

    (b)   The number of craft of all descriptions (other than tender dinghies) moored in the river or stored on the banks shall not exceed 3,000 craft on the Lower Hamble.

    (c)   Further yacht harbours or river moorings will not be permitted until such time as present commitments have been implemented and experience has been gained of river traffic conditions with about 3,000 craft on the river, when a new assessment will be made.

    (d)   The present club controlled water ski-ing will be permitted to continue for the time being; but in the long term an alternative location for water ski-ing should be sought, after which the sport might be prohibited in the Upper reaches of the river. In the interim period the County Council will consider the possibility of the use of by-laws to control this type of recreation.

    (e)   The use of the upper river as a harbour will be discouraged, and powered craft controlled by the imposition of a speed limit, except in the case of water skiers under club control.

    (f)   The moorings below Bursledon Bridge will be reorganised and concentrated so far as possible between the road and railway bridges.

(ii)   Access – Public access to the waterfront will be improved and extended and small car parks and picnic sites established. The timing and method of implementation of these proposals will depend upon the production of more detailed plans, the availability of funds and the co-operation of the landowners concerned. Proposals for new yacht harbours will be required to include provision for public access to the shore and car and tender dinghy parking for users of moorings in the river.

(iii)   Landscape – The analysis has shown that the Hamble valley has a landscape of high quality and, therefore, outside those areas defined on the plan for new facilities, no new development will be permitted which intrudes upon this landscape. The Local Planning Authority in applying this policy will give particularly close scrutiny to any applications within those parts of the valley defined on the map as 'vulnerable' areas and will need to be satisfied that any proposed development does not adversely affect the quality of the existing river scene.

These 'vulnerable' areas are:-

(a) Those lengths of river bank within areas of high landscape or ecological value, where the absorption of new
development is very difficult, often due to the level
terrain or the scarcity of trees.

(b) Prominent areas which are of only average landscape
value and where even small scale development could
bring about a marked deterioration to the river scene.

The protection of these areas will be further ensured through
agreements with landowners and where appropriate by Tree
Preservation Orders. Suggestions for the removal or
screening of features that detract from the valley scene will
be welcomed.

(iv) Implementation – In considering applications for any development of yacht harbours the Local Planning Authority will
have regard to the criteria contained in Appendix 2* and, in
particular, will require comprehensive plans exhibiting a
high standard of layout, design and landscaping. The scale
and phasing of development will be controlled by agreement
under Section 37 of the Town and County Planning Act 1962.

The County Council will also exercise its powers as Harbour
Authority to ensure that the river is used in accordance with
the policies contained in this plan and any rules or bylaws
which may be drawn up. As funds permit it will undertake
works and enter into such agreements as may be necessary
to secure improvements.

---

* Outlined in Section 4 of this paper.

RIVER HAMBLE POLICY PLAN

Proposals Map

Proposed picnic site	●
Proposed car park	▲
Existing footpath	●●●●●●
Footpath maintenance	☐☐☐☐☐☐
Proposed footpath	●●●●●●
Area to be the subject of a more detailed plan	▬ ▬
Moorings reorganisation	▬ ・ ▬
Site for yacht harbour	▬▬▬
Proposed M.27 motorway	▭ ▭
Vulnerable areas	▨▨▨
National Trust	⬭

Scale 1:12500

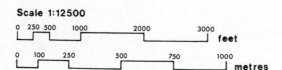

Appendix B

List of existing and proposed marinas serving the Solent (Chichester to Lymington)

Chichester Harbour

Capacity approx. 5,830 craft

	Existing	Proposed	Permitted
Chichester Yacht Basin	800	-	-
Emsworth Yacht Harbour	200	-	-
Birdham Pool	220	-	-

Langstone Harbour

Capacity not assessed

	Existing	Proposed	Permitted
The Kench	-	300	-

Portsmouth Harbour

Capacity not assessed

	Existing	Proposed	Permitted
Camper and Nicholsons	220	60	600
Haslar Lake	-	-	600
Gosport Yacht Marina	70	-	-

Southampton Water — Rivers Itchen and Test

	Existing	Proposed	Permitted
Kemps Marina	87	-	-

Hamble River

Capacity 3,000 craft

	Existing	Proposed	Proposed in Study
Fairey Marine	150	-	200
Port Hamble	230	-	344
Badnam Creek	-	250	250
Swanwick Marina	213	81	294
Crableck Marina	-	-	480

Beaulieu River

	Existing	Proposed	Permitted
Bucklers Hard	76	-	-

Lymington River

	Existing	Proposed	Permitted
Lymington Marina	300	-	-
Harpers Lake	-	450	450

Isle of Wight

Cowes Yacht Haven Marine Co.	-	236	236
		(150 for visitors)	
Minerva Yard (E. Cowes)	-	353	353
Medway Queen Marina			
(Newport)	120	-	317

Marinas and the Developer

A. R. Dale-Harris

Edendale Properties Ltd.

1 Need for a National Policy

1.1 Demand for Berthings

An accurate assessment of the rate of expansion of sailing as a
recreational activity is difficult to obtain. There is no national register
of boats and the Lloyd's Register of Yachts only includes vessels of
approximately 7 tonnes (tons) (Thames Measurement) and over, and,
even then, registration is not obligatory. However, it has become
increasingly important for the Regional Planning Authorities to make
this assessment in order that their long-term planning can adequately
cater for the rapid expansion of this activity. Figures have been
produced by the Royal Yachting Association and other bodies which
show that the number of craft has been increasing annually by about
10%, and it is probable that this rate will increase over the next few
years provided that adequate facilities can be made available.

Once the natural harbours and traditional yachting and boating
centres have become saturated with moorings, which in the more
popular areas has now happened, the problem can only be tackled by
the development of Marinas, that is by high density accommodation
for yachts. There is a parallel to this in housing by way of high rise
flats and in car parking by multi-storey car parks.

In other countries, notably the United States, Canada, Scandinavia
and France, the respective Governments have been quick to realise the
urgent necessity to formulate national policies that will help to promote
the development of Yacht Marinas. Unfortunately, there has not been
much evidence of this happening so far in the United Kingdom. There
are a number of good reasons why such central direction and governmental involvement should materialize. These are outlined in what
follows.

1.2 Planning of the Environment

Yacht Marinas must have the necessary infra-structure; namely, good access by land and water and good lines of communication from the highly populated areas which they are serving. They must be supported by such facilities as car parking areas, yacht repair yards, clubs, hotels, restaurants, shops and new residential development for holiday houses. At the same time, they must detract as little as possible from the areas of natural beauty in which many of them will have to be located. Although this is strictly within the sphere of regional planning, a uniform national policy could greatly speed up the planning decisions required.

1.3 Promotion of Tourism and Leisure

This is a major factor in bringing about the involvement of other European Governments in the development of Yacht Marinas. Tourism and leisure are both major industries and are closely linked. The provision of Yacht Harbours and allied development will become increasingly important in promoting these industries.

1.4 Youth Training and Recreation

The future of any nation depends on the calibre and character of its people; this is decided in the early years of an individual's life. It is generally recognised that sailing, in one form or another, is not surpassed by any other activity in building into the character the qualities which a successful nation would hope to see in its people. Therefore, it will be necessary to provide mooring facilities for the growing number of boat owners who are unable to afford the luxury-type Marina.

1.5 Finance

The construction of new Yacht Harbours in tidal waters is expensive; more will be said about this later. In terms of return on capital investment they are most unlikely to be economically viable unless supported by large-scale land development. This is because there is a limit to the amount of money which yachtsmen are prepared to pay for mooring their yachts, and this limit gets lower the further removed the Yacht Harbour is from the areas of greatest demand. Construction costs (for similar projects), however, remain the same whether the harbour is located in the Solent, the West Country, or anywhere else.

In France, a large number of the new Yacht Harbours are being subsidized or entirely paid for by public funds, either central or local. The supporting services and residential development, where planned, are then hived off to private enterprise. In Canada, an ingenious formula has been devised by the Government whereby it makes a substantial contribution towards the cost of dredging, piling and construction of breakwaters, provided that the Developer puts up an equal sum for the supporting land development.

The British Government realised the need for subsidizing Hotels in order to achieve a rapid expansion of tourist facilities, and, if new Yacht Harbours are to be constructed in areas where large-scale land development is not desirable, then subsidies will have to be forthcoming.

2 The Role of the Developer

2.1 Identity and Purpose

Before elaborating on this, it would be useful to try and define more precisely what is meant by the term 'Developer'. To quite a number of people this immediately conjures up a person, group or company hell bent on exploiting any situation with the sole object of getting rich and getting out as quickly as possible.

The Developer, by definition, is obviously he who carries out the development; but this for example, could be any or a combination of any of the following:

The proprietors of the local Yacht Yard.
The owners of the land and foreshore adjacent to the prospective harbour.
The local Yacht Club.
A group of enthusiastic yachtsmen.
A private investor.
The Local Authority.
The Crown Agents (who probably own the sea-bed).
A Property Company.

The assessment of the viability of a project is likely to vary substantially according to which of these is making the assessment.

If it is the Yacht Yard, they will probably have the advantage of owning land and foreshore which is under-utilized and lowly valued. They are likely to be located in sheltered waters where dredging, some piling and the provision of pontoons are all that is required. The economic viability is based not solely on the revenue from moorings but also on the increased business generated for their Yard.

The other categories would have other criteria on which they would base their assessment, but this short paper is primarily concerned with the last category – the Property Company.

2.2 Function of a Property Company

There are hundreds of Property Companies, ranging in size from the large corporations, having long-term financial arrangements with Insurance Companies running into tens of millions of pounds, down to the one-man band. Sheer size is not a necessary ingredient for success, but sound financial backing, experience and expertise certainly are.

A Property Company has two basic lines of business:

(i) Trading in property.
(ii) Investing in property.

It is usual to decide which line is to be adopted for each project.

If the project is to be a Trading Operation then short-term finance is required to finance the development according to the projected Cash Flow. Almost all Residential Development is of this nature, but also an appreciable amount of Commercial and Industrial Development which is sold, after letting to tenants, usually to Insurance Companies or Pension Funds. In this case, the value of the property bears little relation to the cost but depends on the status of the tenant, the terms of the lease and location of the building.

If the project is to be an Investment Operation, then not only short term, but also long-term finance has to be arranged. The latter is most likely to be forthcoming from an Insurance Company or Pension Fund, who will retain their own professional experts to evaluate the project before it starts. As they are investing Life Funds they will apply very strict criteria in valuing the project. Above all, they will be looking for first class security on their money and an increasing income over the years as a hedge against inflation. The status, expertise and experience of the Property Company are therefore essential to attract this source of finance.

The function of the Property Company could therefore be stated as follows:

(i)   To assemble the Professional Team.
(ii) To prepare a feasibility study on the project.
(iii) To assemble the land.
(iv) To 'master mind' the development.
(v)   To arrange for the necessary finance.
(vi) To find the tenant or eventual purchaser.
(vii) To accept the risks involved.

2.3 Property Companies and Marinas

Where then does the Property Company stand in relation to an expanding Yacht Marina programme? One thing is certain, there is going to be no mad rush of companies eager to get in on the act! Available funds and expertise can at present be more profitably employed elsewhere.

Unfortunately, quite a number of Local Authorities and Regional Planning Officers appear to take the view that Yacht Marinas = Goldmines, and, when a prospective Developer is insistent that he must be allowed land development to make the project viable, they consider he is overplaying his hand to a very large degree. There are, of course, notable exceptions, Brighton Corporation being but one. Even

here, the Developer had his problems, as is evident from the paper on
Brighton Marina at this Symposium.

There is one fundamental difficulty for the Property Company in
assessing the viability of a Yacht Marina which does not present itself
in any other form of development. This is, that a high capital investment is required to construct a Yacht Harbour, often entailing provision
of breakwaters, locks, extensive dredging and piling. And at the end
of the day, what is there to show for the money? – An expanse of water,
albeit smooth, with a conglomeration of floating pontoons connected to
the shore. The whole contraption, costing hundreds of thousands of
pounds, is suitable for one purpose and one purpose only – the mooring
of yachts.

Property Companies don't like specialized buildings let alone
specialized water!

2.4 Property Company – Local Authority Partnerships

From the foregoing remarks, it might be thought that there is no
role for the Property Company in Marina Development. However,
I do not believe this to be the case. If the future need for Yacht Harbours
is to be realised, then Partnerships will have to be formed between
Private Enterprise and Local Authorities to carry out the development
on rather similar lines to Town Centre Development. The land would
have to be acquired by the Local Authority if it does not already own it.
New legislation to give them powers of compulsory purchase may be
required. The land would be leased to the Developer at a peppercorn
rent in the early years and subsequent ground rents would be geared
to the profitability of the venture. By this means, the capital cost
of the Yacht Harbour could be substantially recovered by the profit
on the land development and the subsequent return on capital invested,
shared with the Local Authority, could make the enterprise viable.

All this presupposes that future Marinas will include a substantial
amount of land development, in order to attract the necessary capital
investment from Private Enterprise and allow a programme to proceed
on the scale required.

A number of Planning Authorities are apt to throw up their hands
in horror when Residential Development is proposed as a necessary
adjunct to a Marina and consider that it should be restricted to a
minimum. This attitude is understandable, bearing in mind the dese-
cration that has been perpetrated along our coastline during the last
fifty years. However, provided that a high standard of design is maintained and the residential units are closely linked to the Marina,
possibly to form a waterside village – the development at Port Grimaud
in the South of France is a good example – the resulting development
need not detract from the natural beauty of the surrounding country.

The foregoing points relate primarily to Coastal Marinas where harbour construction costs are high and the cost per berth may be £1500 or more if extensive breakwaters are required. In the case of Inland Marinas, which are usually located in existing waterways or gravel pits connected to rivers, the cost per berth should be much less and large-scale land development is not so necessary, although good facilities, including probably an hotel, a club, shops and repair sheds and car parking are essential.

At this stage, perhaps, it would be worth making a point about the vexed question of Car Parking. It is of course essential to provide adequate car parking to service any particular Marina. The problem here is that Car Parking takes up a considerable area of land and at the same time produces no revenue. It has been suggested that car parking areas can be utilized out of season for dry boat storage, but, with the advent of glass fibre hulls, it is no longer necessary to haul out for the winter and this alternative use is less and less available. No general standards have yet been laid down but from observations of the current use of Marinas which are 100% filled, a car parking requirement of 1·5 car spaces per berth would appear adequate.

3 Marina Development Procedure

3. 1

Having stated the principle functions of a Property Company in carrying out a commercial development project in partnership with a Local Authority, we might look at these more closely in relation to Marina Development.

3. 2 Selecting the Professional Team

This will probably comprise the following:

> Architect,
> Consulting Engineer,
> Quantity Surveyor,
> Chartered Surveyor/Estate Agent,

and this team must work as an integrated whole throughout the project.

The question of whether the Architect or the Consulting Engineer heads the professional team will have to be decided. It will probably depend on the extent of the land development content in the project. It might be wise to select the team from professional firms who have experience in Marina Development or similar work, and for the Architect to have experience in large-scale residential development, hotels, and buildings for the leisure industry. The Consulting Engineer should have experience in harbour works and in the design of mooring arrangements for yachts.

The Quantity Surveyor will most likely only be concerned with the land development, as it is normal for the Consulting Engineer to produce a Cost Estimate for his work. The Quantity Surveyor will produce a Cost Plan for all building work and, subsequently, Bills of Quantities to enable a building contract to be placed.

The Chartered Surveyor will advise on land values, rental values of buildings and Target Sales prices of houses; subsequently, he will find tenants for the buildings and organise the sale of the houses. He may also be involved in the negotiations for the acquisition of the site.

3.3 The Feasibility Study

For any project the first requirement is for the professional team to carry out an investigation and write a report. The object of the report is to set out in some detail the design and method of carrying out the development, together with an estimate of cost and the ultimate value of the completed project. The value will be expressed in terms of the estimated net income from the development year by year over a period of years after allowing for the cost of funding and amortization.

A full scale Feasibility Study requires a lot of work and is therefore costly. It should, however, be possible for an experienced team to apply certain yardsticks at an early stage to see if the project is likely to prove viable. If this is the case, the Feasibility Study would then proceed and would involve such matters as hydrographic and land surveys, ground exploration, and studies of wave and wind behaviours and liability to silting. Should the project ultimately prove abortive, the cost of this Study, amounting to several thousand pounds, would have to be borne largely by the Developer, although it may be possible to persuade the professional firms that they should also be at risk to a certain extent.

3.4 Acquisition of Land

Owing to the fact that the profit on the land development is required largely to finance the harbour work, the initial cost of the land must be relatively low. As mentioned previously, this is most likely to be achieved by leasing the land for a term of 150 years from the Local Authority and paying a very low rent in the early years, but with subsequent increases at agreed dates known as Rent Review dates. These dates have to be negotiated with the Local Authority or owner of the land, but should certainly not be less than seven-year intervals. It may also be possible to reclaim land, but this has the disadvantage that it will probably have to be allowed to consolidate for 2 to 3 years before building can start.

3.5 Assessment of the Market

This entails forecasting occupancy rates for the Marina, the level of mooring charges, the numbers, sizes and types of the vessels to be accommodated. Such factors as to whether berths will be rented on an annual basis or whether a proportion of them will be leased for a number of years on payment of a premium will have to be considered.

In order to make this assessment, which is vital to the project, it will be necessary to obtain as much information as possible from local sources such as Local Authorities, Harbour Boards and River Authorities, Boatyards and Sailing Clubs. Also, national bodies, such as the Royal Yachting Association and the Sports Council, might be able to help in this matter.

4 Conclusion

In conclusion, I would like to stress again that the points, which I have attempted to make, relate primarily to the participation of Property Companies in future Marina Development.

These Companies will only become involved in projects where there is large-scale land development. It appears that the most likely future pattern will be the carrying out of such projects in partnership with Local Authorities, and, it is hoped, with the assistance of subsidies from the Government.

Discussion

(Session 1)

AUTHORS' INTRODUCTION

Mr. J. R. Bryans

The R.Y.A. asked me to give my views on what the yachtsman requires of a modern marina or yacht harbour. Therefore, I must first explain that I have no specialist knowledge of the subject other than that acquired by an ordinary yachtsman who has cruised, raced and pottered in his yacht for the past forty years. Therefore, my attention has been devoted to mooring, laying her up and the like.

My yacht has been in a marina for three years, and has been in permanent commission throughout that time. As a result, I have noted one overall requirement. The marina manager should provide a service to his clients at a reasonable price and in a courteous, understanding manner so that the client is grateful, thereby assuring harmonious relations between both parties.

I know that this sounds very pompous, and it may seem an obvious point. However, it must be remembered that emergencies occur in marinas as well as at sea. Many lives are at risk, and many millions of pounds' worth of yachts. Accordingly, personal relations are of paramount importance.

Having become accustomed and equipped to the marina way of life, one of the things which we want to know is: Where are the other marinas? When I tried to obtain this information a short while ago, it was not forthcoming. When I rang up the National Yacht Harbour Association to ask for their names and addresses, I was told that there were about 30. The R.Y.A. told me that there were about 60, and I think that figure is a practical one.

We want to be able to go from one marina to another, simply plug in and enjoy the same amenities and facilities in other parts of the United Kingdom. A certain amount of standardisation is required before this can become possible. My boat has four plugs. One was for a socket in Helsinki, one has round ends, another has square ends and the fourth is a patent one from America.

What sort of person is the yachtsman, and what special claim has he upon your attention? He follows a way of life which is almost unique. First, he loves the sea. He cherishes his boat, even if she is a 'tore-out', and would rather sleep in her than in Blue Steel. In his activities, he acquires wisdom, vigilance, and a comradeship second to none. Having learned the way of the sea, he is an asset in the Ministry of Defence balance sheet. He is always ready in case of an emergency, as was proved during the last war, to offer his services to his country.

Most of the headings in my paper are obvious, and the ones which you would have expected me to make. Therefore, I will choose only two—those in Sect. 3. 5 and 4. 2.

My first point is the question of noise. The yachtsman is, in general, someone who wants to get away from it all and to find peace and quiet. One of the things which we do not want in any marina is noise. We do not want rowdy parties or dance floors which will keep us awake all night. Last, but not least, we do not want what prevails in every marina today—the ghastly sound of halliards hitting up against masts.

Today, the Government is spending, on the taxpayer's behalf, millions of pounds trying to stop noise and is examining the noise problems obtaining in factories, aircraft and, I hope, in hovercraft. For the cost of two or three short lengths of hambro'-line, costing 3p a metre, any yachtsman can silence his yacht.

When we visit the marinas on Friday, I hope that it is blowing like hell. Then you will discover that nine out of ten halliards or running rigging in the yachtsmen's masts are rove inside the sail cover, and there is then no earthly chance of keeping them silent.

Yachting editors and the Noise Abatement Society are interested in this problem to a considerable extent. I bring it up because it is not only the yachtsman—particularly the newer one—who must be educated to observe what is a normal, seamanlike precaution, but the yacht yards and marina management who must do something about this problem. They may be unwilling to do so, but somehow they must be made to do so, because we are all aware that noise is a deterrent to good health.

Security of tenure is the second very important point. A wise yachtsman will look very carefully at any contract which he is expected to sign. When he goes into a marina, he has often given up a valuable mooring elsewhere. When terms are being drawn up for any prospectus, please ensure that they are terms to which the yachtsman will be agreeable. He will not take it very kindly if the marina manager suddenly takes a dislike to his looks and he finds that the two or three years are up and cannot be renewed. He will then be unable to keep his yacht anywhere, unless there is another new marina being built elsewhere. He has given up an expensive—and probably very good—set of moorings which he will be unable to get back for eight or ten years, if at all.

I conclude by thanking this University, or behalf of the R.Y.A. and all yachtsmen, for putting on this Symposium which gives us a marvellous opportunity to say what we want. I am sure that, with a little goodwill and co-operation, we will get answers from all you gentlemen representing the highly technical side of the business.

Mr. D. H. E. Hockley

The introduction to my paper shows the competing interests in a popular and commercial stretch of water. It also shows that I had bought a new telescope and had spent a pleasant afternoon watching what took place upon the Solent, which is one of the most popular areas in the British Isles for recreational sailing as well as an extremely busy commercial waterway.

In planning appraisal, the first consideration must be that of landscape study. From this, the three types of area which I describe in Sect. 3. 2 emerge clearly. I am indebted to the University of Southampton for including in this paper the River Hamble policy plan of 1971, which incorporates the study of 1965. I believe that this is the earliest of its type. The Chichester Harbour study is a much more weighty document, which certainly bears examination by anyone interested in this subject.

Capacity exercises must include all types of recreational sailor. In Sect. 3. 4, I have attempted a broad definition into three types, which are clearly set out. The sting is in the tail, because I believe that yacht harbour proprietors are primarily interested in my third type, whereas responsible authorities must, somewhere and somehow, provide for all types.

Appendix B shows that, in recent years, Hampshire has seen the construction of quite a number of successful yacht harbours, and I can claim that—with the exception of a single case—all comply with the criteria defined by my Authority.

I do not say that there is no place at all for the more sophisticated development about which we shall hear when the paper on the Brighton Marina is presented. However, I feel that such opportunities will be rare, and would probably need far greater justification on grounds other than that they are demanded by yachtsmen.

I am very keen to see that yacht harbour proprietors provide a service to yachtsmen other than their own berth holders. I am sure that this makes good commercial sense, for this gives that type of customer a taste for the luxury of a yacht harbour compared with his open mooring, and the inconvenience and discomfort which he experiences when taking his guests aboard in a small dinghy in inclement weather.

The practice of discipline at sea and in yacht harbours is of foremost importance from every aspect. Pollution is a hazard, and the time may come when people will feel that each boat must contain its own sewage, with disposal and pumping-out facilities ashore. In considering this, we must remember that a very large number of boat owners live on their boats at weekends in a yacht harbour or at their moorings, and seldom venture to sea.

In Sect. 6, I have been encouraged to include something about the making of a planning application and the manner in which local planning authorities must deal with such applications. The number of authorities which a planning authority must consult on the receipt of an application for a yacht harbour is formidable. These procedures will last for two

years until we have an 'all-change'. We are not sure which authority
will determine the outcome of a yacht harbour application after 1974.
It may be the district planning authority or the county planning authority,
but we will not know the answer until the Local Government Reorganisation Bill appears upon the Statute Book. However, the advice
given to consult the local planning officer, at a very early stage when
considering this form of development will still hold good.

In Sect. 7 I have commented upon the types of further study which
will be needed and upon possible future courses of action. The first
Solent Sailing Conference has already been held, and there is little
doubt that it has been a great success. All concerned agreed to the
need for further studies and confirmed their willingness to participate,
which was very encouraging. The working party is now considering
what should be contained in a report and what sort of studies should be
undertaken to deal with the opportunities, objectives, problems, financial
implications and, possibly, with what longer-term options exist. It will
also consider such aspects as management and education, and it has
considered the possibility of taking aerial photographs at certain times
during the summer months to indicate the number of craft in use, the
number on moorings and, to some extent, even the destination of the
craft that are under way. Consideration is also being given to a sensible, but meaningful, questionnaire to users of the Solent, bearing in
mind the fact that most sailors hate filling in questionnaires.

I set no great store by the examples I have given of possible future
opportunities, except in the case of the site at Hythe, which I consider
to be a starter. I fear that I am likely to be banned from all existing
yacht harbours in Hampshire when I imply that they were easy sites. I
am sure we all know the tremendous difficulties which were encountered
and overcome during the course of their development. Perhaps I should
have said that they were more straightforward projects than many
which have been examined, and are likely to be more popular with
yachtsmen should a period of competition occur.

I am a little saddened to read in some of the papers and to hear
stated this morning that planning authorities are not concerned with the
provision of facilities for yachtsmen. To my knowledge, many planning
officers in this country own their own boats and, therefore, know a great
deal about sailing and the needs of sailors. In Hampshire, the county
staff even have their own yacht club, based upon Calshot, and the Hampshire Education Authority is actively engaged in teaching sailing in its
superb Calshot activity centre. Many other counties are concerned
similarly, and their teaching will produce in this and the following
generation the potential customers for yacht harbours.

Mr. A. R. Dale-Harris

I have tried to look at marina development on a national scale from
the point of view of a property company or financial institution. There-

fore, I have employed the criterion which I would apply to other forms
of commercial development, such as shops, offices, industrial estates
and town centres. I have also tried not to be parochial; by that, I mean
not to look at marina development in the way in which it has been
materialising here in the South-East and, in particular, in the Solent.

The Solent is quite exceptional. One only has to sail down the Hamble
or Lymington estuaries and see the millions of pounds' worth of yachts
of all sizes to realise that it is unique, with the possible exception of
America. Therefore, I had to look at the issue from the point of view of
marinas for all. This is how the paper starts off—with the need for a
national policy.

I am quite convinced, despite what the Minister has said this morning, that the Government must take a far more active and positive outlook and become involved in the development of yacht marinas for the
future. It will call for an investment of millions of pounds. It will need
to attract pension fund and life fund finance—the normal form of long-
term property finance, it will require co-operation and partnership
with local authorities, and it will require a phased programme so that
the larger companies and institutions can become interested, and can
look ahead to see that this is an expanding form of property development and a safe place for their funds.

I am sorry that the Minister is not here now because I was not
terribly impressed with what he held out to us in the form of government help for the marina programme. Like other countries, our government must be prepared to put their hands into their—or the taxpayers'
pockets.

I then dealt with the role of the developer, and set out who the
developer might be. Unfortunately, the sound of the word developer has
unpleasant overtones to many people. When it is said in conjunction
with the word yacht, it implies a state of filthy richness. I have not
expanded upon the new marinas in the Solent area, because the developers are mostly the proprietors of boatyards, that have been in existence
for many years, if not centuries. These marinas are in sheltered
waters, and have a very good captive demand. The land is probably
available at low cost and, although I do not say that it is a bonanza,
they should be doing very well out of it with the present inflationary
situation.

Therefore, my paper has been related to the property company. By
this, I mean the professional, large public company which is backed by
institutional funds. I have looked to see what would induce them to
become interested in such developments. At the moment, it is safe to
say that, with the exception of the Brighton Marina, they do not particularly want to know.

The reason for this is fairly simple. A property company is linked
with institutional funds, such as those providing pensions for widows

and orphans. Therefore, the investment must be safe, secure, and keep pace with inflation, and this means investment in first-class property.

On its own, a yacht harbour is a very specialised piece of property, if it can be called that. It is suitable for only one purpose: parking boats. It is more liable to catastrophe than bricks and mortar. Therefore, I think it safe to say that the property companies and institutional finance will never become interested in investing money purely in yacht harbours.

That leads us to the big bone of contention which prevails throughout the scene. We must have land development to go with yacht harbours. The more expensive the yacht harbour, the cheaper must be the land from the Local Authority or the subsidy coming from the Government. The costs of producing yacht harbours, or marinas for all, will increase all the time. In general, the further westward one goes, the deeper is the water and the more costly the breakwaters become. Therefore, my theme is that this must be a joint enterprise between government, local authorities and private enterprise.

The paper ends with my concept of marina development procedure, which is very short and concise and not controversial.

CONTRIBUTIONS

Mr. J. Hodge (South Western Sports Council)

In making provision for yachtsmen in marinas and yacht harbours we must remember that sailing is practised by people from all walks of life. Many people who started sailing in dinghies in the 1950's now own small cruisers and they find marina charges of between £25 and £33 per metre (£7.50 and £10 per foot) per annum too high. We can no longer expect, of course, to put boats on swinging moorings, which take up a great deal of water area per boat, at a rental as low as £10 per annum in the popular sailing areas. Nevertheless, the sailor should not be faced with a choice of a relatively expensive berth in a marina or no mooring at all.

It is clear that the more easily developed sites in the Solent area have been taken up, new sites for marinas will be more costly to develop and charges for berths will reflect this.

A *national policy* for the provision of yachting facilities is needed to ensure that all types of sailors are catered for. Perhaps it would be possible to provide berths within a marina ranging from the 'luxurious' with every convenience that some yachtsmen require, to the simple mooring that many yachtsmen find sufficient, with a range of fees appropriate to the services provided. Consideration should also be given to moorings outside marinas as some people prefer a quiet anchorage, for example as on the Beaulieu River where moorings are provided in the river for £125 per annum for a boat 7½ m (25 ft) in length.

A *Sports Council Working Party* is looking at the need for yachting facilities nationally and is undertaking certain lines of research and the collation of survey information. It is to be hoped that some guidance will be given by the Sports Council on a hierarchy of provision so that piecemeal development of coastal areas can be avoided. The area of coastal waters is fixed and cannot be reproduced: its development must be carefully planned.

Any Government financial help for facilities is likely to be directed to schemes which take into account any such planning and which offer the best service to the whole sailing community. As from 1st July, 1972, the Sports Council will be able to make grants to Local Authorities and voluntary organisations for the provision of facilities, including those for sailing.

Planners have been asked to be more positive in their approach to planning for sailing facilities. It may well be that planners will have the needs of all types of yachtsmen very much in mind when formulating policies for the provision of sailing facilities.

Mr. D. T. Humphrey (Development Manager, Scottish Tourist Board)

In general terms, Scotland is unlikely to experience much pressure for marina developments comparable to existing development in the South of England. This is because most of Scotland is relatively sparsely populated except for the Central Belt. Demand for marina facilities catering for the resident population of the Central Belt is most likely to be on the Clyde estuary where there is the greatest existing concentration of boating activity, and on the Firth of Forth.

At the present time, most boat owners do not have difficulty in obtaining moorings and even in the most popular areas, waters are not overcrowded. Marinas will therefore depend, to a greater extent, on good berthings and shore based facilities to attract customers than in England. Use by visiting yachtsmen, charter hire boats and casual day or week-end sailors will also be important if properly catered for and will help to ensure economic viability.

The greatest potential for development in Scotland appears to be in exploiting the potential of existing harbours or the natural resources of sea or inland lochs. Throughout Scotland there are many existing under-used harbours which could provide pontoon berths for boats at relatively low cost. Development could follow the example of France with the use of half tide walls or locked basins to provide yachtsmen with good facilities, even if on a small scale.

Sea and inland lochs often have sheltered locations which offer potential for the development of boating centres. Land is normally available for substantial shore based development and sheltered waters should mean economies in providing berths by using floating as opposed to fixed breakwaters. Sea lochs, particularly, provide deep water close inshore which should also eliminate dredging or land reclamation works. At these types of location it is not difficult to imagine the possibilities for exciting holiday villages centred on boating activities, and again perhaps following the example of France as at Port Grimaud.

The first proper marina (300 berths) in Scotland, at Inverkip on the Clyde, will be open in 1973 and several other schemes are being considered or actively planned. One incentive to prospective developers of schemes in Scotland is the possibility of attracting grant or loan assistance from the Scottish Tourist Board*. Under Section 4 of the Development of Tourism Act (1969) the Board are empowered to give financial assistance towards capital expenditure incurred on the development of Tourist Projects. This can include marinas and the development of new facilities or improvement or extension of existing facilities. The type and rate of assistance offered is at the discretion of the Board and will naturally depend on the degree of benefit to tourism of the proposal, but a maximum of 50% of the total cost is available.

Similar schemes are operated by the English Tourist Board and the Wales Tourist Board for the development areas of England and Wales.

Mr. D. W. T. Shannon (R. Travers Morgan and Partners, Consulting
                                                    Engineers, London)

I would like to raise three specific points. The first concerns the yachtsman's viewpoint. Mr. Bryans suggests in Sect. 2. 2 (p. 3) that marinas should have free access at all states of the tide. The cost of doing this would be very great in certain places, and some of the papers give instances where far less than this is provided. Some allow access only at states of the tide above mean low water springs or some similar reduced accessibility. I would like to know the effect of this upon the viability of a marina and to hear the yachtsman's viewpoint concerning the effect of such a restriction.

Secondly, as an engineer, I am concerned not only with providing structures in the water and around the marina but also over water. It will become increasingly the case that bridges crossing our estuaries will be built further downstream. I am concerned with the heights at which these bridges will have to be built, and the restrictions which the problem of height will place upon the masts of yachts.

---

*The explanatory leaflet 'Tourist Development Projects' is available from The Scottish Tourist Board, 23 Ravelston Terrace, Edinburgh.

My preliminary investigations have shown that a 22-metre (70 ft) air clearance will allow 99 per cent of yachts to pass. I would like to hear any other statistics which would support this view. These heights would normally be related to mean high water springs.

Lastly, various aspects must be borne in mind when considering the needs of marinas: accessibility by water and by road, the quality of the sailing, and the cost and the quality of the moorings. I am concerned with developments in the area of the River Thames, which is at the heart of a population of over $7\frac{1}{2}$ million. It could not be more accessible to people, either by road or rail, than that. Perhaps the quality of sailing is not all that we encounter along the South Coast, but I would be interested to hear Mr. Bryans' views on the relative importance of these factors in such an area.

Prof. A. N. Black (Faculty of Engineering, University of Southampton)

My contribution was prepared before I heard the Minister's speech, and I was delighted to hear his remarks. I do not wish to steal any thunder from my talk tomorrow, but I wish to hurl one bolt at Mr. Bryans.

Henry Ford made more money than Rolls-Royce. He did this by ensuring that his wares were made available at a price which could be afforded by the general public. Although I do not question that there is a market for the type of Rolls-Royce marina described by Mr. Bryans, commercial and other considerations suggest that the Model-T Ford type marina should be considered, too.

I agree with the Minister that, socially, it would be unacceptable for yachting to be made once more the privilege of the very rich.

Over much of our coast, the available sheltered water area for berthing is already occupied. The further berths which will be needed by intending newcomers can be provided either by more intensive use of existing deep-water areas, by dredging existing sheltered areas, or by building breakwaters to enclose fresh harbours. Whichever method is used, it will prove unacceptably expensive unless the utmost economy is practised. This applies especially in the use of space, but applies also in relation to the frills provided. I regard the provision of electric power on the pontoons as a frill.

Pontoon berthing of marina type is needed in order to achieve a high intensity of berthing. Two French harbours (Figs. A and B) illustrate the type of thing which I envisage.

Fig. A shows a very intense development at La Rochelle. The end-on berthing can be seen in the foreground, and parallel berthing in tier on the remoter pontoons. There is a very high-intensity use of space in this harbour resulting in serious overcrowding. Another marina for 1 000 craft has now been built outside.

Fig. B shows a development for small craft at Le Croisic which has

(*Photo: Yvon*)

Figure A La Rochelle, France

been achieved by dredging out what has been a very shallow corner at
the upper end of the harbour. Berths have been provided on the pontoons for about 100 small craft in a very compact area. The area
appears exaggerated in the photograph because it had to be taken with a
very wide-angled lens.

This kind of berthing may be far less convenient, but all that a
yachtsman can afford. It will be remembered that the Model-T Ford
was available in any colour the customer wished, as long as it was
black.

Figure B Le Croisic, France

Rear-Admiral P.D.Gick (Director, Emsworth Yacht Harbour Ltd.)

We keep hearing about expensive marinas. I own a 10 m (32 ft) boat, which is at a mooring costing £40 a year. If I lived inLondon, I would have to pay about £95 for laying-up that boat in a yard during the winter. I would have to pay for car parking facilities. I would have to buy a dinghy and outboard, and would have to pay to park that.

The cost of keeping a boat of that size in any one of four marinas of which I know would be £128 only for the whole year. That includes facilities for parking cars, there would be no need for a dinghy, and the boat would be looked after and kept safe from being bashed about by people going up and down the channel. I suggest, therefore, that marinas are not so terribly expensive.

Capt. C. McMullen (Marine Consultant, London)

I do not lay my boat up ashore, and I am on a pile mooring. That is why I am a supporter of an earlier speaker, Professor Black. If one were to make a statistical analysis of the number of keel boats in this country, probably only 3 per cent of these would be berthed in marinas of the more luxurious type. Therefore, although there is a need for this kind of berthing, we should also examine seriously the question of the provision of more cheap moorings for the growing number of small boat owners.

The average person who has to save hard to buy a 7·5 m (25 ft) boat just cannot afford average marina costs. Therefore, I wonder if support not only from the Government but from the County Councils could be forthcoming in support of new small craft harbour developments.

In America a large small craft harbour was built by the Los Angeles Council and parts of it were then hired out to profit making concerns; I refer to the Marina del Rey.

As a start I suggest that a large new small craft harbour could be built in the Solent sponsored by Government and Local Authorities with the aim of providing a multitude of cheap moorings but with part of the harbour hired off to help meet the cost.

Mr. E. W. H. Gifford (E. W. H. Gifford & Partners, Consulting Engineers, Southampton)

In connection with the second half of the title of this Symposium, I was taken by Mr. Hockley's remarks that most of the sites developed so far have been relatively easy sites. This is so from a civil engineering point of view.

It is important to realise that very, very few small craft harbours have been built since mediaeval times. Most of our experience in harbours of any size during recent years has been of the commercial ports. When we consider the building of small craft harbours, it is a very different proposition. A great deal of research and development work will be needed to get anywhere near sensible costs. Small fishing harbours, which are the nearest equivalent, are barely viable on a 60 per cent government grant, whereas governments elsewhere apply a 100 per cent grant. When that happens, I wonder where the developer will enter the picture.

I hope that civil engineers will not despair. Although there are 20,000 yachtsmen in the Solent area, there are 8 million fishermen in the world.

Until a few years ago, there has been a tendency to concentrate fishing boats and fishermen into a small number of very large harbours. Grimsby is a typical example of this. It has been realised that this is not satisfactory, either socially or economically. Therefore, the 7½ or 8 million coastal people of the Bay of Bengal, West Africa, West and Latin America are being encouraged to increase their fishing capacity off their beaches. That means that we must deal with fishermen in those areas who will have bigger boats than they have at present.

This brings me back to small craft harbours, and the absolute need to develop techniques of getting boats off and onto open beaches. Maybe the yachtsman can benefit from this as well, although he may have to buy a slightly more robust craft. This is a line of development which I can recommend to my professional colleagues.

Mr. P. C. Mornement (Bertlin and Partners, Consulting Engineers,
Redhill)

I wish to contribute one statistic which may prove of interest. My
firm has been privileged to examine the records of a large yacht harbour over a number of years since its construction and we found that
the number of boats leaving the harbour on any day expressed as a percentage of the number of boats in the harbour was gradually decreasing.
Thus, on ten Sundays in 1967, more than 35 per cent of boats in the harbour left, whilst on ten Sundays in 1970, only just over 30 per cent
passed through the entrance.

I think that this has an important bearing on the provision of car
parking spaces. If the number of boat movements is known at the
beginning, it is easier to plan realistically for the future. If the number
of visitors to the marina declines, it may be that overcrowding of the
car parks at first may be acceptable. On the other hand, there could be
a number of other reasons for this reduction in boat movement. People
get to know their marina neighbours better and as they become friend-
lier, their interest may change from active sailing to the social, but they
will still need car parking space. More research into this is needed.

Earlier on, Mr. Bryans mentioned safety. I think it is very important when designing pontoons to incorporate some means of climbing
back readily, if one finds oneself in the water. I say this with feeling
because, on Sunday, I went sailing with my daughter on a reservoir and
we capsized. Wearing a life jacket I did not find it too easy myself to
climb back into a dinghy. It would be much harder for a child and the
risk of drowning if one had to climb out on to a pontoon with no ladder
would be high.

My firm often receive requests to design a marina from people who
own a piece of land with water frontage. Usually, we can come up with
a viable proposition, but sometimes the land next door would be better.
We feel that the problem has been presented to us the wrong way
around. If would be far better if the initial brief were given to us by
the County Council or responsible Local Authority who would say, 'Here
is an area. Can you identify the best sites for marinas?' After the best
sites have been identified, the property owners would be approached
and the feasibility study would then be carried out on better sites.

Mr. B. H. Rofe (Rofe Kennard and Lapworth, Consulting Engineers,
London)

In several recent schemes my firm have been concerned with the
use of a surplus body of water arising from construction works for
another purpose.

As an example, we have been considering a situation where a motorway is being constructed adjacent to a river and additional material is
required for construction of the embankments. The material is to be

obtained from a flood plain and it is proposed that the resulting hole, which will automatically fill with ground water, should be used as an inland marina.

In the promotion of this scheme it became apparent that an alternative source of material was available in the form of unburnt colliery shale which might have been cheaper under certain circumstances. Although the local inhabitants were very keen on the possibility of a marina, neither they nor the local authority appeared to be prepared to underwrite this in the form of money. In this sort of situation how does one obtain a potential developer?

The relevant government organisations, in my experience, tend to be frightened of using public money for recreation on the grounds that they are there to 'build motorways and not marinas'.

Another example concerns the use of an old colliery tip area in the Midlands to be developed as an inland marina and pleasure ground. Here the Coal Board are prepared to contribute the money they would have spent on restoration works on their own account.

We have been concerned with several reservoirs in different parts of the country and in these cases it is often easier to obtain support for development and a grant for the development of sailing or fishing facilities. Nevertheless there is still much resistance by public authorities to providing additional funds for this purpose. The Minister has already indicated in his opening address that it is the Government's intention to provide funds for this purpose but it must be said that there is as yet very little money available for recreational facilities alone.

I should also like to refer to the selection of the professional team (Sect. 3.2 (p. 36) of Mr. Dale-Harris's paper). I feel, as an Engineer, that it is vital that the Engineer is brought in at the earliest possible date so that the full dimensions of the problem can be analysed by Engineer's experience in all aspects of it from the beginning. The control of initial surveys, provision of services and control of pollution are all aspects for which the Engineer must be responsible.

Dr. D. J. Kluth (Binnie and Partners, Consulting Engineers, London)

Several papers have contained statements to the effect that marinas are of use only to the boats floating on them and that land development onshore is necessary to make the marinas viable economically.

Marinas provide a body of sheltered water where the sea or river bed may well be of use for such purposes as fish-farming (e.g. shell fish). Not all marinas would be suitable and there are practical difficulties in combining the activities of yachtsmen and fishermen. However such joint usage would be worth some consideration (as for example, in other circumstances, yachtsmen benefit from surface use of reservoirs intended primarily for water supply purposes) and there could be some economic advantage. Perhaps the idea is more suited to small boat harbours designed for normal fishing activities as well as for sailing purposes.

Mr. H. D. Barron (Consulting Engineer, Southampton)

I found Mr. Bryan's paper gave an excellent brief on the requirements and I would like to make a few observations on this topic.

Firstly, I would suggest that the dredged depth should be linked to the requirements of the site and the expected demand.

I note his comments on the need for manoeuvring space and I wonder whether he could suggest rules for calculating the required space for entry and egress.

In respect of access and parking, I wonder whether he could suggest a definite ratio between yacht berths and car parking spaces?

Mr. Hockley has given a most interesting definition of planning objectives and it is noted that, in Sect. 4 (p. 16), the fifth item in the list of criteria for the establishment of yacht harbours suggests that 'ancillary features, such as cabins for yachtsmen, hotels or cafés, would not seem to be needed unless associated with urban areas'. I wonder whether Mr. Hockley could amplify this point, because it seems to me that it is in just such cases, where a yacht harbour is some distance from an urban area, that the facilities outlined would not be readily available and that there may well be a case for their provision.

Capt. A. C. D. Leach (Harbour Master, River Hamble)

If we look at a small yachting estuary, such as the River Hamble, we find that the marina companies are providing the alongside berths for the wealthier yachtsman while the harbour authority provides moorings for the poorer yachtsman, and for those—and I regret to inform you that there is a significant number of them—who just do not like marinas. Since the local council provide public hards for dinghy sailors, all classes of yachtsman are catered for.

In rivers and estuaries, interference with the natural regime can be dangerous, providing undesirable scouring and silting. At the planning and design stage of a new marina it is essential that expert engineering advice should be sought on what is likely to happen if a particular area is dredged or breakwater constructed.

It is also vital not to overcrowd the existing yacht harbours with boats. You may find that you have permission for a marina for 500, and it is possible to increase this to 1 000, but think first—as, I hasten to assure you, the harbour authority will—about the navigation in the entrance and the fairways of that harbour. If, between us—by which I mean the harbour authorities and the marina companies—we allow our harbours to silt up or become overcrowded, and frustrating for the navigator, yachtsmen will take to golf and there will be derelict marinas and—perish the thought!—out-of-work harbour masters.

Capt. H. N. J. Wrigley (Harbour Master, Cowes)

Harbours, like humans, have personalities and their problems and needs are best dealt with by local people who have a feeling for the various interests. My own small harbour, Cowes, is a case in point, and, in view of the considerable yachting activity, some comment on the way in which the needs of the yachtsman have been and are being met may be appropriate to the theme of this Symposium.

It is only within the last year that the income from yachting has very nearly equalled that from commercial shipping. Ten years ago, commercial shipping contributed about twice the revenue of yachting, which shows the rapid development of leisure interests in recent years.

In view of the obvious priority, the Harbour Commission have always regarded it as their primary function to establish and maintain free fairway for commercial vessels using the port or navigating the Medina Estuary to and from Newport.

At the same time we have recognised the needs of the yachtsman by the provision of moorings and by facilitating the development of marinas.

The increased income from yachting, just referred to, has been largely derived from moorings laid out in the harbour and in the Medina Estuary. There is now a capacity for nearly 1 200, including provision for about 500 visiting craft, for it is important to recognise that the Island harbours are extremely popular as places of call from the mainland. The number of moorings has now, however, just about reached the limit of capacity and further accommodation must be in marina berths.

The Harbour Commission has welcomed the development of marinas, whilst insisting that they comply with desirable conservancy requirements. We look upon them rather like storage cupboards in that the craft are tidily stowed away, leaving proper fairway for the passage of all classes of vessel. Two marinas are now operational—Cowes Yacht Haven (240 berths) and Wight Marina (180 berths)—and a third is under construction at East Cowes (300 berths). There are proposals, too, for enlarging the Wight Marina so as to accommodate a further 180 craft.

Thus, by 1973, it is likely that the harbour will be able to afford mooring or berthing accommodation to 2 000 pleasure craft. In spite of this large number in a relatively small harbour and estuary, it is considered that the careful planning which has been given will ensure that there will still be ample fairway space available and that there will be no problem concerning mass entry and exodus of craft.

We feel that we have now made provision for the larger yachts and indeed for the smaller cruising vessels, but we are acutely aware of the lack of facility to meet the needs of the dinghy sailor and those who trail small craft to the water's edge. This is a problem which many harbours are now experiencing. It is extremely difficult to forecast the capacity requirements for the small boat sailor, and one can only hope that, in the future, more landing aprons and facilities for stowage will be made available.

With regard to this problem, we do have one great advantage in Cowes, in that there are many yacht clubs which provide a facility for the smaller craft and this is a great advantage since one can have some appreciation of the numbers involved and through a club one can hope to control the movements of such craft within the harbour bounds.

Mr. G. D. Bent (Assistant Borough Engineer, Torbay County Borough)

With the creation of Torbay County Borough in 1968 the three authorities of Torquay, Paignton and Brixham were amalgamated. This brought the harbours of the three authorities under one control as a result of which a new Harbour Act 1970 was introduced. This created a new enlarged Harbour covering an area of over 9 km² (23 mile²), which embraces the three existing inner harbours.

The County Borough provides the moorings, which consist of ground trots and swing or fore and aft type moorings at Torquay and Paignton. The situation at Brixham, however, was different. Here the Council leased the site and the owner provided and laid his own mooring equipment. Over the years this resulted in a considerable misplacement of moorings with a mixing of different sizes of craft, and, consequently, bumping and uneconomic use of water space.

In 1971, a scheme was prepared for a system of ground trots and brace chains with swing type rising chains. It was not considered practicable to have fore and aft moorings in the Outer Harbour due to the exposed conditions under severe winds from the north.

The existing drop moorings provide accommodation for 390 craft, varying from 3 m (10 ft) motor boats to sailing craft of over 12 m (40 ft) and fishing vessels up to 24 m (80 ft) overall length. A further reduction in mooring space took place when the new Fishmarket and Jetty was constructed at a cost of £375,000 and opened in 1971. Clearly, with the increasing pressure for sailing facilities and with the extension of the M.5 down to Exeter in 1975 there will be a real need for extra moorings in Torbay which already has over 1 200 moorings in the three Harbours.

The new scheme provides for a minimum of 450 moorings on 33 ground chains, 50 mm (2 in.) and 38 mm (1½ in.) dia., with end bridles and 1½ t pick type mooring anchors. The ground chains will be interconnected with a system of 38 mm (1½ in.) brace chains and anchors.

The capacity of the new system is given in the accompanying table and the layout is illustrated in Fig. C.

The scheme which is to cost £79,300 is due to be commenced in October 1972 and should be completed by March 1973. The existing mooring holders have been given the option of either removing their own mooring equipment if it has any further useful life or of leaving it to the contractor to remove and dispose of as scrap. In the new scheme the ground chains and lower pendants will be provided by the Council and the swivel, upper rising chain and flotation gear by the owner.

Table A

Location	Craft size overall		Number available
East of Fairway	Under 6m	(20 ft)	50
	6-9m	(20-30 ft)	103
	9-12m	(30-40 ft)	42
	12-18m	(30-40 ft)	32
West of Fairway	Under 6m	(20 ft)	136
	6-9m	(20-30 ft)	64
	12-18m	(40-60 ft)	23
	30m	(100 ft)	3
	TOTAL		453

With the pattern of moorings adopted it will be possible, within reason, to vary the number of moorings for any particular size range of craft by dropping some moorings and inserting others. Some twelve moorings will be reserved for visiting craft.

In conclusion, it must be emphasized that this scheme is a positive step by the Council to provide increased moorings to meet the rising demand. It must be pointed out that it would be possible, at considerable cost, to provide a pontoon type of marina at Brixham, but due to the harbour's exposure to the northerly winds this would entail the construction of a permanent northern breakwater.

Mr. Wee Keng Chi (Director (Administration), Port of Singapore
Authority)

At Singapore, we have a somewhat unusual situation in that the port is very large, whilst the hinterland is relatively small. It is a very beautiful harbour, with natural deep water, but the available coastal

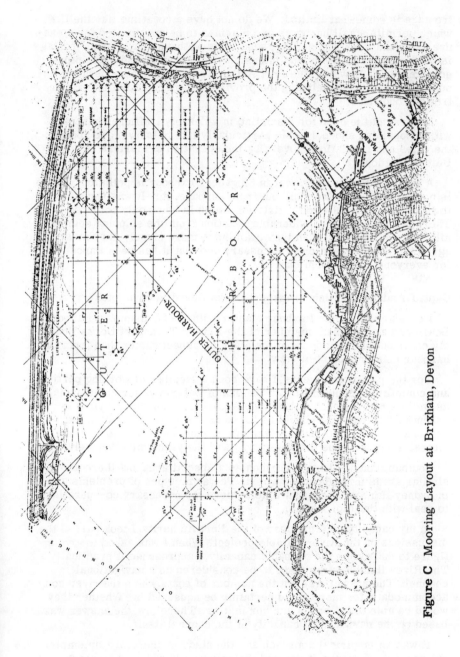

Figure C Mooring Layout at Brixham, Devon

frontage is somewhat limited. We do not have a coastline like the U.K. which permits small harbours and marinas to be constructed for pleasure craft and week-end sailing; what little we have as a coastal frontage is being used extensively and intensively for shipping and other more economic use. However, the Port Authority has under consideration a number of ventures, including the provision of marinas, but under controlled conditions.

Because of the need for discipline in a densely trafficked harbour with a populated shore, I would particularly like to know more about the rules and regulations governing the operation of marinas in the United Kingdom.

A problem that is very real in Singapore harbour is pollution. There is not only pollution from oil, but from garbage, etc. It was necessary to introduce anti-pollution legislation which is being duly enforced. There has been quite considerable reaction from the shipping community, but we think that when they examine it more closely, they must agree that this legislation is necessary and that it has been imposed for everyone's long-term benefit.

Capt. J. Andrew (British Transport Docks Board, Southampton)

I speak as one-time Harbour Master with the Southampton Harbour Board and as a present member of the British Transport Docks Board. My contribution is made from the planning aspect rather than from the harbour master's point of view.

For the past twenty years, I have been a member of working parties and committees concerned with the use of waterways for commercial as well as recreational sailing. My experience has shown that it is essential that planning should be based on discussions between the responsible local authorities—both afloat and ashore, the commercial interests who will use the waterways, and the yachtsmen themselves.

Southampton has been described as a special area, but there are similar areas throughout the world. The same types of problems arise in Sydney Harbour. Our aim is to achieve the necessary co-operation to deal with these problems.

In my capacity as a member of the Port Authority, I took part in the discussions on the River Hamble project. When I was asked to give a figure to determine the probable capacity, I approached it practically. The River Hamble would have to be considered as a navigational channel. The answer was not the number of boats which the river could accommodate, for more could certainly be squeezed in. Whether they would be able to get out is another matter. Therefore, the answer was based on the navigational capacity of the channel itself.

It was an empirical approach and the study is, therefore, an empirical concept. However, it seemed the only way in which to tackle it.

Simply, there were only a certain number of boats. Although several would be using the channel at one time, it was unlikely that they would all wish to use the channel at the same time. Therefore, I gave an estimate of 3000.

Of course, there were several safety valves. The channel was narrow at Bursledon Bridge, and the width at the mouth was only 45 m (150 ft). By sacrificing one row of moorings, this width could become 60 m (200 ft). That was the way in which the navigational side of the River Hamble project was tackled.

Throughout, we worked in close co-operation with the shore planners. The responsible people in port and river authorities should do nothing without holding full discussions with the local planners, and vice-versa. Both the former Southampton Harbour Board and its successor, the British Transport Docks Board have enjoyed close co-operation with the Hampshire County Council.

One other study which Mr. Hockley did not mention was that of Southampton Water. A working party was set up to study the amenity development in the Port of Southampton, and I was invited to become its chairman. We tackled that problem in exactly the same way as we had tackled the Hamble problem. The planners, yachtsmen and sailing associations were represented. Figures were obtained for present capacity and how that capacity was distributed. We studied prospective commercial development. We also took into consideration areas which could be suitably developed for amenity sailing and development.

When we had to fix a figure for the project, we used the same empirical concept. We had a figure of 2 000 boats—similar to the Hamble figure—to which we added another 1 000. This figure of 1 000 was broken down into two divisions of 500 boats, each group of 500 to be allocated a site which would be suitable for future development. When the figure of 6 000 for Southampton Water is reached, we shall then review the position. Everyone's opinion must be considered before deciding whether the sailing capacity can be increased. In this area, it is the navigational capacity which decides how many boats can be accommodated.

This has a direct bearing on any marina developments which are being considered. As the Minister has said, we have reached the stage when development has taken place where the natural harbours have been, or where the boat builders and commercial developments are. It is from development of such an area that our figures have come.

The Minister said that this type of development could not continue, and that we had reached the stage where we must begin to look elsewhere for sites for new developments. Figures such as those which I have given will be reached quickly, and it will be necessary to look elsewhere.

The Solent Sailing Conference is an extension of the Hamble/ Southampton Water study. Any future discussions which we hold in relation to the Solent must take into consideration that it may well become a national and not a local area. In future, it will be far more difficult to find accommodation. Therefore, concerning future marinas, conferences and close consultation are desirable to make sure that we know where we are going.

Mr. D. A. McIntyre (Peter McIntyre (Clyde) Ltd.)

This is not a commercial but, when God made Scotland, he really intended that that was the place where marinas should be built. He was not well-advised, however, and lacked the right civil engineer and geographer. While we have the facilities, we do not have the people. It is on that subject which I wish to speak.

Every now and again, the company which I run has to look after a great number who come periodically, about once in every five years, to complain about the lack of facilities. I wish to find out how other delegates have been able to encourage the developers to go into areas where there should be marinas and where people should be sailing, so that they can be encouraged to sail there again.

How have successful developers managed to involve the municipal undertakings? How have they managed to get the parks departments to create the right number of car parks and plant the trees? How have the water and electricity been brought to the area—obviously, at no cost to the developer? Whenever we wish to get projects off the ground, these are the very reasons why we are stopped.

Mr. D. P. Bertlin (Bertlin and Partners, Consulting Engineers, Redhill)

For a number of years the National Yacht Harbour Association has been pressing the Government to do more to help with the development of yacht harbours. I was very glad to hear from Mr. Eldon Griffiths' speech that the Government are now taking a more positive and helpful approach to marina construction. However, we are still far behind the French, Americans and Canadians, who have done so much to develop yacht harbours. In the United States and Canada, the Government meets the cost of the basic structures (breakwaters, etc.), which usually comprise a substantial proportion of the cost of the development, and enables municipalities or private enterprises to undertake the project economically.

Some developments, such as those at Port Grimaud, La Galère, and José Banus illustrate how housing can be knit into the overall plan to produce an economically viable project. As Mr. Dale-Harris remarked, yacht harbours are not gold mines, and in most cases must be linked to some other development if they are to be made to pay.

Professor Black (p. 49) mentioned that facilities should be provided for all classes of yachts and small boats, and not only for Rolls-Royces. It should, however, be remembered that whereas Fords and Rolls Royces require only slightly different parking facilities, the cost of providing deep draft berths is vastly greater than that needed to provide facilities for small craft, which can use beaches and hards.

Referring to Mr. Hockley's reasons for what one could call his guidelines for yacht harbours on the Hamble (p. 16), I do not see why he gives priority to sites near existing boatyards unless, as is often the case, they are in any case good sites for marinas. Obviously, certain boat repair and maintenance facilities are necessary for any marina but not those of a full scale yacht yard. Quite rightly, he considers navigation and hydrography in relation to the siting of marinas as a prime consideration and, in my view, such aspects should be dominant.

I do not know what Mr. Hockley has in mind in referring to cabins for yachtsmen or what he means by ancillary features. Surely, first-class facilities should be provided and marinas should be provided with far better facilities than they have at present.

Mr. Hockley seems to have a prejudice against locks. A lock provides completely protected water and limits the range of tidal movement. There is no tidal stream in a locked basin, and because of this a larger number of yachts can be accommodated in a given area. A disadvantage is that lock attendants are necessary, and this can prove expensive. Therefore, it seldom pays to have a lock unless the marina which it serves is a fairly large one. An example of a successful lock development is that at Chichester.

Encroachment upon existing moorings can be beneficial, if by so doing far greater accommodation can be provided.

Car parking is always a bone of contention. Mr. Dale-Harris' view (p. 36) that 1½ car parking spaces per yacht are sufficient is the viewpoint of the developer as against that of the planner, who often demands two spaces. Car spaces are very expensive to provide, and land area in the vicinity of a marina is always in short supply. Therefore, the parking area to be provided may make all the difference between a viable marina and one which is not economic. More research is needed and the experience of existing marinas investigated in detail.

A census should be made of categories of yachts in order that the best use may be made of the area of the yacht basin.

Mr. H. T. Hale (J. D. and D. M. Watson, Consulting Engineers, London)

I must congratulate Mr. Dale-Harris for an interesting and concise appraisal of the developer's problems in a marina project.

However, as a member of the Association of Consulting Engineers, it is my duty to point out that the last sentence under his heading 'The Feasibility Study' (Sect. 3. 3, p. 37), is against the professional ethics of independent consultants. The service which the consulting engineer has to sell, apart from his specialized technique in particular fields of engineering is, more importantly, the impartiality which he can bring to bear on engineering projects.

It is the standard practice for consulting engineers to work either by means of a retaining fee or by a fee for a definite service rendered, and, if there is an element of financial risk attached to the performance of that service, it is, in my opinion, impossible for the consultant to remain impartial. This situation could give rise to the consultant not giving a mature and considered engineering judgement on the task in hand.

I am unable to speak for professional firms of other disciplines, but I am sure that the basis of my remarks applies to them as well.

Mr. F. Coombs (Chartered Architect, Manchester)

There is some uncertainty concerning the boundaries of ownership of marinas and other maritime development.

Could Mr. Hockley clarify the ownership of coastal foreshores and the bed and inter-tidal margins of estuaries? *

Mr. M. J. Phelps (Basil Phelps and Partners, Chartered Architects,
Shanklin, Isle of Wight)

As an architect involved in the design of marinas, my particular concern is the lack of direction given by planning authorities and the need for an overall coastal plan, so that the sport of sailing may be open to a greater section of the community, and not restricted to the few who can be accommodated and afford marina berths.

Clearly, the 'sea lane' motorway travellers are an ever growing group of sportsmen, who cannot and do not require permanent berths, but on the other hand need access to the coast, car parking and, ideally, sheltered harbour facilities to leave their boats in the water overnight, and hotel accommodation for the overnight and week-end stay.

Such small craft boat harbours are unlikely to prove commercially viable, but nevertheless there is a real need.

Editor's footnote: The legal position appears far from straightforward and those interested may care to refer to E. Latham, 'Marine Works', Crosby Lockwood, 1922, p. 157. The ownership of the foreshore was originally vested in the Crown, but the latter has in many cases ceded the rights in the form of grants, so that the ownership may be vested in the lord of the manor or in the local authorities.

We have heard much of the crowded estuaries and coastal waters giving rise to boat jams and shortage of sea space. Immediately outside of the sheltered estuaries the sea is vast and provides the breathing space that is apparently required. But to enjoy this with safety it will again be necessary to construct small boat harbours on the more exposed coasts, so as to provide shelter.

Such developments will free the pressure on the rivers and estuaries and allow the coast to be more fully used. With this in mind, I welcome the Brighton marina as a real contribution to the sailing scene.

The development of the small coastal harbour or boat haven meets a definite need. However, it does of necessity mean adjusting the virgin coast line, and this, apart from presenting an interesting engineering problem, provides an opportunity and challenge for our planners to adopt a positive planning approach and overall concept for the use of our coastal waters, thus freeing the commercial harbours and approaches.

My final point concerns the management of marinas and is a plea, that visiting yachtsmen for overnight and week-end stays should be encouraged. The present position is that the success of a marina demands that all berths are permanently let; in consequence, most yacht owners return to their moorings each night, rather than venture further afield to less crowded waters, neighbouring marinas and small harbours.

Mr. N. A. Stead (Director, Gratispool Co. Ltd., Glasgow)

Mr. Hockley, on p. 16 of his paper, refers to marina projects submitted for planning approval where residential development has been the primary objection and the yacht harbour only a secondary consideration. The remark follows: 'that it was not particularly relevant to this country where distances between home and the sea are comparatively short'.

His suggestion seems to be that since people don't have far to go to their boats, there is no reason why they should be permitted to build their houses next to their boats. I for one do not agree with this. It is not necessary for people to have television sets but I would not deny them their luxury. Personally, I believe it very desirable to have my boat tied up next to my front door. If the price of houses, where the garden extends directly to the foreshore, is any yardstick, it would seem that there are many others who share this view. With the development of a marina village, many people can enjoy this luxury on a site which formerly would perhaps have only had room for one or two houses.

I believe also that sociologically it is a desirable thing to have people living, as it were, on top of their hobbies like this. Many families who go boating can barely support the house, the car and the boat in their lives and a bit of amalgamation and integration can result in considerable savings.

Furthermore, mother does not become a 'boatyard widow', since father can pursue his hobby outside the kitchen window. Yet another advantage to the community is the reduction of traffic at week-ends.

A little further on, in the same paper, Mr. Hockley states: 'Areas of high landscape value should not be chosen'. Why ever not? The suggestion seems to be that marinas have to be something ugly!

Hampshire County Council have apparently agreed rules of conduct to be applied by marina proprietors. As the proprietor of a small yacht harbour on Loch Lomond, I would appreciate a copy of these rules.

In his paper, Mr. Dale-Harris states in Sect. 3.4 (p. 37) that: 'Owing to the fact that profit on the land development is required largely to finance the harbour work, the initial cost of the land must be relatively low'. In my experience in trying to acquire land for marina development, the existing land-owners already have a good idea of the potential contained in their land and many of them in fact have an inflated idea of this potential. The result is that they ask for enormous prices and are, apparently, prepared to hang on to their land indefinitely, hoping that the advent of planning permission for some development or other on their land is going to make their fortune for them. What they forget is that the cost of developing the land has to be added to the price of the land for it to realise its full potential.

Mr. Dale-Harris goes on to recommend leasing, which, to my mind, removes the most attractive feature of this type of investment. I believe that I am not alone in being the kind of potential marina developer who, having made his fortune elsewhere, is looking for a viable alternative to entering politics or playing the stock-market, an activity which at best makes one richer than necessary and at worse brings on a coronary through lack of exercise. An investor, such as I, would be wanting to own the land so that he can build the community he would like to live in round about him. The neighbours he would want are the kind who would want to purchase their houses and the land around them. None of this would be possible on rented property.

I recently did a feasibility study on a marina project on the Clyde which, incidentally, we decided not to pursue. This revealed that land which was currently yielding zero revenue in rates to the Local Authority would have yielded £30,000 per year from the first year of the marina development onwards. The total investment on the project in water supplies, sewage and roadways was £120,000 and on the potential increase in rates revenue alone the Local Authorities would have been justified in making the investment in these. I believe this situation is not likely to be unusual and it certainly lends support to the closing remarks in Mr. Dale-Harris's paper.

Mr. J. C. Seabrook (County Planning Dept., East Sussex County Council)

It is a pity that Mr. Bryans, in his paper, did not deal with the important questions of where marinas should be located around our coasts, which areas have potential for increased use by small craft, and which areas are in danger of becoming or have become too overcrowded for proper enjoyment. The RYA could have given a responsible lead on this aspect of marina provision. In my opinion, planning authorities require and should have expert advice on the need or otherwise for further facilities and this should come from a nationally recognised and responsible authority, not in any way connected with commercial interests.

There have been only four applications for marina development in the administrative County of East Sussex, (excluding Brighton, Eastbourne and Hastings). One of the four was approved and is now established at Newhaven (Cresta Marine). The other three schemes were poorly presented and completely lacking in necessary detail. They inspired little confidence in their authors and it was obvious that no study had been given to the practical problems that would inevitably arise.

In 1967, the County Council published their draft Town Map for Rye showing land for a yachting centre on the west bank of the River Rother. There are tidal, ownership and other problems in the Rye Harbour area, but little real interest has been shown in developing this or any other site. I conclude that there is no overriding need at the present time for further facilities on this part of the coast, but I may be wrong and this is why I feel the RYA should give a stronger lead and possibly their encouragement to the use of less popular waters.

AUTHORS' REPLY

Mr. J. R. Bryans

It is impossible to have free access at all states of the tide in every instance. In writing my paper, I tried to put forward what we would like to see. I cannot say how it would affect the viability of a marina if yachts could not enter and depart at various states of the tide. There must be some statistics on this, but I am sure that those who will speak about marina development are in possession of better statistics than anyone else since this is a problem which they have looked into, because a marina must pay.

Mr. Shannon raised the question of masts and bridges. Some yachts have tabernacles allowing the masts to come down. This is a problem which will always be with us, unless we have bridges which open.

Holland has a vast number of such bridges, there are some in France, but there are not so many in this country. The bridge is something which we must put up with—for example it is unthinkable that rail traffic should be disrupted simply in order that we can carry on with our sport.

A typical example of the problem of masts and bridges obtains in the journey to Paris. It is possible to go as far as Rouen with a 30 m (100 ft) mast, but it must come off at or before that point. It is necessary, therefore, to have the mast taken off at Le Havre or Rouen.

Mr. Shannon also mentioned the River Thames. This is a locality which is not ideal for sailing; dinghy sailing is about the only possibility and, in the upper reaches, winds are very flukey. Obviously, though, it is an important area. For the cruising man, I can think of nothing worse than beating up the River Thames. The view is uninteresting, heavy planks and similar debris constitute a constant danger, and one is lucky not to have a damaged hull or, if the engine is being used, prop damage. For these reasons, the Thames area suits the dinghy man rather than the cruising man. However, I am a cruising man, so I realise that much of what I have said may have been coloured because of that.

Professor Black talked about Ford and Rolls-Royce. Of course I agree that, if possible, marinas, yacht anchorages or harbours should be available to yachtsmen of all incomes. There is a particular income group—i.e. the man who has just retired and is living on a pension—who cannot afford high marina charges. However, if marinas are to be built to cater for his pocket, then the facilities available will not be as great, although there may be many to use such marinas if they are provided. I must record, though, that my marina, which has almost every facility, is used by rich and poor, Rolls Royces and Fords!

He considered electricity a frill, and I cannot agree with this—we all have it at home, after all. It is of enormous advantage. Today, it is possible to have a six-tonner, run a wire of about $3\frac{1}{2}$ m (12 ft) in length from it to shore mains, and keep the boat afloat and dry throughout the winter, with all its gear on board. That is one of the ways in which electricity is so valuable today. All that is needed is a thermostat and a tubular heater, and it saves a great deal of money for the owner of such a yacht. The marina provides the meter at a fixed charge.

A point that does require serious attention is the fact that some marina managements are charging for electricity at rates substantially above those allowed by statute. The electricity boards are not empowered to enforce the law. This leaves only one remedy which is for the yachtsman to take the marina management to court.

It is difficult to reply to Prof. Black's sort of question, because we are dealing with the chap who wants everything as well as the one who wants as little as possible so that he can afford it. Both should be catered for.

Mr. McIntyre asked why there were no marinas in Scotland. I can give one very good reason. When I went to Scotland three years ago, I experienced lovely weather until I reached the Clyde. The day I got there, the wind was force 5. The next day it was force 6. By the time I had got through the Canal as far as Crinan it was blowing force 9 and it continued to do so until I had to return, without locking out. Once I had left Scottish waters the weather was fine again, both in Ireland and on the way back to the Solent.

I am sure, however, that Mr. McIntyre had cruising people in mind. In Scandinavia where one generally ties up alongside, it is sometimes a relief to anchor and not to be tied up with a lot of ropes. Do we really want to spoil the Western Isles and their lovely anchorages which offer some of the most beautiful cruising waters in the world? Anyhow, I do not think that marinas would be an economic proposition in that area.

In reply to Mr. Seabrook, I do not consider that the location of marinas is within the terms of reference for my paper.

Mr. D. H. E. Hockley

A number of points have been raised in the discussion which call for comment.

Generally, yachtsmen are extremely busy elsewhere when they are not sailing. Therefore, it is convenient when a marina can be attached to a boatyard and the yachtsman has only to say to the berthing master: 'There is this, that and the other to do, and I want some fuel. I'll be back next week'. It is most advantageous, and—somehow or other—this type of service must be provided at every yacht harbour.

By cabins for yachtsmen I mean the facilities needed by yachtsmen. Minimum facilities would include lavatories, showers, etc., and a very good shop which would provide all essential supplies from food to dinghies. I do not think that a club-house is an absolute essential. Apart from that, in the type of yacht harbour or marina which I en- visage, there seems to be no need for yachtsmen's cabins or hotels save in exceptional circumstances.

I am not entirely against locks. This is a personal preference, and I have been very impressed by the design which Mr. Bertlin showed me this morning among the photographs displayed in the exhibition outside.

On the question of encroachment upon existing moorings, when, in a yacht harbour, several hundred boats displace half a dozen moorings, I agree that we must balance the advantages. This is what we try to do in planning and harbour management.

I am sure that further study of car parking facilities is necessary, and that it will be carried out.

Concerning Scotland, I was amazed when I went up there three years ago to see so much water and hardly any boats or facilities. Then I got out of the car and tried to do some filming. The film is all of a tremble—it's terribly cold in July! In Scotland, the season for this type of activity is really too short. This may be why, even from the Solent, France and Spain are more popular if the yachtsman has the money to get there.

I apologise to Captain Andrew for not having mentioned the Southampton Water study, which is a most important one. He has given me a copy, but my excuse is that I received it after I had written the paper. I wish to take this opportunity to express my thanks to Captain Andrew for all the help which he has given to us in the past in Hampshire.

Public opinion is something which local planning authorities have always to assess. If there are any doubts, the precedure is that the matter is referred to the Department of the Environment, and that Department then makes an assessment to decide whether to hold a public Local Enquiry. It is not always easy to distinguish between those with genuine concern and the 'professional' objectors. However, if a whole district is up in arms about any project, I think that it is possible to sense it.

I am very keen that good behaviour should be observed in marinas. It could be improved upon, and I have advocated rules which are applied by most yacht harbours, and certainly those in Hampshire.

With regard to the question of rules for marina operation, the Hampshire County Council would normally require, as an aspect of planning approval, that a comprehensive set of rules of conduct and management be agreed with the parties concerned. The following set of rules has been prepared by my Department with the advice of the County Clerk.

These rules fall into three parts. Part I comprises general rules of application to a marina as a whole. Part II comprises rules which apply to boat owners and which may appropriately be included as terms of the agreement between a marina authority and individual boat owners. The breach of these rules should be grounds for terminating such agreements. Part III comprises matters which are not the direct concern of the Local Planning Authority but upon which it is recommended that provision should be made in the regulations of a marina.

Part I

(i)   The number of vessels (including barges, pontoons, rafts, sea-planes, hovercraft, aqua-planes and craft of any kind excluding tender dinghies or pontoons forming part of the permanent structure of the marina) to be accommodated in the marina at any one time shall not exceed****.

(ii) No moorings shall be laid within the confines of the marina unless the permission of the Harbour Authority and the Local Planning Authority is first obtained.

(iii) A clear means of access for fire engines to the shore and of jetties shall be maintained at all times.

(iv) The Marina Authority shall keep continuously available a suitable craft for the transport of firemen within the marina.

(v) The Marina Authority shall provide adequate means of escape in the case of fire from all buildings including club rooms and licensed premises within their control.

(vi) The Marina Authority shall continuously maintain an up-to-date record of all vessels accommodated in the marina and the berths to which they have been allocated.

(vii) These rules shall be displayed in a prominent position on the marina and shall not be varied without the prior consent of the Local Planning Authority.

Part II

(i) All persons entering the marina shall comply with these regulations.

(ii) No vessel shall be berthed or made fast in the marina in any place other than in a berth allocated from time to time by the Marina Authority.

(iii) No vessel shall, except in an emergency, be anchored in the marina or placed in any position that my obstruct or interfere with the free movement of any other vessel.

(iv) No person shall cause any obstruction on any jetty in the marina or leave or deposit any equipment dinghies or rubbish thereon, other than in places specially set aside for such purpose.

(v) The banks, slipways, pontoons, jetties and quays are to be kept clear, clean and tidy, and all garbage and rubbish should be placed in the receptacles provided by the Marina Authority.

(vi) No rubbish or waste material may be deposited in the marina.

(vii) Lavatories on board vessels should not be used while vessels are in the marina as adequate toilet facilities are provided on land.

(viii) No washing lines may be put up ashore.

(ix) Radios, record players and musical instruments of any kind shall only be played below deck of any vessel and all such instruments when in use shall be kept at low volume at all times.

(x)   No vessels shall be used as houseboats or for permanent residential purposes.

(xi) All vessels shall have adequate means for the extinguishment of fire and in this connection due regard shall be paid to the recommendations to be found in the appendices to these rules.

(xii) In a fire or other emergency, vessels may be moved clear of other vessels and buildings by the Marina Authority or by the Fire Service.

(xiii) No person may solicit or carry on any business or advertising within the confines of the marina.

Part III

(i)   All vessels occupying berths must carry Third Party Insurance to an amount of not less than £25,000 for any one accident.

(ii) All craft within the confines of the marina shall navigate with due care and attention at a speed not exceeding ** knots.

(iii) The Marina Authority shall provide such lighting and reflectors within the confines of the marina as shall be reasonably necessary to enable vessels to navigate with safety during the hours of darkness.

(iv) All vessels must be maintained in a seaworthy condition and of a good standard of appearance.

(v)   All vessels navigating within the marina during the hours of darkness shall display suitable navigation lights.

Other matters of which provision may be made in the Rules include:-

(i)   Yacht refuelling arrangements, storage of flammable liquids and outboard motors.

(ii) The provision of workshop and maintenance access for boats and safe storage of paint thinner and other equipment.

(iii) The control of car parking.

(iv) Requirements as to identification marks on boats and tenders.

The building of marinas by County Councils may apply in future, but I cannot see it happening for some time. Some years ago, the Hampshire County Council was responsible, with the Gosport Borough Council, for a feasibility study of Stokes Bay. The New Forest R.D.C. has commissioned studies for the possible yacht harbour at Hythe which I have mentioned.

Mr. A. R. Dale-Harris

I seem to have been let off very lightly, possibly because part of my paper dealt with the absolute necessity of obtaining cash from the Government, which is an idea popular with everyone.

I am a bit surprised that some planning officer has not come back rather more strongly on the question of land development. I know that this is a problem in the minds of many regional planning departments. It is a fundamental and serious problem, and perhaps I did not make the point strongly enough in my paper.

Session 2

Chairman: **Mr. D. P. Bertlin**
*(Member of Council, National Yacht
Harbour Association)*

Coastal Engineering Considerations

H. Lundgren

Professor of Harbour and Coastal Engineering
Technical University of Denmark

Scientific Director, Danish Hydraulic Institute

Abstract

The main purpose of this paper is to outline, for the benefit of those concerned with marina and small craft harbour development, the important coastal engineering factors which need to be considered at the planning stage. Experienced harbour designers will not find much that is new in the paper although it may be helpful to those engaged in a study of the subject.

Introduction

1.1 Site Selection

From the coastal engineering viewpoint the ideal site is one that is:

(a) Well protected from waves, and thus not requiring expensive breakwaters.

(b) Not prone to surging due to long period waves.

(c) Free from sedimentation by sand or silt.

(d) Not exposed to ice drifting.

(e) Of adequate depth for navigation and mooring purposes.

(f) Satisfactory with respect to foundation conditions.

If the site is not ideal, the coastal engineer has to consider the problems arising from one or more of the following – waves, currents, sediments, ice and wind.

The best site for a harbour for large vessels is generally at a place where the deep-water contours come close to the coastline, that is to say the nearshore transverse profile should be steep. On the other hand, if a combined reclamation project for a large marina is involved, the profile should be fairly gentle so that there is sufficient area available for the mooring basins between the boundary of land reclamation and the optimum location of the breakwaters. However, the centre portion of an exposed sandy bay is unlikely to be a good site since any approach channel that might be required would tend to trap sand by-passing the harbour in either direction.

Deep harbours are often placed at a headland on the coast where the convex contours result in a concentration of wave energy by refraction. It is likely that a better location for a marina is within a bay on the leeward side of the headland, at some distance from it, where the concave contours tend to laterally disperse the waves.

1.2 Field and Laboratory Investigations

The constructional cost of many harbour projects has been too high because no funds were available for proper investigational work at an early stage. Furthermore, even when funds have been allocated, there has often not been sufficient time to prepare and carry out the necessary studies.

At least one year should be allowed for field investigations of various kinds, including the recording of short and long waves, and tidal currents. It is relevant here to point out that the interpretation of the short wave records may require a knowledge of the currents if they are strong.

Unless the site is well protected, adequate funds should be set aside for model tests, and this money will normally be recouped many times over later on by virtue of the design economies that will result. For small projects, model testing would be confined to regular waves, whereas, for large projects, some of the studies may require the more expensive techniques entailed in the generation of irregular waves.

For a description of this sort of preliminary investigational work, reference should be made to the paper by I.W. Stickland in this Symposium.

1.3 Importance of Statistical Concepts

Whilst land structures are normally designed for prescribed loads, harbours are intimately related to statistical phenomena, such as:

(a) Variation of water level (due to the astronomical tides and wind set-up).

(b) Variation of wind direction, speed and duration – producing variation in direction, mean period and mean height of the waves.

(c) Variation of the individual waves with respect to height, period and shape – producing a wide range of boat motions and wave forces for a given storm.

For a large project, the statistical analysis may involve several parameters, as for example the joint probability distribution of water levels and wave heights.

The aim of the statistical analysis is to predict rare events by extrapolation from data obtained in field investigations of limited duration. Examples of design criteria which require this type of analysis are:

(1) Wave disturbance within a marina to be reduced to such an extent that, on average, a specified boat motion is unlikely to be exceeded more than once in 10 years.

(2) A specified stress level in a structure is unlikely to be exceeded more than once in 100 years.

(3) The forces on a breakwater are unlikely to exceed the limit of stability more than once in 1000 years.

1.4 Factors to be Considered

These may be listed as follows:

(a) Wave and current conditions in the vicinity of the harbour (see Section 2.1).

(b) Wave, current, and wind conditions in the harbour entrance. This evaluation requires consultation with experienced yachtsmen.

(c) Wave motion within the harbour and the resulting motion of moored boats due to wind-generated waves (see Section 2.2).

(d) Water surface variations and the resulting heaving and surging of moored craft because of the response of the harbour to long wave disturbances in the sea. If the conditions are particularly unfavourable, harbour resonance will occur (see Section 3).

(e) Wave forces, particularly on the breakwaters (see Section 4).

(f) Transportation of sediments along the coast (see Section 5).

(g) Wave motion, currents and salimities in river mouths, as well as tidal estuaries and inlets (see Section 6).

(h) Transportation and deposition of sediments in river mouths and estuaries (see Section 7).

(i) Drifting and accumulation of ice floes, as well as the problem of ice forces on structures.

(j) Wind effects on boat manoeuvring and the behaviour of beach sand.

(k) The presence and behaviour locally of marine biological species, such as seaweed.

(l) The effect of marine organisms on the maintenance of structures.

2 Wave Conditions

2.1 *Wave Conditions in the Vicinity of a Harbour*

The siting and planning of marinas should take into account:

(a) Waves generated by the passage of large vessels.

(b) Incoming waves generated by wind.

(c) Reflection of waves from the seaward side of breakwaters.

The two main types of solid breakwater are shown in Fig.1. Type S is a rubble mound breakwater with slopes on both sides and Type V is a vertical face breakwater.

Most of the wave energy impinging on Type S is dissipated by wave breaking and percolation, but on Type V the major part is reflected.

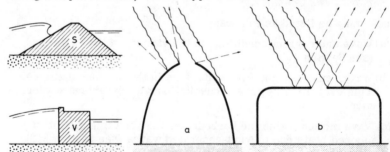

Figure 1   Breakwaters of Types S and V. Reflections from the outside

The configuration in plan of the breakwaters in Harbour (a) is favourable because the reflected waves (shown dashed) are dispersed.

In the case of Harbour (b), wave conditions at the entrance would be unacceptable if the breakwaters are of Type V. During severe storms, craft may also be in serious trouble within a triangular area that extends far out to sea, because breakers occur among both incoming and reflected waves, which cross at an angle. It is very difficult to control a boat in a steep cross sea, and there is a serious risk that the craft will 'broach to', with the result that it may capsize or fill with water. Therefore, the breakwaters for Harbour (b) should be of Type S rather than of Type V.

If Harbour (b) has to be built with Type V breakwaters, the reflections can be reduced by perforating the face. Perforated breakwaters
were conceived in Canada and they have been applied in a few situations.

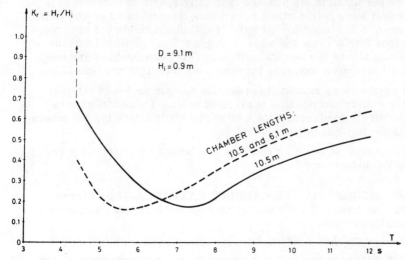

Figure 2   Perforated breakwater: variation of reflection coefficient
with wave period

Fig. 2 presents the reflection characteristics for a perforated
breakwater tested in connection with the Brighton Marina project*.
The lengths of the chambers are perpendicular to the breakwater.
Energy absorption was found to be best for wave periods of between
5 and 8 seconds, shorter and longer periods giving higher reflections.
Incidentally, because of the technique applied, the highest reflection
coefficients have been under-estimated. According to more recent
investigations, a measured coefficient of 0.7 corresponds to almost
100% reflection. In general, it is found that the coefficient of reflection decreases with increasing wave height.

Low reflection for a larger range of wave periods is offered by the
breakwater type in Fig. 13, which has both a permeable face and a
permeable inner wall.

2.2 Wave Disturbance within a Harbour

There are three possible reasons for the presence of wind-generated
waves in a mooring basin:

(A) Ingress via the harbour entrance.

---

* Terrett, F. L., Osorio, J. D. C. and Lean, G. H. (1969), 'Model Studies of a Perforated
Breakwater', *Proc. 11th Conf. on Coastal Eng. (1968)*, 2, Ch. 70, pp. 1104-1120. Am. Soc.
C. E.

(B) Overtopping of the breakwaters.

(C) Generation by wind within the basin.

The permissible disturbance is usually specified in terms of a maximum wave height with a recurrence interval of 10 or 100 years. However, a 5-second period wave of maximum height 0·3 m is more injurious than a 7-second wave of height 0·5 m, provided that the fendering allows the vertical motion. The 'permissible wave height' depends also upon the angle between wave direction and boat axis.

It seems more rational to prescribe certain angles of rotation for the rolling and pitching of selected craft. These movements can be determined from tests with model boats where typical mooring and fendering systems are simulated.

The motion of berthing pontoons may also be a criterion of permissible disturbance.

(A) INGRESS VIA THE HARBOUR ENTRANCE. Since there is a continuous inflow of wave energy through the entrance, a balance is not achieved until

Energy Outflow + Internal Energy Dissipation = Energy Inflow

The outflow is insignificant unless the waves inside the harbour are several times higher than the waves outside. Incidentally, this did sometimes happen decades ago when harbours were built without previous model tests! Thus energy dissipation is of paramount importance. Fig.3 is an example of the provision, at strategic locations, of energy-absorbing slopes, some of which are sited beneath the quays.

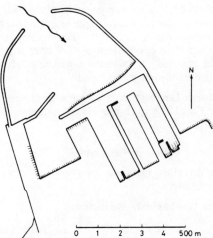

Figure 3   Energy-absorbing slopes inside Hanstholm harbour, Denmark (57° 08'N, 8° 36'E)

In spite of certain shortcomings, model testing with regular waves
is the standard procedure. Since the higher waves are often the
longest ones, their energy is spread over a wider angle by diffraction
when they pass an opening, that is to say more energy 'bends around
the corner'. Hence the tests should comprise periods 80-100%
longer than the mean period of the waves attributable to the severest
gales.

If one of the natural rolling or pitching periods of the moored boats
coincides with one of the wave periods tested, tests with regular waves
may give a too pessimistic picture of the boat motions. On the other
hand, if such resonance does not occur, the motions observed may
be only 30-50% of the motions in irregular waves because of the combinations of long and short waves of varying shapes.

(B) WAVE OVERTOPPING. The crest elevation and the superstructure of the breakwaters should be so designed that the disturbance
generated by the overtopping waves is within acceptable limits.

It is only the highest waves that cause significant overtopping.
Each overtopping water mass generates a very irregular wave train
wherein relatively long waves are followed by many shorter ones.

For reliable prediction of small craft behaviour under these conditions, the testing procedure should include irregular waves and boat
models.

(C) INTERNAL WAVE GENERATION. In the case of long basins,
the cost of model tests may be excessive and it is then necessary to
estimate the characteristics of waves generated by strong winds.

The following formulae apply to open basins of normal dimensions:

$$H_s = U(10^{-5} F/g)^{\frac{1}{2}} \qquad (1)$$
$$\overline{T} = (0 \cdot 04 \ UF/g^2)^{\frac{1}{3}} \qquad (2)$$

where H_s = significant height (mean of highest one-third of the
waves) (m)
$\overline{T}$ = mean wave period (s)
U = wind velocity (m/s)
F = free fetch = length of basin (m)
g = acceleration due to gravity (m/s^2).

3 Harbour Resonance

Harbour resonance is the amplification inside a harbour of waves
in the sea having periods between 20 seconds and 1 hour. Because of
the unsatisfactory conditions in some existing harbours, coastal
engineers are always anxious to avoid this phenomenon in new projects.

Long period oscillations in the sea are generally small, of the order 0·1 m or less. They are often caused by the turbulent pressure fluctuations travelling with the wind during storms, but there may also be other causes such as surf beats.

The resonance period (first mode) of a rectangular basin of length l, open at one end and with depth D, can be calculated from the wave length L (=$4l$) and the wave celerity $C = (gD)^{\frac{1}{2}}$ to be

$$T = 4l / (gD)^{\frac{1}{2}} \qquad (3)$$

If, for example, l = 275 m and D = 3 m, then, in accordance with Eq. (3), T = 200 s. The water surface variations are maximum at the closed end of the basin, where long moorings are required. The currents are maximum at the open end, where excessive surging of the boats may occur and moorings break.

The problems in nature are usually more complex than represented by Eq. (3) because of irregular shapes and varying depths. Fig. 4 shows a fjord where maximum water surface variations of 4 m with a period of 6 min were reported, probably caused by the breeding of the Jakobshavn Glacier (45 km from the harbour). Later, the oscillations were reduced, partly due to the natural retreat of the glacier front and partly as a result of the introduction of the two short breakwaters indicated in the figure.

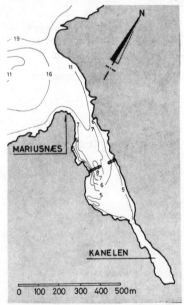

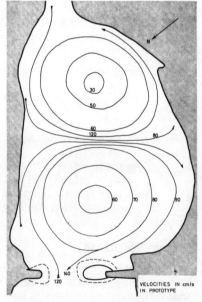

Figure 4   Jakobshavn, Greenland (69° 14'N, 51° 06'W)

Figure 5   Harbour resonance: vortices in Jakobshavn

Fig.5 shows the circulatory currents produced by these oscillations. In addition to the provision of breakwaters it was necessary to align the fishing quays so that all the berths were exposed to uni-directional flow during the entire 6-min period, thus virtually eliminating any surging of the boats.

The usual approach to the problem of harbour resonance is to test small models in very large basins. There are three difficulties which arise:

(a) Ideal boundary conditions are normally not obtainable because of the extreme lengths of waves.

(b) Tests are made with constant period, whereas the natural disturbances from the sea are random.

(c) The amplification factor can vary abruptly (for regular waves) by a change of wave period of less than 1%.

For larger projects it is now possible to circumvent these difficulties by the substitution of a mathematical model for the physical model. System 21 developed by the Computational Hydraulic Centre of the Danish Hydraulic Institute is a large complex of computer programs adaptable to arbitrary topography and arbitrary boundary conditions. By incremental calculation the water surface variations and the current velocities are reproduced over a grid covering the harbour and part of the sea, for an input from an actual sea level record.

4 Wave Forces and Breakwaters

4.1 Types of Breakwater

The selection of a suitable type of breakwater is limited by consideration of water depth and wave height. In general, breakwaters may be classified in order of increasing wave height and/or increasing depth as follows:

(a) Pneumatic breakwater – appropriate only where waves are low and are of length less than 3 × water depth; of rare application.

(b) Floating breakwater – dealt with in the paper by N.B. Webber and R.J.S. Harris in this Symposium.

(c) Rubble mound breakwater (Type S in Fig.1) – see Section 4.2.

(d) Vertical face breakwater (Type V in Fig.1) – see Sections 4.3 to 4.6.

(e) Composite breakwater (Fig.6, lower) – the most economical type for the largest depths.

If the tidal range is small, the rubble mound is the only type of breakwater that need be considered for the majority of coastal marinas.

4.2 Rubble Mound Breakwaters

The discussion here will be brief because the classical rubble mound breakwater is well covered in the technical literature.

The coastal engineering problems posed are:

(a) Method of construction.

(b) Availability of durable materials.

(c) Stability of armour blocks and other parts of the structure exposed permanently or temporarily to wave action.

Preliminary designs can be based upon recognised stability formulae. Model tests are needed where the detailed design of an important structure is entailed. The influence of the angle of wave approach is not well understood.

Hudson's formula is commonly used to establish the required weight W of the armour blocks and may be expressed in the form

$$W = \frac{w_r H^3}{K \left[(w_r / w_w) - 1 \right]^3 \cot \alpha} \tag{4}$$

where H = significant wave height
w_r = specific weight of rock
w_w = specific weight of sea water
α = stable angle of the exposed face of the mound
K = non-dimensional coefficient

Approximate values for K are:

Rounded stone	Quarry rock	Cube	Tetrapod	Akmon	Dolos*
2·5	4	6	8	10	20

Many other shapes of blocks have been used or proposed, such as Tribar, Quadripod, Stabit, Hollow Square, N-Block, Svee Block, Cob, etc.

4.3 Vertical Face Breakwaters

These will be discussed at greater length in view of the developments over the past ten years.

A vertical face breakwater may be justified because of:

(A) Great depth.

(B) Constructional hazards for a rubble mound.

(C) Lack of economical materials for a rubble mound.

---

* Merrifield, E. M. and Zwamborn, J. A. (1967), The Economic Value of a New Breakwater Armour Unit Dolos', *Proc. 10th Conf. on Coastal Eng. (1966)*, 2, Ch. 51, pp. 885-912.

The coastal engineering problems posed are:

(a) Method of construction.

(b) Materials: steel sheet pile walls or reinforced concrete caissons.

(c) Stability against overturning and sliding (including strength of foundation) under the influence of wave forces.

(d) Scour protection of the sea bed.

(e) Settlement.

(f) Stresses in various parts of the structure.

(g) Durability and possibilities of repair.

4.4 Wave Forces on Vertical Face Breakwaters

Most of the waves that approach a vertical face at normal incidence are reflected and cause total or partial clapotis, yielding a quasi-static force, that is to say a force which varies with time approximately as the elevation of the wave profile.

Some of the waves, however, are reflected so that the next wave breaks at a critical distance from the face, resulting in a rapidly rising 'shock' force on the breakwater.

Unless the foundation is particularly soft, the shock forces are the decisive factor for stability. The wall in a caisson always has to be designed for the shock pressures.

It is necessary to distinguish between three different types of shock, identified in Fig. 6.

The 'ventilated shock', where air is entrapped only as bubbles, occurs when the vertical face rises directly from the sea bed.

The 'compression shock', where a larger air pocket is enclosed, occurs when there is a steep slope in front of the vertical face. Under the influence of such a slope many of the waves become plunging breakers, some of which produce particularly high shocks. A composite breakwater of this form should therefore be avoided except in large water depths.

The last type of shock, a 'hammer shock' occurs when a plunging wave, described above, strikes the face. Locally, the shock may be of high intensity.

The forces involved in the shock process are: inertia, gravity, and pressure in air bubbles and pockets. The compressibility of the water is negligible.

If natural wave shapes are generated in the laboratory, shock forces and pressures can be studied by model tests. However, the results are somewhat conservative because the air entrainment is propor-

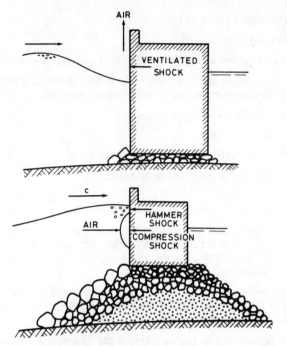

Figure 6   Types of shock forces

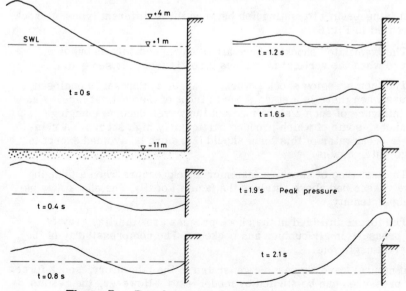

Figure 7   Development of ventilated shock

tionately greater in nature. It is imperative to generate the prototype wave shapes, because, if only the correct wave spectrum were reproduced, there might be no ventilated shocks and the compression shocks would be erroneous.

The development of a ventilated shock is shown in Fig.7. At $t = 0$, with the wave crest approaching the breakwater, the trough of the preceding wave is gradually filled in and there is a simultaneous reduction of the wave crest. The slope of the water surface accelerates the water towards the vertical face until, at $t = 1\cdot2$ s, the maximum velocity is attained. Since the breakwater obstructs the free flow of the water towards the right, the horizontal velocities of the water are changed into vertical velocities, exerting a high pressure on the face ($t = 1.9$ s). The shock pressures can be attributed to the centrifugal forces induced by the curvature of the paths of the water particles.

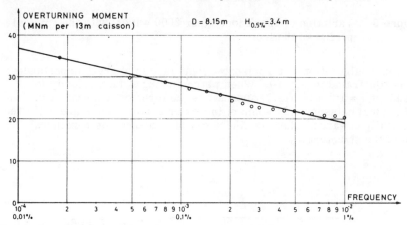

Figure 8   Stability of breakwater: statistical distribution of overturning moment for 3000 waves

The shock forces must be analysed statistically as illustrated in Fig.8, which shows the results of a test on a structure when $H_{0.5\%} = 3\cdot4$ m, that is to say when 0·5% of the heights of the incident waves exceed 3·4 m.

It is important to run a large number of waves in each test, because the greatest shocks are due to rare combinations of shapes of successive waves rather than to a particularly high wave. The latter, incidentally, may break so far from the breakwater that no shock is produced.

4. 5 Influence of Face Geometry on Shock Forces

Even minor differences in the geometry of the face, as in Fig.9, may have a considerable influence on the magnitudes of the shock forces. In the case of a composite face, with the top slope extending below still water level, the shocks may be entirely eliminated.

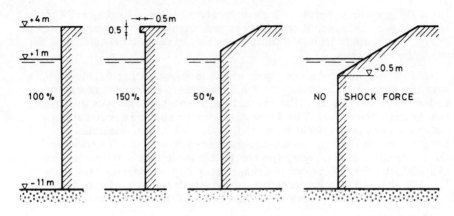

Figure 9   Variation of shock force (per 2000 waves) with the vertical
profile of the face

The configuration in a horizontal plane is also of great importance
as is illustrated in Fig.10. When water moving at high velocity (at
the stage $t = 1 \cdot 2$ s in Fig.7) approaches the foremost generatrix of a
cylindrical caisson, only some of the water particle paths are deflected
vertically upwards, whereas others can bend around the peripheral
arc of the structure.

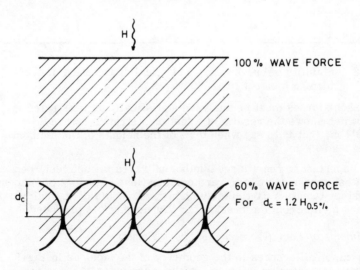

Figure 10   Variation of force with the horizontal profile of a vertical
face

Fig.11 shows typical variations with time of the pressures on a model of a cylindrical caisson in which 20 pressure cells have been installed, arranged in four horizontal rows of five each on a quarter of the peripheral face. Cells 1-5 are in the top row, above still water level. Cells 16-20 form the lowest row.

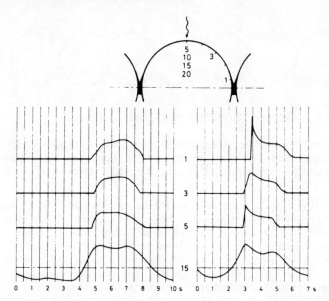

Figure 11   Pressure cell records for a circular caisson breakwater

On the left hand side of Fig.11, the recordings show a typical quasi-static pressure, increasing simultaneously on all cells. On the right hand side there is evidence of a high shock pressure. The time delay from cell 5 (meridian) to cell 1 (corner) is clearly discernible.

Physically, the reduction of shock forces associated with the cylindrical shape may also be explained in the following way. The delay in pressure development around the cylinder indicates a longer time of pressure rise from zero to maximum intensity. Since the horizontal momentum of the water approaching the face is approximately the same for the two breakwaters in Fig.10, the longer shock duration corresponds to a smaller maximum force.

On the grounds of structural economy, the cylindrical caisson also shows to appreciable advantage. For example, in the case of a particular breakwater site, it was found that the provision of rectangular caissons would necessitate a total wall length of 5·7 m per metre run of breakwater, whereas circular caissons would only require 3·0 m. In addition, the rectangular caissons required a 50% thicker outer wall and much more reinforcement.

4.6 *Newer Types of Vertical Face Breakwater*

If long caissons can be floated into position and placed on a prepared bed, the diaphragm type shown in Fig.12 is preferable.

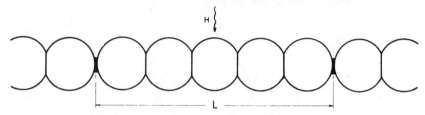

Figure 12   Diaphragm-type breakwater

A most economical breakwater results when one of the cylindrical cell types is provided with a composite face, having an upper portion as in the right hand diagram of Fig.9. This also applies to locations with a large tidal range.

Whilst all the types mentioned so far are sand-filled structures that have already been adopted in practice, the slotted breakwater design in Fig.13 has no sand fill and is still under development. The main purpose of this proposal has been to produce a breakwater with a minimum of wave reflection for all wave directions and periods of practical interest, and, at the same time to maintain the economic advantages of the thin-walled shell caissons described earlier. The variation of the reflection coefficient with wave period is shown in Fig.13 for a typical case.

A complete evaluation of the advantages and disadvantages of the slotted breakwater is beyond the scope of this paper. The more important characteristics are as follows:

(a) There is less wave reflection than with any other vertical face breakwater.

(b) If a composite face is adopted, it is likely that the horizontal shock forces will be almost entirely eliminated – by the top slope when water levels are high and by the slots in the front face when they are low.

(c) Because of the reduced wave forces, stability (without sand fill) can be achieved by placing mass concrete in the bottom of the caisson, or by increasing its diameter.

(d) Structurally, the caisson is still a shell, although the front columns must carry their wave loads as beams.

(e) With small waves there is no hoop tension in the shell, because there is no sand fill – hence tension crack widths are negligible.

(f) The shell is exposed to the marine environment on both sides.

(g) Overtopping and spray on the superstructure are minimised.

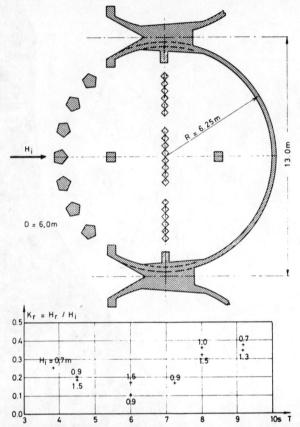

Figure 13   Slotted circular caisson breakwater with internal permeable wall. Variation of reflection coefficient with
wave period

5 Sediment Transport along Coasts

5.1 Factors Determining the Coastal Drift

Sedimentary material is transported along a coast by the combined
effects of waves and currents. Under wave action alone there is
appreciable movement of the finer sediments, but, since the motion
is forwards with the passage of the crest and backwards with the
trough, the net transport is relatively small. However, if a current
is also present, the transportation of sediment takes place along a
zigzag path.

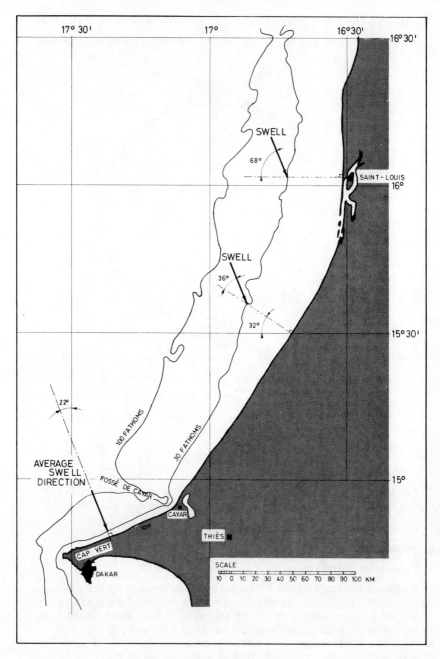

Figure 14   Coast of Senegal

Outside the breaker zone there is usually an offshore current generated by tides or wind and mainly running parallel to the coast. The resulting sediment transport, known as the 'offshore drift', may be of significance if the current is strong.

Between the breaker zone and the coastline, the wave-induced current normally dominates. It is generated by waves of oblique incidence, and the resulting sediment transport is called the 'littoral drift'. This movement may be in the direction opposite to that of the offshore drift.

The littoral drift is particularly large in the breaker and surf zones. If there is a bar along the coast there are two breaker zones. Normally, a strong current flows in the trough between the bar and the coastline. This current is generated by the water masses passing over the bar with the wave crests.

The direction of the drift changes with the longshore current. The net drift is defined as the resultant averaged over many years.

The tidal range has a pronounced influence on the coastal profile; the greater the range, the less is the possibility of the formation of a bar.

For a given wave climate, it is found that the finer the material, the flatter is the profile of a stable beach.

5.2 Variation of Littoral Drift with Wave Direction

In the case of the Senegal coast north of Dakar (Fig.14), it has been possible to estimate the variation of the littoral drift with the angle α_∞ between the wave direction in deep water and the normal to the coast.

Little sediment passes Cap Vert so it may be assumed that the average direction of the swell approaching the coast is normal to the coastline between Cap Vert and Cayar. Hence, north of Cayar the angle of incidence is 36° and the correspondingly larger littoral drift is deposited in the submarine canyon, Fossé de Cayar.

Northwards, along the coastline at Saint Louis, the angle of incidence is 68°. Since the Senegal River, which discharges into the Atlantic south of Saint Louis, does not contribute sediments to the littoral drift, the latter must have the same value for an angle of 68° as for an angle of 36°.

In Fig.15 the sediment transport Q_s has been plotted as a function of the angle of incidence, taking cognizance of the fact that Q_s is zero for the angles 0° and 90°. The maximum value of Q_s corresponds to an angle of incidence of about 53°.

Although the curve in Fig.15 is only really valid for this particular wave climate (and for this coastal sediment), it does give a general

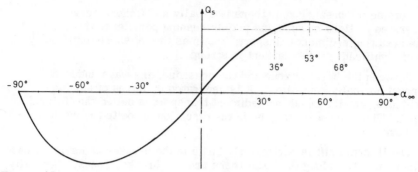

Figure 15   Variation of littoral drift with wave direction in deep
water

idea of the variation of the littoral drift with wave direction relative
to the coast. It leads to a marked difference between harbours on
coasts for which the angle is either materially less than 53° or
materially larger than 53° (see Section 5.5).

5.3 *Sediment Problems at Harbours*

Since the breakwaters of a harbour interfere with the longshore
current, there will normally be an accretion on the updrift (windward)
side and a corresponding erosion on the downdrift (lee) side.

The main sediment problems in connection with the planning of
harbours are:

(a) To maintain the necessary depth in the approach to the harbour
entrance.

(b) To avoid unnecessary accumulation of sediments inside the
harbour.

(c) To avoid detrimental leeside erosion.

A favourable location for a harbour entrance is a point where there
is no net drift (a nodal point).

If the net drift is not zero, a period of time will elapse before the
accretion and erosion regions have reached an equilibrium state.
Thereafter, the problem posed by the net drift must be solved in one
or more of the following ways:

(1) By siting the breakwaters in such positions that the depth maintained by waves and currents at the harbour entrance is
sufficient to allow the drift to pass naturally from the updrift
to the downdrift side.

(2) By artificial by-passing, whereby a stationary or mobile
dredge removes the accumulated sediments from an appropriate
area on the updrift side and pumps them to the other side.

(3) By arresting the sedimentary material in transit before it reaches the harbour entrance, and allowing it to accumulate continuously on the updrift side. This procedure presupposes that the reservoir for accumulation is sufficiently large (or can be enlarged at reasonable cost) and that the steadily developing leeside erosion is acceptable.

(4) By intercepting the drift in a natural or artificial reservoir before it reaches the entrance region. The material is then dredged from the reservoir and dumped in deeper water. This is a common method and often the most economical. However, it has the drawback that most of the dredged material is removed permanently from the coast, where it may be badly needed.

5.4 Harbours on Coasts without a Bar

If there is no bar along a coast, the littoral transport takes place in the breaker and surf zones near the shore. Where there is a breakwater extending beyond the breaker zone, sediments are normally deposited along the structure until the depths are so reduced that a new breaker zone is established. The depth reduction along a vertical face breakwater is relatively small if the angle between the wave fronts and the breakwater is large.

The depth reduction is particularly pronounced on a tropical coast exposed to unidirectional swell, because the breaking of the swell takes place in relatively shallow water.

Fig. 16 shows the extended accumulation on the updrift side of a Peruvian harbour where the littoral drift is of the order of 500,000 m³/annum. The customary swell comes from approximately SSW. Since the sand can be transported by breaking waves only, all the depth contours between 4 and 9 m bend around the breakwater head. A sand barrier is forming across the harbour entrance.

If the entrance is not dredged, the harbour will eventually be closed by a tombolo extending from the breakwater, approximately in the direction of the average swell. This is illustrated in Fig. 17, where a natural harbour in South-West Africa is connected to the sea only through two small inlets maintained by a tide with a range between 0·6 and 1·5 m.

5.5 Harbours on Coasts with a Bar

The breaking of oblique waves on a bar accounts for a major part of the littoral drift. If the bar is cut by a breakwater, it will move seawards and bend around the end of the structure. An example of this is shown in Fig. 18 which refers to a Kattegat harbour where the drift is 25,000 m³/annum and the natural depth over the bar is about 2 m. This is too shallow for dealing with the problem by method (1) of Section 5.3.

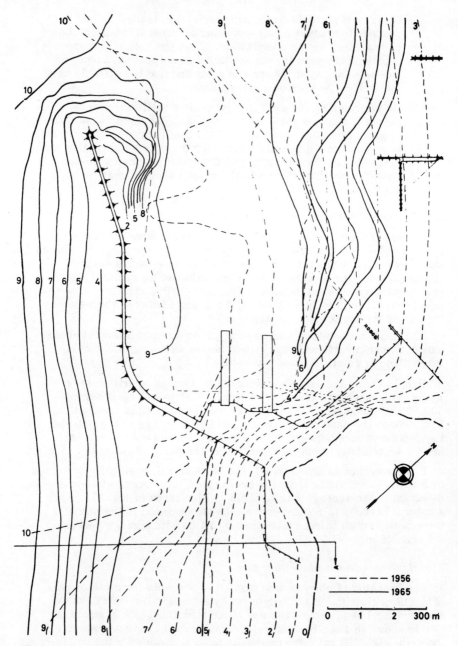

Figure 16   Salaverry harbour, Peru (8°13'S, 79°00'W): depth contours
(in metres) before and after construction of the harbour

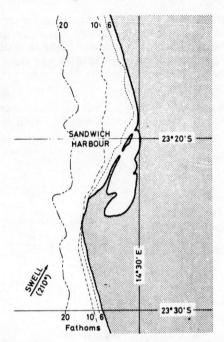

Figure 17 Closure of a natural harbour by littoral drift

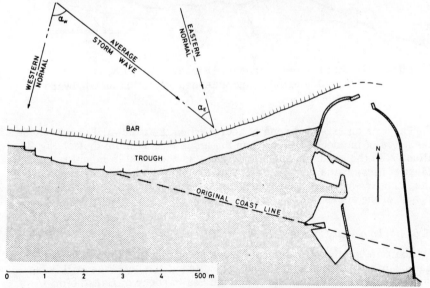

Figure 18 Gilleleje harbour, Denmark (56° 08'N, 12° 19'E):
Short length of accretion on windward side

The angle of incidence α_W for the average storm wave on the original coastline is larger than the angle of maximum drift (cf. Fig.15). The accretion on the windward side is such that the angle α_E offers the same transporting capability as α_W. Consequently, the accretion zone is short and, in fact, it was rapidly filled after the harbour had been constructed.

Fig.19 shows an example of a North Sea harbour, where the drift is more than 500,000 m³ /annum and the natural depth over the bar is about 3.5 m.

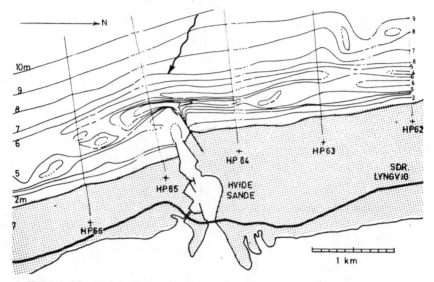

Figure 19   Hvide Sande harbour, Denmark (56° 00'N, 8° 07'E): leeside erosion and extended accretion on windward side

There is an extended zone of accretion on the windward side because the angle of incidence is less than the angle of maximum drift. Fig.20 illustrates the sand transportation paths as observed in model tests. Most of these paths converge towards the bar which is forming across the harbour entrance, subsequent to the erosion which occurred as a result of the accretion on the north side.

5. 6 *Harbours on Coasts with Strong Offshore Currents*

Sometimes, the offshore current is so strong that the net drift can by-pass a harbour, the depth reduction at the entrance still being within an acceptable limit. The North Sea harbour of Hanstholm (Fig.21), located on the 90° headland, is in a situation where this occurs.

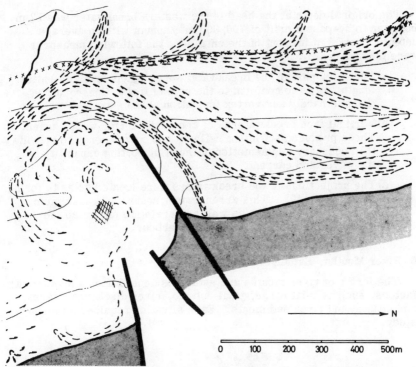

Figure 20 Hvide Sande: sand transportation paths during storms

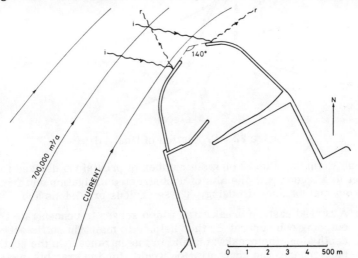

Figure 21 Hanstholm harbour, Denmark (57° 08'N, 8° 36'E): natural by-passing of littoral drift

The original depth at the head of the western breakwater was 12 m. In order to by-pass a drift of 700,000 m³/annum with an average depth of about 9 m in front of the entrance, the following measures were taken:

(a) The outer part of the breakwater was aligned, over its entire length, so as to conform to the path of flow. Consequently, there is hardly any vortex formation at the entrance.

(b) Vertical face breakwaters, of composite form, were chosen. These produced sufficient reflection of wave energy to provide the necessary augmentation of the transporting capability of the waves and current.

(c) The projections of the breakwaters were located so as to form an angle of 140°. This arrangement results in a maximum depth at the entrance, as well as serving to minimise the amount of sand conveyed into the harbour.

6 River Mouths, Estuaries and Inlets

The forms of river mouths and estuaries depend upon a number of factors, such as tidal range, tidal volume, river discharge, waves, and coastal and river sediments. Each situation requires a thorough study.

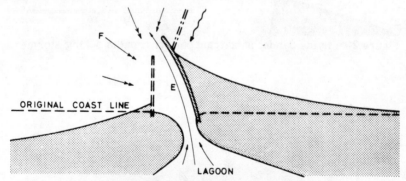

Figure 22   Protection of tidal inlet

As an example, Fig. 22 shows a number of provisions devised for an inlet to a lagoon with the aim of unobstructed navigation and freedom from maintenance dredging. These various provisions are:

(a) A curved eastern breakwater which serves to concentrate the outgoing ebb current E, thus helping to maintain sufficient depth along the breakwater and in the entrance. In the northern hemisphere, the concentration would, for the example quoted, be strengthened by the Coriolis force, a phenomenon associated with the earth's rotation.

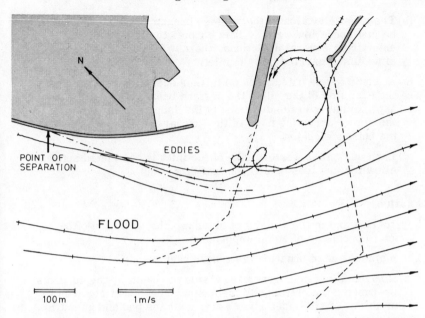

Figure 23 Esbjerg harbour, Denmark (55° 28'N, 8° 26'E): existing entrance with eddies causing siltation

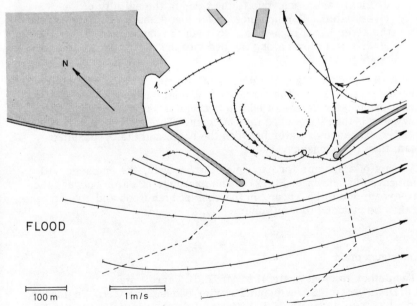

Figure 24 Esbjerg harbour: improved entrance for enlarged harbour

(b) The crest elevation of the western breakwater is arranged to be just above low water. This enables the flood current F to enter from several directions, thereby reducing the amount of sediment carried into the inlet.

(c) At some future date, when no further accretion is possible on the east side of the inlet, the eastern breakwater will be extended approximately in the direction of the incoming waves, with the aim of arresting most of the littoral drift before it reaches the entrance region.

(d) Land use on the western side of the inlet is restricted so as to allow for any leeside erosion that may occur.

7 Siltation

In estuaries and in the vicinity of river mouths, siltation often gives rise to problems of some importance.

The main causes of siltation in harbour basins are:

(a) Horizontal vortices generated inside the basin by the currents by-passing the entrance to the basin. These vortices lead to an inflow of silt-laden river water near the bed and an outflow of clearer water at the surface.

(b) Repeated renewal of the water in the basin as a result of cyclical variations, due to the tide, of the salinity of the river water. For instance, after some hours of flood current the river has a higher salinity than the basin, and silt-laden river water flows along the bed into the basin, where the silt tends to settle.

By appropriate design, the degree of siltation may be materially reduced. Fig. 23 shows the entrance to a tidal harbour where the flood current produces a series of eddies because it separates from the breakwater before it reaches the entrance. This eddying brings about a greater exchange of water between the basin and the by-passing stream than is necessary.

As part of a scheme for expanding the harbour, the entrance will be improved as shown in Fig. 24. The exchange of water between the tidal stream and the harbour, in the case of both flood and ebb currents, will then be reduced to a minimum.

Acknowledgement

The author is most grateful to Mr. F. L. Terrett and Mr. J. D. C. Osorio of Lewis and Duvivier (Consulting Civil Engineers, London) as well as to Mr. N. B. Webber of Southampton University for many valuable amendments to this paper.

Site Investigation
and
Hydraulic Model Studies

I. W. Stickland

*Hydraulics Division, Wimpey Laboratories Ltd.**

1 Introduction

One of the most important factors in the process of planning a yacht harbour is that of obtaining as detailed a knowledge as possible of the physical characteristics of the proposed site. The information is required in order that the Engineer may evaluate the relative merits of a particular site or sites, develop the best layout for a marina, determine its long term effects on the existing coastal regime, and investigate the most effective and economic design for the various marine structures and other facilities.

Factors such as wave action, wind velocities and directions, tidal range, tidal currents, river discharge, littoral drift, siltation problems, the nature of the sea bed and sub-surface strata for foundation problems must all be surveyed and documented.

Some of this information will be required at a very early stage, such as during the feasibility studies which normally precede the selection of a particular site. Other data, particularly wind and wave information, must, if it is to be of value, be recorded over as long a period as possible and preferably in excess of one year. In the event that hydraulic model studies are likely to play a part in the design of the marina, then this too must be taken into account when considering the scope of site investigations.

The data required for model studies fall into two categories, firstly to provide sufficient information to design, construct and operate the model, and secondly to interpret the results and if possible to forecast the frequency of occurrence of certain phenomena or long term effects on the existing regime. To undertake any form of statistical forecasting with any degree of assurance requires as much data as possible

* Mr. Stickland is now Head, Hydraulics Group, British Hovercraft Corporation, Cowes, I.W.

over as long a period as possible. This fact must be recognised and allowed for when preparing a schedule of work for site investigations and therefore it must be considered at the earliest possible point in the design process.

There is in fact a very good case to be put forward for the design engineer and the research and site investigation engineers discussing the scope and requirements of the various studies prior to the preparation of the specifications for their respective work. It should also be possible at this time to prepare some form of flow chart showing the order in which the information is required and establish lines of communication between the various disciplines involved and the main coordinator, who in most instances will be the Consulting Engineer.

2 Organisation of Site Investigations and Research Work

Each particular project will have its own specific problems so that it is not possible to lay down a standard procedure for the field and research work in relation to the design process but experience suggests that the flow diagram shown on Figure 1 is reasonably typical of current practice. It assumes that, in this instance, the Consulting Engineer has already obtained sufficient preliminary information to enable him to prepare an initial feasibility study, select the site and establish, at least, an outline design for the proposed marina. It also assumes that the preliminary work has indicated the need to consider hydraulic model research.

The normal procedure at this stage is for outline specifications to be drawn up for the field work and the model studies, and quotations invited from organisations specialising in the various spheres of work. This may involve either a large number of separate organisations or an individual company capable of undertaking all aspects.

In the case of the former the Consulting Engineer would act as coordinator between the individual organisations, ensuring adequate communication and dovetailing of activities and, perhaps most important of all, ensuring correct cross referencing of such vital items as survey grids, level datums, correct disposition of boreholes for correlation of geophysical data, etc. and the model studies.

If, however, all the various surveys and the model studies are carried out by one organisation it is normal practice for that company to appoint a project co-ordinator who will be responsible to the Consulting Engineer for all matters relating to the activities of the separate sections.

The importance of good co-ordination in the work of site investigations, particularly in a marine environment cannot be stressed too much, and, if handled properly, can lead to considerable economies. For instance, hydrographic survey of sea bed contouring can be carried out simultaneously with the geophysical survey of the sub-surface rock or

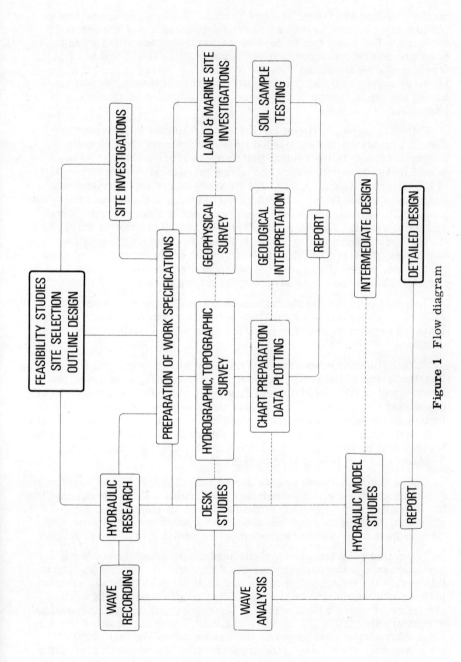

Figure 1 Flow diagram

strata profiling and from the same vessel. Position fixing and track
plotting are common to both as are the determination of the sea bed
contours. The same can be said of marine boreholes although separate
craft are an obvious necessity, but again position fixing and sea bed
levelling can be combined with the work of the survey team. If a geophysical survey is being carried out, co-ordination with the marine
boring survey in the matter of correlation boreholes is absolutely
essential.

This overlapping between the various disciplines is indicated in
Figure 1 by the horizontal dashed lines and includes the hydraulic
research studies in the context that there is every advantage to be
gained by the research engineer visiting the site during the latter part
of the survey. He can, during such a visit, carry out a preliminary
assessment of the information obtained to date and if necessary suggest
modifications, bearing in mind the very specific requirements of the
hydraulic model. This is particularly the case if the initial survey is
the first of a series having as their object the determination of the
movement of the sea bed due to littoral drift or the movement of sand
banks, etc. where the hydraulics of the particular site will dictate
possible alterations in the scope of the survey work.

The next phase of the operations shown on Figure 1 is concerned
with the analysis and interpretation of the data obtained on site and
again it is essential to ensure the free flow of information between
sections.

At this time the hydrographic surveyors will be preparing final
'master' plans of the sea bed contours, tidal curves, float track plots,
diagrams of current velocity and direction, etc. The geophysicists will
commence the interpretation of their seismic records, including geological and borehole correlation, rock head profile cross-sections, and
sediment thickness charts. Samples obtained from the land and marine
borings will be returned to the laboratory for analysis and testing, and
final detailed borehole records prepared.

One of the first requirements during this phase will be to supply the
research engineer with as much data as possible so that the design of
the hydraulic model can be finalised and a start made with the construction, bearing in mind that this latter operation may require anything from 4 to 16 weeks depending on the complexity of the problems.

From this point onwards the site investigation and survey work
continue through the normal process of reporting to the client. During
this period the construction of the hydraulic model will have been completed and a start made on the actual test programme. This work
always commences with a series of tests to establish that the model is
adequately simulating the known site conditions on the basis of the data
obtained from the site surveys. This is known as the 'calibration'
stage and only when satisfactory reproduction has been achieved can a
start be made on the examination of the proposed design of the marina.

With regard to the actual test programme, this frequently takes the form of an initial series of exploratory tests, the object of which is to examine broad schemes of development from which can be distilled one or two preferred layouts. These layouts are studied in greater detail until a final scheme is arrived at, which will then allow the last stage of the test programme to investigate refinements and points of detail.

Very close co-operation between the design engineer and the research organisation is essential throughout the hydraulic model studies as fundamental changes in the design concept may be necessary, the justification for which will depend, not only on the hydraulic requirements, but on economic consideration as well. On the completion of all the above work the engineer should be in possession of sufficient data upon which to prepare final detailed designs for the project.

Having set out in broad terms the overall picture of the organisation and planning of site investigations, it is proposed to discuss the more detailed work involved by relating it to the individual requirements of particular types of model investigations, desk studies, and engineering design requirements.

3 Hydraulic Model Studies

The use of hydraulic model studies in the design of marine works has now become accepted as a significant and useful tool available to engineers working in this field. In experienced hands, the results obtained from a properly conducted investigation can materially assist the engineer in assessing the effectiveness of various proposals and, in a great many cases, indicate the possibilities of substantial savings in costs not only of initial capital outlay but equally important of long term recurring maintenance costs. Hydraulic models also have a part to play in the realm of public relations, particularly where it may be necessary to satisfy local interests that their rights are being safeguarded.

In many ways a hydraulic model can be looked upon as a form of computer. It must for example be designed or programmed to perform a specific task; it must be asked the right questions; it must be given sufficient and adequate data, and, finally, the answers must be interpreted by experienced staff. If the questions that are asked are wrong, the answers will be equally wrong; if there is insufficient or unreliable input data, the answers will be only part answers or unreliable answers.

In short, the model will be as good or as bad as the information that it is supplied with and should be looked upon as an 'aid' to engineering judgement and not a substitute for it.

In the context of the design of marinas or small craft harbours, the type of model normally associated with this work falls into one or more of the following categories:

(i)   Storm wave models
(ii)   Flume studies
(iii)   Long period wave models
(iv)   Littoral drift studies
(v)   River and estuary studies

Each type will be described, setting out the scope of the work which can be undertaken, the possible limitations inherent in certain studies, and the extent of site data required to construct, calibrate and operate the various models.

4 Storm Wave Models

The principal object of storm wave models is to establish the most satisfactory layout for a harbour with particular reference to the dissipation of wave energy. More specifically, studies can be made of wave conditions in the approaches to the harbour, in the entrance, the outer and inner harbour and the effect on adjacent coastal features. In certain instances, depending to some extent on the scale chosen for the model, it is possible to examine and measure wave induced currents and resulting circulation patterns.

It is not, however, the function of this type of investigation to look into the complex problems associated with littoral drift or the effect of tidal currents on the movement of the sea bed. As a result the model is classified as being of the 'rigid bed' type in which the sea bed is contoured using some form of concrete screed.

For hydraulic reasons, which lie outside the scope of this paper, it is possible to construct storm wave models to natural scales without recourse to distortion.

The majority of models have linear scales of between 1:60 and 1:120 full size and frequently require wave basins of around 37m × 30m. In the case of marina studies where natural wave heights of 0·15m may be important it is obviously prudent to adopt as large a scale as possible.

This question of the comparatively low wave heights expected within the berthing area of a marina is extremely important as it calls for a degree of wave reduction far greater than would be necessary in a commercial harbour catering for vessels of between 5000 DWT and 250,000 DWT. It does in fact stress the need for hydraulic model studies.

With this in mind it is obviously essential that the wave conditions fed into the model, and more particularly at the harbour entrance, be realistic in terms of height, period and direction of wave approach.

Because both wave height and directions of approach are, in shallow water, significantly affected by the depth of water it follows that this type of model requires information from the survey work on two main subjects: (a) the wave climate of the area, and (b) the sea bed contours over a considerable distance offshore. Of these two, by far the most difficult to obtain will be the details of the wave climate, the more so because, to be of real value, not only in the design of the model, but also in the interpretation of results, they should cover as long a period as possible. In the case of storm wave models where the method of evaluation of design proposals is on the basis of careful comparative studies using repeatable wave conditions from test to test, the present procedure in all laboratories is to use uniform waves of discrete period. Whilst it is fully appreciated that this is not an exact reproduction of a complex random sea it is nevertheless the best that is available at this time until much more basic research has been done. Provided therefore that the range of wave periods and heights adequately covers the anticipated range in nature, comparative studies can be undertaken.

As far as sea-bed contouring is concerned the important factor here is to ensure that a sufficiently large area is surveyed offshore of the harbour so that the bending or refraction of waves can be correctly reproduced in the model, as the alignment of the wave crests at the entrance to the harbour is critical. In this respect, it is not unusual for the main point of interest, i.e. the harbour, to occupy only $\frac{1}{4}$ to $\frac{1}{6}$ of the contoured area of the model.

The importance of this in terms of the drawing up of the specification for the survey work is obvious and reinforces the previous suggestion that the research engineer be consulted in sufficient time. In certain instances it is, of course, possible to obtain a great deal of useful information from local charts but some caution must be exercised, bearing in mind that the primary function of a chart is navigation.

Before leaving the question of the effect on wave action of water depth it is as well to remember that variation in water level as a result of tidal rise and fall, which in European coastal waters can vary from 0·6m to 12m, must be catered for as not only will it influence the refraction of waves but may also cause incoming waves to break and dissipate a considerable proportion of their energy before reaching the harbour. This can be of the greatest significance and in many cases limits the maximum height of wave reaching a harbour and, therefore, considerably affects the whole design. The author has known of many sites where the highest waves at the harbour resulted from lower waves offshore which did not break.

All these points must be considered when designing a storm wave model together with an assessment of the possible direction of approach of waves to the harbour, and, on the basis of this work, terms of reference for the conduct of the model study agreed with the Consulting Engineers.

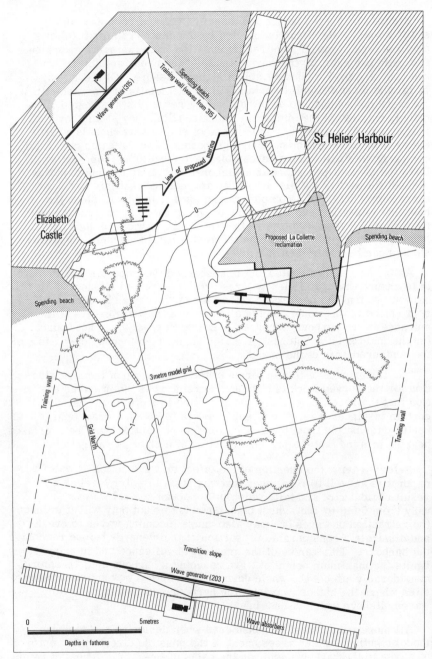

Figure 2 Layout of model of St. Helier Harbour

Figure 3 Model of St. Helier Harbour

Figure 4 Model of St. Helier Harbour

The general arrangement of a typical storm wave model constructed to a scale of 1:100 is shown in Figures 2, 3 and 4. In this case, the wave basin was some 34m long by 25m wide and demonstrates the comparatively small area occupied by the harbour in relation to the contoured bed of the model. It may be of interest that the time required for the construction of this quite detailed model was some 6 weeks.

Various aspects of the design were examined, and were concerned in the main with the most satisfactory alignment of a new breakwater to retain the reclaimed area, proposed new cargo and tanker berths, the influence on the existing harbour and, finally, the additional effect of the construction of further new breakwaters adjacent to both the new works and the existing harbour.

The investigation commenced with a study of the existing wave conditions so that sufficient data would be available for later comparisons with the future development schemes. This was followed by a series of tests in which various alignments of both the breakwater and the new berths were studied, and involved wave measurements in many key areas of the harbour and its approaches. The model indicated that the large area of rocks just offshore of the harbour played a significant part in dissipating wave energy with high waves, but were also responsible for altering the direction of approach of lower waves and focussing them into the area set aside for development. As a result of this work, additional tests were carried out to study what effect these wave conditions would have during the construction of the new works and it was established that modifications to construction procedures would be necessary.

Figure 5 shows the model under test with 7 sec waves approaching the harbour and new works. The bending or refraction of the waves due to the sea bed contours can clearly be seen as well as the diffraction of waves round the new breakwater and into the new berth. Later tests examined the effect of introducing a new vertical solid faced structure on a curving alignment to the west of the existing harbour entrance. This structure resulted in severe reflection of the incoming waves in many directions and caused a deterioration in both the existing harbour and in the new berths (Figure 6). In the approach channel to the existing harbour the reflected waves increased the height of waves by as much as 100% and changed what was previously a following sea into a very difficult combination of a following sea and beam sea. The investigation did not of course end at this point but went on to examine many alternatives until an acceptable solution was found.

The question of reflected waves is, of course, one of the important problems to be studied, particularly in the design of yacht marinas where the general smallness of the craft make them more susceptible to this type of wave motion. In this respect, the design of the structures forming the outer and inner harbour should, if possible, incorporate

Figure 5 Wave studies in St. Helier Harbour model

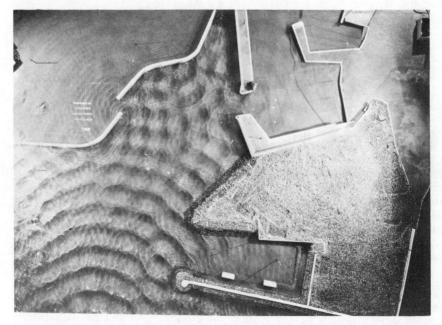

Figure 6 New breakwater under test in St. Helier Harbour model

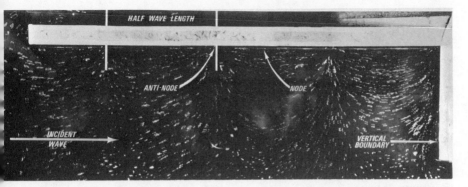

Figure 7 Behaviour of reflected waves

some form of wave absorber, such as a rubble stone slope. If this is not possible a situation may arise similar to that shown on Figure 7 which shows part of a berthing area formed by two vertical faced structures. Incident waves entering the basin from the left hand side of the photograph are reflected back from the vertical boundary at the right hand side through the next and subsequent incident waves.

Where the incident and reflected wave crests meet and pass through each other, i.e. at the antinodes, the movement of water will be in a vertical plane and the apparent wave height almost double the height of the incoming wave. At the nodal points the water movement is horizontal as shown by the orbital movement of the tracers on the water surface and there is little if any apparent wave height. The effect on yachts moored along the finger jetty would be one of considerable vertical movement at the antinodes and equally severe ranging fore and aft at the nodal points.

If in the design of a harbour basin the distance between opposing boundary walls is such that the time required for a wave to travel from one boundary to the other is an integer multiple of half a wave period a standing wave situation will be set up by reflections from each boundary coinciding and a condition of resonant basin oscillation will result.

Resonance, or seiche action basin oscillation, is analogous to the motion of a spring mass system, pendulum, or electrical oscillating system which once started will continue until brought to rest by outside forces. The effect in the harbour basin will be one of severe surging or ranging of boats at their moorings and tests to investigate the possibility of this occurring should be included in the model study. Although resonance can be detected in storm wave models where the range of wave periods may be from 7 to 25 sec, the most significant effects will be related to waves with periods between 30 secs and 5 min and the problems must then be examined in a separate 'long period' wave study.

On the assumption that the storm wave model does demonstrate the existence of resonance in a harbour basin, the engineer is faced with the problem of deciding whether or not to 'de-tune' the harbour by significantly altering the shape and dimensions of the basin. The alteration may well increase the cost of the project considerably so that it will be essential to the process of decision making for the engineer to know 'how often' or 'the frequency of occurrence' of wave conditions likely to result in resonant basin oscillations.

Here again, the existence of adequate wave records and their correct analysis is important in the overall design process.

5 Flume Studies

Having established the layout of the harbour in the storm wave model the engineer will next be concerned with the more detailed design of the actual breakwaters, etc.

Bearing in mind the heavy costs involved in these structures and specific operational requirements, such as the reduction of waves overtopping breakwaters, it may be necessary to examine design proposals to a much larger scale than is possible in the storm wave models. This work is normally carried out in long, relatively narrow wave flumes in which typical cross-sections of the breakwaters are constructed to a natural scale in the region of 1:24 to 1:60 full size.

The flume may be of the order of 30m to 90m long and anything from 1·2 to 2·5m wide with an operating depth of water up to 0·75m.

The wave generator may produce either uniform waves or, more commonly nowadays, the full random sea. Indeed in many of the problems studied in flumes quite erroneous answers will be obtained if random waves are not used; this is particularly true in studies of overtopping. Finally, it may also be necessary to have facilities for generating both wind and tidal currents.

The principal types of investigation carried out in flumes are the stability of rubble mound breakwaters, impact forces on marine structures, efficiency of wave absorbing structures, transmission of waves through permeable construction, performance of tidal gates, and the design of stepped sea walls and curved parapet walls.

Breakwater studies will enable the engineer to determine, in the case of rubble mound structures, the slope, size and weight and type of main armouring for the seaward face, the depth to which this armouring must be taken below water level before changing to a lighter stone, the extent of wave run up and draw down, the crest level of the breakwater and or parapet wall and the extent to which the structure will be overtopped. It is also possible to measure the amount of wave energy which is reflected by the structure, which, in the case of spending beaches inside the harbour, is of special importance in yacht marinas.

Studies may also be carried out of the forces exerted on structures by wave action, which will allow the engineer to determine more precisely his foundation pressures and structural design loadings.

It will be obvious that to obtain the most benefit from such studies very comprehensive data are required on wave conditions, particularly if random seas are involved.

6 Littoral Drift Studies

If the initial feasibility study of a site proposed for a marina has indicated the possibility of littoral drift of beach material as a result of wave action, the engineer is faced with the problem of predicting what effect the new works will have on the existing coastal regime and on the long term operation of the harbour itself.

A number of courses of action are open to him. One may be to attempt a forecast based on a desk study of the information obtained from very detailed hydrographic surveys and mathematical computations with particular reference to the past history of the coastline. A second may seek to combine the above with the additional data which might be obtained from a natural scale rigid bed wave model, with the model being used to predict changes in wave patterns and currents resulting from the new works. A third method may be the use of a fully mobile bed model using sand or some light-weight material, which, with careful design and calibration, may demonstrate likely trends resulting from the introduction of the new harbour.

When considering the use of mobile bed hydraulic model studies for the purpose of examining problems of littoral drift certain limitations have to be accepted. At the outset it must be borne in mind that the question of beach movement resulting from wave action alone or a combination of wave action and tidal current is one of considerable complexity in hydraulic terms, both in nature itself, and, more particularly, in models.

The survey work must provide answers to important questions and the specification for the work will include not only detailed echo sounding of the offshore contours but intensive beach profiling, sampling of bed materials, current metering, float tracking and, of course, wave recording. Moreover, if the existing data is sparse, this survey may have to be repeated at 3 to 4 monthly intervals over at least one year in order to define more correctly the beach movement taking into account seasonal variations. Again, as in the case of the storm wave models, a sufficient length of coastline must be surveyed and although each must be judged on its merits it is not unusual to have to cover 7 to 8 km foreshore. It may also be prudent to include a geophysical survey of the rockhead in the area under consideration as this may play a significant part in determining the long term beach movement.

With regard to model studies, whilst scale laws exist for essential parameters such as time, velocity, discharge, etc., no model laws have yet been developed to enable the type of bed material to be determined in advance, for a particular condition to be reproduced. In addition, there is no mathematical relationship which allows the overall time scale of beach movement to be related in any way to the scales of the model. In fact experience in certain European laboratories has shown that even within a particular model more than one time scale has been necessary because the behaviour of the model changed once man-made structures such as groynes were introduced.

A further limitation is imposed in that it is necessary to distort the vertical scale with reference to the horizontal scale by as much as five or six times. This is brought about by the need to reproduce the correct degree of bed movement with depth of water, and, as a result, the establishment of the required equilibrium profile of the beach.

The existence of the distorted scale raises other associated problems in that the refraction or bending of waves is primarily a function of depth and therefore the vertical scale; diffraction or lateral spreading of waves around a breakwater is dependent more on wave length and therefore the horizontal scale. Of the two, refraction is the more important and therefore some degree of error is normally accepted with respect to diffraction.

These main limitations therefore require to be examined on a trial and error basis until satisfactory performance of the model is established (i.e. the calibration stage).

The extent to which the performance of the model is considered acceptable depends on how well it reproduces known changes in the prototype which have occurred over the years. It also requires that the changes that have occurred in nature have been adequately documented and measured. Normal practice in this respect is to look for a definite feature on the coastline, such as a breakwater, which will retain beach material, and, on the basis of periodic surveys, to determine the rate of build up with time. Additional information at this stage would be some knowledge of predominant wave direction, significant height and period. The model is then set to reproduce these wave conditions and the movement of the bed is monitored at the structure until such time as the required configuration is achieved. Many tests of this nature may be required and refinements made both to the material in the model and to the test conditions before satisfactory results are obtained.

If adequate back history of the coastal regime is not available the model will only demonstrate the mechanics of beach movement and give indications of trends. It is extremely unlikely that mobile bed models of this nature can be expected to give quantitative answers in terms of material in movement which could be relied upon for engineering design.

Because of these limitations and the empirical nature of the approach *mobile bed* wave studies are not so flexible as other types of coastal model studies.

It is not possible for instance to use them to examine questions related to the reduction in wave height resulting from breakwaters, or the protection afforded by harbour configurations. This type of study has to be carried out on a *natural scale rigid bed* model so that wave refraction resulting from variations in contour alignment and diffraction of waves around harbour structures can be correctly simulated.

Mobile bed wave models are also not normally suitable for the study of flow problems resulting from tidal conditions or outfalls where dispersal and mixing are important. In this instance a *rigid bed distorted scale* model is usually employed with sophisticated tide or current generators which control water level to within very fine limits. It is also necessary on the bed of the model to introduce artificial roughness to ensure correct curvature of flow. Such additional roughness, usually by means of stones scattered on the bed of the model, would completely nullify the purpose of a mobile bed model.

Despite however the inherent limitations imposed upon mobile bed wave action studies they can be justified and are necessary if only to indicate trends, more importantly highlight problems of design, to suggest alternative ideas and to permit proposals to be examined.

7 River and Estuary Studies

If the location of a new marina is in a river or estuary the engineer may be called upon to demonstrate that the new works in no way interfere with or significantly alter the existing regime. If, for instance, the new development involves building out into the waterway, the existing flow patterns may be changed quite dramatically and in such a way as to cause scouring or accretion in new areas.

In the worst case this may lead to very long term changes in the river or estuary and the effects felt over a very wide area.

Cases have been known where new structures so altered the velocity distribution in a river that severe siltation occurred many km upstream and downstream of the new works embracing, in the process, commercial berths whose annual maintenance dredging costs multiplied many times.

It is not always possible to forecast on the drawing board the effect of new structures in a dynamic 3-dimensional hydraulic situation such as can be found in any river or estuary with so many unknown variables to contend with.

As in all situations dealt with so far the first requirement is to understand as fully as possible the hydraulic characteristics of the

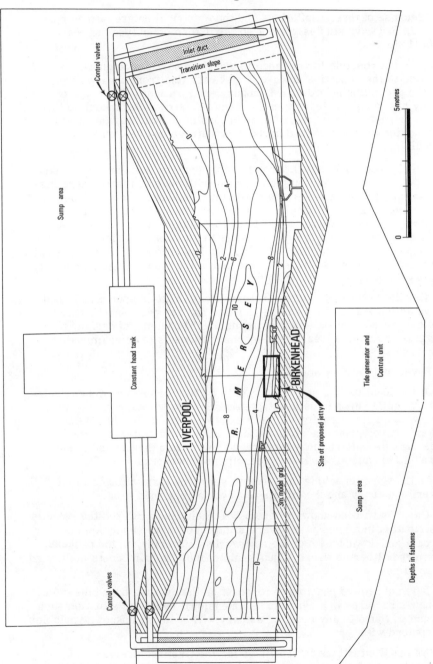

Figure 8 Layout of tidal model of R. Mersey

existing river or estuary, and, if the situation warrants it, to examine the proposed development in a hydraulic model. In this instance we are dealing with either a tidal or non-tidal problem but probably without the added complication of wave action. The preparation of the specification for the survey work again requires careful consideration of the scope of the model studies and these should be examined in some detail. Before discussing the survey work some idea of the area to be covered by the model must be considered, bearing in mind that to obtain the correct hydraulic conditions in the area under examination it will be necessary to include a far greater length of the river or estuary; indeed, in certain studies it may even be necessary to reproduce the entire tidal volume of the river.

Because river and estuary studies invariably cover these large areas it is uneconomic to adopt a natural scale for the model of sufficient size to permit accurate control of tidal levels and adequate measurements of flow velocities. The vertical scale is normally decided by the tidal range on site and the capability of the instrumentation to monitor it and may lie within the range of 1:50 to 1:120 full size. In the case of the horizontal scale this is frequently determined by the space available and may be within the range of 1:300 and 1:2000 full size. However in choosing the final scales due regard must of course be given to insuring that the flow characteristics, i.e. turbulent and laminar, are correct, together with an appreciation as to whether the object of the model studies is to cover conditions over a large area of the estuary or to examine local effects of new structures.

A typical study is shown in Figures 8 and 9. This was a rigid bed tidal model of a section of the River Mersey to study the effect on the tidal regime of a proposed jetty and associated dredged pocket. The horizontal scale for this model was 1:350 and the vertical scale 1:100 giving a 3·5:1 distortion.

The area under detailed examination is shown as the small rectangle and clearly demonstrates the extent of the river which had to be included in order to ensure correct reproduction of flow at this site.

As with all hydraulic model studies, the first part of the test programme must be concerned with calibrating the model to reproduce the flow conditions encountered in nature. More specifically, the tidal curve and the magnitude and distribution of velocities must be correct not only at the area under consideration but some distance upstream and downstream. With regard to velocities, it is normal practice to monitor a number of positions on various cross-sections and at various depths, and it is also essential to ensure that eddy formations existing in nature are adequately simulated. It is obvious that to obtain a comprehensive understanding of the flow conditions at a site it would be necessary to reproduce the complete cycle of tides from springs to neaps. This however would involve an immense amount of survey work and would be completely uneconomic. A com-

Figure 9 Model of R. Mersey

promise is therefore adopted in which the flow conditions are reproduced for a mean spring tide as this will normally produce the maximum
velocities.

From all of the above it will be apparent that it is unwise to expect
complete definitive answers from tidal models and to realise that their
merit lies in indicating trends of behaviour and permitting rapid comparisons of various design proposals.

The value of the answers obtained will however depend to a very
large degree on the coverage possible in the survey work. In the case
of the Mersey model, velocities were measured at 3m vertical intervals from surface to bed at some 20 current meter positions on three
cross-sections at half-hourly intervals over a period of 25 hours for a
mean spring tide.

In larger models covering complete estuaries the survey work may
be multiplied many times by comparison with the above; it may also
include observations of temperature, salinity, silt content, freshwater
discharge, float tracking and tidal data from a number of stations
throughout the estuary.

The preliminary design work for this type of model, which can be
looked upon as a desk study, will examine the past history of the
estuary from charts, etc., particularly if mobile bed studies of bed movement are contemplated and in order to obtain at least an initial assessment of the hydraulic factors.

It is perhaps essential to realise that this type of model study is probably the most complex in this field, and requires considerable experience in the design, operation and interpretation of results. By the very nature of the problem it is unwise to expect immediate results from this type of model and this must be taken into account when preparing the overall programme of research and site investigation, and indeed their relation to the design process as a whole.

8 Wave Data

Throughout this paper the need for adequate data on the wave climate at a particular site has been repeatedly stressed together with the insistence that records should be available over as long a period as possible.

It is probably safe to say that little or no information on waves will be available at any site when the project is first considered so that if the engineer is not to be severely restricted in his design work one of the first items to be decided should be the installation of a wave recorder. This should either precede the survey work or be the first task on arrival at site. In this way, a continuous flow of data will be recorded throughout the survey, site investigations, and the model study. This may well occupy a period of 6 to 9 months and at least goes part way to achieving the ideal long-term approach. It would of course be prudent to continue recording throughout the inevitable committee stages, planning enquiries and parliamentary submissions so that when detailed design commences there will be better chance of producing reliable forecasts of wave conditions.

At the same time as records are being obtained on site a desk study can be put in hand to forecast wave conditions on the basis of hourly wind record from Government Authorities using techniques developed by the National Institute of Oceanography and various researches in America. Whilst this will not provide such reliable data as actual records from site it will assist the engineer to ascertain dominant directions of wave attack and the variation of various parameters over a period of many years. This latter point is particularly important as the author has been concerned with a number of studies where one year's record gave misleading answers as to the predominant direction of wave approach when considered in the light of five years records. The importance of this in preparing specifications for model studies is obvious.

With regard to wave recording instruments it is regrettably true that their reliability in terms of continuity of data output has left a lot to be desired in the past but newer models now on the market are showing considerable improvement in this direction. Other problems however remain to be solved, particularly in the direction of mooring systems and the many natural hazards such as removal by dredgers, demolition by collision with vessels, and the tendency to be collected in fishing nets and the consequent claim for salvage.

Assuming, however, that despite these hazards records are available the subsequent analysis and presentation of results will still occupy a considerable amount of time and manpower.

When dealing with the analysis of wave data much time can be saved if the object of the work is clearly defined, i.e. whether it is required as input data for a random wave generator, say in flume studies of overtopping, or statistical data on the frequency of occurrence of wave heights and periods, or the determination of the design wave height or 100-year forecast for structural design.

As an indication of the amount of data to be handled and on the optimistic assumption that the instrument remains operational for a complete year, then on the basis of a 10 minute record every 3 hours, which is the normal sampling time, some 2900 records will require processing and the data plotted. There is therefore a very good case to be made out for the designers of wave recorders including a punch tape output as part of the installation such as is available with the 'waverider' buoy.

With this volume of data a computer becomes essential not only for the individual analysis of each 10 minute record but the subsequent storage and further analysis of the complete year's data.

It is not the purpose of this paper to set out the many methods currently employed for the analysis of wave data, particularly as this work is still the subject of much research effort, but more perhaps to make a plea for this very vital aspect of applied research to be recognised as basic design data and funds set aside as part of the overall investigation.

9 Conclusion

With the ever increasing cost of construction work, particularly in the marine environment, the engineer is increasingly under pressure to refine his design to examine new methods of construction and give assurance as to the long term efficiency of the project. He will also be called upon to provide expert advice to committees during the planning stage where the interests of other parties is in question.

All of this requires basic fundamental data about the site and its particular characteristics which can only be obtained from a properly co-ordinated site investigation and model study.

It is not unusual for considerable difficulty to be experienced in convincing authorities and developers to release sufficient funds for this work at what must be inevitably a very early stage in the project. If, however, a viable economic solution is to be sought in the design and development of a marina the design and research engineers must be given the tools with which to work. It is in fact a situation where the developer must 'spend money to save money'.

Acknowledgements

The author would like to place on record his thanks to the Department of Public Building and Works, States of Jersey, and their Consulting Engineers, Messrs. Coode and Partners, for permission to use information on the storm wave model of St. Helier Harbour; and also the Engineer in Chief, Mersey Docks and Harbour Board for permission to reproduce details of a tidal flow study.

Floating Breakwaters

N. B. Webber and R. J. S. Harris

Department of Civil Engineering, University of Southampton

Synopsis

Floating breakwaters have received the attention of engineers and scientists for a number of years and many ingenious designs have been proposed. Although quite an appreciable amount of investigational work, both analytical and experimental, has been undertaken, very few such structures have actually been installed so that operational experience is relatively limited.

In this paper, the basic principles by which a floating structure can be designed to attenuate wave energy are discussed. The problems presented are of considerable complexity and a wide variety of structural form is possible. Some typical designs are described.

1 Introduction

Sheltered berthage is an important consideration in the siting and layout of boat harbours. A desirable criterion is that wave heights in a mooring area should not exceed a maximum of approximately 0·15 to 0·3 m (0·5 to 1·0 ft)[1, 2]. In small estuaries or in sheltered locations in larger ones, this condition may well exist and there is no need for the construction of a breakwater. But where the fetch, or expanse of water in the direction of maximum exposure exceeds about 0·8 km ($\frac{1}{2}$ mile), acceptable wave conditions can often only be achieved by some form of artificial structure. Apart from wind waves, shelter may be needed from the waves created by passing vessels in a busy waterway.

There are various forms of breakwater, but broadly speaking they can be classified as fixed or mobile. Apart from open structures such as permeable wave screens, the former are the conventional solid type, comprising concrete structures and protective embankments, usually of rock; the latter include caissons, pneumatic systems and floating structures. Caissons have very limited application, requiring most careful preparation of the foundations and placing, whilst the pneumatic, bubble-type, breakwater is generally quite uneconomic owing to the large quantities of compressed air that are needed for creating the counter currents which bring about wave damping[3]. Our consideration here is limited to the floating structure.

A conventional, fixed type of breakwater is capable of providing a high standard of protection against the severest of storm waves. Whilst maintenance costs may well be low, the capital cost of construction is generally high, and particularly so if the water is relatively deep. The massive nature of this kind of structure makes it a permanent feature so that the initial location requires most careful consideration, and any subsequent expansion of the harbour will to some extent render it redundant.

A floating breakwater, on the other hand, can be pre-fabricated on a slipway, favouring a high standard of workmanship and a low con-structional cost. Mooring arrangements require the most careful design, although in general the cost of installation is largely indepen-dent of depth. The initial position for the structure may not be the final, because the performance in several locations may be investigated before the optimum is established; later on, if the demand for sheltered berthage warrants it, the breakwater may be moved further seaward and additional units introduced. Sometimes, temporary protection is all that is required; for example a dredging activity, or perhaps a small craft harbour operates only on a seasonal basis so that the breakwater can be removed and overhauled during the winter period. A further important factor in its favour is that it causes minimal interference with the regime of tidal currents of the particular estuary or coastline where it is situated. Siltation and scour do not therefore generally present a problem.

The floating breakwater is not necessarily an alternative to a fixed structure, but can serve as a useful complement. For instance, the entrance channel to a harbour, protected against the highest waves by a solid outer breakwater, may well admit a small proportion of wave energy, not sufficient to cause embarrassment to commercial vessels but quite possibly so to the small pleasure craft. In this sort of situation a mobile breakwater can be introduced to create a sheltered inner harbour with all the advantage of easy subsequent expansion if circumstances demand. Also, there must be many instances of deep-water areas, such as fjordic type inlets and reservoir sites, where a solid structure would be prohibitively expensive and a mobile structure offers the only possibility.

Summarising, then, the relative merits of solid and floating break-waters are broadly as follows:

	Solid Breakwater	Floating Breakwater
Advantages:	High degree of security	Mobility
	Low maintenance cost	Relatively low capital cost
		Pre-fabrication
		Minimal interference with hydraulic regime
		Can be installed in deep water
Disadvantages:	High capital cost	Waves only partially damped
	Immobility	Mooring problems
	Possible siltation, scour and pollution problems	Maintenance can be expensive
	Cost increases sharply with water depth	Little operational experience

It is perhaps unfortunate that the well-known Bombardon breakwater employed in the Normandy landings failed when subjected to an exceptionally severe storm (for which incidentally it was not designed) because this has, somewhat understandably, made harbour authorities hesitant about the general concept of floating breakwaters. It is felt, however, that the potential advantages which have been outlined and the many design proposals put forward in recent years fully justify a closer look at the basic principles and practical means of attenuating waves by this sort of device.

2 Wave Characteristics

Since the objective is to attenuate waves it is important to consider the mechanics of waves and more particularly their inherent energy and power.

Waves in nature are, of course, irregular and especially so under storm conditions. It is now possible to record sea waves and simulate them realistically in the laboratory. A reasonable period of prototype wave recording is necessary in order to establish the design criteria; data analysis computers are useful for this purpose. As a very simplified statistical representation, the term 'significant wave' has been introduced. This wave has a height equal to the average of the highest one-third of the waves and a corresponding period. Thus a less realistic alternative to testing in irregular waves is to examine the performance in a train of significant waves.

Regular waves are amenable to mathematical analysis and, for the simplest case, that of a low sinusoidal wave and irrotational motion (Figure 1) the following relationships may be derived[4,5]:

The wave form relative to still water level is

$$\eta = \frac{H}{2} \cos 2\pi \left(\frac{x}{L} - \frac{t}{T} \right) \tag{1}$$

where H is the wave height (crest to trough), L is the wave length, T is the period and t is time, with coordinates x and y as indicated.

The speed of propagation of the waves is given by

$$c = \left(\frac{gL}{2\pi} \tanh \frac{2\pi d}{L} \right)^{\frac{1}{2}} \tag{2}$$

where d is the still water depth

The water particles describe ellipses with major and minor axes, respectively —

$$A = H \frac{\cosh 2\pi(d + y)/L}{\sinh 2\pi d/L} \tag{3}$$

$$B = H \frac{\sinh 2\pi(d + y)/L}{\sinh 2\pi d/L} \tag{4}$$

and the corresponding particle velocities in the horizontal and vertical directions are:

$$u = \frac{\pi H}{T} \frac{\cosh 2\pi(d + y)/L}{\sinh 2\pi d/L} \cos 2\pi \left(\frac{x}{L} - \frac{t}{T} \right) \tag{5}$$

$$v = \frac{\pi H}{T} \frac{\sinh 2\pi(d + y)/L}{\sinh 2\pi d/L} \sin 2\pi \left(\frac{x}{L} - \frac{t}{T} \right) \tag{6}$$

The energy of the waves per wave length per unit length of crest is

$$E = \frac{wLH^2}{8} \tag{7}$$

where w is the specific weight of the water. It is made up of potential and kinetic energy in equal proportions, and the corresponding power transmitted is

$$P = \frac{nE}{T} \tag{8}$$

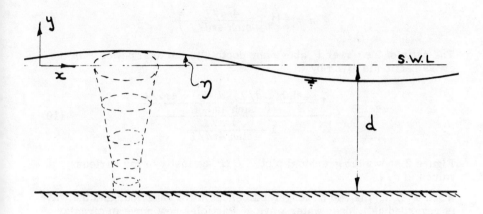

Figure 1   Low sinusoidal wave in water of finite depth

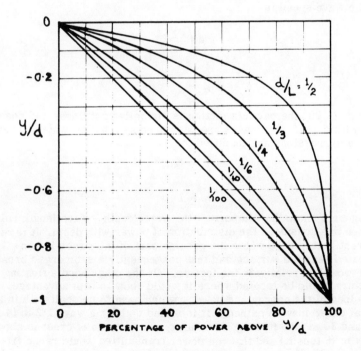

Figure 2   Distribution of power with depth

where n is a coefficient dependent on water depth, being given by

$$n = \tfrac{1}{2}\left(1 + \frac{4\pi d/L}{\sinh 4\pi d/L}\right) \tag{9}$$

The ratio of the power P_y above any depth y to the total power P in the cross section is given by

$$\frac{P_y}{P} = \frac{1 - \dfrac{\sinh(4\pi d/L)\,(d + y) + 4\pi y/L}{\sinh 4\pi d/L}}{1 + \dfrac{4\pi d/L}{\sinh 4\pi d/L}} \tag{10}$$

Figure 2 shows the graphical plot of P_y/P against y/d for various values of d/L.

When $d < L/2$, the bed no longer influences wave behaviour and the wave is regarded as a 'deep water wave'. Particles now move in circular orbits, with radius

$$r = \frac{H}{2}\,e^{2\pi y/L} \tag{11}$$

and the wave speed is

$$c = \left(\frac{gL}{2\pi}\right)^{\frac{1}{2}} \tag{12}$$

with

$$n = \tfrac{1}{2} \tag{13}$$

When $d < L/20$, the particle motion is virtually rectilinear and does not vary with depth. The waves are described as 'shallow water waves' and the expressions are modified to

$$c = (gd)^{1/2} \tag{14}$$

and

$$n = 1 \tag{15}$$

Figure 2 shows how important the water depth − wave length relation is when one considers the distribution of power with depth. It is readily apparent that in deep water the greater part of the power is concentrated near the surface and that consequently a submerged breakwater would be relatively ineffective. On the other hand a floating structure would be located where it would show to best advantage. Some idea of the energy and power, which have to be dealt with in a typical case, may be gained if it is stated that for a wave 1·2 m (4 ft) high and 30 m (100 ft) long, the energy per foot run of crest is about 18 kN m (6 tons ft) and that the power transmitted would range from about 1·9 kW (2½ horsepower) to 3·8 kW (5 horsepower) according to whether the water is very shallow ($d < L/20$) or deep ($d > L/2$).

It is wave height which we aim to reduce and it will be noted from these expressions that the energy and power of waves vary as the square of the wave height and are directly proportional to wave length. Therefore, if the energy or power is reduced by one half, the wave height is only reduced by one quarter, indicating that some very large reductions of energy are needed if there is to be effective wave attenuation.

3 Wave Attenuation

The schematic diagram (Figure 3) shows a partial barrier (fixed or free) interposed in regular waves of height H_I and period T.

A portion E_R of the incident wave energy E_I is reflected at a barrier and produces a train of waves, travelling in the reverse direction, of height H_R and of the same period T, but with a phase difference of 180°. However, if a series of reflecting surfaces are present, the reflected waves will comprise a number of small amplitude waves of different phases but the same period. A further portion E_D of the incident wave energy is dissipated as a result of interaction with the structure, and the residual energy E_T is transmitted to the lee, creating waves which can be represented by a regular train of height H_t and period T. The wave form here may be rather irregular owing to non-linear interaction with the structure; however, it would normally be composed of harmonics of the incident wave with the fundamental harmonic predominant.

From these considerations, a number of relationships may be formulated:

The transmission coefficient is

$$K_T = \frac{H_T}{H_I} \tag{16}$$

The breakwater efficiency is

$$\eta_B = 1 - K_T \tag{17}$$

The reflection coefficient is

$$K_R = \frac{H_R}{H_I} \tag{18}$$

For conservation of energy:

$$E_T = E_I - E_R - E_D \tag{19}$$

so that

$$H_T^2 = H_I^2 - H_R^2 - \frac{8E_D}{wL} \tag{20}$$

Likewise, introducing power, it may be shown that

$$H_T^{\;2} = H_I^{\;2} - H_R^{\;2} - \frac{8P_D}{wncH_I^{\;2}} \tag{21}$$

or

$$K_T = \left[1 - K_R^{\;2} - \frac{8P_D}{wncH_I^{\;2}}\right]^{\frac{1}{2}} \tag{22}$$

It is thus evident that a reduction of wave height may be effected by reflection and/or energy dissipation. These are discussed in the following sections.

4 Wave Reflection

When there is no loss of energy due to breaking, the wave reflection at a fixed vertical barrier, extending over the entire depth, is perfect. The resultant wave form is given by:

$$\eta_{RES} = \frac{H_I}{2}\, \sin 2\pi\left(\frac{x}{L} - \frac{t}{T}\right) + \frac{H_I}{2}\, \sin 2\pi\left(\frac{x}{L} + \frac{t}{T}\right)$$

which simplifies to

$$\eta_{RES} = H_I \sin \frac{2\pi x}{L}\, \cos \frac{2\pi t}{L} \tag{23}$$

indicating that the resultant wave height is twice that of the incident waves. This is the familiar standing wave or clapotis condition, which is manifested by the unpleasantly steep waves in proximity to a steep or vertical faced structure.

The reflection phenomenon involves a reversal of momentum, producing, in accordance with Newton's second law, a large periodic reaction force at the barrier. It may be shown[6] that the maximum force/unit length is approximately

$$F_{max} = \frac{wH_I L}{2\pi}\, \tanh \frac{2\pi d}{L} \tag{24}$$

For deep water $(d > L/2)$ the expression becomes

$$F_{max} = \frac{wH_I L}{2\pi} \tag{25}$$

Whilst for shallow water $(d < L/20)$ it is

$$F_{max} = wdH_I \tag{26}$$

This means, for example, that a 1·2 m (4 ft) high wave, 45 m (150 ft) long would induce a force of about 65 kN/m (2 tons/ft) run in a vertical barrier, whether the water is deep or relatively shallow. This is a by no means small force to be catered for.

If the barrier extends for only a portion of the water depth, the maximum force on it, in shallow water conditions, is approximately[7]

$$F_{max} = wdH_R \qquad (27)$$

This indicates that the force will be nearly as high as for the full depth, otherwise it will not be effective.

Clearly, then, where the efficiency of a floating breakwater largely depends on wave reflection, horizontal motions must be restrained with the result that the forces on the mooring lines will be relatively high and this may pose difficult problems.

Some appreciable reduction in the reflective properties of a vertical breakwater can be achieved by introducing perforations on the seaward face, thereby allowing water to flow to and fro an inner chamber with solid rear wall. With a suitably designed structure, fixed or floating, the restraining forces that are needed can be significantly reduced.[8]

5 Energy Dissipation

There are a number of ways in which energy may be expended – not destroyed, but converted into other forms such as heat and mechanical energy. The principal ways are as follows:

(a) Forced Instability

By changes in water depth, configuration of a structure, or other means, waves may be made to become unstable and break. A deep water wave breaks when the steepness (H/L) is greater than about $1/10$ and a shallow water wave when the water depth d is slightly more than the wave height. There are various forms of breaking wave, but all involve a loss of energy through turbulent eddying and the creation of foam and spray. The most familiar example is the breaking of waves on a shoreline; normally, the breaker zone is close inshore, but sometimes it is at offshore bars where the protection afforded may approach that of a conventional breakwater.

Violent interaction with a structure results in shock forces of considerable magnitude, which may be fully comparable with or in excess of the longer duration forces caused by reflection. On the other hand, if waves are induced to break over a reasonable distance, such as for example on a horizontal or gradually sloping face, the forces applied to the structure will be much smaller and will be distributed over a greater period of time. But the drawback is that large surface areas are required.

(b) Interference with Orbital Motion

In order to avoid unwanted reflections from the vertical bulkhead at the end of a laboratory wave channel it is customary practice to install a permeable wave absorber, consisting of such material as rubberised mattress, aluminium shavings, or an open-textured gravel. This sort of device serves to impede the orbital motion of the water particles, thereby absorbing wave energy, and, if very efficient, eliminating the waves.

Comparable arrangements, such as fascine mattresses, perforated curtains, or horizontal immersed platforms may be employed in the full-scale situation. As in case (a), a relatively large volume or surface area is required if particle motion is to be rendered sufficiently random and the transmitted wave height thereby appreciably reduced, all at the expense of only moderate restraining forces.

(c) Out of Phase Damping

The principle here is that a change of phase is introduced by the structure so that the transmitted wave has a different phase to the incident wave. It is well known that when a regular wave train has a phase difference of 180° with another train of similar height and period, travelling in the same direction, the two trains are self-cancelling. This is not a practicable proposition, but it is nevertheless a fact that a floating structure with a long natural period of oscillation relative to the waves will have a relatively small amplitude of oscillation and thus effect a considerable reduction in wave height. The implications of this concept, both in respect of the structure and the mooring forces, are discussed in the next section.

(d) Viscous Damping

This is the sort of wave attenuation that is produced by skin friction resistance associated with the presence of a boundary layer. By introducing a number of closely spaced vertical plates in the longitudinal direction, a significant reduction in wave height may be achieved,[9] but more particularly of the short-period waves rather than the longer waves. A thin flexible membrane on the surface[10] and artificial seaweed fronds,[11] seem to have a rather similar effect.

In all cases a very large surface area is required and for this reason it is hardly a practical proposition. But it would have the advantage of no reflection and negligible restraining force.

In practice, wave attenuation by a floating breakwater would in most cases be achieved by a combination of reflection and the various processes of energy dissipation just enumerated.

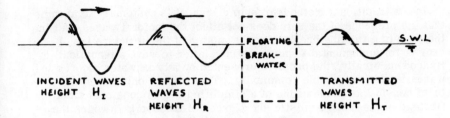

Figure 3 Schematic diagram of wave trains

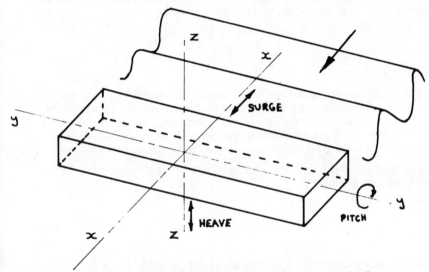

Figure 4 Two-dimensional motion of a floating body

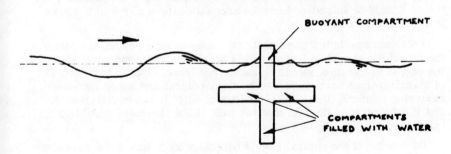

Figure 5 Bombardon breakwater

6 Dynamics of a Floating Breakwater

In the traditional methods of ship design, it is customary to assume that the presence of the ship does not affect the incident waves, but in the case of a floating breakwater the motion of the structure is, of course, of fundamental importance in relation to wave attenuation. Hydrodynamically, the problem presented by a breakwater moored in waves is of considerable complexity. Thus, space only permits a brief consideration in outline of a simplified two-dimensional situation (instead of the more realistic six degrees of freedom), in which the general requirements for effective out-of-phase damping are assessed.

A floating breakwater aligned normal to the waves exhibits the linear motions of heave and surge, and the angular motion of pitch (Figure 4). These motions are in fact coupled, but for small amplitudes they can be regarded as separate. Considering each in turn:

Pitching

The pitching behaviour is a most important characteristic, for this represents the principal interaction with the waves and is primarily due to the vertical motion of the water particles. As stated previously, for effective out of phase damping the natural period of oscillation must be long compared with the period of the waves.

For a small angle of pitch, the natural period of oscillation about the yy axis is given by

$$(T_N)_{yy} = 2\pi \left(\frac{I_{yy}}{W\overline{GM}}\right)^{\frac{1}{2}} = \frac{2\pi k_{yy}}{(g\overline{GM})^{1/2}} \tag{28}$$

where I_{yy} is the moment of inertia about the yy axis, k_{yy} is the corresponding radius of gyration, W is the weight of water displaced, and $\overline{GM}$ is the metacentric height for pitching motion. In practice, a factor should be introduced to take account of the water which moves with the breakwater.

This expression indicates that for a long natural period, the mass of the structure should be large, with a small restoring moment; also that the radius of gyration should be relatively large. But, as an increase of mass involves some increase in displacement and hence increased restoring moment, there is an obvious conflict in the requirements. But it does point to the fact that the bulk of the structure should be immersed.

Of course, if the natural period coincides with that of the waves, the pitching amplitude becomes considerable and the structure acts as a paddle transmitting the waves with almost undiminished energy.

Heaving

Heaving motion is generally of relatively small amplitude, the natural period being given by:

$$(T_N)_{zz} = 2\pi \left(\frac{W}{wgA_w}\right)^{\frac{1}{2}} \tag{29}$$

where A_w is the water-plane area.

Surging

This motion is mainly of importance because of its effect on the moorings. The natural period of the breakwater-mooring system is

$$(T_N)_{xx} = 2\pi \left(\frac{W}{Kg}\right)^{\frac{1}{2}} \tag{30}$$

where K is the damping constant for the mooring lines.

Thus the less the stiffness of the mooring line, the greater is the period. If the period coincides with that of the waves, the longitudinal movement can be considerable.

A phenomenon which sometimes accompanies the above motions is 'slamming'. This is a description applied to the impact or momentary high pressure of water on the underside of the leading portion of a floating body. High water velocities in proximity to a structure of shallow draft are conducive to this condition. Clearly, the area concerned requires adequate strengthening to resist these temporary forces.

An elastic mooring system has a complicated non-linear response to waves, so that the problem of evaluating mooring forces does not lend itself to theoretical analysis. It is, however, one of the major considerations in any floating breakwater proposal. The tension in the mooring lines is attributable to the normal oscillatory motion of the structure and the impact blows of breaking waves. Mooring forces generally increase with wave height, and are particularly large under conditions of resonance.

In order to counter any tendency to drift with or against the waves, fore and aft moorings are needed. Experiments have shown that provided the mooring cable length is in excess of about 4 × water depth, suspended in the usual catenary anchor line form, variations of length have little influence on breakwater efficiency[12]. This is because a portion of the mooring line always remains in contact with the bed. But the decision as to the optimum mooring arrangement is very much a matter of empirical good judgement, backed if necessary by model tests. A compromise must be made between the stiffness of mooring line needed to maintain a breakwater in position at all states of the tide and the extensibility which is desirable in order to avoid excessive forces being induced. It is important that horizontal move-ment should be sufficient to absorb any snatching action and to reduce load variation. As stated previously, a reflective structure necessarily entails high mooring forces; it also follows that for a structure to be strongly reflective, stiff mooring lines are needed. Light-weight structures offer the advantage of relatively low mooring forces.

7 Types of Floating Breakwater

7.1 Design Considerations

A floating breakwater has as its primary objective the satisfactory attenuation of wave height, but in its design there are other important considerations:

(1)   The structure should be sufficiently robust to withstand the severest wave conditions at the particular site, and these may not be easy to assess. They will almost certainly be in excess of the incident wave height values used as a criterion for wave attenuation.

(2)   The mooring system should be of sufficient strength to maintain the structure in position under all possible conditions of wind, waves and tide.

(3)   Maintenance requirements should be minimal.

(4)   Where space is valuable – a situation which might well pertain in the case of a sheltered basin within a harbour – the structure should be designed with a view to economy of superficial area.

(5)   The cost of construction should be as low as possible compatible with fulfilment of the other requirements.

Numerous forms of floating breakwater have been proposed, as is evidenced by a recent review of the literature[13]. Several designs have been patented. Detailed comparison would involve a consideration of different site conditions and constructional costs. These, of course, are not readily assessed, and in this paper an outline only is given of a few fairly representative types of structure.

7.2 Bombardon Breakwater[14]

This design is of historic significance, because it is one of the few instances where a full-scale version has been tested under field conditions – in the extreme, the war-time hazards of an invasion beach.

The structure was of cruciform section (Figure 5) with approximate dimensions as indicated; the length of each unit was 61 m (200 ft). By filling the unit partly full of water, a large mass with a small restoring force was achieved. As has been explained earlier, this results in a relatively long period of oscillation and a high degree of reflection.

The performance criterion was that it should withstand deep water waves 2·5 m (8 ft) high and 37 m (120 ft) long. Tests in Weymouth Bay showed that under these conditions waves were attenuated to about 0·6 m (2 ft) high in the lee. At Arromanches in Normandy in 1944, the structure performed satisfactorily until, only a short while after installation, a storm of exceptional severity occurred which destroyed it. The waves in this storm were estimated to be up to 4·5 m (15 ft) in height and 90 m (300 ft) in length, with a period near to that of the natural period of oscillation. Consequently, a large amplitude of motion resulted, inducing stresses of about 8 times those for which the structure was designed.

7.3 Shallow-Draft Breakwaters

The main advantage of this type of design is that the mooring forces are reasonably small. In general, the maximum mooring force is not significantly greater than the average. Energy dissipation is by induced wave breaking; also by interference with the vertical component of the orbital motion, thus creating a pressure disturbance and the damping of the transmitted wave. Some reflection occurs, not so much due to the small vertical face in the fore part of the structure, but mainly attributable to the mass inertia of the water adjacent to the underside of the structure. Surface area, which in this case means length (in the direction of wave advance) is the principal criterion for breakwater efficiency.

The simplest form of shallow-draft structure is the impermeable rigid type. Certain aspects are amenable to analysis for the case of long waves. Figure 6 shows the results of small-scale experiments carried out recently at Southampton University. It will be noted that the efficiency is about 50 per cent when the length of the raft is equal to the wave length, and improves appreciably for greater proportionate raft lengths. Performance improves slightly with increasing wave steepness (H/L), increasing mass, and increasing inertia. The mooring force (results not yet fully evaluated) increases with wave steepness, and, to a lesser extent, is also influenced by wave length.

There are many refinements of this basic concept, introduced with the aim of improving efficiency without increasing overall length.[15] These may take the form of roughness elements, perforations, or subsidiary rafts. Energy dissipation takes place as the waves interact with the impediments, but the net result of the turbulence and eddying seems to be to reduce the amplitude of the reflected wave rather than to markedly improve breakwater performance. But, of course, perforations will reduce the amount of material that is needed and hence the cost of construction.

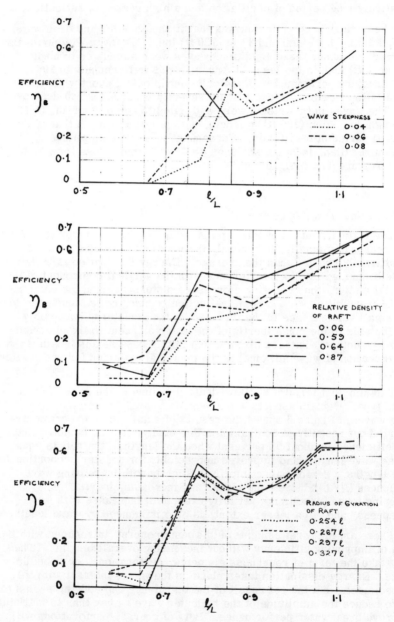

Figure 6 Plain raft − effect of wave steepness, mass and radius of gyration for various values of raft length/wave length

A large scale model test of a perforated structure designed by the consulting engineers Harris and Sutherland has been undertaken at the National Physical Laboratory[16]. More recently, the same consultants in association with Archibald Shaw and Partners have organised field trials (Figure 7) of a slightly different design of perforated structure. The Department of Civil Engineering of Southampton University has collaborated in this investigation, the results of which are currently being analysed.

An interesting form of breakwater 'The Seabreaker'[17] has been devised by Col. H. G. Hasler and sponsored by the N.R.D.C., who have filed patents and granted an exclusive licence to manufacture. It consists (Figure 8) of a long, shallow pontoon moored broadside-on to the direction of wave advance, and connected to an outrigger float on its leeward side, whose function is to minimise rolling and to obviate any risk of capsizing. A tubular superstructure has the main function of limiting vertical flexing, and it also limits horizontal flexing and torsion.

For effective wave attenuation, the main pontoon must remain as stationary as possible in the waves and this is achieved by the fact that the dimension (normal to direction of wave advance) of each Seabreaker unit, if the scale has been correctly chosen, is much greater than the significant crest length of the incident wind-driven waves. Each wave will then break over part of the unit only.

Figure 7 Field trials of perforated shallow-draft breakwater
(Harris and Sutherland and Archibald Shaw)

It is claimed that a breakwater unit of this design, whose main pontoon has dimensions 40 m × 2·4 m (130 ft × 7·75 ft) with 0·15 m (6 in.) draft and 0·08 m (3 in.) freeboard, will provide attenuation of the order of 66% of the height of wind-driven waves up to a significant wave height of about 0·6 m (2 ft) (equivalent to a maximum wave height of about 0·9 m (3 ft)).

Tests of models have been performed in the laboratory and in Portsmouth Harbour, and a prototype unit has been moored continuously in Stokes Bay (East Solent) from February 1971 to the time of writing (Figure 14).

Several investigators have reported on the success achieved by flexible structures. Kennedy and Marsalek[18] have examined the behaviour in the laboratory of simulated log jams. They found that such an arrangement extending over two or more wave lengths can greatly attenuate waves of moderate length, this effect being attributable to energy dissipation through interaction with the porous structure, and out of phase and viscous damping.

Fascine mattresses have also been shown to be effective[19]. Model tests have indicated that if the length of the mattress is about the same as the wave length, a reduction of wave height to about 40 to 45% of the incident waves may be expected.

Another interesting flexible form, although having a draft rather greater than can reasonably be called shallow, is the 'wave-maze', which is in effect an assemblage of discarded heavy vehicle tyres. Kamel and Davidson[20] have reported on laboratory tests on this design.

7.4 Fluid-Filled Bags

About ten years ago an extensive programme of research on transportable breakwaters was conducted by the St. Anthony Falls Hydraulic Laboratory, University of Minnesota, and the Hydraulic Engineering Laboratory, University of California (Berkeley), on behalf of the U.S. Navy[21]. These studies became directed towards fluid-filled bags ('hovering' breakwater), with their top at the water surface (Figure 9), the principle being that the restoring force is only proportional to the weight of the enclosing fabric while the enclosed fluid provides the mass. Many plan shapes and orientations for the bags were examined. Disadvantages of the device were considered to be the vulnerability of the flexible fabric and the mooring line problem.

New, durable and strong, rubber nylon fabrics have become available in recent years, and this has prompted Fredericksen[22] to investigate, in the laboratory, the performance of a floating blanket consisting of several individual bags joined together. He found that whilst bag thickness, fluid viscosity, and amount of bag fill influence performance, the major factor is bag length. His tests in regular waves showed that

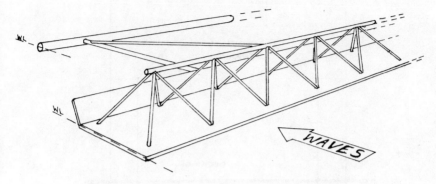

Figure 8 'Seabreaker' floating breakwater

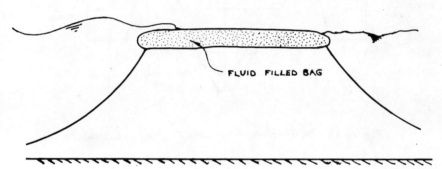

Figure 9 'Hovering' breakwater

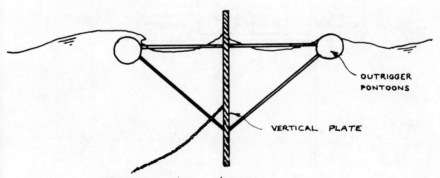

Figure 10 A-Frame floating breakwater

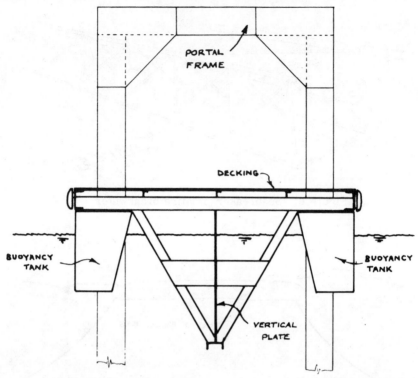

Figure 11   'Winter' dual-purpose floating breakwater

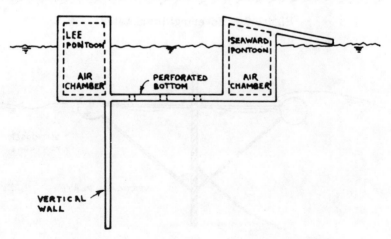

Figure 12   Reservoir-marina floating breakwater

an efficiency of 80% requires a bag length of about twice the incident wave length, whilst up to 40% can be achieved with a bag length of half the wave length.

7.5 A-Frame Breakwater

This form of structure, proposed by the Department of Public Works of Canada, consists essentially of a central vertical plate with one or more cylinders located symmetrically on either side (Figure 10).

The underlying concept is that large mass is replaced by large moment of inertia of mass. Wave attenuation is achieved through the processes of reflection, turbulence and orbital interference.

Brebner and Ofuya[23] have investigated the performance of this type of structure in the laboratory and have found that the efficiency is of the order of 70% when the distance apart of the cylinders is $\frac{1}{2}$ wave length. Reflection can account for as much as 35% of the incident energy and the mooring force is then relatively high. Maximum mooring forces, however, were found to be only about twice the average.

A variation of this theme has been developed by Winter, a marine consultant at Cowes, with the aim of incorporating a breakwater and a pontoon landing stage in the same structure (Figure 11). A battery of these composite structures has been recently installed in a marina at Cowes (Figure 13).

Although not strictly of the A-frame type, the Resa breakwater (Figure 15) is also a dual-purpose structure especially intended for marina sites. It incorporates a curved wave-return profile on the weather side and is available in prefabricated units.

7.6 Reservoir-Marina Breakwater

The breakwater shown in Figure 12 is among a number of designs whose performance was investigated at model scale by Chen and Wiegel[24]. Their intended application was to reservoir-marina sites where wave heights and wave lengths might be expected to have dimensions of up to 1·5 m (5 ft) and 18 m (60 ft), respectively The underlying concept of this particular design is that it offers a large entrained moment of inertia with a good potential for absorbing wave energy.

It consists of two pontoons separated by a perforated base. A vertical barrier is attached below the lee side of the perforated section; the weather-side pontoon has a sloping upper face. Energy is dissipated by forced instability on the sloping face, by turbulence and eddying in the water channel and perforations, and by the turbulent inter-mixture of air and water in the vicinity of the underside of the sloping face.

(Beken of Cowes)

Figure 13   Winter pontoon breakwater unit at Cowes

Figure 14   Field trials of 'Seabreaker' floating breakwater

(Col. H. G. Hasler)

Figure 15   'Resa' floating breakwater

(Resabo International)

The efficiency was found to be in excess of 80% when the ratio, wave length/overall length of structure (L/l), is less than 2·7. Efficiency diminishes with increasing values of L/l until at 3·8 it is about 35 to 40%.

In these experiments, mooring forces were not measured, but it was observed that the impulses associated with pitching and wave impact were not in phase and that the reflected waves were of apparent higher frequency than the incident waves. This suggests that the ratio, peak mooring force/average mooring force, may not be very much in excess of unity.

8 Conclusions

(1)   Floating breakwaters are worthy of consideration where there is a need for the attenuation of short period waves. Unless the structure is extremely large they are not capable of attenuating long swell waves, although they may be expected to dampen any steep chop superimposed on them. They show to particular advantage where mobility is desirable or the water is fairly deep.

(2)   Waves in nature are irregular, so that the selection of design criteria should be based on the statistical analysis of a representative period of wave observation. The concept of the 'significant wave' is useful as a simplifying assumption.

(3)   A floating breakwater may effect a reduction in wave height by reflection and/or by promoting energy dissipation. In general, the higher the proportionate reflection, the greater is the mooring force.

(4)   A variety of structural form is possible. Design should be based on the wave attenuation required, and on other factors such as space availability, and economy of construction and maintenance.

(5)   Safety demands that the structure and the mooring system be designed to withstand the severest possible storms.

(6)   Because of the complex nature of the behaviour of a moored structure in waves, hydrodynamical analysis offers only general guidance as to actual performance, but is very helpful in an understanding of the mechanics of wave attenuation and reflection. Model testing is therefore nearly always essential, and because of the limitations here too – as for example the representation of an irregular sea by regular waves, or the difficulties of stress determination – field trials are a most desirable prerequisite to prototype installation.

References

1. ——— (1969), *Small Craft Harbours*, Am. Soc. C. E. Rpt. on Eng. Practice No. 50, p. 55.
2. Lee, C. E. (1967), 'Wave Damping in Harbours', *Proc. 10th Conf. on Coastal Eng. (1966)*, 2, Ch. 46, p. 804. Am. Soc. C. E.
3. Bulson, P. S. (1969), 'The Theory and Design of Bubble Breakwaters', *Proc. 11th Conf. on Coastal Eng. (1968)*, 2, Ch. 64, pp. 994-1031. Am. Soc. C. E.
4. Ippen, A. T. (Ed.) (1966), *Estuary and Coastline Hydrodynamics*. McGraw-Hill.
5. Wiegel, R. L. (1964), *Oceanographical Engineering*. Prentice-Hall.
6. Ippen, A. T. and Bourodimos, E. L. (1964), *Breakwater Characteristics of Open-tube Systems*, Mass. Inst. Tech. Hyd. Lab. Rpt. No. 73.
7. Carr, J. H. (1952), 'Mobile Breakwaters', *Proc. 2nd Conf. on Coastal Eng. (1951)*, Ch. 25, pp. 281-295. Council on Wave Research.
8. Marks, W. (1967), 'A Perforated Mobile Breakwater for Fixed and Floating Application', *Proc. 10th Conf. on Coastal Eng. (1968)*, 2, Ch. 64, pp. 1079-1129. Am. Soc. C. E.
9. ——— (1948), 'The Wave Filter', *La Houille Blanche*, 3, No. 3, pp. 285-290.
10. Ref. 5, p. 141.
11. Price, W. A., Tomlinson, K. W. and Hunt, J. N. (1969). 'The Effect of Artificial Seaweed on Promoting the Build-Up of Beaches', *Proc. 11th Conf. on Coastal Eng. (1968)*, 1, Ch. 36, pp. 570-578. Am. Soc. C. E.
12. Homma, M., Horikawa, K. and Mochizuki, H. (1964), 'An Experimental Study on Floating Breakwaters', *Coastal Engineering in Japan*, 7, pp. 85-94.
13. Harris, R. J. S. (1970), *Summary of Present Knowledge of Floating Breakwaters*, Univ. of Southampton, Dept. of Civil Eng. Rpt. No. 2/70.
14. Lochner, R., Faber, O. and Penney, W. G. (1948), 'The Bombardon Floating Breakwater', *The Civil Engineer in War*, 2, pp. 256-290, Inst. C. E.
15. Harris, A. J. and Webber, N. B. (1969), 'A Floating Breakwater', *Proc. 11th Conf. on Coastal Eng. (1968)*, 2, Ch. 67, pp. 1049-1054.
16. Bury, M. R. C. and Clarke, J. L. (1967), *Floating Breakwater – Large Scale Model Investigation at N. P. L.*, Taylor Woodrow Rpt. No. 147/67/1275 (Unpublished).
17. Frost, J. (1971), 'Floating Breakwater has Many Applications', *The Dock and Harbour Authority*, 51, pp. 474-475.
18. Kennedy, R. J. and Marsalek, J. (1969), 'Flexible Porous Floating Breakwaters', *Proc. 11th Conf. on Coastal Eng. (1968)*, 2, Ch. 69, pp. 1095-1103.

19. Vinje, J. J. (1966), *Increase of Effective Working Time during Operations at Sea by Means of Movable Structures*, Delft Hyd. Lab. Pub. No. 42.

20. Kamel, A. M. and Davidson, D. D. (1968), *Hydraulic Characteristics of Mobile Breakwaters Composed of Tyres or Spheres*, U.S. Army Eng. Waterways Exp. Sta. Tech. Rpt. H-68-2.

21. Wiegel, R. L., Shen, H. W. and Cumming, J. D. (1961), *Final Report on Hovering Breakwater*, Univ. of Calif. (Berkeley), Hyd. Eng. Lab. Tech. Rpt. Series 140, Issues 5.

22. Frederiksen, H. D. (1971), 'Wave Attenuation by Fluid-Filled Bags', *Proc. Am. Soc. C. E.*, **97**, No. WW1, pp. 73-90.

23. Brebner, A. and Ofuya, A. O. (1969), 'Floating Breakwaters', *Proc. 11th Conf. on Coastal Eng. (1968)*, **2**, Ch. 68, pp. 1055-1094. Am. Soc. C. E.

24. Chen, K. and Wiegel, R. L. (1971), 'Floating Breakwater for Reservoir Marinas', *Proc. 12th Conf. on Coastal Eng. (1970)*, **2**, Ch. 100, pp. 1647-1666, Am. Soc. C. E.

Discussion

(Session 2)

AUTHORS' INTRODUCTION

Prof. H. Lundgren

Selection of a harbour site involves consideration of a number of coastal engineering factors. To obtain the ideal site, one must ensure that there are no waves. This implies that there would be no need for breakwaters. There should be no surging so as to avoid the risk of broken moorings. There should be no sedimentation, thus obviating maintenance dredging. There should be no currents in order that boats will not collide. There should be no silt in the water to ensure that there will be no mud. There should be no tides which would require the use of pontoons. There should be no ice to ensure that there is no winter damage.

When these ideal requirements have been met there is no need for the coastal engineer with his hydraulic laboratory!

Therefore, my subject is the simplest of all. Fortunately for the coastal engineer, however, the need for marinas in some localities is so great, and some investors have so much money to spend, that it is possible to choose sites where there are, in any combination, high waves, large sand drifts, strong currents, muddy water, large tidal range, or ice.

As Mr. Stickland emphasises in his paper, it is important to reduce wave motions within a marina to the smallest possible amount. Instead of thinking in terms of permissible boat motions the coastal engineer adopts, as a criterion, the maximum permissible wave height. Hydraulic model tests would be undertaken with a view to reducing wave heights to about $0 \cdot 2 - 0 \cdot 4$ m ($0 \cdot 65 - 1 \cdot 3$ ft), dependent upon the wave period. When considering very small craft, even lower wave heights may be required.

Whilst everyone is fully aware of the importance of the wave height aspect, I would also like to stress the importance of considering the wave heights in the approaches to a marina, and this has been discussed in Sect. 2.1.

Not all wave problems need to be studied with the aid of hydraulic models. The Danish Hydraulic Institute is currently developing what we call 'computational hydraulics' with the aid of Dr. M. B. Abbott, formerly of Southampton University.

An example of the application of mathematical techniques is to be found in our recent report on the extension of the port of Karachi. As coastal engineers will understand, we had to consider very seriously the possibility of disturbance in the harbour by long waves, i.e. waves having a period of several minutes. We fed into the mathematical model the water level variations at the entrance to the harbour as registered by a long wave recorder. As an output, we computed the wave conditions at various points within the proposed harbour.

We have undertaken extensive research on the subject of the optimum form of breakwater and this is discussed in the paper. Breakwaters are expensive items and there is a possibility of considerable saving on the conventional type.

Mr. I. W. Stickland

The underlying theme of my paper is the need, on the part of the Consulting Engineer, to obtain data for the design of a marina. Sufficient data must be obtained to enable not only an efficient design to be formulated but also a prediction to be made of any possible long-term effects.

There is everything to be said for introducing all the specialists at an as early a stage as possible. I have been concerned on one or two occasions with projects in which we have had to go back to site again to seek additional data which the model study has indicated as being absolutely vital to the performance of future tests. Therefore, co-ordination must be a very important feature of the design operation.

On the question of hydraulic model studies and their role in design, it does not follow—and I certainly do not advocate it—that every marina which is built should first be the subject of hydraulic model testing.

In the paper, the principal types of model study are described. The storm wave model is the most basic. In this model, the performance of the harbour is examined under short period waves, that is to say in the short steep sea state resulting from locally generated storms. The constructional arrangement and operation of the model must be sufficiently flexible to enable the Consulting Engineer to visit the laboratory and observe the behaviour of a number of alternative designs. The one thing which such a model will often reveal is the unexpected. It is possible to predict the expected, but to be able to observe the unexpected is one of the benefits associated with hydraulic model studies.

Maximum wave heights of 0·4 and 0·2 m (1·3 and 0·65 ft) have been quoted. In fact, some developers have stipulated that the wave height inside a marina must not exceed 0·15 m (0·5 ft). Thus the design requirement for a marina is more exacting than that for a commercial harbour where wave heights of 0·6 m (2 ft) or so are usually acceptable.

In the design of a harbour entrance, the engineer aims to restrict the access of waves whilst providing sufficient navigational channel to allow as many vessels as possible to enter and leave the harbour an any one time.

These requirements are in conflict so that some compromise is called for. This often results in an outer harbour where wave heights are reduced by expansion. The storm wave model is very useful in such a case, enabling the best layout of the harbour and breakwater location to be observed.

Wave reflection should be reduced to a minimum and this is particularly important in the case of yacht harbours, since small craft are usually relatively short in length and narrow in the beam. Suitable energy-absorbent structures, such as rubble-mound breakwaters should be provided and their detailed performance may be observed in a wave-channel facility. Tests in irregular waves rather than regular waves are important where overtopping is a critical factor.

To ensure that satisfactory results are obtained from models, the data which are fed to them must be correct. This is where site information is of primary importance. I know that I speak for most consulting engineers present when I appeal to the promoters of marina projects to let us have sufficient money to obtain adequate records of site conditions, and, in particular, wave records, both with regard to height and direction. My final plea is for more time in which to do this.

Mr. N. B. Webber

Floating breakwaters have for a long time presented a challenge-the quest for a device that will reflect or dissipate incident wave energy, in such a way that relatively calm conditions exist in the lee, whilst at the same time the operating forces are not excessive.

From our examination of the literature, it appears that a floating breakwater was first proposed in 1842 by a Captain Graves. It consisted of a vertical heavily weighted blanket suspended from a buoyant cylindrical tank. Since then, many ingenious designs have been proposed, a limited number have been the subject of model tests, a few have been tested under field conditions, whilst a still smaller proportion have actually been installed as a harbour feature.

A great deal of laboratory research was sponsored by the U. S. Navy during the late 1950's and early 1960's, but the terms of reference were rather restrictive. The objective was to reduce waves 4·5 m (15 ft high and about 250 m (750 ft) long to waves about 1·2 m (4 ft) high, and there were certain military requirements which had to be met, such as speed of assembly. No economic practical solution was found. In fact, it is fair to say that long waves such as these can only be dealt with at considerable expense, quite beyond the normal resources of a small craft harbour undertaking.

However, in general, it is not the long waves that are the problem in small craft harbours—it is the short steep waves say up to 1·2 m (4 ft) high and 30 m (100 ft) long that are objectionable and need to be reduced to something like 1·15 m (6 in.) maximum height. Recent research in this country and the United States has been directed to this end.

Here, in Southampton, we have been studying a particular form of breakwater—a raft type of structure, which has the merit of very low mooring forces. This basic research was the sequel to some specific investigations sponsored by the consulting engineers Harris and Sutherland, and it is described in the paper.

Fig. A shows the experimental set-up. Noteworthy features are the considerable reduction in wave height and the water flowing over the surface of the structure, the latter being a characteristic of this form of breakwater.

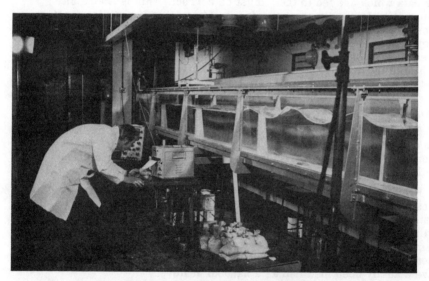

Figure A Model tests of a floating breakwater

In 1971, the same consulting engineers, in association with Archibald Shaw and Partners, conducted field trials in the Solent of a perforated raft structure (Fig. 7 in the paper) and we were very glad to assist in this work, our principal task being the analysis of the data.

It was fabricated in timber ply (Fig.B) and was 45 m (150 ft) long by 15 m (50 ft) wide. The object of the tests was to establish the breakwater efficiency, the mooring loads and the principal structural stresses, with a view to affording guidance to the design of a permanent structure in a durable material such as concrete.

Figure B Floating breakwater prior to field trials

(Harris and Sutherland and Archibald Shaw)

Wave heights on the weather and lee side were measured by 'waverider' buoys, which transmitted the information by short wave radio either to a receiver at Browndown or to the Hovercraft Research Station at Hythe. Deflections of the structure were obtained by cine-recordings, whilst maximum mooring forces were measured by a calibrated turnbuckle.

A great many problems were encountered, which it would be inappropriate to mention here—suffice it to say that model studies in a laboratory are not particulary easy, but in such a hostile environment as a storm sea one's problems are at least of a further order of difficulty. I think it is a tribute to the resourcefulness of Richard Harris and Peter Shaw, who did almost all the work, that useful data were obtained.

Fig. C is fairly typical of the results. It is a spectral diagram and shows wave energy plotted against frequency. The waves are predominantly of 2 sec period and their height, proportional to the square root of the energy, has been reduced to about one third of the incident. It may be noted that the smaller frequency (longer period) components are apparently passing through the structure with little attenuation.

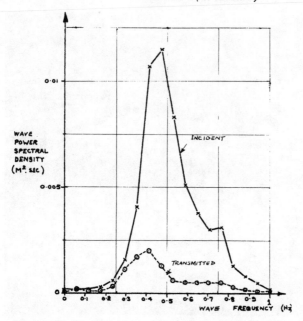

Figure C Comparison of incident and transmitted wave spectra

Since writing this paper, another type of composite floating break-water has come to our notice. A twin pontoon unit has been devised by the U.S. Army Corps of Engineers for Oak Harbour near Seattle.[*]
Each module is 13 m (42·5 ft) long, 3 m (10 ft) wide and has 1·5 m·
(5 ft) draft (Fig. D). There is timber decking on the top and sides, with concrete beams for ballast and polystyrene for Flotation. Model tests have been undertaken for both an anchor chain and a mooring pile system. It was found that waves of height 0·6 m (2 ft) and of length about 9 m (30 ft) could be reduced to 0·15 m (6 in.) height

It is not possible to give any quick answer as to the best type of floating breakwater for a small craft harbour. It depends on the site conditions, the attenuation desired, what is acceptable in terms of maintenance, and, perhaps most important of all, the cost. This last aspect has been deliberately avoided in the paper, but in the accompanying table there are a few statistics that people have been good enough to supply.

---

[*] Davidson, D. D. (1971), *Wave Transmission and Mooring Force Tests of Floating Break-water, Oak Harbor, Washington,* U.S. Army Eng. Waterways Exp. Sta. Tech. Rpt. H-71-3.

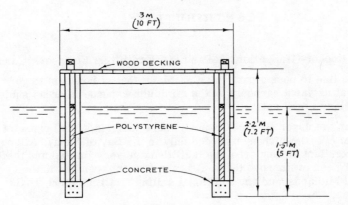

Figure D Proposed floating breakwater for Oak Harbour, Washington State

(*U.S. Army Engineer Waterways Expt. Sta.*)

Table A

Specification: Incident storm-type waves of approx. 1 metre (3 ft) maximum height are to be reduced to a height not exceeding 0·3 metre (1 ft)

Type	Quotating Authority	Approx. Cost (incl. moorings, etc. per metre	per ft
Seabreaker	Sea Services Agency	£148	£45
Perforated raft	Archibald Shaw & Partners	£150	£46
Resa	Resabo International	£242*	£74*

* excluding moorings, but including leeside berthage

From our viewpoint, there is scope for further interesting study which could well be directed to useful practical ends, but probably more in the way of optimising a design and understanding the mechanics of behaviour, rather than creating a new concept. There appears to be little or no prospect of developing something small and of low cost which will damp, in any acceptable degree, the great energies contained in large waves.

CONTRIBUTIONS

Mr. A. V. Hooker (W. S. Atkins & Partners, Consulting Engineers, Cardiff)

I would like to pose a particular problem: that of how best to go about creating yacht harbours at the minimum expense in areas subject to a very large tidal range.

I sail in the upper Bristol Channel, where there is a tidal range of up to 12 m (39 ft), which is exceeded only in the Bay of Fundy. Although it is an excellent sailing area, the facilities are very limited and there is a great need to improve them. It is the nearest open sea to the industrial Midlands, and any additional sailing facilities there would be taken up.

Fig. E shows the old harbour at Barry. Originally, Barry Island was separated from the mainland by a tidal channel. When the docks were built during the last century, the channel was closed and the old harbour remained. The almost horizontal dark line is the causeway, which takes the road and closes off the channel. Barry old harbour has gradually silted up and is no longer maintained as a harbour of refuge, but is capable of development as a yacht harbour to take at least 200 boats.

The essential problem is whether to impound or dredge. If a breakwater were built right across, it would have to be more than 12 m (39 ft) in height and might be more than 30 m (100 ft) wide at its base. The cost of such a breakwater would be enormous, together with the deep lock which would be necessary.

Another solution would be a half-tide wall, but this might produce the worst of both worlds. There would still be a rise and fall of about 6 m and difficulties of access.

The solution put forward is to dredge out a pool which is some 2 m (7 ft) deeper than the approach channel so that, as the approach channel dries out, an area is left in which boats of up to about 1·5 m (5 ft) draft can lie afloat. This has been done on a very small scale on the other side of the Bristol Channel at Porlock Weir. It is appreciated that there will be siltation problems which will require careful investigation.

I wish to end on a lighter note by telling an anecdote of an occurrence in Scotland some years ago. I stopped to give a lift to a yachtsman who told me that he had just come over from Ireland and, from his description of it, the boat seemed a very small one. This was long before the days of piped water in marinas, and I asked him how he had coped with the problem of water storage. He said, 'We don't shave, we cook our potatoes in sea water and we use gin for drinking, so we don't need very much water'.

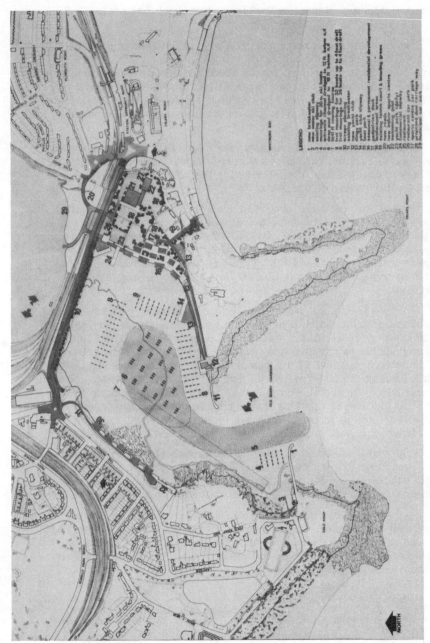

Figure E Redevelopment of Old Barry Harbour, S. Wales

Mr. J. D. Mettam (Bertlin & Partners, Consulting Engineers, Redhill)

I wish to ask Professor Lundgren why, in the case of Hanstholm, there is a harbour where not only boats but waves can enter from any direction. This was very common about a hundred years ago, when most vessels had to make harbour under sail and had to use various directions of approach, but why in this age were the new breakwaters at Hanstholm not provided with an overlap so as to exclude most of the waves ?

In harbour design, one has to be very fortunate to have available a few years' reliable recordings of wave height. Then the only problem is how to decide from this information the height for which the breakwater should be designed.

Until a few years ago, everyone used probability paper to extrapolate wave records. This assumes that the wave phenomenon follows a Gaussian distribution. Nowadays, this is unfashionable and we use graph paper for the Weibull distribution*, or exponential distribution†. These give different answers and no one knows which is the right one. In some cases we use three different methods and take the average.

If the wave data are not available one must have recourse to wind information from which it is possible to calculate wave heights. In this country, we are fairly well placed for wind information and it is often possible to calculate the probable wave height. Mr. Shellard‡, of the Meteorological Office, has produced some valuable data on the magnitude of the 100-year winds that can be expected in this country. These are quite useful, except that they are not expressed in terms of different directions. Most harbours are only exposed from a few directions so that, unless a harbour is facing towards the strongest winds, generally directly south-west, the forecasts may be exaggerated.

Another difficulty, which may cause waves to be under-estimated, is that the winds are mostly measured on land, whilst we are concerned with conditions over the sea. There are not very many weather ships at sea and those that there are do not always produce good wind data.

As an extreme example of the difficulty of forecasting waves, I would like to mention a harbour which we are studying at the moment in Jamestown, St. Helena. All the local winds are from the south-east, and the harbour is open only to the north-west. There is no locally generated wind. The harbour is troubled by waves generated off

---

* Battjes, J. A. (1970), *Long Term Wave Height Distribution,* N. I. O. Int. Rpt.
† Mayençon (May 1969), *Etude Statistique des Observations de Vague,* Cahiers Oceano-graphiques, 21.
‡ Shellard H. C., (1965) *Extreme Wind Speeds over the U.K. for Periods Ending 1963,* Meteorological Office Climatological Memo. No. 50.

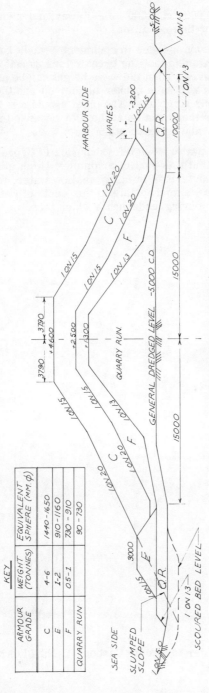

Figure F Breakwater for Larnaca, Cyprus

Newfoundland about 13, 000 km (8000 miles) away, and we aim to select a design wave for that condition.

Another approach recommended in considering yacht harbours is to site them in shallow water so that the breakwaters cannot be exposed to extremely severe waves. Then the wave height can be assessed by considering what waves will have broken further off and those that will break at the harbour structure. The chief problem is then to assess how much surge there can be at the site, because this will give an extra depth of water and an extra strength of wave.

Fig. F shows a breakwater design for Larnaca in Cyprus, where a yacht harbour is being built as part of a complex which includes a large commercial harbour. It is in fairly shallow water, and is designed to resist the largest waves appropriate to this depth of water. Rock of 4 to 6 t is the main armouring, underneath which there is ½ to 1 t

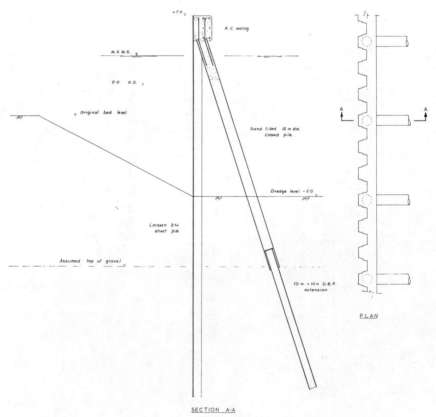

SECTION A-A

Figure G Breakwater for Poole Harbour Yacht Club Marina

stone and then quarry run. In this case, it is an economical solution, in part because the main harbour is also being built with armour stone over a rubble core, which will effectively absorb wave energy.

Fig. G shows a totally different solution for a marina at Poole Harbour, which is exposed to a fetch of only about 3 km (2 miles) so that the design wave is calculated from the maximum expected wind. In this case, it is possible to adopt an economical form of construction in the form of a vertical line of sheet piling, the top of which is supported by a concrete waling strutted by a steel pile. This type of solution is possible only where the wave action is very limited.

Mr. N. H. Searle (Director, Wimpey Laboratories Limited)

A few years ago, Mr. Mettam and I were involved in a hydraulic model investigation into wave action in Shoreham Harbour. We were both attracted by the idea behind a device called a 'resonator' because it appeared to be a beautifully simple method of using nature to counteract her own forces.

Fig. H shows the layout of breakwaters which protect the inner harbour at Shoreham. During certain sea conditions the wave heights at the lock entrance caused some difficulties and a significant reduction of wave height in the eastern arm was achieved by constructing three 'resonators' at the position shown. These were simple open-ended box-like structures set into the quay wall with dimensions such that the rear wall was one quarter of a wave length from the face of the quay (Fig. I). Wave crests entering the box were reflected by the rear wall, and emerged half a wavelength later. In other words, the crests

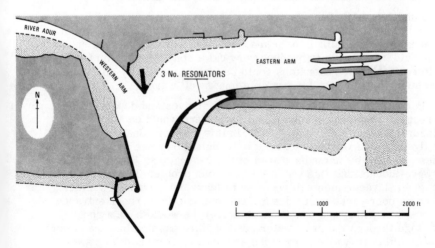

Figure H Layout of Shoreham Harbour, Sussex

Figure I Resonators for Shoreham Harbour under model test

were used to fill in the troughs; three different sized resonators were constructed to cover the natural spread of wave periods.

I understand that the device worked very well on site and Fig. 13 (p. 93) in Prof. Lundgren's paper reminded me of this principle. If resonators were built into the main breakwaters of a marina entrance, it should be possible to produce very calm conditions within the harbour. Alternatively, the resonators could be tuned to virtually eliminate certain wave periods—for example long swell waves.

In conventional ports, where shipping arrives and departs almost irrespective of offshore sea conditions, there would be a particular disadvantage with resonators built in this manner. Sea conditions at the entrance would be extremely turbulent because wave energy is dissipated in the immediate area of the resonators. However, I have always thought that this was a less serious problem in marinas since, in general, yachtsmen will not wish to leave port in rough weather. If some poor yachtsman finds himself outside the harbour entrance during worsening sea conditions, however, he would have a rough passage through the breakwater heads before passing into the calmer water, although where resonators are used to eliminate long swell only, the entrance conditions should not be troublesome.

Resonators are a subject requiring further research. If Fig. 13 depicts some form of resonator, I would be interested to hear from Prof. Lundgren whether he is working along these lines or intends doing so.

Mr. J. G. Berry (Bertlin and Partners, Consulting Engineers, Redhill)

When Mr. Stickland told us of the necessary investigations for carrying out a job properly, I felt rather like a taxi-meter ticking away the cost. I felt this particularly when I read in Sect. 6.4 of hydrographic surveyors preparing 'master plans' of the sea bed contours, tidal curves, float track plots, etc. Then come the geophysicists, with another list of studies. Unfortunately, the amount of money which it would be necessary to spend on these sorts of investigation is not generally available in the case of yacht harbours.

Yacht harbours present the same design problems for the engineer as commercial harbours ten times their value but funds available for adequate investigations are usually very limited.

A problem which sometimes arises in the case of rubble-mound breakwaters is settlement. Where there is a sandy bed, it is difficult to ensure that the whole structure does not settle into the sea bed. This can be particularly serious for a yacht harbour where water depths are usually small.

The new breakwater under construction at Larnaca (Fig. F, p. 167) is a typical example. Rock armour sinks about 0·5 m (1½ ft) or so into the sea bed after it has been subjected to wave action for some time. We have, therefore, designed the toe in such a way that it can settle by up to 1 m (3 ft) but still provide support to the 4 to 6t rock armour. The assumed line of the slumped slope is shown in Fig. F.

It is interesting to compare this solution with that adopted for a large commercial project-the southern mole at Europoort in Holland. Fig. J shows the elaborate filters provided to blanket the sandy sea-bed in order to prevent settlement of the breakwater. Such a solution would not normally be economic for a yacht harbour.

Turning to breakwater type, there is a lot to be said for the rubble mound type, although it is not so attractive visually as the vertical form.

If there are a few waves which are much larger than have been forecast—and we know how wrong forecasts can be—they are not as susceptible to damage in that, although the armour may be disturbed, it can be replaced after the storm has passed. Once a vertical-face breakwater has overturned, it has failed and there is nothing that can be done about it.

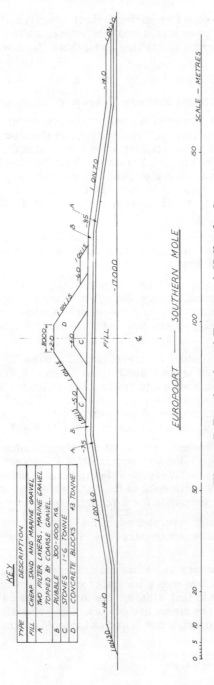

Figure J Breakwater at Europoort, Netherlands

Mr. A. W. White (Assistant Borough Engineer, Poole)

The use of aerial survey techniques has recently been employed in carrying out a hydrographical survey of Poole Harbour. The survey was carried out with the assistance of the Coastal Sedimentation Research Unit at Taunton and, when completed, will give direction and speed of harbour currents for spring and neap tidal ranges on the ebb and flood tides.

Fifteen minutes before each flight was scheduled four high speed launches were used to seed the harbour with flat cardboard floats 0·45 m (18 in.) square. These craft travelled on separate predetermined courses and launched between them 1300 floats, each craft launching floats at 12·5 s intervals.

As soon as this operation was completed the photographic flight commenced, the aircraft flying a series of parallel runs to obtain vertical photographs (Fig. K) from a timed camera with generous overlap on all of the photographs. The direction and speed of each float could then be plotted by measuring the relative movement and relating the distance moved to the time recorded on each frame of the film.

Photography was carried out at heights of 1200 m (4000 ft) and 3000 m (10, 000 ft) to produce a plot to scales of 1 : 3000 and 1 : 10, 500 respectively, the latter being the scale used for the local Admiralty charts. The final survey drawings will be available during October.

Mr. P. G. R. Barlow (Coode & Partners, Consulting Engineers, London)

I wish to add a note to what Mr. Stickland said in his paper about the breakwater layout in the St. Helier Harbour model. The marina breakwaters at the top left-hand corner of Fig. 6 (p. 116) were put on that alignment as a first shot in design because that alignment represented the optimum layout from the point of view of minimising rock breaking.

Furthermore, a vertical-sided breakwater was reproduced in the model because the very large tidal range-and this is another place with a range of 12 m (39 ft) at springs-made this design attractive from the point of view of construction costs. However - regrettably and not surprisingly - the reflections were unacceptably confused in the harbour entrance. Mr. Stickland showed this particular illustration to demonstrate his point.

We then played around with the alignment, and reverted to a rather more expensive, wave-absorbing type of breakwater and the problem was solved.

The really valuable use of the hydraulic model technique can be experienced only when the consulting engineer and the model specialist work together all the way through, using the benefit of each other's

(*Fairey Surveys Ltd.*)

Figure K Float tracking by aerial photography, Poole Harbour

experience and optimising the layouts; so I would make a plea to those who hold the purse strings not to stint expenditure on model testing because, if a testing programme has to be curtailed, this can be done only at the expense of the optimisation tests. It is these tests, in the final stages of the programme, where the money-saving process really begins.

Capt. C. McMullen (Marine Consultant, London)

I am sure Mr. Stickland would agree with me in saying that the prototype is the best form of model.

In certain rivers on the south coast, notably the Hamble, Beaulieu and Lymington Rivers, various large holes are being dug without, it is believed, sufficient knowledge as to what the ultimate effect will be on the estuary regime as a whole.

Two of these estuaries, the Hamble and Beaulieu, have been donated by nature as beautiful self-maintaining estuaries and man may be in danger of desecrating them.

To list the various works: on the Hamble, marinas have been dug at Port Hamble, Mercury Yacht Harbour, Port Swanwick, with additional ones planned in three other places. On the Beaulieu River, a large hole has recently been dug above Bucklers Hard with a 'whisper' that another may be excavated elsewhere. On the Lymington River, three large 'holes' have been dug; the Lymington Marina has altered the tidal currents of the river, a large crossing place has been dug to allow ferries to pass in the lower part of the river and the Lymington Yacht Haven Marina is just completing.

It seems important that harbour authorities keep a close check by frequent soundings on the effects of these works on the rivers as a whole and the circulation of these results would be of great interest to other authorities and marina firms.

Interchange of information regarding siltation and maintenance dredging inside the various marinas might also be of great interest to present and future marina operators and although it is unlikely that two marinas would ever be exactly similar, such interchange of information might be extremely useful.

I understood the Minister to say that the Government was keen to help generally and I have suggested that assistance with new public small craft harbours might be one field of activity.

Might the building of a model, perhaps of the Hamble River as a start, be another sphere in which the Government could help? It is believed that such a model, preferably permanently established in Southampton University, would greatly add to our knowledge regarding our estuaries and help to ensure that they are not irreparably damaged in the future.

Mr. E. W. H. Gifford (Gifford and Partners, Consulting Engineers, Southampton)

There is something which seems to have been forgotten in recent years - a timber wave screen. It is a device which the Victorians used

Figure L   Timber wave screen at Brixham Harbour, Devon

happily and it consists simply of a series of long, thick vertical timber planks with gaps between.

An example of this device is to be found at Brixham in our design of the new Fish Quay where it has proved extraordinarily effective in attenuating the waves (Fig. L).

I am quite certain that by installing a double screen, the millpond stillness evidently expected by contemporary boat-owners could be achieved.

Col. H. G. Hasler (Sea Services Agency, Folkestone)

I am responsible for the 'Seabreaker' design, and wish to give a few more details about what has been done and what we are trying to do.

The sloping face at the shoreward side of the main float not only prevents overtopping of the waves but also traps a lot of water on deck in bad weather. This water pours continuously off the seaward face. The fact that water is trapped also causes the whole 'Seabreaker' to trim down lower. We believe that both effects help the attenuation.

The vertical forces induced by the waves on the main float are very great. We considered it necessary to provide the large girder along the top in order to contain these forces.

The prototype is built entirely of steel, except for the main float, which consists of 52 blocks of moulded polystyrene foam sheathed in GRP. These have proved successful so far, and we have had no measurable loss of buoyancy, even when on a certain occasion the wave pole drove a 75 mm hole through it.

The whole structure (Fig. 14, p. 151) has been continually on station in Stokes Bay for 14 months. It is moored in 8 m (26 ft) average water depth, and its moorings to seaward consist of two 16 mm (0·63 in.) chains, one at each end, going down to a 1·5 t stockless anchor. We have had difficulty in measuring loadings on the device, but we have at least established that, in the recent series of S.W. gales - which I think went up to force 9 more than once - the loading in one chain did not exceed 7 t and may have been considerably less.

For a breakwater perimeter, it is obviously necessary to join two or more units together and we envisage using a heavy universal joint between them. This is arranged so that they can take an angle of 90 degrees to shoreward, or up to 30 degrees to seaward, thus enabling any desired curve or angle to be laid out in the perimeter.

It also enables one, should it be wished, to use one section of 'Seabreaker' as a gate which can be closed if bad weather comes from a particular quarter. It operates just like a wartime boom gate.

We consider that we can moor the device in a tide of up to 4 knots in any direction, but we assume that very few designers of small craft harbours would relish such a current in a mooring area. It is very easy to tow, and this particular one was towed from Kent, where it was launched, at a speed of 4 knots behind a 20 m (66 ft) M.F.V.

It is important to emphasise that the dimensions of the breakwater unit must be increased in proportion to the height of the predicted wave. Here I am referring only to local, wind-driven, waves. The question of a low swell is a different, and far more difficult, problem. It is of course, implicit that the 'Seabreaker' will have to survive any weather.

We envisage four different applications for the 'Seabreaker':

(i)   Permanent installation - a perimeter about a small harbour.

(ii) Temporary installation - one or two units moored to protect harbour constructional works while they are in progress.

(iii) Semi-mobile use - one or two units provided with their own system of winches and anchors, and capable of being winched along to keep pace with some slowly advancing vessel, such as a dredger or pipelayer.

(iv) Fully mobile use - a self-propelled sea-going vessel capable of proceeding to any site where it is temporarily required and able to hold itself on station without moorings.

To add to the small craft harbour application previously mentioned, we also envisage enclosing a bay in such a way that it is sufficiently sheltered for yachts to lie on swinging moorings, but not sheltered enough for them to lie alongside.

It is also hoped that there will be dinghy clubs on open beaches who can benefit from having one or two units moored off the beach. We assume that the requirement there would be to reduce the wave height to about 0·5 m (1½ ft) in winds up to about force 5. Beyond force 5, nobody would want to launch off the beach.

We intend to offer 'Seabreaker' units for charter, if the demand warrants it.

Mr. P. Winter (Chartered Architect and Marine Consultant, Cowes)

In the paper on 'Floating Breakwaters' there is an illustration (Fig. 13, p. 150) of a floating breakwater under trial at Cowes. This was the first experimental part of the breakwater periphery of Cowes Yacht Haven (Fig. M), which, so far as I know, is the only marina which relies for its protection entirely upon floating breakwaters.

It is important to realise that, in this instance, the breakwater performs two functions—it serves as a breakwater but also earns an income as a mooring pontoon. When considering costs, one must bear in mind its dual role. The cost of this installation was about £260 per metre (£80 per ft) though I am quite sure that it could be built for considerably less.

Fig. 13 presents rather an alarming view since the breakwater is swaying around a good deal. This was an extreme test in a force 8 gale from the most exposed quarter which occurred before the mooring arrangements were completed. Since then, in similar waves, the motion of the breakwater has been very much less.

In addition to the north-facing breakwater, there is a lighter, east-facing breakwater which does not have to withstand such high waves. Its basic function is to brush aside the waves which have already been attenuated by the north-facing breakwater and to deal with the wash from traffic passing up and down the Medina estuary.

The question of the efficiency of a floating breakwater will probably be of interest. The tests carried out on a scale model of the Cowes Yacht Haven breakwater in Southampton University indicated an efficiency of 75%-85% on short period waves. These experimental results have been confirmed in practice as the breakwaters have proved most effective in attenuating the short waves which are so troublesome in Cowes Harbour. They are less effective in dealing with waves having a wavelength of 15 m (50 ft) or more, so that the overall effect of the breakwaters is to 'filter off' the shorter waves. The best measure of a breakwater's efficiency is the practical one. Last

Figure M Cowes Yacht Haven, showing floating breakwater/pontoon units at seaward periphery

weekend, there were a number of boats in the marina, although it was by no means full, when a northerly gale of force 6 or 7 sprang up. Inside the marina, parties held on board boats went on in comfort, while outside the marina everyone looked pretty green.

In listing the rival merits of the different types of breakwater - solid versus floating - the paper did not mention aesthetic considerations, which are important when considering marinas. The sight of large weed covered walls outside a marina is not pleasing to those inside. With a floating breakwater all that can be seen is the walkway, and even this is usually obscured by boats.

Mr. Stickland, in his paper, mentioned site investigation costs. Our site investigation costs at Cowes were measured in tens or hundreds, and not in thousands of pounds. I agree with the principle of fullest site investigations, but the expenditure must be related to the scale of the subsequent operation. Local knowledge can, of course, be invaluable though it is notoriously unreliable where the height of the waves are concerned.

A subject on which further research seems necessary is the design of the entrances to marinas. Clearly the larger the entrance the more weather one will let in but the entrances must be wide enough for boats to enter and leave in safety. I was interested therefore to hear Col. Hasler's suggestions about a 'Sea gate'.

Mr. H. Pokorny (Resabo International, Hamburg)

I am a General Manager of the German branch of the Swiss-German Company that manufactures the 'Resa' floating breakwater and I would like to amplify the brief comments on it given in the paper on 'Floating Breakwaters'.

Our breakwater (Fig. N) is available in prefabricated units, which means that no consulting engineer or contractor needs to prepare a design, nor is skilled labour required in fabrication. All that is necessary is to purchase pre-packed parts which only require assembly on site. No welding, sawing or bending are involved and the only tools required are wrenches. In other words, the device is simply screwed together.

All our pontoons, even those made from individual prefabricated sections, are assembled as rigid units. Movement of floating Resa jetties, independent of actual length and with or without floating breakwater system, is limited to about that which occurs in the wing of an aeroplane when subjected to vertical air currents.

There are two wave-braking shields. The weather side shield consists of individual bent sections whilst that on the leeward side comprises a submerged vertical grille (Fig. O). As a result, very

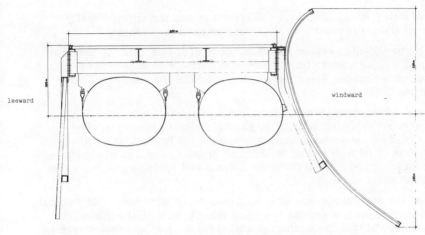

Figure N Cross-section of Resa floating breakwater

Figure O Resa floating jetty, 2m (6·6 ft) wide, showing leeward breakwater profile with aluminium vertical members

little water is splashed over the structure and the space directly
behind the breakwater may therefore be used for mooring yachts.

No breakwater system, solid or floating, can prevent the penetration
of long period waves. But these will constitute no danger to vessels
moored behind the 'Resa' breakwater because the entire system is
floating.

On the Starnbergersee, near Munich, there is a complete floating
yacht harbour constructed of Resa prefabricated elements. The
floating breakwater is designed to protect the harbour from waves up
to 1·5 m (5 ft) high and up to about 10 m (33 ft) long. It was installed
last autumn and has survived the autumn and spring gales, and even
a short spell of ice.

At the Starnbergersee site, we would never have been able to obtain
a permit to build a marina if we had interfered with the natural
currents and this is an inherent advantage of floating breakwaters
which has perhaps not been sufficiently emphasised.

AUTHORS' REPLY

Prof. H. Lundgren

The Bristol Channel poses a difficult problem because of tidal
range. The cost of a breakwater to cope with a tidal range of 12m
(39 ft) and a minimum depth of 3m (10 ft) at low water would, for
constructional reasons, be quite excessive.

It is, however, a problem of considerable scientific interest and I
invite Mr. Hooker to join me for cocktails before dinner when we can
talk about it, although I must advise him that it could easily lead to a
few years' discussion between two consulting engineers.

Mr. Mettam asked a very interesting question about the entrance to
Hanstholm harbour, which incidentally was designed in 1960. It is true
that wave protection is a very important consideration, since this is the
most exposed corner of Denmark. However, the over-riding factor
in this case is the need to bypass the littoral drift of 700, 000 m^3
(900, 000 yd^3) per annum in a natural manner, without interception at
the harbour.

Fig. 21 (p. 101) illustrates the flow of sediments during a westerly
storm. There has been a build-up of sediments in certain areas, until
a new equilibrium has been reached, but the alignment of the breakwaters represents an optimum with respect to the difficult sand
problem.

Since north-westerly gales are the most severe ones, a solution with an overlapping western breakwater was also studied. For this solution there was heavy sedimentation in the entrance area outside the end of the eastern breakwater where the eastbound current running along the western breakwater produced an eddy.

It must be admitted that experience has shown that the wave conditions in the commercial harbour (the westernmost basin in Fig. 3, p. 82) are not satisfactory during gales from the north-west in spite of the many steps taken as a result of the model tests. As the person responsible for these tests in 1960, I may add that the unsatisfactory results are due to an inadequate understanding of the behaviour of irregular waves at a time when three-dimensional model tests were run with regular waves only.

Even with the experience we have today about wave disturbance inside the harbour, it can be stated that the shape of the entrance is the best possible one. Any shape that gives heavy sedimentation in the entrance area would be unacceptable not only for economic reasons, but also because winter dredging after a gale is impracticable.

To Mr. Berry I should like to comment that there is no controversy between the type 'S' sloping breakwater and the type 'V' vertical face breakwater. I believe that the most commonly installed breakwater of the future will be the 'S' type. Recently, I read a Dutch report on Europoort which stated that various types of breakwater had been investigated and it had been found that the most economical one comprised circular caissons with sloping face.

Mr. Searle spoke about resonators, but in a rather different sense to that which I have in mind. I am concerned with eliminating the reflection of waves from the seaward face of breakwaters in order to reduce disturbance in the vicinity of the structure. Wave action in such a case can, of course, never be reduced to less than the incoming waves, but reflected waves would make navigation more difficult.

The idea of a perforated-faced structure to reduce reflection was first conceived in Canada. It was modified at the Danish Hydraulic Institute to take care of the higher reflection occurring at small wave periods. The result is that 90% of the incident energy is absorbed by turbulence through the openings. This means that the very difficult conditions induced at a harbour entrance by resonators of the form described by Mr. Searle would not arise in our case.

With regard to Capt. McMullen's plea for an exchange of information on the effects of marina construction in estuaries and on their siltation, I consider that factual data from the site should be analysed very carefully by people who have some appreciation of the basic physics of what is undoubtedly a very difficult problem. Whilst I am in favour of an exchange of information between the owners of marinas, I would prefer to see a flow of information and criticism between hydraulic experts.

Mr. I. W. Stickland

I apologise to Mr. Barlow for not explaining fully the extent of the testing on the vertical breakwaters. At the same time, I think he was a little modest in not suggesting that the reduction in wave height can be accomplished, not necessarily by the use of Dolos units, but by another type which he has developed, and which I think he would claim to be more effective than Dolos. This is perhaps an indication of the fact that there are many kinds of prefabricated armouring block which can be used on breakwaters and that stone is not the only material.

It may have sounded to Mr. Berry that money was being clicked up on a till when he read the list of professional skills that are needed in site investigation. Unfortunately, specialist advice is essential to any project, although it may not be easy to convince a developer that the money expended in site investigation work is good value.

I appreciate that in the case of small marinas it is difficult to extract that sort of money. Obviously, investigations must be tailored to the finance available, but it must be remembered that the answers and interpretations which are passed back to the developer are only as good as the data obtained from the investigations they have authorised.

I agree with Capt. McMullen that the prototype is the best model. But there are difficulties, as in the case of a yacht marina at Malta with a water depth of 36 m (120 ft), with which he and I were both concerned. Moving the breakwaters around to find the optimum alignment would be rather impracticable in the prototype.

I also agree that the results of creating large dredged areas in estuaries for marinas should be monitored wherever possible. These sort of data would prove most useful, and their analysis might well form the subject of a paper.

We have been very interested in trying to get data back from the site after a harbour has been constructed. Unfortunately, this again raises the question of money. It is perhaps asking too much when one tries to persuade a client to authorise further expenditure so that a scientist can have more data from which he can gauge the effects of what has been done.

Mr. N. B. Webber

There were no questions specifically directed to us, but we are grateful for the additional information furnished by Col. H. G. Hasler, Mr. P. Winter and Mr. H. Pokorny concerning their particular forms of floating breakwater.

Undoubtedly, one of the principal advantages of the floating break-water is its mobility and this may have a particular appeal to marina developers. With full berths and a high degree of profitability it should be a relatively simple matter to extend a breakwater system so as to enlarge the area of a marina. At the more gloomy extreme there should at least be an asset to be dismantled or towed elsewhere.

Also, in the case of small craft harbours in relatively deep water, a floating breakwater may afford the only possibility of providing some measure of protection at acceptable cost.

Perhaps the major disadvantage, apart from only partial attenuation, is the present lack of operational experience, particularly in respect of maintenance. It might help to overcome the conservatism of harbour masters and others if breakwater firms, instead of selling their structures, were to lease them under terms which were inclusive of maintenance. At the end of a certain number of years the marina operator would have the option of purchasing or dispensing with the device.

Turning to a rather different topic, Capt. McMullen has raised the important question of the effects on regime of creating large marina basins on the margins of our estuaries. This draws attention to the need for hydrographic studies and research on these small craft estuaries which up till now have received little or no attention, because they have not been considered of significance from the commercial navigation point of view. It is only in the light of adequate factual data that satisfactory answers can be given to this sort of question.

Session 3

Chairman: **Mr. N. H. Searle**
(*Director, Wimpey Laboratories Ltd.*)

Marina Design and Construction

D. P. Bertlin

Bertlin and Partners, Consulting Engineers, London

1 Introduction

A marina must have a protected area of water of sufficient extent and depth, free from excessive siltation, with good access from both sea and land, and an adequate adjacent area for such facilities as parking and yacht yards. It must fit into the general environment, be attractive to yachtsmen and be within reasonable distance both of the population it is intended to serve and to an attractive sailing area.

The provision of berths and other facilities must be given adequate attention. It is important to obtain the maximum reasonable density of craft and the most economic structural design, as these items make up a substantial element of the total cost. The project has to be planned so as to make the marina an attractive financial proposition as well as one which will appeal to the planners – or at least not attract adverse criticism from reasonable people.

This paper is an attempt to assess a number of the engineering problems involved and suggest some solutions.

No detailed consideration is given to aspects of marina construction which come within the scope of standard civil engineering practice or are covered in more detail in other papers in this Symposium.

2 Environment

A marina must be well placed from the point of view of access both from land and sea (or river or canal). The more interesting the sailing area in its vicinity the greater will be the attraction. England is fortunate in having long lengths of coast which are of great interest to yachtsmen and the south coast has the additional advantage of the proximity of the many delightful small harbours of the French north and west coasts.

Yacht harbours situated close to large centres of population have obvious advantages. The Solent area has developed rapidly as a

yachting centre not only because of its wonderful sailing waters but
also because it is within a reasonable distance from London.

However, as motor roads and other facilities for fast travel are
developed, more and more marinas will be built further afield; this
is particularly so with those associated with residential development.

Road access and provision for parking often involve major expense.
Whilst obviously it is important that adequate parking should be provided, insistence by planning authorities on an excessive ratio of car
space to berths can ruin the chances of a marina being a viable proposition.

3 Master Plan

Frequently, a site is of sufficient area to permit the layout of a large
marina and associated development, but the immediate demand may
be limited. It is then desirable to prepare a Master Plan for the full
development and undertake implementation by stages. The initial
stage may entail a disproportionate capital outlay but growth will
bring good returns. The forecasting of the growth rate has been and
is likely to be somewhat hazardous and based on few hard facts.
However, experience in this country is that marinas are soon filled,
though one as large as, for example, Chichester, may take several
years to reach capacity utilization.

4 Protection of Marinas – Breakwaters

If any extensive artificial protection is required, its cost is likely
to be the largest single item of capital expenditure. The design and
siting of breakwaters must therefore be most carefully planned;
large savings can be made by extensive design studies supported by
adequate field work and models.

It is only in rare cases in this country that it is possible to justify
building a yacht harbour on an open coast. Brighton is such a case,
as its proximity to London and the scope of the associated development is of such magnitude as to make it a reasonable proposition.
In the United States and Mediterranean countries a number of yacht
harbours involving substantial breakwater construction have been
undertaken. However, the Mediterranean has a tidal range which
does not exceed one metre, which makes breakwater construction less
costly than in most places. In the case of many American marinas
a major part of the cost is borne by Federal and/or State Governments.

Many marinas have been constructed in rivers or estuaries where no
breakwaters are necessary, but such favourable locations are becoming progressively fewer. Some have been optimistically developed
without adequate protection and it is now being found that better protection is necessary.

Assuming that the orientation of the berths is such that it is perpendicular to the wave front of the maximum height waves to be expected, the degree of protection may be either:

(1) The completely protected harbour. This is one where the berthing area is more or less completely protected from waves by adequate breakwaters or its situation (e.g. in a river). The maximum wave height should not exceed 0·4 m under the very worst conditions and normally it would not exceed 0·25 m. The dimension of such a harbour is unlikely to exceed 500 m.

(2) The partially protected harbour. This is one where shelter is provided from the prevailing winds by natural features (sometimes assisted by existing breakwaters) but the moorings would be exposed to waves from open water from some directions. If one assumes a maximum permissible wave height of 1·2 m, the uninterrupted fetch from the most exposed direction should not be more than about 8 km, but this is dependent on the effects of refraction which would permit much larger fetches if they are from directions more or less parallel to the coastline. However, the conditions are usually complex and each situation has to be considered on its merits.

Whilst, naturally, the Class (1) harbour is to be preferred, there are locations where the extra cost of providing such good conditions is prohibitive and one has to accept the Class (2) type. One can design for these less favourable conditions but the cost of providing berths will be greater, more area per boat will be required and the berth conditions will not be as good as with the more protected type. However, the overall cost may be so reduced, owing to omission or reduction in cost of breakwaters, that such a solution is either the only practical one or by far the most economical.

Breakwater design is fundamentally the same for commercial harbours and marinas, the difference being the lesser depth required in marinas but the more exacting requirements of wave reduction within the harbour. This involves a consideration, not only of wave diffraction and refraction, but of reflection and resonance. If a harbour is exposed to open sea waves, a regular shape should be avoided so as to reduce resonance.

This is not the place to develop breakwater theory, which is a subject in itself. However, the following points, which particularly pertain to yacht harbours, might be mentioned:

(i) In a large marina, the fetch across the marina itself may be such as to warrant the division of the area into two or more basins.

(ii) In view of the comparatively shallow breakwaters, it is of great importance to ensure that they are not undermined, as this is a more acute problem than with deep breakwaters.

(iii) Single sheet breakwaters may be an inexpensive way of providing a breakwater, particularly where clapotic forces are likely to be small.

(iv) With marinas in rivers, it may be necessary to provide against floating ice, which may be done by booms and pneumatic air breakwaters.

5 Dredging, Reclamation and Siltation

In developing an area for a marina, dredging often has to be undertaken to provide a sufficently deep basin. If the dredged material is suitable, it may be used for reclamation. Sand and ballast are the best materials for this purpose but stiff clay may also be used. Alternatively, ballast or sand, instead of being reclaimed, could be sold to the advantage of the marina budget. This has been done in the case of a large number of inland marinas, such as that at Penton Hook on the Thames. If the dredged material is silt it can either be disposed of at sea or pumped to a suitable area for long term reclamation after drainage. There are a number of problems concerning pumped reclamation and each situation has to be considered on its merits, but if the location and materials are suitable, pumped dredging combined with reclamation, particularly if on a reasonably large scale, can lead to very economic results. The Larnaca (Cyprus) and Beirut yacht harbours are examples of such development.

Siltation can be an important factor and constant maintenance dredging expensive and a nuisance. If a marina is situated in a river or estuary of a river, siltation is obviously a problem. Yarmouth, Port Hamble and Swanwick are all examples of marinas which have dredging maintenance problems.

If marinas are carefully sited, siltation can be reduced to a minimum, but, in some instances, they seem to have been planned with no regard to this aspect and frequent maintenance dredging has to be carried out. Naturally, in some cases, there is no alternative solution and siltation has to be lived with, but this is not always so, and by careful siting, incorporation of training walls and other expedients, it is usually possible to reduce it to an acceptable degree.

In the case of coastal marinas, there is almost always the problem of littoral drift, leading to the carriage of bed material across the entrance of the harbour, causing siltation at the entrance and possibly carriage of material into the harbour itself. This is a more acute

problem than with deep water commercial harbours as most movement takes place in shallow water. On some coasts, wind currents
may be in one direction at one season and the reverse at another, so
that, although there may be considerable movement of shore material,
the nett result is not great. However, to avoid entrance siltation,
even in these conditions it may be necessary to take the entrance
some way to seaward of that required by the maximum draft of yacht.
Alternatively, and this will normally be the case, it will be better to
accept dredging of the entrance at fairly frequent intervals.

Sediment transport caused by waves may be estimated by the formula
of the U.S. Army Coastal Engineering Research Centre, which is:

$$S = k \, H_e^{\,2} \, C_o \, k_r \, \sin\phi \, \cos\phi$$

where S = transport rate (m^3 /s)
   H_e = equivalent wave height (m)
   C_o = velocity of deep water waves (m/s)
   ϕ = angle of incidence of wave
   k = coefficient, depending on the shore material: $1\cdot4 \times 10^{-2}$
      for sand (but very much smaller for shingle)
   k_r = coefficient of refraction
   (for a wind driven sea, $H_e = H_s /\sqrt{2}$ approx. , where $H_s =$
   significant wave height and $C_o = g \, T/ (2\pi)$, T being the wave
   period (s))

However, even if one can obtain a reasonably accurate figure for the
transport of bed material, to proceed from this to an assessment of
the dredging required, cannot be done with any degree of certainty
without a thorough study of the coastal regime which would take several
years and is normally outside the scope of a marina feasibility study.

Provided that, from a study of the site and the history of coastal
movements, tides and storm, it is anticipated that accretion in the
entrance channel will not be excessive, it can usually be accepted
that there will be some siltation and maintenance dredging will have
to be undertaken as required. However, such accretion can be minimised by carefully planning the entrance channel and a current model
study can be of great help in doing this. The José Banús Marina is
an example of such careful study, where it is estimated that sand will
not enter the harbour before 2060, and then only in small quantities.

6 Locked Harbours

When the tide range is large and dredging a basin expensive, it is
frequently more economical to provide a locked basin rather than a
tidal one. The main disadvantage of a lock is that it requires atten-

dance, unless it be made user operated, which is not practicable in
many cases. However, a complete, fast operating locking system,
such as that at Chichester, is normally only employed for large
marinas, where the cost of an attendant is not unduly burdensome.
Another disadvantage is the time taken for a boat to pass through the
lock; if the capacity of the lock is not sufficiently large, queueing
may be experienced.

There are, however, many advantages, such as

    (i)   A completely protected basin.
    (ii) Constant, or near constant, water level.
    (iii) No maintenance dredging (except, possibly, of the
           entrance channel).
    (iv) Reduction in height of walls around the basin.

Sector lock gates have two big advantages as compared with mitre
gates. One is that they are very fast in their operation; for example,
at Chichester, the adjustment of level of water and opening only takes
about a minute. The other, is that they can operate with a head of
water in either direction, enabling them to be used for free flow operation for a considerable time each side of high tide and also as a flood
protection gate during periods of extreme high water.

There are a number of variants of the complete lock system. For
example, a single pair of gates may be used, allowing entrance only
during 2-3 hours at high water. The basins at Honfleur, Courseulles
and Morlaix are examples of this system. Sometimes, existing locked
basins which are no longer fully used commercially have been turned
into marinas, such as at St. Malo and Calais.

It is also possible to dispense with a lock entirely and trap the re-
ceding tide above a dam at low water, such as with the Emsworth
Marina. This system, however, is very restrictive and does not have
the advantage of a near constant water level in the basin. A gate may
be used in place of the dam or in addition to it. This arrangement
considerably improves conditions and is suitable for small basins.

7 Classification of Yachts

When designing a marina, it is important to know as closely as
possible the categories and numbers by category of the yachts which
will use it. It is then possible to arrange berths economically, both
for depth and length. This is important as the optimum development of
the water area is essential if the marina is to be financially successful.
At the present time, there are few reliable statistics on which to base
an estimate and we can only hope that the authorities concerned will
eventually agree to a census, say, every 4 years, which would be of
great help to marina designers.

The categories proposed by the International Commission for Sport and Pleasure Navigation of P. I. A. N. C. * are shown in Table 1. For classification purposes it is assumed that craft above 7 metres in length have living quarters and those less than 5 metres do not. From the point of view of the marina designer a more practical classification is given in Table 2.

The depth and width of berths are assumed normal maxima for the class which will only be exceeded in a small percentage of cases. The dredged depth should be taken from extreme low water and increased appropriately to allow for wave action, dredging tolerance and siltation. The amount allowed for wave action should be half the wave height plus a tolerance of 0·3 m in soft material and 0·5 m in rock. In some cases, particularly if the entrance channel is a long one, it may be necessary to allow for squat. The width quoted should be increased by an appropriate amount to include tolerance, etc., depending on the type of berth, e.g. alongside, finger piers or stern mooring.

The percentage of the different classes varies widely in different countries and regions. In the United States there are yacht harbours with no sailing yachts at all, whilst in the Mediterranean the motor boat dominates the scene. In England, the size distribution varies considerably and a forecast of categories and types to be expected in a projected marina has to be based on experience of similar situations. There are comparatively few vessels in Classes V and VI and those in Class VI are rare in this country but must be catered for in the larger yacht centres in the Mediterranean. A large coastal marina in this country should certainly provide facilities for Class V and VI yachts as, although the percentage is small, it is not negligible and such craft bring a worthwhile trade to the harbour.

A count by size (related to the classes quoted in Table 2 overleaf) of the yachts in the marinas of Swanwick, Chichester and Emsworth is shown in Table 3. For comparison, the assessment of boat sizes expected in the Languedoc-Roussillon marinas is also given.

---

*This is an International Commission appointed by P.I.A.N.C. (Permanent International Association of Navigation Congresses). Some sixteen countries are represented on this Commission which meets once a year with each country represented by one member. The British delegate is chairman of a committee of the British National Committee of P.I.A.N.C., which has eleven members who represent respectively the Department of Trade and Industry, Department of the Environment, British Waterways Board, the Dock and Harbour Authorities Association, the Royal Yachting Association, the Ship and Boat Builders' National Federation and the National Yacht Harbour Association.

Table 1 Classification of pleasure boats proposed by P.I.A.N.C.

Class	Length overall L (metres)	Sub-classes
I	$L < 5$	Motor boats Sailing yachts Motor/Sailing
II	$5 < L < 8$	Motor boats with living quarters Motor boats without living quarters Sailing yachts with living quarters Sailing yachts without living quarters Motor/Sailing with living quarters Motor/Sailing without living quarters
III	$8 < L < 15$	Motor boats Sailing yachts Motor/Sailing
IV	$L > 15$	Motor boats Sailing yachts Motor/Sailing

Table 2 Proposed yacht classification

Length overall L	Sailing yachts and motor/sailing			Motor boats and centreboards			Trimarans and Catamarans		
	Class	Berth depth	Berth width	Class	Berth depth	Berth width	Class	Berth depth	Berth width
$L < 8$	IS	1·5	2·8	IM	1·0	3·3	IT	0·6	4·5
$8 \leqslant L < 10$	IIS	1·6	3·0	IIM	1·0	3·5	IIT	0·8	5·0
$10 \leqslant L < 12$	IIIS	1·7	3·2	IIIM	1·0	4·0	IIIT	1·0	5·5
$12 \leqslant L < 15$	IVS	2·0	3·8	IVM	1·3	4·6	IVT	1·2	7·0
$15 \leqslant L < 18$	VS	2·5	4·5	VM	1·5	5·0	VT	-	-
$18 \leqslant L < 25$	VIS	3·0	5·5	VIM	2·0	5·5	VIT	-	-
$L \geqslant 25$	VIIS	4·5	7·0	VIIM	2·5	7·0	VIIT	-	-

All dimensions are in metres

Table 3 Size distribution in three English marinas

Class	Swanwick		Chichester		Emsworth		Languedoc-Roussillon (forecast)			
							Large harbours		Medium harbours	
	S	M	S	M	S	M	S	M	S	M
I	13	5	30	14	46	10	30	45	45	65
II	25	9	24	15	30	4	24	24	30	24
III	19	2	4	6	4	2	23	20	15	9
IV	12	7	2	3	2	2	16	7	10	2
V	3	4	-	1	-	-	3	2	-	-
VI	-	1	-	1	-	-	3	2	-	-
VII	-	-	-	-	-	-	1	-	-	-
	72	28	60	40	82	18	100	100	100	100
	100		100		100					

All figures are percentages. Multihull craft account for less than 1%.

Size distribution by percentage distribution of boat lengths for a
number of marinas is given in Fig. 1.

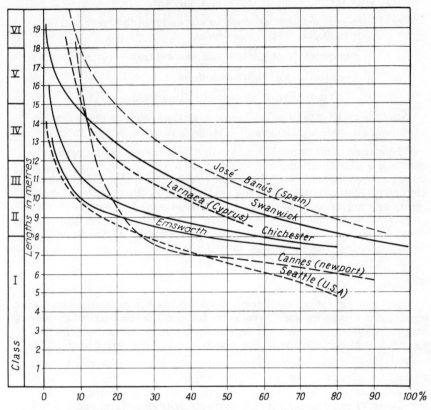

Figure 1 Yacht lengths, percentage distribution

8 Berths

8.1 Layout

Having decided on the anticipated class distribution, the layout of
the berths within the marina can be planned. Berth rentals provide
by far the largest income producing element (rents for berths are now
as high as £33 per metre (£10 per foot) per annum in some popular
marinas). It is, therefore, obvious that the greatest care must be taken
in planning the layout so as to maximise the capacity of the marina
whilst maintaining good access and facilities.

The first aspect to be considered is the orientation of the berths which should be as follows:

(1) With the current, if there is a current.

(2) If no current, but exposed to waves from the open sea, perpendicular to the wave front.

(3) In a completely protected marina preferably either

    (i) parallel with the longest side

or (ii) in the direction of the prevailing wind.

A number of types of berth layout are illustrated in Fig. 2. Some advantages and disadvantages of such layouts are given in Table 4.

The choice must depend on a detailed assessment of the requirements of a particular site and an analysis of costs of various possible layouts, remembering that the overall return per berth should be the criterion, taking into account the capital cost of the complete development, and not the cost of the berths themselves. Due weight should be given to the convenience to users of some types of berth as compared to others. In some instances, a combination of types may have advantages, such as in the new Larnaca marina.

8.2 Clearance

Widths of channels, clearances between vessels at berths and turning areas for manoeuvring have to be decided for the particular marina under consideration, and will depend on a number of factors, such as the size of harbour, entrance conditions and degree of protection.

Entrance: A width of entrance of 12 to 18 m for Class I to V yachts is usually adequate, but the channel leading to the entrance should be not less than 15 m and preferably 20 to 30 m. If provision is made for Class VI yachts, then it should be not less than 22 m and for Class VII 30 m, and the channel should be proportionately wider, depending on its length and exposure.

Where there is a lock, lay-by berths should be provided, particularly if the entrance is exposed. Normally, an adequate arrangement is a row of piles, with a catwalk or floating boom.

Channels within the Marina: There should be an area immediately within the entrance for manoeuvring and turning, the size of which will depend on the protection, maximum size of craft and general situation. Main channels should be not less than 18 m wide.

Clearances: Clearances between jetties or pontoons should be fixed according to size of craft, type of berth and situation. Degree of exposure and existence of a current are also important considerations. Table 5 gives clearances applicable to some of the berth arrangements shown in Fig. 2.

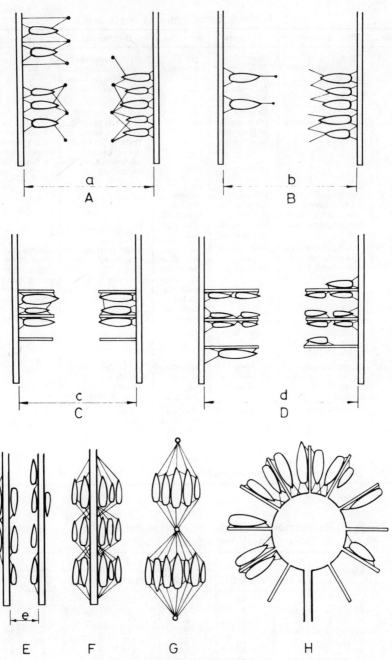

Figure 2 Types of berth layout

Table 4 Some types of berth layout

Ref.	Type of mooring	Examples	Advantages	Disadvantages	Remarks
A	Stern to quay, jetty or pontoon, bows to piles	Chichester Le Grande Motte Rotterdam Kristiansund	jetty economy	not as convenient for embarking as alongside jetties or pontoons	
B	-do- but bows moored to anchors or buoys	Deauville & the majority of Mediterranean marinas	jetty economy	not suitable with large tide range as excessive space required for head warps; danger of propellers being entangled in head warps	particularly suitable for large yachts in basins with little tide range where gangways can be attached to sterns
C	Alongside finger piers or catwalks one yacht on each side of each finger	Cherbourg, Larnaca (Cyprus) & many American marinas	convenient for embarking & disembarking		
D	-do- but more than one yacht on each side of each finger	Port Hamble Swanwick Lymington	-do- also allow flexibility in accommodating yachts of different lengths	finger piers must be spaced wider apart than in 'C' though this may be compensated for by the larger number of craft between jetties	fingers may be long enough for two or three vessels: if more than three then provision should be made for turning at the root of the berths
E	Alongside quays jetties or pontoons single banked	Granville	-do-		
F	Alongside quays jetties or pontoons up to 3 or 4 abreast	St. Malo Ouistreham St. Rochelle	economical in space and pontoons	crew from outer yachts have to climb over inner berthed yachts	
G	Between piles	Yarmouth Hamble River Cowes	cheapest system as no walkways, also high density	no dry access to land; difficulty in leaving mooring if outer yachts are not manned	not recommended except for special situations such as exist in the example quoted
H	Star finger berths	San Francisco			

Table 5 Recommended minimum clearances for the layouts proposed in Table 4 (well protected still water basins)

Class	a	b	c	d	e	
	S & M	S & M	S & M	S & M	S	M
I	32	30	26	40	9·7	11·3
II	37	35	32	53	10·5	12
III	44	42	40	62	11	13·5
IV	58	55	52	82	13·5	15·5
V	72	66	64	100	15·5	17·5
VI	100	90	90	140	25	25

All dimensions are in metres

Density: The number of berths per hectare which may be accommodated in a basin naturally varies according to size of yacht and other factors, but an average yacht basin usually accommodates anything from 75 to 175 yachts (30 to 70 per acre).

8.3 Types of jetty

Jetties may be fixed or floating. In tideless waters or where the tidal range is less than about one metre, the normal practice is to use fixed jetties usually of reinforced concrete piled construction suitably fendered. Where a large tidal range has to be accommodated, floating pontoons must be used. They entail more maintenance than fixed jetties, but in some circumstances are somewhat cheaper in first cost. They are also more flexible, and enable a layout to be modified if the categories of yacht are found to vary from those originally anticipated.

Jetties should not be less than 2m in width, except in the case of short finger jetties between pairs of boats, when the width may be reduced to 0·5 m or even less. If a jetty is over 100 m the land end should be increased to 2·5 m in width. If over 200 m then the land end should start at 3 m. Live load for fixed jetties should be a distributed load of 250 kg/m^2. Horizontal forces are difficult to estimate with any precision and should be estimated according to the type of craft for which the marina is designed. A figure of 300 decanewtons (0·3 tons) is used in the design of the Languedoc-Roussillon marinas.

Floating jetties should preferably be not less than 2·5 m in width, though 1·8 to 2 m wide pontoons are sometimes used. A design live load of 150 kg/m^2 may be used. They should be designed so that they will tilt less than 15^0 when the total design load is applied to half the width. It is possible to reduce the width of pontoon in the case of Type C and D layouts by making the finger piers (or part of them) act as catamarans. An economical pontoon arrangement based on the finger jetty principle is shown in Fig.3.

A variety of materials have been used for pontoons: steel, concrete, plastics and timber being the usual ones. The cheapest, oil drums with a timber deck, is not recommended as the maintenance is prohibitive. Expanded polystyrene is an inexpensive material for floats and may be used with various coatings, such as glass reinforced plastic or glass or fibre reinforced concrete or without any coating. The location of a marina is important when deciding on the type of pontoons and float to be adopted. Table 6 gives particulars of a number of pontoons on the market.

As compared to using standard pontoons, considerable savings can be made by designing for the requirements and conditions of a particular marina. For some pontoon arrangements, for example, Type 'C' in Table 4 and Fig. 2, width of boat is of great importance. The clearances shown in Table 7 can be adopted for this layout.

Table 6 Types of commercially marketed pontoons

Maker	Dimensions of standard pontoon unit(s)	Flotation unit	Dimensions of flotation unit	Deck	Width of deck	Approx. cost, ex works	Remarks
Dibben Structural Engineers	12·2 m × 1·83 m	steel rectangular	1·83 m × 1·0 m (6' × 5'6" × 3'3")	timber (keruing) on steel frames	1·83 m	£30–£33/metre run (£9–£10/ft)	
Walcon Limited WINCHESTER	1·9 m (6'3") width overall	expanded polystyrene encased in 19 mm (¾") polypropylene fibre reinforced concrete	1·83 m × 1·2 m × 0·9 m (6' × 4' × 3'), wt. 9 cwts, draft (sea water) 9", displacement (sea water) 128 lb/in	timber on steel frame	1·9 m (6'3")	£45 per flotation unit	
Thos. Storey (Engineers) Limited LONDON	12 m × 2 m 12 m × 2·5 m 12 m × 3 m	polystyrene coated with plastic or concrete	2 m (2·5 m, 3 m) × 1·25 m × 0·65 m	hardwood timber in modular mats	2 m 2·5 m 3 m	£14–£16/m² (£1·3–£1·5/ft²)	'Acrow-berth' system
United Flotation Systems		steel pontoon filled with polystyrene foam					
Magnum (Engineering) Ltd.	9·1 m × 2·4 m (30' × 8') 13·7 m × 2·4 m (45' × 8')	expanded polystyrene encased in elkalite	1·83 m × 0·53 m × 0·76 m (6' × 1'9" × 2'6")	elkalite	2·4 m 1·2 m fingers	£16/m² (£1·48/ft²)	elkalite is made with high alumina cement and synthetic fibre
Concrete Utilities	7·3 m (24') and over	expanded polystyrene encased in 13 mm (½") ferro-cement		concrete timber or steel	0·9 m to 2·4 m (3' to 8')	£22 to £35/ m² (62p to 99p/cu ft)	price is for delivery within 100 miles

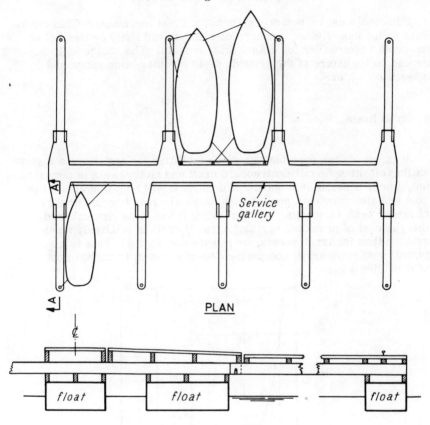

PLAN

SECTION A-A

Figure 3 Trimaran pontoon

Table 7 Dimensions for construction of Type 'C' layout

Ref.	Class of yacht			Spacing of finger jetties	
				between fingers	centres of fingers
a	IS	IIS	IM	6·8	7·5
b	IIIS	IIM		8	8·8
c	IVS	VS	IIIM IVM	9·5	10·5
d	VIS	VM	VIM	11	13
e	VIIS	VIIM		16	18·5

All dimensions are in metres

Pontoons must be restrained from too great movement. This can be done by the use of piles, anchors or clamps, end fixity or ties below the depth required for maximum draft vessels. The choice will depend on the nature of the ground, depth of water, tide range and other such factors.

9 Small Boats

9. 1

It is not always possible to include facilities for small boats such as sailing dinghies, small centreboard craft and motor boats in a marina, but, where possible this should be done as it will help to animate the port and also provide a pool of yachtsmen who may become owners of larger craft in due course. However, it has to be remembered that the cost of providing berths for small craft is relatively much greater than for large yachts, as is shown in Fig. 4. This is a typical cost ratio graph comparing cost of a vessel to capital cost of providing a berth.

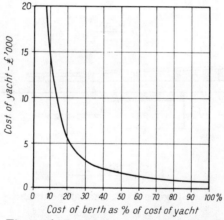

Figure 4 Cost ratio of berth to yacht

As small boats can be handled ashore more readily than larger craft, the possibilities of storage ashore should be exploited.

9. 2 Small Motor Boats

The most economical stowage for boats under about 6 m is shelf stowage with a gantry crane to place and retrieve craft, using an arrangement such as that shown in Fig. 5. This system has been successfully used in Spain, where it was estimated that the installation cost 30% of the capital cost of the boats, of which 10% was the cost of the quay and 20% that of the shed, gantry, etc. This allows quick stowage and retrieval and can be used both in winter and summer.

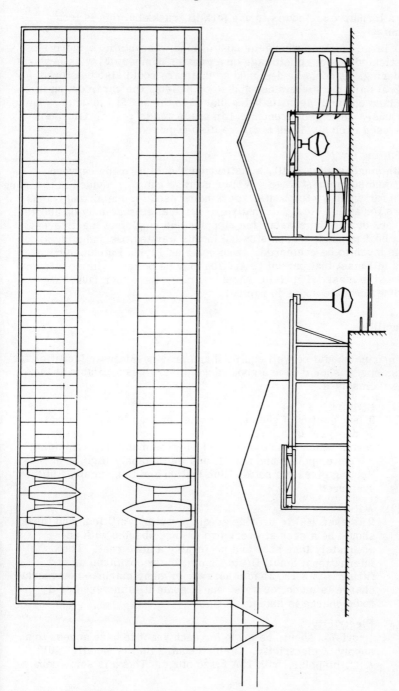

Figure 5 Storage for small motor boats

An alternative method is to use forklift trucks but this is less economical.

For large marinas where the cost of land warrants it, a more sophisticated system of stowage on a greater number of levels is worth considering. It could be designed so that cars could also be stored. Both boats and cars would be handled on pallets, the cars coming in at the land end and the boats being placed in the sea at the other. This is obviously extremely economical in space and is very flexible as it can be used exclusively as a garage if so required.

9.3 Sailing Craft

With small sailing craft, a distinction should be made between winter and summer storage. Winter storage can be provided in the same way as for small motor boats, racks being used for masts and booms, lockers for sails, etc. Alternatively, vertical storage may be adopted. However, during the season, the stepping and rigging of masts every time a boat is used, makes stowage in this way tedious and a high roof shed is much to be preferred. Such boats as Flying Dutchmen have such a tall mast that partial protection may be better, with no attempt to cover the mast. Provision should be made for owner launching, including adequate non-slip ramps.

10 Facilities

10.1

A marina should be well equipped and provide adequate facilities for yachtsmen. It should have a good range of services available at the berths themselves.

(1) Lighting
It is a matter of choice as to whether high level illumination be provided or a large number of low power lights on the berths which can be combined with the manifolds containing the power points and sometimes water taps. High level lighting gives the better illumination and is normally to be preferred.

(2) Water
It is essential to provide adequate water facilities, and these should be a cock at every two or three berths with an adequately long hose and preferably a hose reel. The International Small Boats Committee recommend an end fitting with a 15/21 mm screw. In many marinas no separate charge is made for water but in some it is metered or a fixed charge is made.

(3) Electricity
Provision should be made for each yacht to have access to a supply of electricity. In this country this is usually 240V, A.C. bi-polar, with 13A fused plugs. There is some debate

as to whether 240V or 110V should be adopted and in the U.S.A. and France the lower voltage is normally used, though there is no evidence that 240V should not be reasonably safe; it is certainly less expensive and more convenient. However, the installation must be to a high standard, bearing in mind the marine environment.

The distribution network should be isolated from the electricity authority's network by an isolating transformer. Supply points should preferably be split into sections of 150 to 200 with sub-sections covering 5 to 8 points, each being provided with a circuit breaker.

Electricity may be charged at a daily rate, no separate charge may be levied, or it can be metered. In England it is usual to use a meter, which is placed within the yacht. The P.I.A.N.C. Committee recommends that a fixed rate should be made for craft less than 8m in length and the charge should be by meter for larger boats.

(4) Telephone and Television
In the more luxurious marinas, telephone and television points are installed and it is hoped that this will become usual practice in this country.

Water, electricity, telephones and television may be combined into a manifold as shown in Fig. 6.

Figure 6 Services manifold installed in the José Banús Marina

(5) Waste Disposal
Waste disposal receptacles should be provided at frequent
intervals.

(6) Fire Precautions
Fire extinguishers should be placed at strategic points. Fire
hydrants should be installed and on long piers one or two
hydrants should be located on the piers.

(7) Bunkers
Normally fuels are not piped to each berth and a separate
bunkering berth should be provided. However, in marinas
catering for the largest classes of motor yachts, it is sometimes convenient to provide a piped diesel supply to the
berths allotted for these craft.

There are administrative advantages in siting the bunkering
berth adjacent to the yacht yard and some provisions and
chandlery may be profitably sold at the bunkering point.

10.2 Land Based Facilities

Land based facilities, such as car parks and yacht yards are essential to any marina and call for careful planning with both economic and
environmental considerations in mind. As a first approximation, it
may be assumed that the land area required will equal the yacht basin
area.

(1) Parking and Hardstandings
The cost of the provision and construction of parking areas
is usually a major proportion of the total cost of the marina.
The number of car spaces to be provided is usually related
to the number of berths. Some authorities in this country
insist on as many as 2 car spaces per berth, whilst others
are satisfied with a much smaller proportion (at Brighton,
for example, 0.6) .

In the United States, standard practice is to allow 1-1·25
spaces per berth, whereas in France it is 0·5 per berth,
though it is accepted that in some marinas the ratio should
be increased to 1·5 or even 2.

The ratio should be determined for the particular marina
concerned, taking into account such factors as size of
average yacht and other transport facilities available.

On the basis of 1·5 and a density of 100 yachts per hectare
(40 per acre), assuming 300 cars per hectare (120 per acre),
the area of parking to be provided will equal half the area
of the yacht basin.

Special consideration should be given to parking cars with
trailers, if provision is made for dinghies. Only a small

area is needed for hibernation as part of the car park can be used for this purpose during the winter and, in this plastic age, fewer and fewer boats are removed from the water except for a scrub, anti-fouling treatment and inspection of hull, propeller and rudder.

The surfacing of the parking area may be concrete, asphaltic concrete, bituminous macadam, water-bound macadam or soil stabilised. Soil stabilisation is the least expensive and may be satisfactory if the underlying soils are suitable.

(2) Buildings

(i) Administration

(ii) Social centre or clubhouse: lounge, cloakrooms, bar, snack-bar, dining room, kitchen, pantry, laundry, men's dressing room and showers, ladies dressing room and showers, bedrooms, etc.

(iii) Shops: provisions, chandlery, yacht outfitters, news-agents, etc.

(iv) Ablution blocks: lavatories, baths, showers, etc.

It has been amply demonstrated that there is no danger to health due to yachts in marinas, whether or not there is any restriction regarding the use of their 'heads'. The amount of marine pollution is microscopic as compared with that caused by municipal sewer outfalls and industrial waste. However, the result of the use of unsuitable W.C.'s on board yachts may cause a nuisance and shore based ones are usually more comfortable, quite apart from any regula-tions the local health authorities may insist on. Ample lavatories should therefore be provided and it may be necessary in some cases to provide tanks for receiving sewage from yachts that have holding tanks.

(3) Yacht Yard

Some marinas are built with no yard, others are extensions of existing yards. All marinas should have some facilities for handling yacht repairs and, if efficiently managed, the yacht yard should be a profitable business. Every yacht will need to be lifted from the water at least once a year and, in this country, as this operation is usually carried out in the spring and confined to, say, three months, it means that, with say a marina of 500 yachts, about 6 craft per day will need attention in the early months of the year. This can be done with a comparatively small yard but only if it is very well organised with a precise drill. A yacht lift, such as the 'travelift' or the Renner is justified for a large marina, as they are manoeuvrable and give good flexibility, but with the

smaller marina or where comparatively few Class V, VI
and VII yachts have to be handled, other methods are cheaper
and give adequate flexibility. For example, a derrick or a
boat hoist (such as a "shift-a-lift") may be used for the
smaller yachts and a stationery lift installed for larger
craft. A type of stationery lift suitable for large yachts is
shown in Fig. 7.

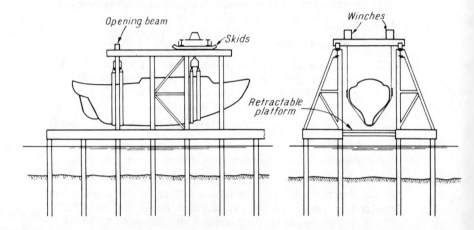

Figure 7 Static yacht lift

In the case of marinas where space is expensive or the area
around the basin congested, it is worth considering more
sophisticated types of boat handling equipment, which
restrict the area required for yacht maintenance and redu
running costs. A yacht scraping and painting facility on these
lines is shown in Fig. 8.

11 Examples of Marinas

The marinas briefly described below have been selected to illustrate
some of the different types mentioned in this paper.

Swanwick Marina

This is a typical riverside marina, developed as an extension to an
existing yacht yard. All that had to be done to produce the yacht basin
was to drive a line of steel piling and dredge an area of tidal foreshore. This was done in two stages and the berths were filled to
capacity almost as soon as the pontoons were placed.

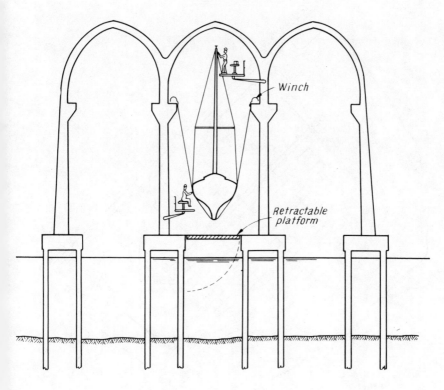

Figure 8 Yacht hanger

Chichester Yacht Basin

This marina could not have been developed economically without a lock, as the excavation required for a tidal basin would have been very large and siltation a constant problem. The lock is of a novel sector gate design; it is very fast acting and has proved very successful. The free flow period over high water when both gates are open lasts for up to 5 hours.

Emsworth Yacht Harbour

Emsworth Yacht Harbour is an example of a marina developed very economically by constructing a tidal basin with a dam at its entrance which submerges at H.W. This allows ingress and egress for about $2\frac{1}{2}$ hours either side of H.W., the height of the dam being 0·5 m above Chart Datum. Further development is possible either by dredging or constructing a lock or a tidal gate.

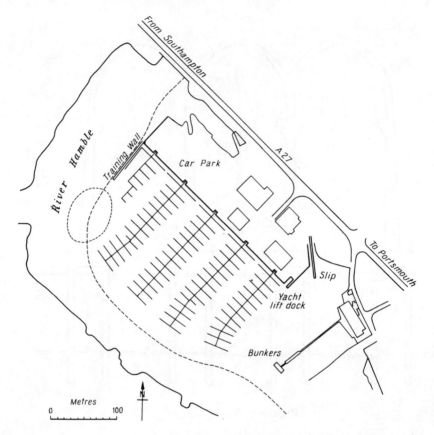

Figure 9 Swanwick Marina

José Banús, Marbella, Spain

The José Banús Marina, having a capacity of 915 yachts, is 30 nautical miles from Gibraltar and 35 from Malaga, and has been constructed on a sea front with no assistance from natural features. However, its cost, of a little over £2M, is most reasonable and the berth charges are comparable with marinas in the Solent area. The sand dredged from the harbour has been pumped to form beaches to the west of the harbour.

Larnaca, Cyprus

This is a yacht harbour for 300 yachts which has just been constructed in a country where yachting is in its infancy but where there are great potentialities. It is an example of the way in which dredged material may be used for reclaiming land around the harbour so that it may be used for requirements of the marina and for tourist development.

Figure 10 Chichester Yacht Basin with the Itenchor River in the background

Figure 11 Chichester Yacht Basin: the outer pair of lock gates

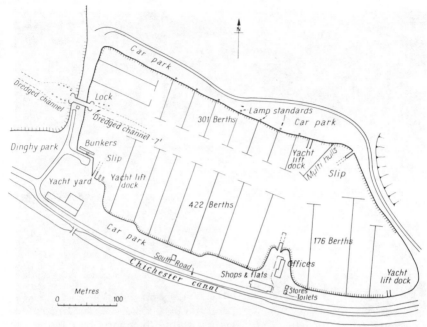

Figure 12 Chichester Yacht Basin

Figure 13 Emsworth Yacht Harbour

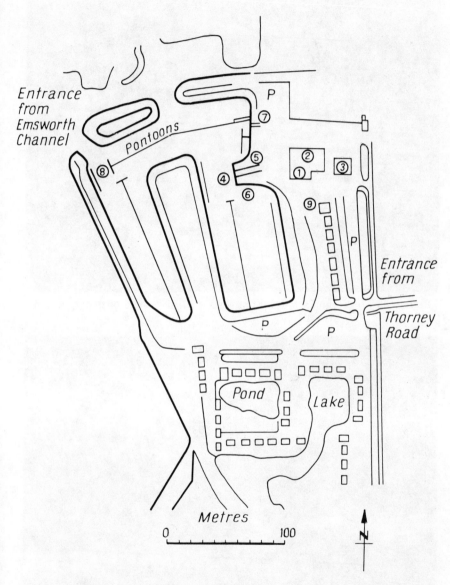

Figure 14 Emsworth Yacht Harbour

1 Office and chandlery   2 Repair shop   3 Engine shop   4 Bunkers and quay (15t crane)
5 50t. slip   6 Grid   7 Slip (1:6)   8 Visitor's berth   9 Club house   P Parking

Figure 15 José Banús Marina: houses still in course of construction

Figure 16 José Banús Marina: yacht moored with Type A mooring (Fig. 2)

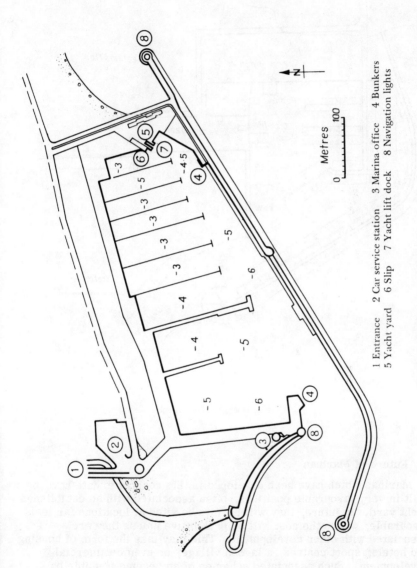

Figure 17 José Banús Marina

1 Entrance 2 Car service station 3 Marina office 4 Bunkers
5 Yacht yard 6 Slip 7 Yacht lift dock 8 Navigation lights

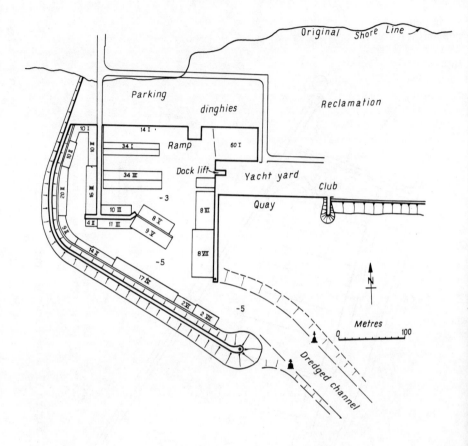

Figure 18 Larnaca

12 Future of Marinas

Marinas which have been developed in this country to date have been built in very favourable positions, often associated with an established yacht yard. In future, they will have to be sited at locations far less favourable, where the cost will be prohibitive unless they are associated with other development. This may take the form of housing and hotels, sport centres, a lagoon village, or even commercial development. Such associated schemes often become possible by developing reclaimed land in the vicinity of the marina, the reclamation material being obtained by dredging the marina basin. Alternatively, use may be made of adjoining land, the value of which would be increased by the construction of the marina.

In general, the overall cost per berth must not exceed £800 to £2000 depending on the situation, size and attraction of the marina. A small marina will entail a larger overhead running cost per berth and this must be taken into account.

If a yacht harbour with 400 berths costs £500,000 (i. e. £1250 per berth) and can earn £200 per yacht per annum with a 90% occupancy, the return will be 14·5% before charging running costs and maintenance. If one can add residential accommodation or a yachtsmen's village, the project would look decidedly more attractive financially.

The lagoon type of development, which enables the creation of yachtmen's villages, is best exemplified by Port Grimaud at the head of the Gulf of St. Tropez, some 50 miles west of Nice. Here, 25 hectares (62 acres) have been developed to harbour 1500 yachts in a water area of 16 hectares (40 acres). Each of the 500 houses and apartments has its own berth and the project has been most attractively planned. Once the extension inland is complete, it will cover 60 hectares (150 acres) with 1700 houses and 8 km of quay.

There are a number of places in this country where this type of development could be carried out to produce most attractive yachting centres and yachtsmen's villages.

Acknowledgments

The author wishes to thank Admiral P. D. Gick, Mr. D. H. Sessions and Mr. G. Young for supplying information regarding Emsworth, Swanwick and Chichester Marinas, respectively, and Mr. Gerald Lewis, F.I.E.E. for his help with reference to matters electrical.

Bibliography

Chaney, C.A. (1961), *Marinas: Recommendations for Design, Construction and Maintenance.* Nat. Assoc. of Engine and Boat Manuf. (U.S.A.) (2nd Edition).
————(1969), *Small Craft Harbours,* Report on Eng. Practice No. 50, Am. Soc. Civil Eng.
—— (1965), *Problems Arising from the Increasing Use of Yachts and Other Small Boats for Sport and Recreation,* Proc. XXIst Int. Nav. Cong. (Stockholm), Section 1, Subject 6
Vian, R. *General Layout of Pleasure Ports,* Service Maritime et de Navigation du Languedoc-Roussillon.
—— *Yacht Harbour Guide,* National Yacht Harbour Association.

Dredging Equipment and Techniques

J. H. Sargent

Dredging Investigations Ltd.

1 Introduction

1.1 General Remarks

It is an aim of this Symposium that the opportunity be taken for healthy discussion between people with different interests concerning the subject of marinas and small craft harbours.

When considering the development of a marina or small craft harbour, the required mix of disciplines to produce an economically constructed and commercially viable business may be a problem. Although this is often true for many civil engineering jobs, a particular feature with projects of the type under discussion is that it appears essential to ensure an inter-disciplinary approach.

The organisers of this Symposium have noted this and refer in their introductory notes to the need to involve planners, developers, architects, engineers, operators, harbour masters and others. Before proceeding with the following paper on dredging aspects the author would also like to make a plea for an early and intelligent liaison on the planning and design of marinas and small craft harbours. The initial approach must come from the prime client, that individual (or company) who sees the need for the project and is willing to raise the capital cost, but once under way the client should require his first appointed professional (whether he be architect, engineer or planner) to decide on the early composition of the planning and design team. By planning the project together from the outset, stupid and elementary mistakes can often be avoided which frequently occur when the project is designed piece by piece and day by day. Clients please take note!

1.2 Dredging Plant and Techniques

The following text is concerned with an important aspect of the civil engineering requirement where water areas, depths or land areas may be insufficient. In essence, dredging concerns itself with the excava-

tion of materials under water and their transport, either to a spoil
area to be dumped or to a site for use as a reclamation fill.

The intention in the following review is to give a general introduction to the types of plant available, the more important factors in
choosing the plant, and some applications which have been made of
dredging plant.

2 Review of Dredging Plant Suitable for Marinas and Small Craft Harbours

2.1 *Choice of Plant*

Many factors affect the final choice of dredging plant for any particular project. With respect to marinas and small craft harbours,
limitations will normally be imposed in particular by available or
required water depths, existing soil conditions, and the need, if necessary, to undertake reclamation works.

Where bucket or grab dredgers are used, shallow draft pontoons
or hulls may be available, but care will be needed that attendant
hoppers or barges can move in a fully-loaded condition. It may often
be found necessary in dredging works for small craft harbours to
resort to tidal working, that is to say, working only when the tide is
above a certain level and provides water depth sufficient for the plant.
In this case, production will suffer.

The effect of soil conditions and the requirements for reclamation
are noted in more detail in Section 3.1 of the paper.

A restriction on programme time which influences choice of plant
in the context of this paper is that in some localities the available working season for dredging works will be limited. Dredging plant is often
cumbersome, and, because of the difficulties of widespread lines and
anchors plus the actual working plant, it may be impracticable or even
dangerous to carry out dredging works during a yachting season in the
vicinity of small dinghies which may be in the hands of relatively
inexperienced crews. Because of this problem, dredging works for
marinas may often be confined to the period between the end of one
season and the start of the next. Under these circumstances, the contractor will wish, whenever possible, to work over the full twenty-four
hour period in order to reduce his downtime to a minimum. In the
South of England, this limitation on available time could mean that only
four to five months are left in each year in which practical construction
work can be carried out.

A further feature of marinas is that it is necessary to produce a bed
after dredging which is level. Although this point is important in all
dredging works, it may assume an exaggerated importance for marinas
which are of relatively shallow depth and with a large area coverage by
small vessels.

2.2 Bucket Dredgers

The bucket dredger (Fig. 1) is very much the 'layman's dredger'. The vessel digs with a chain of continuously revolving buckets which discharge material through a side chute into the wells of attendant barges or self-propelled hoppers. The vessel is usually non-propelled and requires a tug in attendance for towage and to assist with moves into working positions, being held by a series of wires both to hold the position and to provide the forward flexible reaction required to pull the dredger into the working face.

The particular usefulness of a bucket dredger is its ability to excavate a wide variety of materials. Buckets will vary in size and type depending on the parent craft and on the type of material being excavated.

A useful feature of many bucket dredgers for work on small craft harbours is that the vessel is comparatively shallow-drafted, although the actual dimension will vary, related to the size of plant. Of value when considering the use of bucket dredgers in this context is the ability to work very close inshore or alongside existing structures. Production will be affected, but nevertheless a skilled dredgemaster will be able to organise the dredger to work tightly to a profile or, for example, a sheet-piled wall (Fig. 11).

A disadvantage of the bucket dredger to the general public in the locality of the project is the noise produced by its grinding bucket chain, reminiscent of few other sounds!

Bucket dredgers suffer badly when exposed to strong winds or heavy swell conditions. However, small craft harbours will often be sited in sheltered locations to protect the resident craft without extensive or expensive protective works and the location may therefore often be ideal for dredging units of this type.

2.3 Hoppers

For most bucket dredging and much grab and suction dredging work, it is usual to use attendant hoppers. These may be modern, large self-propelled units (Fig. 2) or small dumb craft requiring towage. Hoppers for use with dredging plant will usually have a series of bottom-opening doors to allow dumping at sea or over shallow reclamation. A more recent development is the split hopper with massive hinges fore and aft and opening up to about 60° along its entire length to facilitate the discharge of materials with high adhesion characteristic, such as boulder clays.

A feature, much used for major sand reclamation jobs, is the towed dumb hopper (Fig. 3) which is taken to a shore plant and then pumped out through a second handling system.

Figure 1   Typical bucket dredger

Figure 2   Self-propelled hopper alongside bucket dredger

(Aerofilms Ltd.)

Figure 3 Installation for pump-ashore plant, with sand barges alongside towed into position by tug

Available also for small craft harbours, when needed, is a hopper design which allows loading of rock on the deck, the material being 'pushed' overboard by the use of hydraulic rams. Plant of this type will be used mainly when dumping stone for protective works.

2.4 Pump-ashore Plant

The purpose of this equipment is to take the dredged material from the filled hopper, emptying the hopper by suction process (Fig. 4). The material may then either be pumped into deposit areas (for poor quality material) or into reclamation areas for sandfill development.

Small plant of this type can be applied for small craft harbour projects where usable land acreage is limited. If dredging is also needed to extend or deepen water areas and providing the material is of a suitable type, its use as reclamation fill can be attractive financially since 'work is making work'.

Although less likely to apply to small craft harbours, it is possible to boost pumped sand over long distances through a pipeline system where the reclamation area is distant from the borrow or the siting of the pump-ashore plant.

2.5 Grab Dredging

This technique is nearest in its approach to traditional civil engineering muck shifting, in which a prime mover is pontoon- or vessel-mounted (Fig. 15). As with civil engineering plant, a very wide range of grab units are available, and it is important to match against the job the potential production of the unit, the soil type and site exposure.

A useful feature of grab dredging in relation to small craft harbour construction is the shallow draft of most pontoons, enabling acess to be attained into creeks and shallow mud-flat areas, a favourite environment for a marina development!

All pontoon-mounted grabs will require ancillary plant for the disposal of excavated material. A common technique is to use an attendant hopper, which, as for bucket dredging, will either dump useless material at sea or take good quality material to a pump-ashore plant or to another rehandling installation for removal into the land reclamation site.

Many self-propelled grab dredgers are available, some being built as self-loading hoppers. Where several grabs are mounted on a single vessel, great skill is needed to obtain optimum production by careful placing of the vessel during the dredging operations.

2.6 Conveyor Systems

The installation of a conveyor system is usually very costly, requiring sufficient total quantities of material for handling to make the initial outlay and installation economically viable. However, with

Figure 4 Pump-ashore plant showing self-propelled hopper being emptied by water jet and suction pipe

Figure 5 Trailing suction hopper dredger

respect to small craft harbours, it is conceivable that for a specific
project, the use of a limited conveyor system could be at least considered.

Where water depths are shallow, it may be practicable to erect a
system which is fed by grab or bucket dredger excavating granular
material which is to be used for fill, the material being rehandled
from a stock-pile by bulldozer into the necessary areas.

2.7 Suction Dredgers

The majority of the world's dredging fleets are comprised of craft
in this category. Some confusion usually occurs with this class since
suction dredgers are of various types and cover a wide range of sizes.
All however use the same basic mechanical technique of a centrifugal
pump mounted in a pontoon or hull with a suction pipe lowered to the
sea, river or lake bed, the material being dredged up through the pump
into a discharge unit. At this point, designs begin to alter considerably.

Of premier importance in the dredging industry, although of less
application to the present consideration of small craft harbour construction, is the trailer dredger (Fig. 5). Modern trailers are built
and behave in the same manner as a normal ship operating as self-
contained, self-propelled hoppers into which a flexible suction pipe
(trailed alongside) discharges its cargo. Doors are built into the
bottom of the hopper, and, after loading, the trailer sails to the dumping or discharging site. Trailers may also have the facility (besides
being able to dump through the doors) of pumping out the cargo directly
into a connected shoreline to the deposit or reclamation ground.

From our viewpoint at this Symposium, the application of this type
of vessel is likely to be limited due to at least three reasons: draft,
manoeuvring room and available quantities of material for excavation.
Trailers require water depths equivalent to a normal ship; for example,
a small trailer of about 1200 cu. metres capacity will frequently have
a draft of about 2·5 m unloaded and 4·5 m in a fully-loaded condition.
With respect to manoeuvring, the vessel will be typically about 70 m
in length, and, although it is possible to turn very tightly, maximum
production will only be possible if reasonable manoeuvring room is
available.

Of direct interest for the present Symposium is the use of plain or
cutter suction dredgers (Figs. 6 and 7). These units basically comprise
the mounting of a pump into a pontoon or hull with the suction pipe
lowered to the bed on a steel ladder, usually from the forward end.
The dredger works from anchors, spuds and wires and is usually non-
propelled. When the working end of a suction-pipe ladder is fitted
with a rotary cutter head, the unit becomes a cutter suction dredger.

Suction and cutter dredgers range over a wide size from two-men
mini-dredgers, through dismantlable units, to large cutter suction

Figure 6 Cutter suction dredger showing pontoon-mounted discharge
pipeline

Figure 7 Cutter suction dredger for reclamation works

dredgers capable of excavating strong materials and pumping directly over long distances.

Of particular application for projects such as small craft harbours, where dredging is to be combined with reclamation, will be the small to medium-sized dismantlable suction or cutter suction unit. Various sizes with corresponding production potential are now available on the market. The unit may be broken down into component parts for road transport, although it is normally more economical to tow direct to the site in assembled form if this is possible. The I.H.C. line of standardised dismantlable dredgers are well known and include the Cub, King and Giant, in ascending order of size. As a rough guide, the I.H.C. 'Beaver Cub' is a 200 mm suction dredger, reputedly capable under good conditions and at maximum engine power of pumping at the rate of about 125 cu. metres of reclamation sand per hour over a distance of about 1500 m. This dredger has overall dimensions of approximately 12 m × 5m with 0·83 m draft, the dredging depth being limited to about 8 m.

3 Technical Aspects

3.1 Geotechnical Conditions

The early study work required for determining the feasibility of the marina or small craft harbour should have indicated from a site investigation the types of soil or rock which exist at the site.

Depending on the topography and the design, water areas and depths and land areas will be planned. Projects of this type are usually in the lower cost range and it is unlikely that high costs can be accepted for the dredging or any land reclamation requirements. In this respect, the nature of the existing soil conditions will be important to costing, since, for example, dredging of sand will be relatively easy and the borrow will also provide an excellent material for reclamation fill.

If encountered, rock is expensive to move whether by direct dredging or by pre-treatment followed by dredging. The presence of large quantities of rock will therefore count against the economic viability of the project and in most cases it will be necessary to try to relocate the marina.

In many cases, the site will be in an estuarine environment and considerable quantities of soft silt/clays will be present. Whilst these are relatively easy dredging materials, they are totally unsuitable as a reclamation fill and in most instances it will be necessary to remove these materials either to a spoil dump distant from the site or to a suitable deposit site on land. In the latter case, it is possible that a conflict will arise with, on the one hand, the development of a prestige marina and, on the other hand, an unsightly deposit area. It should however be noted in passing, that deposits containing poor quality materials can, with suitable husbandry and treatment, be converted into areas of reasonable appearance which will even accommodate agricultural development.

Nature is generally unkind in the geological sense and mixtures of soils will often be encountered. It is difficult and expensive to separate different types of material during a dredging process since the dredging technique thrives on large productions of material which can be excavated without unnecessary downtime of the plant. Each site and geotechnical condition will require separate treatment and consideration.

From a reclamation viewpoint, the use of granular material is normally ideal, since the optimum density will be attained quickly with free drainage above tide levels. Various ground engineering expedients can be used to hasten the consolidation process of poorer quality fills, but this adds cost to the job and is normally unattractive economically.

3.2 *Surveys and Investigations*

Surveys and investigations for marinas and small craft harbours can follow the normal civil engineering approach with basic land and hydrographic surveys required on which to plan the scheme, followed by site investigation borings from which samples will be selected for laboratory testing and analysis. Unless the site is particularly exposed to wind or sea, or is large and complex, it is not usually necessary to collect other than basic information on the hydraulic conditions, although, even for the relatively shallow depths occurring at these sites, care must be taken that maintenance dredging to remove siltation will not prove unnecessarily expensive in the long term.

Acknowledgements

The author is grateful for assistance in obtaining illustrated matter to Mr. Douglas Bartram of the Bos Kalis Westminster Dredging Group and Mr. Denis Brown of Westminster Dredging Company Ltd.

Acknowledgement is made to Eileen Ramsay, Southampton, for the use of the photographs in Figs. 8-13.

Figures 8 to 13 illustrate construction stages of the Berthon Lymington Marina (1967-68).

Figures 14 and 15 illustrate dredging work in progress for Lymington Yacht Haven Marina (1971-72).

Figure 8 Sheet-piled wall under construction

Figure 9 Floating walkway with polystyrene buoyancy tanks

Figure 10   Greenheart piling in progress

Figure 11   Bucket dredging close inshore

Figure 12 Completed walkway arrangement

Figure 13 General view of completed Berthon Lymington marina

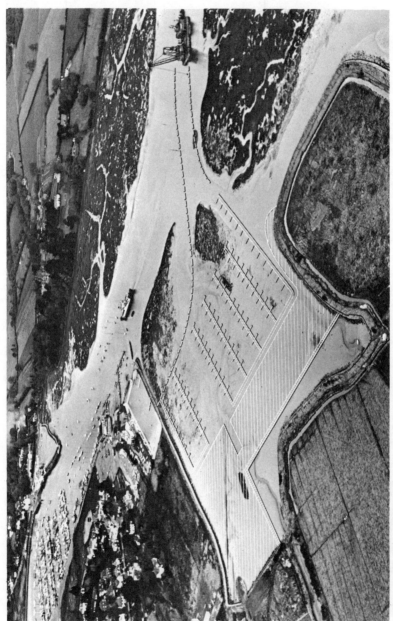

Figure 14 General layout of 450-berth marina under construction at Harpers Lake, Lymington. (The overlay shows the position of the approach channels, the pontoons and berths, and the area being reclaimed for land facilities)

Figure 15 Large capacity grab dredger excavating the approach channel to the site of the new Lymington Yacht Haven Marina

Discussion

(Session 3)

AUTHORS' INTRODUCTION

Mr. D. P. Bertlin

I would like to follow up the last paragraph of my paper by suggesting some places where marinas might be built in the future. I would also like to show some ways in which they may be adapted to the particular site in question.

River Blackwater
Fig. A shows how a marina may be constructed at little cost in a river. Although there is a considerable fetch up and down the river, yachts, being berthed parallel with the stream, will not come to harm and a fairway is left for the small amount of river traffic.

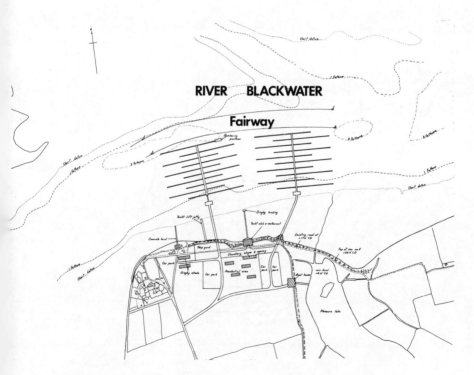

Figure A Proposal for a marina on R. Blackwater, Essex

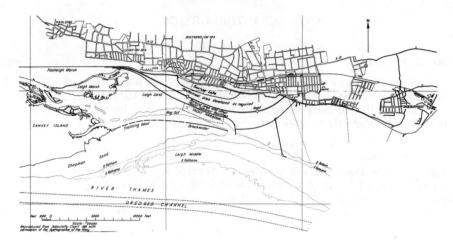

Figure B Proposal for marina development at Southend

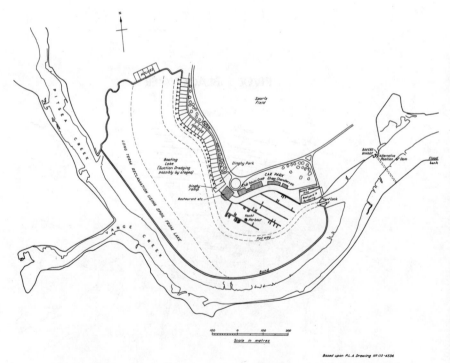

Figure C Proposal for marina development at Basildon, Essex

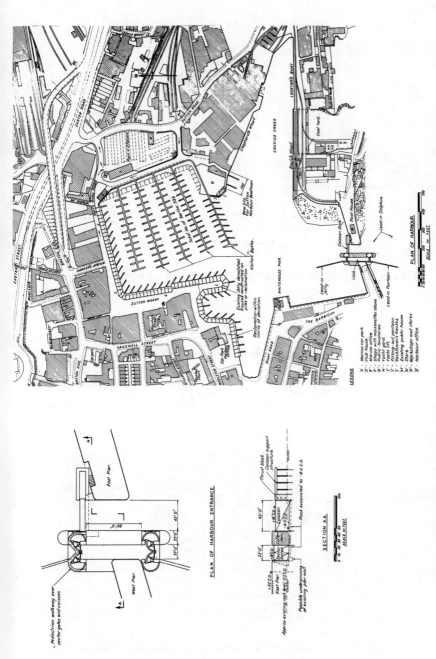

Figure D Proposal for marina development at Sutton Harbour, Plymouth

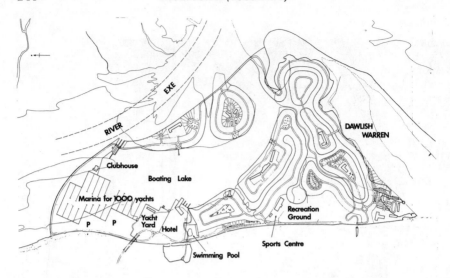

Figure E Proposal for marina development at Dawlish Devon

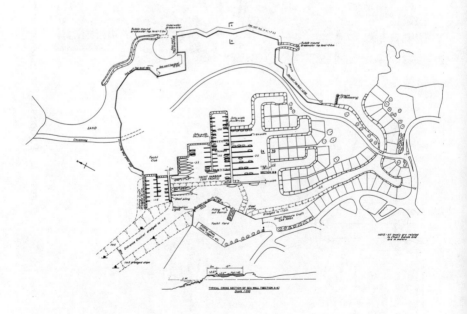

Figure F Proposal for a marina at Famagusta, Cyprus

Southend

A much more ambitious scheme might be undertaken at Southend (Fig. B), provided the results of soils investigation proved satisfactory. Not only could a yacht harbour for 2,000 yachts be developed, but a most valuable area of land developed attractively.

Basildon

At the present time, an area of land near Basildon is being used as a refuse tip. It could be developed (Fig. C) to provide both recreational facilities and much needed housing.

Plymouth

There is a demand in the west country for more and better yachting facilities. The proposal for developing Sutton Harbour, right in the middle of Plymouth, illustrated in Fig. D, would go some way to meet this demand.

Dawlish, Devon

With the linking of Devon with the Midlands by a new motorway, the possibility of attractive developments at such places as Dawlish becomes tenable. This project (Fig. E) would require considerable engineering investigation, involving, as it does, a re-routing of a fast moving river near its mouth. It would, however, provide extensive recreational facilities and would be most convenient to yachtsmen and others from the Midlands.

Famagusta, Cyprus

There is only space for one example of a possible development overseas. This project (Fig. F) involves reclamation, sea walls, artificial beaches and dredging for a yacht harbour, making use of an island situated between the harbour of Famagusta and the beaches to the south which have already been converted into the tourist resort.

The above examples are only a few of the many possibilities of developing boating and other facilities around our coasts and elsewhere. The technical problems are many—there is no time to discuss these here—but they are by no means insurmountable.

There will be considerable opposition to many of the schemes; no such development can be carried through without such opposition. But I am convinced that eventually the balance of advantage and disadvantage will show overwhelmingly in favour of such developments, as increasing numbers of boating enthusiasts, with more and more leisure, call for the opportunities for recreation and sport that such centres provide. The way has been shown by America and France, and England has a long way to catch up.

Mr. J. H. Sargent

Mr. Sargent introduced his paper by showing a number of slides depicting various types of dredging plant and projects in progress.

These illustrations included marine works in the Lymington River and in St. Lucia, Windward Islands, where a major marina project is under construction by the Caribbean and Jamaica Dredging Co., using a large cutter suction dredger.

CONTRIBUTIONS

Mr. D. L. Pope (Livesey and Henderson, Consulting Engineers, London)

I would like to thank Mr. Bertlin for his excellent paper which brings together in one place much information not previously published. In the past the 'bible' for the designer of small craft harbours has been the American Society of Civil Engineers Report on Small Craft Harbours. I think it likely that in the coming years the proceedings of this conference will replace it as our 'bible'.

My remarks refer to Table 7 (p. 203) in Mr. Bertlin's paper, which gives dimensions of the spacing of finger piers for various classes of yacht. In Table A I have extended this table to include water depth, and the area and volume of water occupied by each berth.

I would like to exhort all designers of yacht marinas to think in three dimensions. It is very easy, when faced with a plan of a possible development, to think in terms of fitting the maximum number of berths on the plan. There are two reasons why this should be avoided:-

(i)   Dredging is frequently the largest single item of expenditure in a proposed marina development.

(ii)   There is a continuing trend for a larger proportion of motor vessels in any marina. I note that Chichester now has 40% motor vessels, and there are marinas in the U.S.A. with up to 90% motor vessels.

A yacht basin is a volume of water. To the developers and operators of marinas I would emphasise that this volume of sheltered water will be your principal asset in the years to come, and it is essential that it should be fully utilised in depth as well as in plan area.

Table 7 groups classes of yacht principally by length and beam. If vessels are grouped in this way in a marina, it follows that motor vessels, which have much greater beam in proportion to their depth, will have an excess of water beneath them. As an alternative, I have tried in the second part of my table a grouping by draft, and allowed sufficient space between the finger piers to accept the largest motor vessel which could use that depth of water. For convenience let us call the former approach *Area Optimisation* and the latter *Volume Optimisation.*

Table A Grouping of berths by vessel categories for Type 'C' layout— finger piers

Classes of yacht	Between fingers (m)	Between walkways (m)	Minimum depth (m)	Area (m²)	Volume (m³)
	Limiting berth dimensions			Water per berth (including slips)	
(1) Grouping by length and beam	*area optimisation*				
a IS, IIS, IM	7·5	32	1·6	60	96
b IIIS, IIM	8·8	40	1·7	88	150
c IVS, VS, IIIM, IVM	10·5	64	2·5	168	420
d VIS, VM, VIM	13·9	90	3·0	291	850
e VIIS, VIIM	18·5	120	4·5	555	2500
(2) Grouping by depth	*volume optimisation*				
A IM, IIM, IIIM	9·3	40	1·0	93	93
B IVM	10·5	52	1·3	136	177
C IS, IIS, IIIS, VM	12·0	64	1·7	192	326
D IVS, VIM	13·0	90	2·0	291	582
E VS, VIS, VIIM	18·5	120	3·0	555	1665
F VIIS	18·5	120	4·5	555	2500

With a normal yacht population, similar to that for a larger Languedoc-Roussillon marina (Table 3 in Mr. Bertlin's paper), having 50% motor vessels, *Volume Optimisation* layout produces a yacht basin requiring 40% more area but only 2% more dredging. If the proportion of motor vessels is increased to 66%, i.e. 200 motor vessels to 100 sailing yachts, the *Volume Optimisation* layout requires 30% more water area, but 2% less dredging.

Moreover, a yacht basin laid out in this way would be much more flexible for the operator, in that as the proportion of motor vessels increases he would be able to utilise the full depth of his dredged area without finding the spacing of the finger piers a restriction. This would be particularly important for a marina with jetties on piles, which cannot be adjusted like pontoons.

I had hoped to prove by this exercise that *Volume Optimisation* makes a significant saving in dredging. This is not the case. What it does prove, I believe, is that the finger pier layout, by introducing three restraints on boat dimension, namely depth, length and beam, makes the most efficient use of the yacht basin impossible.

If low cost marinas are required, it is necessary to forget finger piers, and concentrate on some other type of layout like end-on mooring (Layouts A or B), which does not limit the beam as well as the draught and length of vessels.

Mr. G. Lewis (Heap and Digby, Consulting Electrical Engineers,
Wallington, Surrey)

My concern is with Sect. 10 of Mr. Bertlin's paper, in which he deals with facilities.

I would like first to refer to the question of electricity services. One of the important matters which the designers and engineers concerned with marinas must decide is just what electrical energy is likely to be required aboard a leisure craft. It can range between the order of a few watts for lighting—possibly with a little heating—up to a quite considerable amount for cooking, etc.

I commend the yacht designers and the engineers concerned with the development of services in marinas to give thought, at the design stage, to the demands for shore-based power which are likely to be made.

It is clear that pleasure craft moored alongside will not want to have their own generating or battery plant working continually and will invariably wish to take a shore-based supply.

Mr. Bertlin referred to the use of 110-volt systems, as is customary on the Continent, and to 240 volts which would be customary in the United Kingdom. Both can be perfectly safe providing that the installations are designed correctly and it is a matter for the designers, both of craft and marinas, to ensure that the installations are safe. There are adequate regulations available, issued by the Institution of Electrical Engineers, concerning the standards of workmanship and materials. There is a section therein dealing with caravans, which, with very little adjustment, could be adapted for floating craft.

Another problem which faces the design engineers and owners of marinas is the distribution of electrical energy about the marina, i.e. from the Electricity Board's service point to the ashore supply points to which the moored craft make their connections. As Mr. Bertlin very properly pointed out, it is most important to ensure that the distribution system about the marina is isolated by means of a transformer from the shore system, which invariably has one line earthed.

Turning to the question of sanitary arrangements for marinas (p.209),

I am inclined to disagree with Mr. Bertlin's views on the subject of the disposal of faecal matter. He says that yachts in marinas constitute no danger to health.

With the utmost respect, I disagree in the case of enclosed marinas where there may be no orders regarding the sealing of marine heads and the use of shore heads.

I ask those engineers concerned with the design of marinas and yacht basins, to give very careful attention to the reception of human waste material and to arrange for its pumping, if necessary, into the nearest public sewer.

Mr. H. T. Hale (J. D. & D. M. Watson, Consulting Engineers, London)

Before joining my present firm of consulting engineers twenty years ago, I had the honour to serve an oil sheikh, for whom I had great respect, in the Gulf. It struck me that perhaps one project of a small boat harbour with which we had to cope in our immediate development was two-staged, in that I had something like eight consultants working for me on major long-term projects, but there were certain things which we had to do locally and rapidly.

Doha Bay had a small shallow entrance from the east with a then depth of 4·5 m (15 ft).

The Bay itself was almost completely surrounded by land with the City on the southern and western seaboards. The Bay was about 10 km (6 miles) in diameter and in the early days of development all trading, produce and building materials came in by dhow or lighter which necessitated the building of a small boat harbour so that materials could be landed in safety.

The prevailing wind is the Shamal blowing from the Nor Nor West at anything up to 45 knots and line squalls in excess of this speed. The fetch being about 10 km (6 miles) and water in some areas up to 11 m (6 fathoms) deep gave rise to severe wave problems.

In some of yesterday's papers, we seemed to be trying to resist the forces of nature and not harnessing them. The harbour was sited so that the wave energy was dissipated by division of wave fronts and by using a splendid material occurring in the Gulf and other tropical waters called ferroush or very thin coral occurring in layers anything up to about 200 mm (8 in.) thick. In the old days, it was possible to get divers to cut this material into approximately 1·2 m × 0·9 m (4 ft × 3 ft) slabs and between 50 mm (2 in.) and 200 mm (8 in.) thick.

The merit of the coral was that it had all sorts of wiggly shaped holes. Usually one face was flat, the other wiggly, but it had millions and millions of interstices. A jetty built of this material presents something which can absorb and let out water and air rapidly, generally out-of-phase with the incoming waves so that considerable damping is achieved.

Unfortunately, ferroush does not exist in this part of the world, but I have cited this case because I feel that there may be scope for research on an aerated, porous concrete or plastic which could serve as an economical energy absorber or breakwater in a marina situation.

Secondly, I wish to touch on pollution. To be healthy, we must all produce pollutants. We cannot help it. Generally, for degradation, about 73 g of oxygen per person per day are required. In the context of the marine environment, it is usually not the biological oxygen demand which is the critical parameter but the coliform count. Crude sewage has a coliform count of about 20×10^7. At present, there are no British standards for areas of water contact sports. Generally, we work to what we consider an acceptable standard of $2 \cdot 4 \times 10^3$. This means that it is necessary to have a reduction in the order of 8×10^4 before the stage is reached when it is reasonably safe to fall overboard in a marina.

Luckily, the situation is not quite as bad as that because coliforms do decay in the sea water, and it is possible to have about a 90 per cent reduction in something like 4 to 6 hours. From what I have just said, and from Mr. Lewis' remarks, the immediate local pollution near a marina of about 3000 boats is not a thing to be dismissed lightly.

Mr. R. G. Walters (Managing Director, Walcon Ltd., Winchester)

My firm of civil engineering contractors has constructed a number of marinas and also manufactures and markets a patented concrete flotation unit. We therefore have a keen interest in the subject of Mr. Bertlin's paper.

I acknowledge that consulting engineers and architects are needed for the design of marinas. However, when Mr. Dale-Harris implied yesterday that the combination of a yachtsman and a developer could be spelled as 'rogue', he did not include a contractor in his team. Perhaps he thought that having two rogues in one team was not good practice!

As contractors, we are often asked to price, in a few weeks, jobs which have perhaps taken years and years to develop and draw up. If we knew earlier a little more of the history behind a particular job, we would often be able to give a more competitive price.

I know that some consultants may not agree with me, but I feel that it would be an advantage if a contractor could be appointed during the early stages of the designing of a marina. This could help, because we have an up-to-date knowledge of plant and we are very experienced in programming.

Mr. P. G. R. Barlow (Coode and Partners, Consulting Engineers, London)

As Mr. Bertlin has said in his paper, the problem of sites with a large tidal range can be dealt with in a number of ways. At some stage, however, a decision must be taken as to how far it will be possible to meet all the highly desirable criteria of accessibility at all stages of the tide on every day of the year. This subject has also been raised in connection with Mr. Bryans' paper.

How is this decision taken? The engineer has to demonstrate, to the people who will be paying, just how much accessibility time will be lost by accepting various levels of tide restraint.

For example, anyone could look at the year's tables and find out that a zero tide occurs maybe one day a year, a plus 0·3 m (1 ft) low tide maybe three days a year, and so on. Obviously, closure for an hour or two for only a few days of the year will be acceptable, if it means saving the cost and inconvenience of having a lock. But how far can we go?

The common way of dealing with this problem is to produce a tidal exceedance curve which shows the percentage of time in the whole year when the tide is predicted to be above a given level. From this, one can read off the percentage of time during which the marina will be open for a given depth criterion.

The example which I quote relates to channel dredging for very large ships, but the principle applies just as well to marinas, although, obviously, it only affects small ships when the tidal range is large.

In such a problem, it became apparent that, if we could persuade container ship operators to accept a plus 2 m (6·5 ft) minimum tide level in a 5 m (16 ft) tidal range, the port authority would only need to dredge a very short section of channel over the bar. If the shipping people had insisted on even an extra 0·3 m (1 ft) of water at low tide, then the dredging would have had to be carried out over the whole approach channel, which is several km long. Therefore, there was a very definite reason for trying to sell the idea of accepting a plus 2m (6·5 ft) tidal restraint.

The ordinary tidal exceedance curves showed that this plus 2 m (6·5 ft) tide would provide 70 per cent accessibility with an average waiting time of two hours and a maximum waiting time of five hours on those occasions when vessels were caught and were held up at all.

'What does 70 per cent mean in relation to our actual schedules?' said the shipping companies.

To try to show them what it meant, we produced a computer record showing the level of tide in relation to time of day for a year's tides. We then put the data into diagrammatic form, as in Fig. A in which the shaded area represents the periods during which the port is closed to vessels requiring a minimum tidal height of 2 m (6·5 ft) to permit access. The time of day is across the top, and working from top to bottom of the diagram each line represents a day of the year. The diagram covers the whole year 1970, and the panels marked A and B

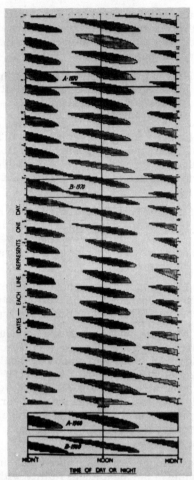

Figure G Typical tidal exceedance diagram for a port with 5·4 m
              (18 ft) extreme tidal ranges

have been introduced to enable a comparison to be made of the patterns at the same time of year in 1960 and 1970, indicating that the
general picture is unaltered.

The most surprising feature of this diagram is the existence of
the two continuous (or almost continuous) light bands running down
the page about halfway between midnight and noon, and again between
noon and midnight. These indicate that in the morning and evening of
every day of the year there will be a period when there is at least 2 m
(6·5 ft) of tide—an excellent feature from the point of view of schedul-
ing a shipping service. Even in the worst months, when the light bands

in the diagram are briefly interrupted by black areas, it will be seen that the time of interruption is at its shortest in these morning and evening periods, and there is always a reasonable period of 2 m (6·5 ft) tide either before or after the closure.

The existence of this sort of diurnal regularity in the tidal pattern is not always fully appreciated. It happens because the tides are produced by the combined effect of sun and moon, and whereas the *times* of high and low water progress steadily around the clock in time with the moon's cycle, the *amplitudes* of these tides depend on the combined effect of sun and moon. The peak springs, for example, only occur when the sun and moon are in a fixed relationship to each other, and as the sun is always high about the same time of each day (midday) the peak springs are similarly more-or-less fixed in relation to the clock. I think I have said enough to show how one can make out a logical case for accepting given tidal restraints in a marina, for the consideration of a finance committee.

There is one more point which I would like to mention in connection with this matter. It will have been obvious that in the case I have quoted a lot of effort was devoted in the feasibility study towards dissuading the Client from embarking on a large dredging contract, thereby depriving ourselves of an opportunity to earn substantial fees. No special credit is claimed for this; it is the attitude you should expect of any British Consulting Engineer. But I would plead with Mr. Dale-Harris not to prejudice such an attitude by expecting his professional advisers to be at risk in the feasibility study to the extent of possibly not being paid any fee at all, if, at the end of that study they have to give him the same advice on the implementation of his scheme as Mr. Punch gave to those about to get married—'Don't'.

Capt. J. Andrew (British Transport Docks Board, Southampton)

When considering accessibility periods to a marina where the depths in the approach channels or the entrance to the marina are critical, it must be remembered that there is a period of 19 years called the Metonic cycle or long period tidal oscillation, which is allowed for in the prediction of tides. For further information of this long period tidal oscillation, reference should be made to Ch. 5—'Motions of the Sun and Moon'—Sect. 5.1 of the Admiralty Manual of Tides*.

The predicted heights of tide are not the same from one year to another. I have plotted in Fig. H the number of occasions in each year for a 19-year period from 1946 to 1964, inclusive, when the predicted tide fell below Chart Datum. The maximum number of occurrences was 103 in 1947 and the minimum number was 67 in 1952. The largest fall of the tide below Chart Datum was 0·5 m (1·6 ft). The 19-year period prior to 1965 was chosen, as the Chart Datum at Southampton

---

* Doodson, A. T. and Warburg, H. D. (1941), *Admiralty Manual of Tides*. H.M.S.O.

was revised in 1965. The resultant curve has a resemblance to a
19-year cycle, although the curve does not return to the same com-
mencing point.

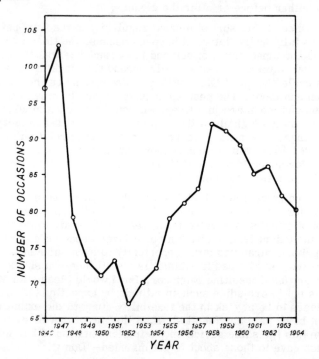

Figure H The number of occasions when the predicted tide fell below
chart datum at Southampton in each year over a 19-year
period (1946-64).

The predicted tide can be influenced by abrupt changes in meteorological conditions and the resulting oscillations are referred to as
Seiches. Local tables are sometimes available to apply meteorological
corrections to predicted tide levels. For example, at Southampton,
when the barometer is standing at 965 Mb (28·50 in.) the correction is
+0·79 m (+2·5 ft) and when it is standing at 1041 Mb (30·75 in.) the
correction is −0·55 m (−1·8 ft) and when the wind is N.E. force 5, the
correction is −0·21 m (−0·7 ft).

One cannot express explicitly or generalise on the variation in tidal
levels from year to year resulting from the 19-year oscillation, as
other changes take place within the 19-year period and two successive
19-year periods of tidal levels would not necessarily be the same. It
would be wrong to apply the result obtained in one geographical position to that of another.

We have seen how the height of the tide can be affected by the 19-year oscillation and meteorological conditions and the difficulty in allowing for the former when considering tidal levels over a long period. A practical suggestion would be to browse through the recorded tidal curves over a period of years for the area being studied if they are available. A number of ports keep recorded tidal levels. This method would give a true picture of tidal behaviour at a particular place.

Mr. P. G. R. Barlow (Coode and Partners, Consulting Engineers, London)

In the light of Captain Andrews' warning about the long-term variations in tide levels, I would like to demonstrate that the long-term changes do not affect the general principle, though, indeed, they do make it undesirable to apply the principle too precisely as far as minimum drafts and levels are concerned.

For marina planning, this principle is of interest only in places where the tidal range is large enough to make full-time accessibility very difficult or very expensive to provide (for example in the Channel Islands or Bristol Channel). The planners then have to decide exactly what the operational effect will be if access to and from the marina is restricted to the periods when the tide is at or above a certain selected level. The point I want to make is that for a given tide level at any given place there are certain fixed periods of the day and night when accessibility is distinctly more favourable than others.

In the example (Table A) I have shown, full time accessibility in the periods of approximately 6-8 a.m. and 6-8 p.m. results from the fact that the selected level is just above Low Water Neaps, which, at that particular port, always occur in the early mornings and early evenings. The Low Water Springs *never* occur at these particular times, so the tides never fall below the level in question at these times. Stated another way—although the *time* of Low Water progresses steadily around the clock, day by day, the *range* of the tide varies cyclically between Spring and Neaps, and it happens that whenever the time of Low Tide falls between 6-8 a.m. and 6-8 p.m. (at this particular place) it is always a Neap Tide; never a Spring.

It is quite an easy matter to find out the most favourable times for the place in which you are interested, just by looking through the tide tables and picking out the highest values of Low Tide (i.e. the middle of the Neaps) in every column of the table. For example, looking at the daytime tides for 1972 at Southampton, the times and heights are:-

11.1.72	1304 h	1·9 m	6.7.72	1233 h	1·4 m
25.1.72	1215	1·6	21.7.72	1313	2·0
9.2.72	1157	2·0	4.8.72	1211	1·7
24.2.72	1330	1·7	19.8.72	1223	2·2
9.3.72	1106	2·0	2.9.72	1203	1·9
24.3.72	1317	1·7	17.9.72	1142	2·3

8.4.72	1208	1·9	1.10.72	1159	1·9
22.4.72	1249	1·6	16.10.72	1107	2·2
7.5.72	1131	1·6	30.10.72	1141	1·8
22.5.72	1313	1·6	14.11.72	1031	2·0
6.6.72	1201	1·4	29.11.72	1215	1·7
21.6.72	1308	1·7	14.12.72	1057	1·7

It can be seen that, in 1972, the highest values of daytime Low Tide always occur within 2 hours either side of noon, and the height varies between +1.4 m and +2.3 m above Datum, which is within plus or minus half a metre of M.L.W.N. (+1·8 m).

This statement, moreover, is true for any year. Taking, for example, the first fortnight in June and examining the times and heights of the highest Low Water over the past 20 years, we obtain the following (corrected for datum changes):-

2.6.52	1103 h	1·8 m	1.6.63	1208 h	1·7 m
6.6.53	1111	1·2	4.6.64	1036	1·6
11.6.54	1232	1·7	8.6.65	1145	1·3
14.6.55	1011	1·5	12.6.66	1046	1·7
3.6.56	1100	1·6	1.6.67	1107	1·7
7.6.57	1139	1·2	4.6.68	0946	1·5
11.6.58	1130	1·7	9.6.69	1159	1·3
1.6.59	1252	1·5	13.6.70	1140	1·7
3.6.60	1014	1·6	2.6.71	1156	1·7
7.6.61	1108	1·2	6.6.72	1201	1·4
11.6.62	1045	1·7			

It should be noted that neither the times nor the heights change progressively over the years. Both remain within the broad bands observed above, i.e. noon plus or minus about 2 hours and M.L.W.N. plus or minus half a metre.

I have used Southampton as an illustration merely because it is the centre for our Symposium. In practice the exercise is of marginal value for small boat harbours in a place such as this, where the difference between Mean Low Water at Springs and at Neaps is only about 1·3 m. For areas where this difference is greater, such as in the vicinity of Liverpool (1·9 m), Cardiff (2·5 m), Bristol (2·6 m) and St. Helier (2·8 m), the investigation may, however, prove well worth the trouble.

A quick examination of the tables shows that Liverpool, like Southampton, has its most favourable tides in the middle of the day and night, whereas the Cardiff, Bristol and St. Helier areas have them in the forenoon and evenings, which would seem to be the most attractive times for touring craft to arrive and depart. In cases like these a close investigation would seem to be a very useful exercise, but it may only be necessary to go to the length illustrated in my diagram, and plot out a full year, if you have to convince somebody else of your conclusions.

Mr. M. V. Woolley (E. W. H. Gifford and Partners, Consulting Engineers, Southampton)

Fig. I shows the location of a half-tide harbour, car park and hover-craft terminal which my firm have been commissioned to design for Ryde Borough Council, Isle of Wight. The work is currently being submitted for planning approval and it is anticipated that construction will commence in the autumn of 1973.

Fig. J illustrates the scheme in more detail.

In addition to providing for terminal facilities for hovercraft travellers up to a peak density of 8000 people per day, the scheme provides for car parking facilities for 300 cars and 40 coaches, and the half-tide harbour accommodates a nominal 80 small craft. The project is valued at just under £500,000.

Ryde, situated on the north coast of the Isle of Wight, is protected off-shore by a considerable area of flat sand exposed at low water. This results in a relatively low prediction of 0·6 to 0·9 m (2 to 3 ft) for the wave height in the region of the harbour mouth. A narrower harbour entrance would have ensured a self-clearing channel but it was considered that the 16 m (52 ft) opening provided was the minimum width suitable for access. The entrance is angled to give the best

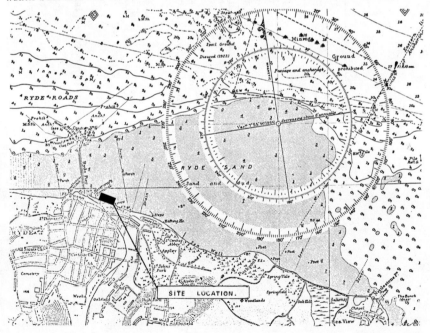

Figure I Location of proposed half-tide harbour at Ryde, Isle of Wight

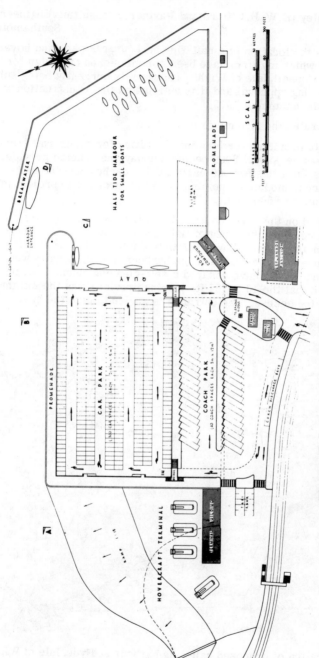

Figure J Layout of proposed half-tide harbour at Ryde

possible protection from north and east exposure, Ryde pier providing a convenient breakwater for weather from the north-west.

The breakwater is aligned to give the best compromise between the conflicting requirements of harbour protection, harbour access and siltation. The trapezoidal shape of the harbour is intended to reduce the effects of surge at or near high water.

The car park is constructed on reclaimed land, the perimeter of which is supported by steel sheet piling. Similarly the breakwater is constructed using conventional steel sheet piling. It is hoped that it will prove economic to carry out the reclamation work using dredged material from offshore. No dredging is intended within the harbour which will dry out at mean tide level. The primary object of the harbour is to provide accommodation for the small boats which at present lie at moorings offshore. These boats tend to be in the 3-6 m (10-20 ft) category drawing only up to 1 m (3 ft) of water.

The provision of this new facility will undoubtedly attract larger vessels, and, at some time in the future, it may be desirable to provide a full marina-type facility. However, at the present time, it is considered that any form of lock gate or wall at the harbour entrance restricting access would tend to detract rather than add to the facility from the point of view of the local boat owners. The alternative of providing a minimum permanent depth of water by dredging is made extremely difficult and expensive, due to the poor subsoil conditions. It is for these reasons that the scheme takes the form proposed.

Mr. K. J. Flemons (Sir Frederick Snow and Partners, Consulting Engineers, London)

I would like to join the earlier speakers and congratulate the author on an extremely good paper on marina design and construction. There are, however, three points I would like to raise on the contents of the paper.

Firstly, no mention is made in the paper on the planned life of marinas or their structures and I would be pleased if Mr. Bertlin could give some indication as to what figure he adopts or is generally laid down by the developer. Is this 50 years or longer?

This factor could well dictate the form of construction used and the materials chosen for the various structures and buildings. For instance, in the case of breakwaters, reference is made of single sheet breakwaters, but if the life is to be over a certain number of years the sheet piling may not be adequate, and consequently a more substantial form of breakwater might be selected in order to eliminate heavier maintenance costs at a later date.

The second point is the question of bunkering referred to on p. 208. Could Mr. Bertlin say what precautions are normally provided to avoid fuel spillage causing pollution within the marina?

On land, the local authorities stipulate oil traps to control such accidental spillage, but if it should occur on board a vessel or over the water then the oil could spread across the surface of the marina and possibly pass out of the enclosed harbour to adjacent beaches.

Oil is a major problem along our coasts and anything that can be done to minimise this form of pollution problem is certainly worthy of consideration. Has thought been given to the use of pneumatic air barriers to contain the oil within the marina?

Thirdly, I cannot agree with Mr. Bertlin that there is no danger to health in the discharge of sewage from yachts. Many marinas are protected by breakwaters with only a narrow outlet to the sea or controlled by locks. Discharge of sewage into such water with little or no interchange of the water in the harbour with that outside would lead to a minimum replenishment of the oxygen, and the oxygen is needed to assist with the dispersion of the accumulation of wastes. Although many of our coastal outfalls leave a lot to be desired they do at least discharge into flowing rivers or tidal waters.

In conclusion, it is unlikely that many river authorities would accept the discharge of untreated sewage, certainly not the Port of London Authority.

Mr. A. E. Weeks (Principal Design Engineer, Thames Conservancy)

The Thames Conservancy, amongst other statutory roles, is the navigation authority for the non-tidal part of the R. Thames above Teddington Weir. A quoted statistic which may well be correct is that, of all the known registered boats on inland water, about 40 per cent are on the R. Thames. It seems likely, therefore, that we shall also see about 40 per cent of the inland marina development in the same region.

There are a few engineering points I would like to draw to your attention which affect the siting and design of marinas on inland waters, particularly on such navigable rivers as the Thames.

Navigable rivers are, generally, of very flat gradient and have fairly extensive flood plains. Where the river is impounded to provide navigable depths, considerable sections of the river are perched above the surrounding ground levels. This gives rise to a problem when it is proposed to produce a marina basin by excavating alongside the river bank and then cutting through it. It is possible that surrounding ground levels will be lower than the existing river bank level. Great care must be taken—and this point must be borne in mind during the marina planning stages, both by the designer and developer—that, in the site chosen, the flood risk is not materially increased.

To give some idea of scale, if ground levels which would form the bank of the marina—about 60 m (200 ft) away from the river—are about

0·3 m (1 ft) below the existing river bank levels, the flood risk to adjoining properties could increase fivefold. Clearly, the owners of adjacent properties would not consider this acceptable.

A similar problem—although perhaps not so apparent—exists in relation to the effect of ground water levels adjoining marina developments. In developing a marina, the effect is to translate what are normal river water levels to points at a distance from the river, still within the flood plain. Flood plains are, generally, formed of pervious alluvial deposits. The translation of river water levels some distance away from the river can have a marked and possibly adverse effect on the adjoining ground water levels. This is a point to watch very carefully during the design stages.

The third point is the question of siltation. It was touched on in the papers dealing with coastal marinas, where certain methods were suggested for dealing with the problem. It is likely to be a very similar and difficult problem for the marina operators in river sites, where frequently it is common practice to form a marina basin and a perpendicular cut through the bank of the river to provide access. I suspect that this situation will give rise to considerable silting problems at the entrance.

I consider that this last point should be the subject of further study. It seems likely that the solution will have to be based on careful alignment rather than the construction of solid training walls projecting into the body of the river, which I am sure most river authorities would not be prepared to accept.

M. Francois Julou (Ingénieur Civil des Ponts et Chaussées of Societé d'études de la Terre Armée

A method of constructing embankments with vertical faces but without massive retaining walls has recently been developed by a French engineer, Henri Vidal.

Reinforced Earth is a material formed by combining soil and reinforcement. The soil must be granular (less than 15% passing the 200 sieve) so that it can transfer internal forces to the reinforcement by friction.

The reinforcement is placed in horizontal layers at right angles to the face of the fill and it usually consists of corrosion-resistant metal strips. At the face itself some covering is required to prevent erosion of the soil and this is provided either by metal sheets or by precast concrete panels.

In marina construction the facing is usually of precast concrete panel 1·5 m (4·9 ft) square and 180 mm (7·1 in.) thick. Each panel weighs 1 t and is easily handled by a light mobile crane. The panels are interlocked and pinned together so as to allow small relative movements. Special care is taken in marina construction to seal the joints in the facing to prevent leaching.

The reinforcement is placed on top of alternate compacted layers of fill and connected to the back of the facing panels by bolting to metal tabs cast into the concrete. Both the reinforcing strips and the tabs are usually made of aluminium alloy for marine work (Fig. K).

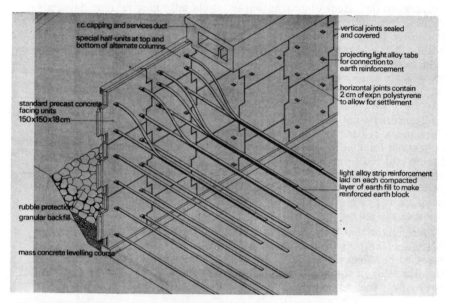

Figure K Typical quay construction in reinforced earth—detail as at Cap d'Agde, Languedoc, France

The main advantages of *Reinforced Earth* in marina construction are:—

(i)   Reduced cost: All elements are prefabricated and mass produced. The quantity of concrete and metal required is much less than for a conventional retaining wall. Suitable fill is generally available on or near the site.

(ii) Easy erection: Handling and erection of units is quick and simple. Output is governed by the capacity of earthmoving and compacting equipment (Fig. L).

(iii) Flexibility: The reinforced earth mass and the subsoil on which it rests can settle freely without any stress being induced, unlike a rigid reinforced concrete wall.

However, reinforced earth quays of this type must be built in the dry. This is very commonly possible for marinas, and dry construction has so many advantages that it may be adopted in any case (Fig. M).

(M. Julou then showed a short film)

Figure L Construction work in reinforced earth in progress

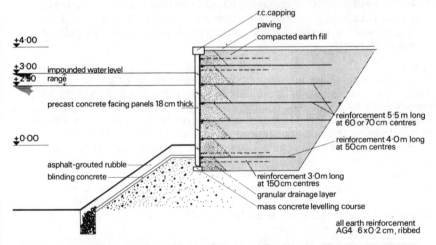

Figure M Proposed alternative construction for inner basin quays at
Brighton Marina

Mr. E. W. Jacomb-Hood (C. H. Dobbie and Partners, Consulting
Engineers, London):

Mr. D. P. Bertlin's paper excluded mention of an important subject,
namely slipways and launching ramps for boats, although he did refer
to stationary lifts for large yachts and to a yacht hanger as a scraping
and painting facility.

I do not wish here to expand on slipways because it raises many
issues such as rails, trolleys, winching arrangements, etc. But simple

launching ramps are a basic requirement wherever boats or yachts are
to be handled in or out of water. Ramps are, naturally, simplest in
non-tidal waters; the selected launching area may be un-paved but
clearly a timber, concrete or other man-made pavement will be preferable, although heavy canvas is a valuable aid on pebble beaches.

It is suggested that the gradient of the ramp should be in the range
1 in 15 to 1 in 20 and the width in the range four to eight metres.
Should timber be used this must be suitably treated and 25 mm × 75 mm
(1 in. × 3 in.) battens may be added to lessen slipping or skidding.
Naturally, steel fixings should be galvanised or sherardised; concrete
ramps, for the same reason, should be roughened with a brush finish.
Algae can be a serious cause of slipping on concrete, in which case
regular spraying with chemicals or applications of Ordinary Portland
cement are recommended.

In sheltered positions, a satisfactory ramp may be provided with
'monobgslabs' the effectiveness of which is in part the facility for
marram grass or other vegetation, amenable to salt water, to grow
within the grid profile. Vegetation should provide sufficient anchorage,
otherwise it is suggested that a simple anchor block be formed at the
top of the ramp to resist the tractive force of motor vehicles pulling
boats up the ramp.

Assuming a solid concrete structure is adopted, pre-cast concrete
blocks hexagonal in plan may be set on a concrete blinding; alternatively, on a steeper slope, pre-cast concrete planks, which overlap and
support each other thereby jointly resisting the uplift of waves, may
be placed on 'saw-tooth' longitudinal concrete ties, again set on a concrete blinding. Overall concrete thickness should not be less than
200 mm (8 in.) and reinforcement should be avoided other than that
required to secure a bond, say, to a buried anchor block. Recommendations on quality of concrete and an indication of types of interlocking
pre-cast concrete planking are contained in the Cement and Concrete
Association's helpful leaflet 93.007, 1971, entitled 'Launching Ramps
for Boats' from which Figs. N and O are extracted.

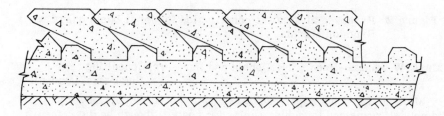

Figure N Precast planks resting on precast 'saw-tooth' longitudinal
ties and shaped so as to overlap and support each other
(Cement and Concrete Association)

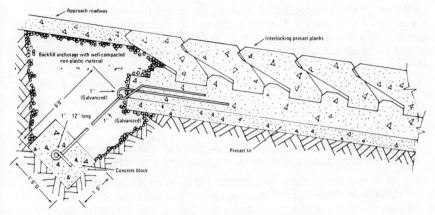

Figure O   Upper terminal feature consisting of an anchor block located
at the top of each line of ties

(Cement and Concrete Association)

In tidal waters, there are many more considerations, such as degree
of exposure to wave action, extent of littoral drift, etc. If there is
littoral drift, then the construction of a solid ramp, will tend to cause
accretion updrift, and scour downdrift, of the ramp. Consequently,
the coastal engineer will be sensitive to a design of open or floating
construction. Assumptions as to width and gradient and measures to
combat slipping can be taken as already stated. On a pebble beach, a
clearing operation by a bulldozer of the ramp may be a frequent
requirement.

Mr. H. D. Barron (Consulting Engineer, Southampton)

I would like to comment on certain aspects of Mr. Bertlin's excellent paper. Could he offer some amplification and explanation of
the recommended clearances, particularly with respect to the dimensions between the opposing finger piers on adjacent pontoon walkways
(Fig. 2, p. 199)

It would appear by reference to Table 5, (p. 200) that the width of the
fairway (F) is in many cases considerably less than twice the length
(L) of the berth and I would suggest that this is considerably tighter
than in many of the marinas in the Solent area.

Would Mr. Bertlin agree that, as a general rule, finger piers which
are of approximately the same length as the boats berthed against
them, should have a pitch (P) not less than $0 \cdot 8L$ centre to centre, the
fairway (F) between opposing ends should not be less than $2L$, and
that F should be increased whenever cross currents are likely to
occur?

With regard to the design of floating pontoons, I would agree with the suggested dimensions for the width of the walkways, but would suggest that a live load of 150 kg/m^2 (31 lb/ft^2) is rather excessive and that because yacht harbours have the advantage that live load is self-correcting, this can be considerably reduced.

I would also suggest that to impose an arbitrary restriction of a 15 degree tilt on the finger piers would seem unnecessary when it is considered that yachtsmen are used to a tilt in their boat of considerably more than this.

A brief description of some of the design and construction problems at Mercury Yacht Harbour, River Hamble, may be of interest.

Fig. P shows the completed harbour between areas of saltings on the west bank of the estuary. All the excavated material, consisting of a mixture of clay and gravel, was deposited in the areas to the west and south of the new harbour.

The western area was subsequently surfaced with hardcore and limestone scalpings so as to form a car park. The sheet pile retaining wall to this area can be identified.

Figure P Mercury Yacht Harbour, Hamble River

The southern area has been landscaped around a natural tree belt with drainage channels connecting to the estuary. Subsequently, further landscaping and planting will be carried out in this reclamation area. Retaining bunds for all of this material were built using the upper sedge layers and subsequently reinforcing this with the pumped dredged material.

Variations in the estuary bed necessitated the use of mooring piles of lengths varying between 12 and 19·5 m (40 and 64 ft). During dredging it was found that certain areas were particularly soft and it was decided that steel piles be used at the outer ends of the centre and northern piers. It was not, however, necessary to extend and re-drive any of these piles.

The three access bridges, which have a maximum slope of 1 : 4 at low water, have been located in line with the three piers, and are fixed by a hinged joint at their lower ends and are free to roll in a horizontal channel at the shore ends. This method was chosen so as to avoid differential loading on the pontoons, which could have caused variations in freeboard.

The whole floating system was designed to carry a live load of 73 kg/m^2 (15 lb/ft^2) and this has been found satisfactory even for heavy point loads. The important factor in the assessment of the design live load is the type of joint; at Mercury, all joints are capable of transmitting a large proportion of horizontal and vertical moments.

Spacing of the finger piers, of up to 12 m (40 ft) in length is generally 10 m (33 ft), except in the centre pier where the fingers are at 11 m (36 ft) centres. The 21 m (70 ft) finger piers which are situated at the fairway end of the southern pier and on the northern side of the northern pier, are spaced at either 17 or 16 m (56 or 52 ft) centres.

Considerable additional stability in the 2 and 2·5 m (6·5 and 8·2 ft) wide pontoons has been achieved by the use of a catamaran arrangement for the floats. This system was not possible for the 1·2 m (4 ft) wide finger piers and these had to be stabilised during the construction period with the addition of a float attached to each side of the pontoon.

Mr. K. Montgomery-Smith (Consulting Engineer, Harpenden, Herts)

I am glad to see that the advantages of expanded polystyrene floats are now being more generally recognised. At the time of construction of Lymington Marina* (1968/1969) the price of XPS was about £7 per metre^3 (£0.2 per ft^3), the American type Styrofoam was about £16 (£0.45), both of these needing protection against petrol and oil, and Urethane was about £22 (£0.63).

---

*Lymington Marina was visited during the marina tour on 21st April and is described on pp. 482-486. There are also photographs of the construction stages in Mr. Sargent's paper (pp. 233-235).

With steel tanks or other hollow shells the money is in the outer surface and the cost increases the more one leaves the cube in shape. With XPS, 80% of the cost is in the volume and the shape does not much affect the cost in the volumes required.

The result is that one can obtain a better ratio of deck area to float water line plane area with a smaller increase in cost with XPS than with a hollow shell. I got the ratio down to about 2 at Lymington, to suit the flexibility of the system.

The material is, of course, rather soft and is easily pressed in with the finger and seems to mark at about 7000 kg/m^2 (10 lb/in^2), so for safety it is better not to exceed about 0·75 m (2·5 ft) draft. Care also has to be taken in limiting the bearing pressure at supports. At Lymington, I provided top support for about 70% of the float area. This avoided imposing any other stresses on the material except pure compression.

If a hard cover is put on either fibreglass or concrete then it must be strong enough to do the whole work or else it will fail.

In order that the floats could follow the deflections of the bearing boards, the casing to protect the floats against petrol and oil was soft so as to keep the pressures even. I found that hard cases were much too expensive if strong enough to do the work required.

Mr. Taylor of Gunac advised me about the covering before his firm was taken over and another company he had started called Surface Developments Ltd., now of Doncaster, supplied a fibre reinforced emulsion which is applied directly to the XPS without the normal sealing coat I normally use on buildings, and four coats of this emulsion seems to stand and do the job very economically. Some of the floats have now been in the water about five years from the initial tests and there does not seem to be any change visible although some did get damaged in the early stages before launching.

Midland Structures Ltd., Bedford, took complete responsibility in the later works for the whole of the floating unit fabrication and there is now in the latest designs a considerable improvement in detail resulting from our earlier experiences.

Regarding the decking, there is a point to watch if one is using the cantilever system I thought out for Lymington (Fig. K). This is designed primarily for single docking not tandem, and in the 17 m (55 ft) long arms the root forces approach 30 t coupled with lift forces from warps to high freeboard vessels on the lee side which practically carry the weight of the arm and require the torsion strength provided.

The horizontal shear in the main walkway panel opposite the arm, if the opposite berth is vacant, requires a diagonal for about 40 t force if not taken another way.

Figure Q 17m (55 ft) cantilevered berthings at Lymington Marina

To provide a flexible joint at the root fixing may be dangerous in these conditions with little weight left to stop the struts buckling upwards, particularly if the joint is lifted on a wave or wash and the far side is in a trough.

It is I think better to avoid a flexible joint in this position and at Lymington I have provided a fully continuous joint up to the full strength of the members joined.

I find this greatly improves the damping of movement and makes for great steadiness in the whole system.

The piles are not held in collars but are purposely kept some distance away from the units so as to allow the whole system to surge under load.

Mr. T. R. de Zoete (Manager, Marina Division, Thos. Storey (Engineers) Ltd.)

Marina construction can be divided into three phases; providing the basin; the contractural work in pile driving and building shore facilities, and, finally, the provision of berth pontoons—'the floating side of the story'.

Figure R 'Acrowberth' pontoon units at Mercury Yacht Harbour, Hamble River

The history of marina pontoons in this country can be portrayed by a series of designs ranging from timber walkways supported on oil drums to sophisticated special structural steel decks fabricated at a high rate, supported on blocks of expanded polystyrene or steel tanks. Today the required specification for marina pontoons has been raised, as yachtsmen paying high south coast berthing fees quite rightly expect a high standard of accommodation for their yachts; furthermore, the marina operator is looking for a system whereby he can obtain maximum revenue from his marina by virtue of its flexibility of layout. Finally, the standard of a marina is determined by the pontoon equipment which forms the visible aspect of a marina (Fig. R).

In 1970, Thos. Storey (Engineers) Ltd. formed the Marina Division as it was decided that their manufacture of marina equipment would be a natural extension to the bridging and heavy pontoon equipment field, in which the Company was already involved. The first brief of the new Division was to design a pontoon system suitable for marinas, landing stages, and floating walkways. Considerable time was spent in the formulation of ideas for the design of a pontoon system to meet the requirements of a modern marina. The *Acrowberth Marina Pontoon System* was thus designed around the following guide lines.

The pontoon system must consist of a series of standarised units which can be built up to conform to the clients' required layout, using an absolute minimum of special components. Whilst satisfying this requirement the system should also be able to accommodate changes in berthing requirements and the possibility of future extensions.

It was decided that the system should be designed on a metric module and that the main walkway pontoon units should be available in three standard widths, 2·00, 2·50 and 3·00 m (6·5, 8·2 and 9·8 ft). Built into the side members of the main walkway should be a facility allowing the connection of finger piers and walkways at right angles; this was achieved by the provision of bolting positions pre-drilled at 1 m (3·3 ft) centres along the length of the side members. This fact of the design would allow the marina operator to position or re-position the finger piers correctly to allow the required space to accommodate the beams of the craft moored alongside the finger piers.

This system ensures the maximum use of the costly water space created within the marina, as well as dispensing with the guess-work of arriving at the correct width between fingers by means of local craft statistics and various inconclusive tables. To allow for this changing of position of finger piers the anchorage piles must be spaced along the main walkway rather than at the extremities of the finger, which had been the accepted practice in the past. The finger pier must thus be designed to accept an impact loading at its extremity and transfer the load back to the main walkway and then to the anchorage piles. The maximum length of finger pier to be cantilevered from the main walkway without an anchorage pile at its end would be 12 m (39 ft).

The superstructure of the Acrowberth pontoon units are to be constructed from standard bolt-together components. This idea produced many inherent advantages: 'Flow-line' manufacture can be organised, using jigs to ensure interchangeability of components and thus the guarantee that the completed pontoon units will connect without difficulty on site.

Individual components can be more easily handled than a welded deck structure within the confines of a factory; furthermore, great savings can be made in overland transport. For lasting protection against the hostile marine environment the components can be easily hot-dipped galvanised.

Finally, in a manufacturing venture of this type, economies of scale can be rigorously applied, by virtue of the manufacture of standarised components.

Once the Acrowberth pontoon superstructure was designed, a detailed study was made of the flotation and the super load it should be designed to accept. It was decided that the main walkways should be designed for a distributed load of 100 kg/m^2 (20·5 lb/ft^2) in their own right without the assistance of any adjoining finger piers. Whilst this loading does not represent crowd loading it was considered adequate to accommodate the pedestrian traffic calculated to use the pontoons.

Various flotation materials were considered and it was determined that it must be inert and thus maintenance free. Expanded polystyrene of 16 kg/m^3 (1 lb/ft^3) density provides the most economical core for any flotation unit. This material can be used in a raw state; however, replacement of the untreated polystyrene blocks may have to be undertaken after a relatively short period. The ultimate in flotation is undoubtedly a block of polystyrene covered in a protective finish and the following suggestions were made; concrete, glass fibre reinforced coating, or plastic. Concrete was not seriously considered as it would add considerable weight to the flotation unit and the curing time would cause delays in the manufacturing cycle. Glass fibre reinforced coatings have the disadvantage that the resins attack the polystyrene and therefore an intermediate coating has to be first applied, thus creating a costly double manufacturing operation. Finally, a plastic coating was found that could be sprayed directly onto the polystyrene, having quick curing time, forming an adhesion to the polystyrene and a tough, coloured finish.

In conclusion, what has been achieved with the design of *Acrowberth* is a marina pontoon system, which can be manufactured at a reasonable cost, whilst giving many new advantages to the marina operator by virtue of its new patented design concept.

Mr. J. M. Kent (Monsanto Chemicals Ltd.)

In general, a marina basically consists of floating pontoons providing convenient and easy access to boats, irrespective of the tide and weather conditions.

The key element in a pontoon is the medium used to provide the buoyancy enabling the access walkways to float and adjust to the various tide conditions.

Until recently, the traditional solution has been to use hollow airtight compartments either specially constructed or adapted from existing vessels to provide the required buoyancy. The problems of leakage, damage, material corrosion and associated deadweight has resulted in the development of more robust permanent materials for this service.

VoidForm expanded polstyrene by Monsanto is one such material and this has found ready acceptance because it is able to provide the basic properties required to fulfil the buoyancy function.

Expanded polystyrene is a closed cell material having extremely high strength to weight characteristics and for marina applications is normally supplied at a density of 16 kg/m^3 (1 lb/ft^3). The cellular structure at this density consists of approximately 98% by volume of entrapped air and therefore the buoyancy potential when using the material is considerable.

The physical properties of this lightweight rigid material, which if necessary can be manufactured to a wide variety of profile shapes, are set out in Table B.

The material is white, chemically inert, non-toxic and odourless. It is easy to handle and can be cut with simple woodworking tools.

VoidForm used bare has a totally immersed buoyancy of approximately 0·9 t/m^3: a standard-production block of the material 2·44 m × 1·22 m × 0·61 m (nominally 8 ft × 4 ft × 2 ft) will give a free-board of 400 mm (nominally 16 in.) under an evenly distributed load of 600 kg (1200 lb). A further imposed load of 150 kg, representing for example 2 persons standing on the block, reduces the freeboard by only 50 mm (2 in.).

It will be appreciated that in the construction of such a pontoon the use of a solid, virtually non-water absorbent material of extremely low density gives the designer considerable scope for combining expanded polystyrene with other materials to meet his requirements.

It should be pointed out, however, that VoidForm expanded polystyrene has been used successfully on its own for some years now and Fig. S shows VoidForm block installed under timber decking at Chichester Yacht Basin. Several hundred cubic metres of VoidForm have been supplied over the past five years and some of the original blocks are still giving excellent service despite the severity of the operating conditions in this busy marina.

Whilst VoidForm has a relatively high resistance to impact damage it is obviously an advantage if a skin of G.R.P. or concrete covers the exterior surfaces. The exceptionally good bond formed between concrete and the surface of the material results in an integral skin/core structure of very high strength. The same can be said of the G.R.P./ polystyrene combinations, although the incompatibility of the cheaper polyester resins used for the G.R.P. can pose some construction problems. As an alternative to polyester resins, solvent free epoxies can be used, although at a considerably increased cost: a polythene film barrier between polystyrene and the G.R.P. enables the polyester resins to be used satisfactorily. In the area of practice between using the VoidForm bare and applying G.R.P. or concrete coatings, there are a number of brush coating materials mostly synthetic emulsions, which provide a water-tight seal at very low cost. Whilst relatively cheap and easily applied, these do not of course give the greatly increased strength which the pontoon unit acquires with heavier forms of coating.

The unit size of the expanded polystyrene buoyancy block is of prime importance in determining the eventual cost of this element

Table B Physical properties of VoidForm Expanded
Polystyrene

PROPERTY	UNIT	VALUE
Nominal apparent density	kg/m^3 (lb/ft^3)	16·0 (1·0)
Cross breaking strength	kN/m^2 (lbf/in^2)	min. 137·0 (20)
Compressive stress to give 10% compression	kN/m^2 (lbf/in^2)	min. 69·0 (10)
Modulus of elasticity	kN/m^2 (lbf/in^2)	min. 6894 (1000)
Modulus of rigidity	kN/m^2 (lbf/in^2)	min. 2758 (400)
Water absorption: 7 days total immersion at room temperature	Per cent by volume	max. 4

of the structure. The material is produced in large blocks of 2·44 m × 1·22 m × 0·61 m (8 ft × 4 ft × 2 ft) and as indicated earlier it can be built up or cut down from this basic size.

The design of a pontoon unit which fits the above module range will of course produce the most economical material utilisation and therefore the lowest cost per unit volume of material.

Monsanto in addition to being able to supply rectangular blocks of expanded polystyrene, are unique in that the material is also available as a solid moulded cylinder. Cylinders are available in 2·4 m (8 ft) lengths from 300 mm (12 in.) to 1050 mm (42 in.) diameter. These units have found ready acceptance in replacing the more traditional cylindrical materials during refurbishing.

Monsanto provide full technical support in respect of VoidForm for marina applications and maintain close contacts with other manufacturers who specialise in coating techniques.

Figure S 'VoidForm' buoyancy units at Chichester Yacht Basin

Mr. E. Seaton (Chartered Architect, Coleraine, N.I.)

I sense that the organisers are a little uneasy in their reference to engineers and architects. Perhaps this is because there is no school of architecture at this University, or it may be for other reasons, but, in my opinion, the person to design a marina is the person whose feelings and thoughts are most akin to the people who use it and/or live there. That person may well be an engineer or, equally, he may be an architect. There is no difference, as long as all the skills which go into the designing of marinas are employed.

These skills are very varied. For example, I have heard no mention of salmon rights, which need to be taken into account in many places. No one has mentioned water skiing or dinghy racing. In other word, there are many factors which have not yet been brought out and which affect the design of marinas.

Mr. Bertlin has said (p. 201) that pontoons consisting of oil drums with a timber deck are not recommended. Compared with prefabricated arrangements they may not be so good, but, if price is included in the calculation, they are certainly worth consideration. A jetty of this form in my marina at Coleraine has been in place for five years and has required no maintenance. Capital investment into a marina should be related to the acceptable mooring charges, and these are less as one operates further north.

Mr. R. H. Mims (Senior Project Architect, Retail Services Division, Shell-Mex and B.P. Ltd.)

On the subject of 'bunkering' (p. 208 in Mr. Bertlin's paper) it is felt that the addition of some basic technical information would be of assistance.

The kind of bunkering facility to be provided and its location depend on the numbers and types of motor-propelled boats to be accommodated. The provision of floating refuellers and direct filling by road tanker are not to be recommended mainly due to safety and operational reasons.

Petroleum products by their very nature are highly inflammable, smelly and dirty, and the fact that they float on water makes their use at marinas the more dangerous due to possible spillage, ignition on the water and consequent spread of fire among closely moored boats. Safety precautions, therefore, must be stringently applied in respect of the method of construction, location and operation of the bunkering facilities provided.

It follows that due to the very technical nature of bunkering facilities and the strict controls applied on their location, the necessary details and locations of the various components involved should be decided and approved at an early stage in planning a marina development. Many marinas now operating have completely inadequate bunkering facilities which often are the direct result of inadequate or late consideration being given to the provision of this facility

The statutory conditions that must be complied with when considering bunkering facilities and equipment are the Petroleum (Consolidation) Act 1928 (revised 1968) Parts I and II.* These conditions cover the principles of construction and licensing conditions at petrol filling stations and depots and cover the location of storage tanks, above or below ground, and the pumping equipment connected to them.

Storage tanks for petroleum spirit, diesel, gas oil, etc., should be of 4500-23, 000 litres (1000-5000 gal) capacity, depending on demand to be met and any rebates that may be offered by the supplying company on bulk deliveries of fuel. Petroleum spirit is stored in cylindrical tanks, of approved specification, installed normally below ground and encased in 0·15 m minimum cover of sand or 1 : 2 : 4 concrete with adequate provision made to prevent corrosion or flotation of the tank. If installed above ground the petroleum storage tank must be contained within a bund wall to an enclosure large enough to contain the full capacity of the tank should a leak occur. Tanks for diesel and gas oil storage can be either cylindrical or rectangular and installed above or below ground. If above ground, bunded enclosures must be provided as for spirit tanks.

The location of spirit tanks is governed by recommendations contained in the Petroleum (Consolidation) Act 1928 and administered by the Petroleum Officer or Fire Officer responsible to the Local Licensing Authority. The tank fills must be within 9 m (30 ft) of the road tanker access position and a minimum of 4·3 m (14 ft) from site boundaries or any building within the site, unless the building concerned is constructed of extra fire resisting materials to the satisfaction of the local licensing authority. Diesel and gas oil tanks are not covered by these conditions on location, although the distance of 9 m maximum from the tanker off-loading position still applies.

Similarly, the position of spirit pumps is governed by the same regulations, but, in addition, the suction pipe from tank to pump in a normal installation should rise a minimum of 38 mm (1½ in.) in 3 m (10 ft) and the overall length of suction line should not exceed 30 m (100 ft). Pumps are capable of working over distances well in excess of 30 m (100 ft) but this is not to be recommended if heavy maintenance and possible replacement of pump motors is to be kept to a minimum. If distances greater than 30 m (100 ft) are necessary a system of booster pumps may be required.

In many cases it may not be possible to locate the storage tank

---

*Obtainable from H.M.S.O., Part I—15p, Part II—5p.

below the level of the pump and a falling suction line will result. To avoid pressure build up in such situations a pressure reducing valve must be fitted in the line prior to connection to the pump. The petroleum regulations will not permit the use of flexible suction lines between tank and pump, and this will prevent pumps being fitted on a floating pontoon attached to a fixed jetty, unless the pumps have separate tanks within the pontoon which are replenished from the main storage tanks at set positions of the tide.

In respect of marinas, additional difficulties arise due to dispensing problems in refuelling boats, which are increased further if the bunkering location is subject to tidal conditions. Boats of various sizes and layout have to be catered for, with fuel tank fill pipes of varying sizes situated anywhere on the deck and often obstructed by deck equipment and rigging. Rise and fall of the tide, possibly as great as 12 m (40 ft) may have to be contended with in tidal waters. All these problems cannot be met or overcome without the design of special dispensing equipment. Standard filling station type pumps with longer hoses or swing arm attachments are used on most marinas, but the lack of hose length and obstruction by the swing arm of rigging make operations difficult and often unsatisfactory. The use of pumps with long recoiling hoses could possibly go a long way to overcome many of the problems.*

It is important that any fire within the vicinity of the bunkering area should be contained and prevented from spreading over the surface of the water to the main mooring areas by the provision of floating booms, forming a bund around the refuelling mooring. These booms can be of specialist design or made up of suitable lengths of 100 mm × 75 mm (4 in. × 3 in.) timber linked together with canvas strips arranged in such a way as to form an arc around the boat being refuelled, yet allow an opening section for access and exit of the boat.

Pollution of sea and rivers is the subject of an intensive study by the River Authorities at the moment. Resulting from this study, conditions could be applied more stringently in future on marina developments, especially on inland waterways, to prevent pollution. The bunding of bunkering areas by suitable booms may well be one of the conditions applied.

Adequate fire extinguishers must be provided and kept properly maintained in positions adjacent to the pumps and tanks in accordance with the Petroleum Licence conditions. Also, means of access for fire fighting appliances must be allowed for, both to the bunkering area and to suitable access positions throughout the marina development.

---

*Such a pump is manufactured by the Tokheim Corporation (U.K. Division), Newark Road, Glenrothes, Fife, Scotland, for light aircraft refuelling, which can be adopted for marine work with 15 m (50 ft) hose and electric rewind mechanism.

Advice on suitable equipment and means of access can be obtained from the Local Fire Officer.

When designing bunkering installations, provision should be made for a small operator's kiosk containing all the necessary electrical switch gear associated with the pumps and situated in such a position that from it the whole refuelling operation can be supervised. In addition, provision should be made for storage of bulk or canned lubricants, and bottled gas, which are products also controlled under the Petroleum Regulations. The provision of an adequate fresh water main at the bunkering position is an advantage, the dispensing of which could be by a recoiling hose unit if costs will allow.

The layout of a typical marina bunkering facility is shown in Fig. T,

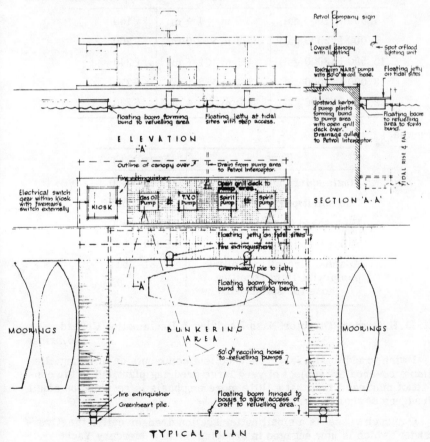

Figure T Details of a typical marina bunkering area
(Shell-Mex and B.P. Ltd.)

but, of course, each installation must be carefully planned to suit the particular conditions. In this respect my Company would always be prepared to advise.

The following are some average cost details (applicable May 1972) which may be of assistance, but care should be taken to use these only as a guide.

Table C Cost of bunkering equipment

Tanks:

Cylindrical fuel storage tanks for installation above or below ground (single compartment)

Capacity	Size	Approx. Cost
4, 500 1 (1000 gal)	3·5 m × 1·4 m	£140
9, 000 1 (2000 gal)	3·3 m × 2·0 m	£200
13, 500 1 (3000 gal)	4·1 m × 2·1 m	£240
18, 000 1 (4000 gal)	5·4 m × 2·1 m	£270
22, 500 1 (5000 gal)	5·2 m × 2·4 m	£290

Pumps:

Type	Approx. Cost
Single spirit pump	£340-£350
Duo spirit pump	£670-£685
High speed Derv pump	£370-£400
Spirit blender pump	£820-£930
Adapted aircraft refuelling pump with 15 m recoiling hose for spirit or Derv	£581-£611

Mr. J. H. Gordon (Director, Nash Dredging & Reclamation Co. Ltd., Weybridge)

I wish to add to Mr. Sargent's excellent comments on dredging. He amply covered the subject of very large dredging plant, but in the context of marinas I feel that a little more emphasis is required on small dredgers of shallow draft.

One such vessel is a small cutter suction dredger called the 'Overlander' which is now engaged in dredging the new Mercury Yacht Harbour in the Hamble River (Fig. U). We call her the 'Overlander' because she can be taken into seven parts, loaded on lorries and taken to another site in a matter of days. She is 28 m (93 ft) overall, draws only 1·1 m (3·5 ft), has a main engine of 272 kW (365 hp) and an auxiliary engine of 179 kW (240 hp) which makes her quite a powerful machine. She is not a toy, and not of the type which could be constructed from Dinky Toy or Meccano. She is ideal for the type of marina being constructed in this country.

Figure U Cutter-suction dredger in operation at Mercury Yacht Harbour Hamble River

It must be apparent to everyone here that the greatest economic advantage is to be obtained by balancing cut and fill. If the dredged material can be put ashore and the buildings put on it, the marina will be built far more cheaply than if the material has to be dumped miles out at sea. This balanced cut-and-fill operation is the job done by the small cutter suction dredger.

Some people have written off silts, alluvial material and certain clays as being quite useless. But if one is prepared to wait two, three or four years and to take special measures, such as laying porous pipes, introducing peat, and sowing the material after a period with a type of rape grass that can stand up to salt water, then to re-plant, re-sow, and let each rainy season wash away the salt, it is possible to get a material which can take ordinary grass at first, and, more gradually, heavier and heavier loading. It is possible to place buildings upon this by putting short sand piles through it or using other appropriate methods. A surface can be laid upon it to take traffic and, eventually, a car park.

This is essentially a long-term process, but after a period of perhaps 20 years the marina owner could well possess an area of land of enormous value, and something that was not taken into account when making the original cost-benefit analysis.

The techniques which we are employing in the Hamble River, where the strata vary considerably, show that it is possible to separate the materials that are dredged. We do this by means of an arrangement of pipelines and valves thus enabling any desired separation of material in the vertical or horizontal dimension. In this way, full advantage can be taken of the material which is encountered in dredging. A good soil mechanics engineer can soon tell how long each particular type of material will take to become consolidated and capable of bearing applied loads.

AUTHORS' REPLY

Mr.D.P.Bertlin

Mr. Pope raised the question of the importance of depth, with which I agree and for this reason I have given in Table 2 (p.196) the depth which should be allowed for craft of different sizes. The limitations of dredging craft have to be borne in mind when designing a yacht harbour as sufficient depth of water must be allowed for such craft.

Motor vessels draw less water than sailing craft and marinas ought to take this into account, e.g., at Poole each berth is either a motor or a sailing vessel berth.

The question of end-on mooring as compared to finger berths is a debatable one. Finger moorings have many advantages, certainly from the yachtsman's point of view. If a first class marina is to be constructed the best possible facilities should be provided and alongside mooring takes up little more space in terms of water area than end-on mooring. Although boats may be placed closer together with end-on mooring, piles or buoys to hold the vessels off the pontoon are necessary.

On the French Riviera, end-on mooring was almost universal, but finger mooring is being used increasingly. M. Vian, who designed the Languedoc Rousillon harbours used end-on moorings with piles at intervals to take bow warps, but in marinas he has recently designed he has used finger moorings.

As I have mentioned earlier there are some instances where end-on mooring can prove more satisfactory. This applies particularly where there is a certain amount of ranging due to incomplete protection.

Mr. Lewis raised the question of electricity. The caravan committee which he mentioned is also dealing with marinas and the National Yacht Harbour Association, which has prepared its own code, has a representative on this committee.

I cannot agree with Mr. Lewis on the subject of pollution. This question has been continuously and actively considered by the National Yacht Harbour Association for four or five years. The Association's honorary consultant, Dr. R. F. Crampton, a very well-known bacteriologist, has studied the subject in detail. He concludes that there is no danger from pollution in general in yacht harbours, even if one swims in the harbour. In view of the danger from yachts moving in marinas, swimming should be prohibited. The danger to health from pollution is therefore practically non-existent. Moreover, all yacht harbours have good lavatory accommodation, which, it is found from experience, is used by yachtsmen. By comparison with the tons of untreated sewage pouring into the sea all around the coast, marinas are clean indeed and the lack of a sense of proportion in discussing this question is quite amazing.

Mr. Hales made some very interesting remarks about the use of ferroush in constructing breakwaters which might well pay following up.

Mr. Walters suggested that the contractor should be appointed early in the development. The most satisfactory way of building any civil engineering work is undoubtedly to appoint a consulting engineer experienced in the type of work in question and ask for competitive tenders. The appointment of a contractor, without tendering, cuts out competition and increases cost.

Mr. Barlow raised the question of access. With commercial vessels, a cost benefit analysis can be done in the way suggested by Mr. Barlow. This is not easy in the case of yacht harbours, because there is the personal factor. How attractive is a berth in a yacht harbour which is only open for one hour or six hours a day? This is where the judgement of the developer, advised by the consulting engineer, comes in.

Mr. Weeks raised the subject of flood plains, siltation and the river regime. These are all important subjects and I agree with him that consideration must be given to them. Obviously, one must have advice from a consulting engineer when these aspects arise.

Mr. Montgomery-Smith's interesting discussion of the usefulness of expanded polystyrene floats makes one doubt whether any treatment of the expanded polystyrene is necessary. I believe that more experience is necessary before we can say positively whether surface treatment is advisable.

The design of pontoons is far from simple if an economical design is to be achieved—that is economical both in cost and space required.

Mr. Flemons raised the question of planned life for marina structures. I would refer him to the *Research Project on Port Structures* published by the National Ports Council, where this aspect is particularly studied. If it is practicable and cheaper to use piles for breakwaters and quays then, in almost all cases, in view of high interest rates, it is preferable to do this rather than adopt a longer life structure.

It is possible to prevent oil pollution entering a yacht harbour by a floating boom and this is adopted in some harbours. The most convenient form is a pneumatic air barrier such as that provided at the new Poole Yatch Club Marina.

Mr. Barron apparently considers the width of fairway between finger piers which I have proposed is too small. I would emphasise that the figures I suggest are a minimum and should only be adopted in well protected waters without any current. In many marinas in the Solent area, such as those in the River Hamble, the current is considerable and I agree that in such cases a greater fairway width is advisable. I do, however, consider that the spacing of pontoons in many marinas is uneconomical and that both their design and layout leave much to be desired.

I agree that a design live load of less than 150 kg/m^2 may be satisfactory for pontoons. I consider, however, that 150 kg/m^2 should be adopted for brows. The angle of tilt of 15° is that recommended by the P.I.A.N.C. Small Boats Commission.

Mr. Mims technical information on bunkering is most useful. However, the provision of a bunkering area with a floating boom is not normal practice and appears to overdo the precautions necessary in view of the extremely unlikely event of spillage at a bunkering quay.

Mr. J. H. Sargent

Mr. Gordon raised the question of using poor quality materials for reclamation purposes. I am fully in agreement with his statements that, with careful husbandry, silts and soft alluvial deposits can be improved over a period of time. The degree of improvement will depend on many factors including the grain size and permeability of the material used for reclamation and the amount of husbandry undertaken over the years following the placing of the reclamation material in the deposit area. If the area is to be used in later periods for development by industry, it will probably be essential to pump a sand blanket over the entire area and to pile for all load-bearing structures.

An unidentified speaker asked about the cost of dredging jobs, but this is a complex subject and there is insufficient time available to discuss the matter at length. The factors which affect cost in relation to dredging works cover the complete range of engineering factors including in particular the geological conditions, the exposure of the site, the time available for the work and the necessity to use the material for reclamation or alternatively its disposal at sea by dumping. The size of the project in terms of volume will also be of importance, since a major cost of the dredging contract is the expenditure on mobilisation of dredging plant and the necessary ancillary equipment.

Session 4

Chairman: **Mr. N. H. Searle**
(*Director, Wimpey Laboratories Ltd.*)

Marina Architecture

Sidney Kaye

Sidney Kaye, Eric Firmin and Partners, Chartered Architects, London

1 Introduction

We are on a relatively small island surrounded by the sea, with an abundance of rivers which have all contributed to making us a truly maritime nation. This has been invaluable in time of war. But in times of peace we have not exploited our natural facilities. As affluence has spread with more leisure time available, so has the increase in the demand for marine facilities; for this is a sporting activity that can be available at very reasonable cost to anyone. It offers a challenge and excitement to relieve the montony which too many have to face in their everyday lives.

The surprising fact is that whilst this country has such a major maritime background, the spread of marina development has been relatively slow compared to other nations. France and the United States have leaped ahead of us in this field.

The name 'marina' sprung into being in 1928. It was conceived by the American National Association of Engine and Boat Manufacturers to describe waterside facilities for boating. This new word was accepted by the British National Yacht Harbour Association as a harbour for leisure craft providing sheltered and easily accessible 'alongside' mooring and facilities.

This new word 'marina' reflected the slight change from rowing out to a boat moored offshore, to having a boat moored alongside a jetty together with adjoining minimal facilities such as a place to get a shower, some food and possibly accessible to telephones and transportation.

The present day concept of a marina is more advanced. No longer does a boat owner expect to carry all his requirements down to his boat by car. Today he expects to be able to obtain all that he wishes at or about the place where his boat is moored. The modern marina concept will boast of several refuelling facilities, boat repair yards, boat showrooms, shops, restaurants, housing accommodation, a school for yachtsmen and even an hotel.

With the improving road systems in the British Isles, it should be possible for 'marina townships' to be available to all, not merely as a week-end retreat, but as a permanent feature of everyday life. This is a far cry from the early concept of marinas, but is in line with what has gone ahead in other countries and gives us the lead as to what can be done here, as well as helping us to profit by the mistakes made by others.

2 American Marinas

Before continuing with further detail it might be as well to refer to some of the marinas constructed in other countries. One luxurious example is: Huntington Harbour, California, which is south of Los Angeles and consists of a well built-up system of water inlets, man-made, off the coast. Most of the water frontage is taken up by luxury private housing, each with its own private mooring. There are a relatively small number of homes which do not have mooring alongside, being without water frontage, but these have mooring facilities in special basins.

Most of the houses here are of timber frame but of contemporary design, each house differing from its neighbour.

This particular development is on quite a large scale and boasts all the amenities of a township with its own club, shopping centre, repair yards, boat showrooms, schools, etc. The unusual feature is that the people, for the most part, live here permanently and commute to their place of work, which may be as much as 110 km (70 miles) away on the fabulous freeways which are so much in evidence in the Los Angeles area.

Another example, the Marina Del Rey, Los Angeles, is one of the largest marina developments in California and takes up almost 10 km^2 (4 sq miles) (Fig.1). It caters at the moment for well over 3,000 vessels but with plans afoot for further extensions. Apart from the enormous number of moorings, are blocks of apartments of varying size, town houses, small house units and all the facilities one could possibly wish for. There is adequate provision of toilets and shower facilities at all convenient points. Each mooring berth has points for connecting up to fresh water supply, power and telephone, each separately metered to that mooring position.

In most American marinas it is expressly forbidden to discharge sewage into the marina waters and this is strictly enforced at the Marina Del Rey.

In California, marina development is encouraged by the excellent weather conditions which prevail there, the small differentiation between

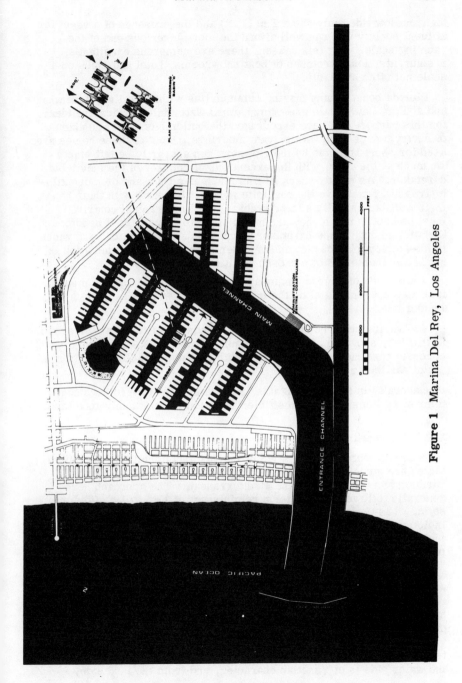

Figure 1 Marina Del Rey, Los Angeles

high and low tide (only about 2 m (7 ft)) and the presence of a very
affluent society who can well afford the more luxurious end of the
yachting scale. For this reason, there are numerous excellent
restaurants, long stretches of boat showrooms, hotel and clubs on a
scale not often available.

Florida boasts many marina communities within the Everglades,
and at Fort Lauderdale are many natural water inlets which are ideal
for this purpose and have encouraged the building of a vast number
of luxury homes each with private moorings. Most of these homes are
used for short holidays by their owners and appear to be left empty
for much of the year, with the exception, of course, of the inevitable
caretaker. As most owners live as much as a thousand or more kilo-
metres away and have the requisite wealth, they have with their house,
their cadillac as well as their yacht. As all mechanical contrivances
must be kept in use if they are not to fall into disrepair, it becomes
the allotted duty of the caretaker to make full use of the car and yacht
in his employer's absence and one therefore wonders if such a job is
not better than one's own chosen vocation.

There are, of course, many apartment developments with mooring
facilities both in Miami on the Indian Creek as well as at Fort
Lauderdale.

The various boat houses and repair sheds in this area are interesting
in that they show the change from timber frame to steel and reinforced
concrete construction. Boat sales buildings and refuelling points are
not of particular note.

Generally in the United States, marina architecture follows contemporary lines serving an efficient function in reasonably good taste.

3 Mediterranean Marinas

In sharp contrast to the style of marina architecture in the United
States are some of the recent developments in the South of France,
Sardinia and elsewhere in the Mediterranean. The approach here
generally follows a design form reminiscent of 17th to 19th Century
style. It is obviously very popular as a style and is something of an
indictment against contemporary designers who have obviously not
met the requirement of the public in the Mediterranean, who seem to
prefer the romanticism of earlier architectural styles.

Port Grimaud is one of the most prominent examples of this
approach (Fig. 2). It is quite a large enterprise involving the use of
reclaimed land. It provides a very romantic setting (Fig. 3) for
housing and boating along narrow waterways, mindful to some extent
of the canals of Venice with its quaint bridges connecting up the
various housing peninsulas. The housing is quite varied both in content, height and shape, yet for the most part attached. The view from
the water side is of Venetian character, and from the land side,

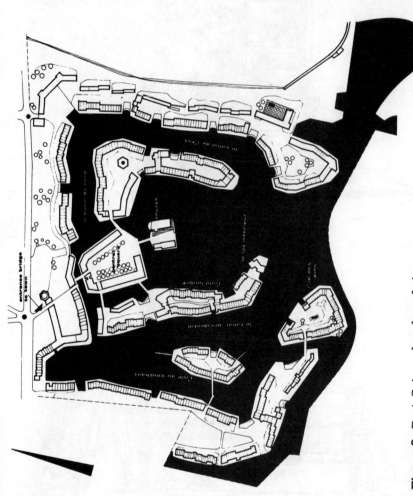

Figure 2 Port Grimaud – plan of stage one

Figure 3 Harbour scene at Port Grimaud

Southern French Mediterranean, perhaps most akin to the housing around St. Paul De Vence. Everything looks as though it had been built ages ago and not within the last few years.

The demand has been great for these properties and the development appears to be financially successful, having created a new community between St. Maxime and St. Tropez. The Port boasts a church, shopping centre, entertainments, school for sailing and other nautical sports, a hotel, numerous cafés and has provision at the moment for 1000 boats. The waterways vary in depth from 2·7 m (9 ft) and 4·6 m (15 ft) and there is a scheme of windmill pumps to avoid stagnation by keeping water flowing through to the lagoon. There are many other developments of a similar nature in the area, such as Port Cogolin, Port La Galere and Port Mandelieu.

In Sardinia, in similar style, is Porto Cervo, but this has nothing like the number of boating facilities at the moment. It is more in the nature of a new Mediterranean seaside town, but as in the case of Port Grimaud, designed in 18th Century Mediterranean romantic, for want of a better term. There is also Porto Rotundo and other new villages of this nature arising in Sardinia.

In sharp contrast to this is the development of mammoth residential apartments with boat facilities in the vicinity of Nice Airport. The scale of this concept is somewhat inhuman and is hardly a commendable example of contemporary design. It is curvilinear in form with the ends terraced but in spite of its shape does not echo the romanticism so much sought after in this part of the world.

A more contemporary and not quite so massive a scale of marina development is that at La Grande Motte in the Languedoc area. This has an unusual pyramidal form of flat development with cleverly contrived terraces producing somewhat novel architecture.

4 Marina Development in Britain

4.1 Planning Control and Finance

The Languedoc development together with the others on the Riviera have been fostered by the French Authorities who have provided the whole infra-structure of roads, services, etc., to make such developments possible. This is in complete contrast to the procedure adopted by the authorities over here.

Now, why have we been unable to produce comparable marina development here? There are many reasons, but one of the most important is that created by planning control. In this country, permission for such development has been extremely slow in forthcoming and it is perhaps as well at this point, to go into the background.

We are a small island that has been going through something of a building boom, partly accentuated by the blitz of the Second World War,

but also by the urgent need for urban renewal. This has resulted in
the passing of Acts of Parliament to control planning, so as to prevent
the spread of urbanism into our rural areas. For this reason a 'Green
Belt Policy' was evolved to surround out major towns and cities.
Unfortunately, this 'Policy' nullifies the ideal location for marinas,
which, by their very nature need to be sited in 'Green Belt Areas'
which are sacrosanct as far as planning policy is concerned.

One can perhaps appreciate the anomaly all the more, when one
realises that the sole purpose of green belt is to create **recreational**
area.

Immediately after the last war there was the act of 1947 which
introduced betterment levy resulting in a massive charge on any rural
land which was used for development. This has now been rescinded
but, coupled with green belt inviolability, did undoubtedly hold up
marina development.

The next reason is one of finance. As marinas are a fairly recent
concept, they were a less desirable subject for finance or loans,
particularly as the market was as yet untapped. Financial institutions
were more certain of adequate rewards if they used their money on
the current spate of office and shop developments.

To sum up then, the marina developer had first to contend with a
relatively unknown market, a much higher rate of interest charge
because of the lack of experience of marina viability, availability of
only a small proportion of the total finance required (for the same
reason) and above all stiff and almost impenetrable planning opposition.
Numerous planning applications have been turned down as being development within and contrary to our green belt policy, but lately smaller
local authorities are beginning to realise the wisdom of having marinas
within their areas. This, however, has still not filtered upwards to
their planning authorities, who only appear prepared to concede to
small additions to boating facilities.

It is hardly conducive to development to have to appeal unsuccess-
fully to the Minister every time one wishes to develop a marina and
the short and only answer is for an **organised** approach by all the
Associations close to yachting to the Minister for Environment for
serious consideration of the provision of special marina village zones.

It should be the duty of planning officers to assess the catchment
areas within their regions and to allocate suitable zones for the
encouragement of marina development after due consultation with the
appropriate specialists in this field. It is high time that the planner's
duty became more positive in approach rather than the negative effect
shown to date.

In this connection, it should be noted that whilst marinas abroad
have grown, there has been a steady decline of some of our seaside
towns. With the ease of air transport, holidays abroad are more

common, with the resultant decline in our obsolete boarding house resorts, which are in urgent need of revitalization, and what better way than by the change to marina villages.

The problem of finance will be eased considerably when special governmental consideration becomes the order of the day for marinas, and this will undoubtedly happen if the re-zoning action mentioned earlier is followed through. No financier will speculate more than is necessary and his finance will more likely be forthcoming if he knows that:

(a) There are no planning difficulties.
(b) The site chosen has a large catchment area.
(c) There is a good road system to the site.

The average financier will know that with these hurdles overcome and with the obvious demand shown in other countries already, he is assured of reasonable success if the design is carefully planned to meet the public requirement. This is the ideal time for such developments, as we have nearly reached the peak for shop and office development and the financial institutions are now more prepared to entertain new ideas.

4.2 *Location*

The question then arises as to where marinas should be created. There are three main areas, the first being in suitable coastal locations, the second in rivers and the third in internal situations such as lakes, water-filled excavations, etc. There are numerous sites available but they should be within reasonable distance of a major town or catchment population area. Some sites will require considerable expenditure to make them suitable, other will require less. Unquestionably, much in the way of what one might call infra-structure will have to be provided in retaining walls, piles, moorings, services and roads. Often it will be necessary to cut and fill in order to make a location more suitable and more attractive.

Owing to the high rise and fall of tide around this country, it is usually advisable to resort to locks to control water levels. For example, a tidal difference of 4·5 m (15 ft) would require gangways of 30 m (100 ft) in length which must result in either wasteful frontages or extravagant use of waterways.

All such expenditure has to be paid for by the back-up of residential and commercial building that will form the marina village or township.

Obviously, the larger the community the cheaper proportionately is the resultant cost per unit, as the cost of the infra-structure is spread further. Great care is needed in the selection of sites to ensure that there is a minimum of expenditure on non-revenue producing work. Fortunately, however, the most suitable sites are usually in rural areas, with the result that by the time the infra-structure is paid for the cost per plot of land after due allowance is not that much more than normal housing land.

Again one has to appreciate that it takes a reasonable size of residential community to warrant sufficient size of ancillary commercial development and it is the latter item which is usually the more profitable part of such a marina development.

5 A Typical Marina Village

Now to deal with the various types of development within a marina village it might be best to describe the ideal (Fig. 4).

One could imagine entering from the sea via one of the many locks, which are all electrically operated with traffic light controls either by a coin or by a specially cut disc which is paid for annually. The boat would be brought through and either moored outside one's house or in a boat basin alongside a block of flats or in the boat basin of the hotel or restaurant or club. There would be an ample number of refuelling positions and when the boat is finally moored there would be the facility of fresh water, power and telephone, all laid on. Adjoining the jetties would be ample toilets, wash and shower rooms. Within close proximity would be the village shopping centre and, nearby, adequate variety of pubs and restaurants. Off the centre would be a school for sailing, navigation and diving and, nearby, the marina club with all its amenities. The hotel, which could be reached by boat or car, would also be close by and it would have reasonable banquet facilities as well as the usual hotel amenities. If one were mooring beside one's week-end cottage, flat or home, one should be able to go from the boat immediately to the car and drive to one's permanent house. If the marina village were large enough, one would expect to have, in addition, schools, churches, tennis courts and even a golf course. If one had no place of residence, one would expect to either moor one's boat or to have it taken out of the water and stacked by fork lift truck in a multi-tiered boat store where it would be cleaned down ready for use next time.

To be a little more specific, the residential accommodation could take the form of say 20% detached housing with private moorings, mostly for people living there permanently, 20% week-end units also with private moorings and the balance in small apartment blocks with moorings at private jetties in a boat basin.

The cheapest form of unit development is, of course, flats. Not only is it cheaper in building cost, but it uses less land and less water frontage. Conversely the large detached house is the most expensive. A careful balance has to be achieved and a well balanced community is most desirable, to both meet the variety in demand and to lend colour to the concept.

Small week-end units could be provided by about 45 m^2 (500 ft^2) at first floor comprising a lounge, bedroom, bathroom and pullman kitchen sited over the car port and boat mooring position (Fig. 5).

Town houses attached to each other, taking up 80 to 95 m^2 (850 to 1000 ft^2), would cater for larger famililies, and larger private houses, completely detached, could be provided for those requiring such properties.

Flat developments catering for all combinations, from the bachelor flatlet to the large unit, would also be desirable.

The commercial part of the development would comprise the shopping centre, with, say a 1400 m^2 (15,000 ft^2) supermarket and numerous shop units varying from 55 m^2 (600 ft^2) to 185 m^2 (2000 ft^2) according to the size of the marina village. In all, the total area would be any- thing from 3700 m^2 (40,000 ft^2) upwards according to population demand. This would include restaurants, pubs and a small school. The boat store would probably be a portal framed structure capable of taking two tiers of boats stacked in threes – and would have wash-down and refuelling facilities (Fig. 6).

The club would be the focal point of the village and should, perhaps be adjacent to the hotel to have ready access to its banqueting facilities. As for the hotel itself, much would depend on the size of the ancillary boat-mooring pool, which could easily warrant bedroom accommodation for weekend visitors in the order of 200. Such hotels are, however, not anything like as viable as hotels in major towns and much would depend on the nearness of commercial towns to keep the rooms in full use during the week.

Finally, it would be as well to refer to some of the problems in marina architecture itself. Design forms will grow from the plan and location. Excitement in design will be created by making full use of contemporary materials to get the best visual effects inside and outside. The views over water, and particularly in boating locations, can, as we all know, be fascinating and will make their own effect on the architectural treatment to be adopted, and this will no doubt be enhanced by greater use of the cantilever. Above all, one must avoid the phoney liner treatment complete with dummy lifebelts used so much in the 1930's, particularly in our seaside resorts.

One note of caution, however, is in the use of materials in exposed marina locations. We are all well aware of examples of steel windows rusting, rods in reinforced concrete rusting through to the surface, incorrect use of timber which has distorted and, of course, cement renderings that have come away through incorrect specification. There is less excuse for such errors today with the knowledge which exists and the existence of an efficient Building Research Station.

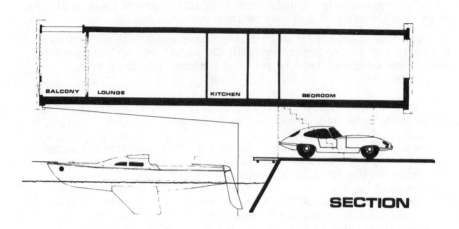

SECTION

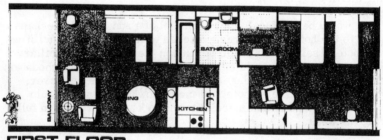

FIRST FLOOR

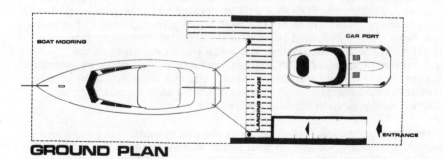

GROUND PLAN

Figure 5 Week-end house unit

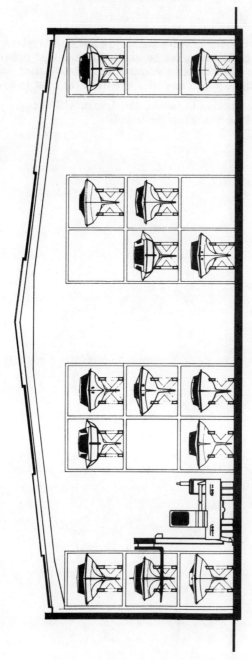

Figure 6 Section through boat store

6 Conclusion

The growth of marina developments presents an inspiring challenge to us all and one cannot help but be excited by the vast possibilities in the provision of well-oriented communities in fascinating and well-planned surroundings which can be a credit to the best in architecture.

If the necessary action is taken, the dream will become reality and the Nation as a whole will reap the benefit.

Discussion
(Session 4)

AUTHOR'S INTRODUCTION

Mr. Sidney Kaye

The main object of the paper is to illustrate the need for viability - to make the project happen-in order to emphasise the planning problems about which so much needs to be done and, in particular, to try to get the Ministry of the Environment to do thinking along these lines

One problem which arises when presenting a paper on marina architecture is that it is not something which can be dealt with in words. It is necessary to have the visual impact which can only come from seeing the building. Therefore I propose to show some slides.

(These slides illustrated a number of marinas and associated development in the United States and the French Riviera)

CONTRIBUTIONS

Mr. B. Poole (Second Deputy County Planning Officer, West Sussex
C.C.)

My impression of the excellent slides of American marinas which Mr. Kaye has shown is that they demonstrate more what not to do than how to do it.

There are a number of points in Sect. 4. 1 (Planning Control and Finance) of the paper that I would like to take up.

He has stated that 'the sole purpose of green belt is to create recreational area'. Of course, this is not so. The purpose of the green belt is to contain the spread of towns, and the only one which we have in this country is the metropolitan green belt. What we must preserve is important landscape-national parks and areas of outstanding natural beauty.

He refers to the Act of 1947 as holding up marina development. This Act was repealed in 1952 and I do not believe that much marina development was held up between 1947 and 1952.

I refute his comment of 'stiff and almost impenetrable planning opposition' which I do not believe to be the case at all.

Then we learn that it is the duty of planning officers to 'allocate suitable zones for the encouragement of marina development'. I believe that this is the responsibility of the developer and his advisers.

I do not think that the developer can expect planning officers to do all
the work and then say: 'This is where you can have your marina'.

Later, he describes the planner's approach as having a 'negative
effect' and expresses the view that it should be more positive in
future. I hope Mr. Kaye will realise, since attending this Symposium,
that with such studies as those of the Hamble River, Southampton
Water and Chichester Harbour, that there has been a great deal of
positive planning on the part of local planning authorities. It is
certainly not fair to say that all planning is negative.

The problem which the planner has is to try to fit the needs of
pleasure sailing and racing into the wider pattern of recreational and
environmental interest. I am thinking here of the interest of the
naturalist, the wildfowler, the walker and so on. In a case such as
Chichester Harbour this problem is very great indeed. Not only must
he try to reconcile these interests but to concern himself with the
wider implications of regional planning. He must be concerned with
matters of public and private investment, with highway planning and
public services and the cost of providing these services needs also
to be considered.

In fact, the planner's job is a fairly unenviable one. It is trying to
make sure that the right balance is struck between all the different
interests. This is something which this Symposium has brought out.
The theme is very one-sided, and it is fair enough that it should be,
but I would like to urge those concerned with planning for sailing
to try to consider not only the benefits to the sailing fraternity but to
consider the far-reaching implications for all the other interests
involved.

In Chichester Harbour, we have just completed a feasibility study
into a further marina development, which is again something on the
positive side. It seems likely that the people who will oppose it
will number thousands, and the people in favour of it will be in the
hundreds. Nevertheless, the Planning Officer thinks that it is the right
thing to happen.

The Planning Officer is the man in the middle, or the meat in the
sandwich. He is the person who has to take the kicks. I would like
some of you to look upon the Planning Officer, not so much as your
enemy but as someone who is trying to help and ensure that everybody's interest is taken care of.

Mr. A. R. M. Bryer (Senior Planning Assistant (Recreation), Hampshire
C.C. and Secretary Solent Sailing Conference)

I come from an office of sailors who happen to be part-time planners. I am delighted that Mr. Poole of West Sussex has, to a certain
extent said most of what I had intended to say.

It will not suprise you that I speak mainly with regard to Sect. 4. 1 in Mr. Kaye's paper. I agree that marina development need not necessarily be alien to green belts or areas of outstanding natural beauty. I can think of two marinas in Hampshire which are in such areas. One is at Bucklers Hard and the other is being developed at Harpers Lake in the Lymington River.

I sympathise with his feeling that planners have been laying a dead hand on marina development. My deputy chief, Mr. Hockley, who was here yesterday, has had the task of dealing with the early marina applications in our County. He had to tread delicately and aim to achieve a balance of interests.

It was the misfortune of pioneers in the marina field that they were dealing with a type of application to which planners were not accustomed. As pioneers, they had—regrettably—to pay the price. Caution means delay, delay means cost and, very often, what were possibly very sound proposals went under water simply because planning delays meant that they were no longer viable.

I agree that, in the past, planning control of marinas has tended to be negative. I also agree that the planner should fulfil a role of positive planning-not only in marina development, but in water development as a whole.

It was partly as a result of this that my chief, Gerald Smart, whom the Minister quoted yesterday, brought together a working party and then a conference, held a month ago, of those organisations concerned with the Solent.

It was evidence of how the planners have neglected the planning of water that there were so many different organisations which had to be got together to study this problem. However, it is a problem at which we are looking carefully, and we realise that we are not just planning for Hampshire; that we are not only concerned with Portsmouth, Southampton or the Isle of Wight. There happens to be water in between which has to be planned and that scarce resource-the coastline-which must be considered.

The constraints and opportunities for the Solent are shown in Fig. A. This map goes some way to showing future developers where they should be looking for development of yacht harbours and where they should not look. It indicates where the balance of interests favours the sailing man or where the balance of interests works in opposition to him.

I hope that from this sort of study, already pioneered in Chichester Harbour, the planner will give a more positive hand in planning for marinas.

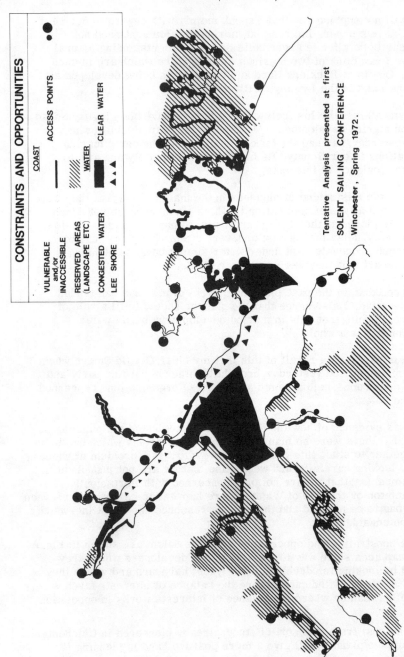

Figure A Map of the Solent showing sailing constraints and opportunities

Many pleas have been made by all professions represented here.
Mine is for early consultation of planners. The business of getting
planning permission is lengthy and costly, but there is no need to go
through a long process to employ consultants at great expense to
produce glossy, finished drawings and then have a heart-to-heart talk
with the planning officer concerned. The procedure becomes far simp-
-ler when the whole scheme has got no further than the back of an
envelope if discussions can be held at that stage.

I would like to have a quick jibe at the remarks made by the
Minister yesterday. He said, in effect, that people need marinas;
therefore, people must have marinas. I have a suspicion that he may
have chosen his platform carefully, and that his words would have been
different had he been addressing the Council for the Protection of
Rural England. In that case, it might not have been with such pride
that he read out the account of the Minister's rejection of his
Inspector's recommendations following a recent marina enquiry.

We must also remember that we are talking of a balance of scarce
resource and a balance of interests. Understandably, this balance is
heavily overweighted today by those interested in marinas. As planners,
we must look more closely at marinas and sailing as a whole, and at
the way in which marinas are used. Mr. Kaye showed us marina
villages, which are fine. However, if we are to develop marina
villages, they must meet the criteria of village development as well
as of marina development.

We must also look at the manner in which people use their boats.
As planners, we might discover that many people use their boats not
as boats but as country cottages and never take them out of the marinas
in which they are berthed. In future years, we could indicate areas
for marina development, such as north of Basingstoke, sunk in
concrete and close to the main road to London!

Mr. D. S. Tucker (Tucker Joyce Laws, Chartered Architects, Tunbridge
Wells)

Some years ago we were involved in a scheme to rehabilitate
Richborough as a small port, like Shoreham or the nearby Ramsgate
Harbour, for light coastal traffic and we planned to incorporate a
marina.

Unfortunately, this scheme did not go ahead and a large industrial
concern has subsequently developed the site for warehousing. This
is a pity, because if the R. Stour, which was last dredged in 1926,
could be dredged again the port could be opened to small coastal
traffic. However, the cost of dredging to Ramsgate Buoy would be of
the order of £ ½ million.

My client (a Dover yacht company) was offered another site, on
saltings, nearer to Pegwell Bay and a scheme has been prepared for

that location. The intended method of construction is to use a dragline to form a basin with depth varying from 1 m (3·5 ft) at landward end to 2·1 m (7 ft) at the river end.

It has been interesting during the course of the Symposium to learn how many schemes are linked with big developments in order to make them viable. By contrast, my client is basically working on a shoe-string and we are not relying upon waterfront houses or similar development. Only a chandlery, boat building and repair facilities, a shop and licensed premises are being considered.

The essential idea is to create an economical marina that yachtsmen can afford in terms of boat-length rental. If constructed, it will afford shelter for those who may be caught in bad weather in the English Channel.

Mr. K. J. Steel (Steel, Coleman and Davis, Chartered Architects, Taunton)

I feel that Mr. Kaye, in his paper, has not sufficiently underlined the severe responsibilities facing architects in the problems of marina design, particularly concerning buildings.

The theme which runs through many papers has been that, to make a marina viable, building development must be associated with it, and these are not buildings needed to service the marina. This is a very different concept from the waterside development which has grown up in this country over many years and maybe centuries, whereby buildings on our waterfronts have come about because of need—cottages for seamen, and buildings for the processing of fish, for the storing and maintenance of net and tackle, for boat storage and repair, and for lifeboats. These buildings have arrived upon the scene because they have been needed as a result of what is happening upon the water.

The buildings have been in existence for a very long period of time. In the majority of cases, they have been built of materials to hand locally. Therefore, they fit into the local quality of the landscape and environment without much friction.

We are now faced with providing buildings in relation to marina developments which are imposed upon those marinas for another need entirely. There is a real danger of a lack of understanding as to why those buildings are needed and of definition of their relationship to marinas.

There is also the grave danger that architects may fail to understand the impact of these buildings upon the landscape. They must be extremely careful in marina building—and this applies to marina building more than perhaps any other aspect of modern building techniques—to look very carefully, indeed, at the local vernacular, at the colour, texture and quality of local materials, and so on.

I stress this because marinas will be seen from the sea. In some localities-and this is a very good area in which to say this-many marinas will be seen in juxtaposition with each other from the sea.

One could create a quite disastrous situation where, visually, the marinas vied with each other and were very poor neighbours to each other, the waterside and landscape as a whole.

Therefore, I have every sympathy with planning officers—although it may seem strange that an architect should say this—in their concern at the possible problems arising from marina developments. There have been sufficient marinas built in America and France, and sufficient marinas development started in England for us to be able to look at it pretty carefully and anlyse what is good and what is bad about it. This country has been slow in getting off the ground in marina development. We may start late, but, in the end, we could do very much better than many other people, provided that real care and skill is exercised.

I hope that architects will realise their responsibility in this matter and look very carefully at our marina buildings so that they may be a good example to the rest of the world.

Mr. I. Noble (Renton Howard Wood Associates, Chartered Architects,
London)

Like Mr. Steel, I am particularly concerned with the importance of the aspect of a marina from the sea. In this country, many of our possible marina sites are located on some of the loveliest parts of our coastline, where there is a very flat and very beautiful environment. When one studies the various means of storing boats and considers the varied building installations which go with marinas, it is necessary to consider carefully the dramatic effect that such buildings will have upon the landscape.

It will be quite a task for designers—architects, engineers and everyone involved in the total design team—to take these environmental factors into consideration.

It is clear from the various papers which have been presented that the economics of the problems obtaining in marinas tend to be like those of the multi-storey car park. It is essential that as many boats as possible can be packed in. This means stacking them in high buildings which might prove disastrous to a beautiful, natural landscaped area of the coastline.

Many of these problems must be gone into very carefully. Otherwise, we will have marinas which vie from the sea for business in a manner which can ruin the landscape, environment and the natural urban development occurring in these places. As we have seen from some of Mr. Kaye's photographs, there will be large building complexes commercially advertising for business by sheer scale with disastrous results on shore landscape and environment.

That cannot possibly be the right solution.

Mr. I. L. Bailey (Bailey, Piper, Stevens Partnership, Chartered
Architects, Southampton)

I would like to describe the Eastney Lake project at Langstone, Portsmouth, (Figs. B and C) which after 10 years of gestation has at last received the approval of the Portsmouth City Council.

Figure B Site of proposed Langstone Marina, Portsmouth

The proposals are for a yacht harbour for some 800 craft lying at finger pontoons, together with piled or trot moorings for some 300 craft now enjoying the existing user 'rights' in the Lake itself.

The proposals, however, are for what might well be described as a new generation of marinas—the urban marina—since it also involves the planning and layout of some 1500 dwellings with all the facilities of a small village within the boundaries of the development. About one-half of the total area of 60 hectares (150 acres) will be reclaimed from the existing mud flats to create a yacht harbour complex which will include

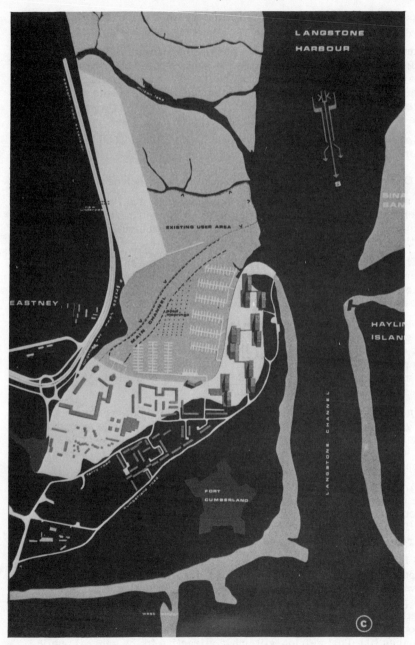

Figure C Layout of proposed Langstone Marina

shops, offices, community centre, chandlery and repair facilities, lay-up areas, a 200 bedroom hotel, restaurants, a pub, and so on.

At the present time the scheme has been approved in principle by the Portsmouth Corporation and is the subject of a Public Enquiry to be held shortly, and of an Act of Parliament which it is hoped will receive early consideration. Should the necessary consents be received by the middle of 1973 the initial dredging contracts are likely to be started in the autumn of the same year.

Later developments envisage expansion to 2000 or 3000 berthings and moorings overall.

Mr. O. E. Will (Halcrow and Partners, Consulting Engineers, London)

I am an architect, employed by civil engineers, and I would like to refer to the problem of a marina in an urban setting, a typical example of which is a scheme that my firm has designed for Hastings (Fig. D).

The general problems of access to a marina and the provision of essential services (sewage, public utilities, etc.) do not arise to the same extent, but there is the problem that in order to keep down the cost of the berths, there must be fairly massive onshore development.

Much thought must be given to this aspect. As Mr. Kaye has said, our seaside towns are tending to decay. They do not attract the same sort of business as they did and they have to make an attempt to recover some of their popularity. Here is where the urban marina has a role, and, located in a seaside town, there is likely to be easy access for a hinterland population.

In Sect. 5 of Mr. Kaye's paper some percentages of development are given but a question I would like to ask is: What sort of proportion of demand is there from boat owners for cottages, week-end units or self-catering units actually associated with their boats? And does this demand really exist?

Another problem which needs a lot of thought is the question of long access ramps and how to deal with them. With a housing unit associated with each berth the situation will arise at some states of the tide that the craft is not nicely in view of the house, but 8 or 9 metres down the quayside and out of sight.

I fully agree with previous speakers that architects have a great responsibility in the development of marina architecture. Mr. Kaye has shown us that, as a profession, we have a challenge to produce an acceptable contemporary style, although I would prefer the words 'contemprary idiom'. Port Grimaud and other developments are, undoubtedly, exceedingly popular; it is conceivable that development at places like Portmeirion will prove attractive to the general public and be viable economically.

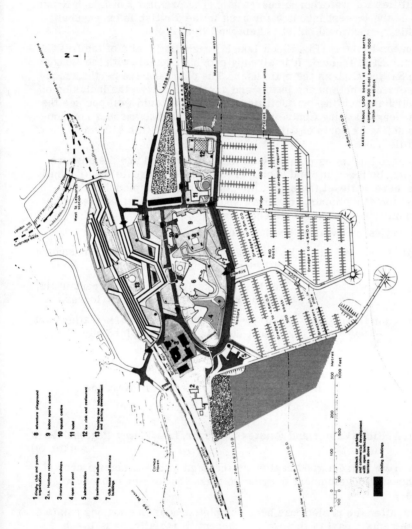

Figure D Proposed Marina at Hastings, Sussex

Mr. A. H. Bannerman (Chief Architect Planner, Craigavon Development
Commission, Portadown, N. Ireland)

The plans of the Development Commission include the provision
of facilities for waterborne recreation. The proximity of Lough Neagh,
which is the largest inland water area in the British Isles, ensures
that this recreational outlet is kept well to the fore.

Kinnego harbour (Fig. E), on Lough Neagh, is the site of the first inland marina in Ireland. It is already proving popular, with the Lough
Neagh Sailing Club as the main user. The plans include berths, moorings, services, both at the jetties and ashore, and, with the inclusion of
boat yard and hauling-out facilities, the marina could well become the
Lough Neagh Boating Centre with lower key Marina/harbour developments acting as ports of call around the shores of this 410 km^2
(160 mile^2) lake.

Kinnego Marina is planned with the user in mind and the onshore
facilities, both boating and social, are designed to create the all family
atmosphere while, at the same time, through proper planning and
disposition of elements, creating a specialist centre attractive to the
very demanding water sports enthusiast.

Facilities included in the plan are:

Central Services:	Water, power (electric), fuel, crane, launching facilities, car parking, moorings.
Social Facilities:	Club/bar/snacks, function rooms, restaurant, changing rooms, toilets, showers, lockers.
Commercial/Boat yard:	Do-it-yourself area, dinghy park/trailer park, keelboat storage, chandlery, food store, gas sail loft.
Sailing School:	Classroom, dormitory, galley.
Caravan/Camping Site:	Toilets, amenity facilities. Wardens accommodation.

Mr. F. A. Rice (Valuer and Estates Surveyor, Lee Valley Regional Park
Authority)

We have heard a good deal about the need to link a marina project
with housing development in order to make the former economically
viable.

But, after the project has been completed, does the housing estate or
village remain part of the overall concept financially, or is it subsequently hived off and the 'uneconomical' marina allowed to silt up or
go into disrepair?

This problem, which probably worries local planning authorities
when considering applications, will have to be faced if there is to be
the type of marina development proposed by Mr. Kaye.

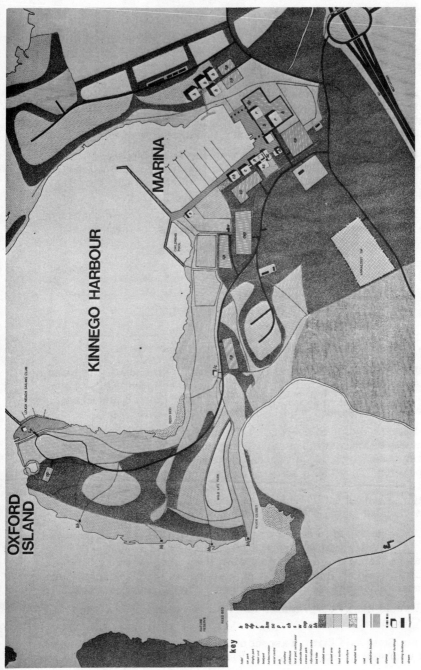

Figure E Kinnego Harbour Marina, Lough Neagh

Mr. J. G. Berry (Bertlin and Partners, Consulting Engineers, Redhill)

The motor car in a marina village can be an awful nuisance.
Perhaps Mr. Kaye could say how this problem is dealt with at places
such as Port Grimaud.

Mr. J. R. Barrett (City Planning Department, Bristol)
Mr. Kaye's slides showed that most developments abroad came
right up to the water front and there appeared to be no facility for
pedestrian access to allow the general public to the watersides.

In the urban situation, this is a very important facility. Walking by
the waterside affords a very agreeable passive recreational pastime to
many, and we in Bristol tend to treat our watersides as a very
valuable resource.

How far is it necessary for the developer's control to extend over
the waterfronts and need he curtail public access to these areas?

AUTHOR'S REPLY

Mr. Sidney Kaye

Mr. Poole mentioned that I had referred to green belt. My reference
was taken from an official document which mentioned that they were
intended primarily for the promotion of recreation. If that is not
correct, then the document is incorrect.

I referred to the betterment levy only as an example of the difficulties which we encounter. It is not the major reason, and was
never meant to be. I did say that there was stiff and impenetrable
opposition. This I have actually experienced when I have spoken to
town planners. I should not really blame them, because I think that
they are hedged with a number of circulars from the Ministry of the
Environment laying down their terms of reference.

I was delighted to hear from Mr. Bryer that their first conference
to deal with the future of yacht harbours was held a month ago. This
is along the right lines. As an architect standing outside all this,
I naturally do not know what is in the minds of the planning officers or
what they plan for the future. I can only quote from my own experience.

I would like to congratulate Mr. Poole on what is being attempted
at Chichester.

Mr. Steel said that the aspect of the architect's responsibility was
not emphasised enough. Whilst I agree in principle, I think that most

architects have a strong sense of responsibility, and that they would treat a development of this nature with the greatest of care.

He mentioned that buildings arrive through a need and that such buildings use local material which fits into the landscape. I agree with this comment. This has been the reason for the type of architecture seen on the north-east coast of the United States which is peculiar to that coast. It sprang from a natural need.

I refrained particularly from showing anything of what I would suggest, because I believe that this must arise from a particular requirement in a particular locality which would make use of local material in the way mentioned by Mr. Steel.

He also mentioned the building of marinas within the landscape. I stressed this when showing Fig. 4 (p. 299) to prove that it whould be landscaped, sheltered and treated well.

The interesting points made by Mr. Bryer seemed in contrast to those made by Mr. Poole. With Mr. Bryer, I felt that active consideration was being given to the question of marinas. I feel that this is a very hopeful sign. I agree that there should be early consultation with planners and that marina villages should be subject to the same sort of control that applies to village development. Here I think we are speaking with one voice.

Mr. Noble mentioned that many marinas are on flat coastline, and the effect of these upon the coastline needs to be examined. This is a very valid point and one which I have covered already in connection with the problem of landscaping, using raised ground to shield the marina village.

I could not agree more about the problem posed by the prospect of blocks of flats dominating the skyline. These would be bad, and would be wrong in every sense, architecturally speaking.

Mr. Will asked about the percentage of development quoted in the paper. The demand will be arrived at by market research among the people likely to go there. In that way, the actual figures can be ascertained.

The important question of freedom of access is a matter on which I cannot comment, other than to say that much must depend upon the actual location.

Mr. Rice mentioned the fear of development taking place to the detriment of the marina. I would have thought that any sensible developer would not wish to do that, because the success of that development must depend on providing boat positions, boat moorings and so on. In any case, I am sure that this could be covered by town planning regulations.

Mr. Berry asked about the way in which the motor car problem is dealt with in Port Grimaud. I must say that I did not see very good provision there. In the main, there were open car parks, and cars were often left in the street or yard in front of the owners' houses.

Mr. Barrett mentioned pedestrian access to the coastline, particularly in urban areas. Again, the example which I showed in Fig. 4 (p. 299) was purely an illustration, and was not meant to be a definite form of policy. There are many areas in which pedestrians must be catered for by attractive walks, and there are many areas where this would be totally unsuitable-rocky areas, and so on. Wherever we have carried out London developments along the River Thames, pedestrian walkways were a must-and a jolly good thing too. I cannot believe that planners and architects are unconscious of this need.

Session 5

Chairman: **Rear-Admiral P. D. Gick, O.B.E., D.S.C.**
(President, National Yacht Harbour Association)

Economics of the Marina

D. H. Sessions

Marina Management Ltd.

1 Introduction

It has been said that a doctor should be paid only when his patient remains in good health. The marina consultant, like the doctor, is too often called in when the patient is sick, and, although he may be paid for his services, he would prefer to prescribe for a healthy client.

There are occasions, however, when the consultant needs to be clairvoyant, as witness an enquiry recently received in my office. "Please send me", the letter said, "all the information about this sort of project (a marina) i.e. designs, capital costs, expected return on invested capital, etc., etc."

I am not at all sure that the sponsors of this Symposium have not posed a similar question when inviting me to present a paper on marina economics.

Some day, perhaps with the aid of the inevitable computer, we shall be able to devise the instant marina, but for the time being we have to struggle with the multiplicity of variables in a more pedestrian fashion.

As far back as 1928, the National Association of Engine and Boat Manufacturers of the United States defined a marina as 'the modern water front facility for recreational boats'. I like this definition because it is succinct and aptly descriptive of something which may lie somewhere between a crowded beach and a waterside city.

2 Objectives

What are the considerations which prompt people to go into the marina business? Their aims may be as follows:

    (i)   Development of an existing waterside enterprise.
    (ii) Getting in on the 'boating boom'.

(iii) Complementing a property development.
(iv) An advertising medium.
(v) Creating a tourist attraction.
(iv) Making a short-term capital profit.

Whatever the underlying motives which project people into this business, I think we may assume that, if there is a common factor, it must be profitability, and I want to try to put into perspective this aspect of the marina.

There are many fine marinas in various parts of the world and I have had the privilege of learning something about some of them. They reflect, to a great extent, the nature of the society which exists about them and for which they exist. Not all of them are an unqualified success from an engineering or financial point of view, and in one country I was told "we no longer build marinas, we buy them up after the third bankruptcy".

In the United Kingdom, we have been late to come into marinas and nowhere yet have we rivalled some of our overseas colleagues' grandiose achievements. We obtain no governmental assistance, we have no pleasure harbours created by the State, and, for the most part, we have to fight to be allowed to spend our own money. Nevertheless, we are quietly producing 'modern waterfront facilities for recreational boats,' which, if unglamorous, are functional, if costly, are well patronised and which, for the most part, are profitably meeting their objectives.

3 Elements of the Marina

A marina may consist of some or all of these facilities:

(1) Berthing.
(2) Direct services (car parking, electricity supplies, fresh water supplies, toilets, refuse collection, telephone, attendance, administration, and security).
(3) Indirect services (haul-out, storage, repairs and refitting, chandlery shops, bunkering, new and used boat sales).
(4) Ancillary services (yacht club, hotel, restaurant, launderette, swimming pool, chalets).

As far as the ancillary services are concerned, I do not feel that these come within the marina orbit. They are properly the concern of specialists in the hotel and catering field and their relevance to the marina is no greater than to many other locations.

Therefore, I propose to consider the three elements of berthing, direct services and indirect services, all of which, in some form, are a necessary or desirable part of any marina complex, whether under common management or as separate components.

4 Berthing

There are many types of dormitory accommodation for boats, but we are concerned essentially with something more sophisticated than moorings and anchorages. The justification for the marina is that it offers convenience to the boat user and this means facilitating the use of the boat by making it accessible from the shore, enabling it to be sailed when required and providing such services as are necessary to achieve these ends.

The haul-out or dry land marina which relies upon 'instant' launching and hauling up has been successfully exploited, particularly where there are a great number of small motor boats which can be stacked when out of use and put into the water by fork lift in a very short time. This system, for larger and more diverse types of craft, has its limitations, but it has been in operation on the Hamble River for some time in a somewhat modified form.

For the most part, marinas provide access to the boat afloat by fixed structures in non-tidal waters and by floating walkways where there is appreciable relative movement between the water level and the land.

The method of mooring boats has been largely dictated by the rise and fall of water level, whether resulting from natural causes as in the Mediterranean or from artificial conditions as with a locked basin. Thus, it is normal to find boats moored bow or stern to the walkway where there is virtually no regular water level change and alongside in tidal locations.

It is very often desirable to employ floating walkways even for inland marinas where the water level of a river or lake may vary in times of flood or drought, but, provided such variation is seasonal rather than from day to day or hour to hour, the method of mooring to be employed may be 'end-on' to the pontoon, with outer fasts on to piles or buoys. This configuration is essentially more economical of space and less costly to construct. It is not, however, quite so convenient to the user, particularly in the case of medium and large-sized craft, as is the 'finger' configuration which enables the boat to be moored alongside.

As this latter is the most common layout in the United Kingdom, let us consider such a marina, what it offers the boat owner and what it can do for its proprietor.

One of the problems facing the marina designer is to determine a compromise between the desirable and the commercially viable. It might be desirable to construct a floating structure with such width of walkways that they would, in fact, become roadways, but this may not be practicable. We need walkways which are stable but of sufficient width only to provide ready access to the boats. We need fairways which are adequate for the passage and manoeuvring of boats, but not wasteful of space.

We have to consider the area of land and foreshore available to us, its configuration, what weather protection it can offer and how best to use the space. Berths can be constructed for a range of specific boat sizes or for multiple occupation. The amount of space required for indirect services must be considered together with car parking requirements, access and services.

We can be sure of one thing – no two marinas are likely to be identical in layout any more than two sites are likely to offer the same problems. It is for this reason that we cannot state that the capital costs of berths should not exceed a certain amount, although we can arrive at a range of costs which relate satisfactorily to the rate to be obtained from tenants or, according to our objectives, the price for which they must be sold.

The berths must, of course, be suitable for the type, size and draft of boats expected to use them, and the water approaches to the marina must be adequate for these craft. In many cases, dredging is a necessity, and, because of its high cost, the optimum use of a dredged basin is most important.

5 Direct Services

5.1 Car Parking

Even if we wanted to produce a marina without car parking space, we are unlikely to be allowed to do so in this country.

The maximum peak loading of marina car parks may be taken to be $1\frac{1}{2}$ cars per boat, but in some areas, such as Hampshire, it appears to be a uniform condition of planning approval that 2 car spaces be provided.

It is, of course, desirable that car park areas should be adequately drained and surfaced in some manner to prevent dust. Not less than 23 m² (250 ft²) of car park should be allocated to each car.

5.2 Electricity Supplies

There has been a considerable amount of controversy regarding the supply of electrical power to boats. Without going into details of the available systems it must be conceded that safety is all-important. The general demand is for mains voltage supplies and such a c rrent is lethal within a very short time if passed through the human body.

Undoubtedly, the best safety equipment we have installed to date includes current operated earth leakage circuit breakers, and, unless a better protective device can be found, such equipment should be considered essential.

The cost of an electrical distribution system can be high and may be aggravated by the necessity for a mains supply transformer installation. On the other hand there should be recovery of costs from the end users which will greatly reduce the bill for consumption. Apart from electrical power supplies to the boats, we must provide for general lighting of the berths and walkways, car parks and buildings.

5.3 Toilets

It is necessary to provide toilets and showers at all marinas, and, if legislation precludes the use of discharge toilets in boats, the incidence of shore facilities will need to be increased. On inland sites it may also be necessary to provide facilities for emptying chemical toilets.

I would suggest that provision be made for six W.C.'s and six showers per 100 boats in the marina. As most marina sites will be low-lying there is also the problem of sewage disposal even when main drainage is available in the vicinity.

5.4 Refuse Collection

It is always surprising that so much refuse arises from a boat. Most of it used to go over the side, but, in the marina, people must not be allowed to jettison anything insoluble or even remotely indestructible.

Fortunately, the provision of paper sacks and receptacles is not a particularly costly operation. Sacks can be handled easily when full and replaced quickly. Nevertheless, this is a service we cannot neglect and adequate provision of receptacles must be included in our budget.

5.5 Telephone

Although it may be considered essential in some very sophisticated marinas for piped T.V. and telephone facilities to be plugged into each boat on arrival, in this country the boat owner appears to be glad to get away from this particular aspect of civilization.

Nevertheless, a telephone connection to the national network may be arranged as a direct contract between the boat owner and Post Office Telephones, or, if the marina complex boasts a PBX, arrangements may be made for internal as well as external connections. Generally, in the United Kingdom, the demand for direct telephone service in our marinas is not as yet of major importance, but should not be ignored at the planning stage.

5.6 Attendance

This is a very important service indeed. Marina staff are responsible for a great deal of the goodwill of the enterprise. They are the prime point of contact between the organisation and its customers.

Duties of pier or dock masters will generally include assistance to
berth holders, direction of visitors, refuse collection, watering, the
issue and receipt of keys, taking instructions for work to be done,
taking messages, recording movements, giving weather and tidal
information, and minor maintenance work.

In view of the importance of their duties and their effect on customer
relations, a great deal of care should be given to the choice of such
personnel.

Security will be largely in the hands of dockmasters, and, ideally
their duty periods should be arranged to cover the whole of the 24 hours.
It must be remembered that berth holders will require access to and
from their boats at all hours, and, however good security may be
ashore, the marina will always be accessible from the water.

5.7 Administration

Whether the marina is concerned only with berthing or is a part of
a larger complex it is important that one person or one office should
have complete control of dealings with berth holders.

Good management of berths can make an appreciable difference to
revenue, particularly in the case of multi-berthing where there is
greater flexibility in space usage.

The marina office will be responsible for dealing with enquiries,
completing agreements, invoicing, correspondence, supervision of
staff, keeping records of boat movements, obtaining supplies and
general clerical work. Customers should be able to contact the
person in charge of the marina when necessary.

Boat owners have to pay high prices for marina berths; their boating
is recreational and they wish to enjoy it. In a small community one
dissatisfied customer can very quickly make his complaints known,
and, therefore, personal relationships between the customers and the
marina manager and staff are all important. The running of a marina
is very different, in this respect, to a motor repair shop. Whereas
car owners have been conditioned to accept what they are given, the
boat owner expects service of a much higher standard.

6 Indirect Services

6.1

Those services I have termed 'direct' are really essential to the
berthing of boats, but they are not sufficient, in isolation, to attract
customers unless other services are available.

In certain conditions it may be that additional services are available
from others, but it is generally a good principle to provide as much
as possible of a customer's requirements, particularly if such

additional services can be made profitable. The majority of marinas in this country are of boatyard parentage and in this case many of the indirect services may be available. It is likely, however, that they will need to be amplified or improved.

6.2 Haul-Out

The first requirement is to provide some method of hauling out and launching.

Traditionally this is done by a slipway and winch but in the marina where hard standing may have had to be made at considerable cost the slipway can be very wasteful of space. Where it can be used to advantage, however, it is desirable to install some form of trolley or boat carrier which is capable of transporting the boat ashore as well as removing it from the water.

Alternatives to the slipway are the fixed hoist with transporter, the mobile hoist, a crane and transporter or a fork lift in the case of small boats. Of these, probably the most versatile is the self-powered mobile hoist.

Whatever plant is installed it must be kept employed. If the need for lifting is minimal, a slipway may be the most suitable, but, in conditions where a thousand or more operations are called for in a year, the more sophisticated machinery should be much more satisfactory.

6.3 Storage

With a large area of hard standing necessarily provided for car parking, it is most important that this land is put to work. Boat storage is the obvious alternative to car parking as the two uses are required at different times of the year.

However many marina berths are available there will always be a great many boats on piles or moorings and a large proportion of these will require winter storage ashore. Also, some of the boats in the marina will need to be put ashore for the winter. Thus there will be demand for this service, and, if the haul-out facility can meet the peak spring and autumn demand, the storage capacity of the car park can be profitably utilised.

Covered storage is also in demand, but it is doubtful whether newly constructed sheds devoted to winter storage and summer car parking could pay their way unless there is an additional use for these buildings.

6.4 Repairs and Refitting

Storage buildings can, of course, become viable if used for repair work. Ideally, these buildings should be divided into weatherproof shelters where general repairs and refitting can be undertaken, and

heated buildings where painting, varnishing and gluing can be undertaken at any time.

Provided a satisfactory method of boat handling is available for
hauling-out and transporting it is possible to move boats into a heated
workshop from their outside storage position, carry out the work and
return them. In this way, the incidence of fitting out work can be
spread over a much longer period than if dependent on weather.

It is thus possible to obtain a better return from the repair section
of the business while providing an essential service within the marina
complex.

There will, of course, be a need for workshops, stores, offices and
plant to equip the appropriate labour force, and the introduction of
this activity represents a major addition to the marina. The alternatives are to depend upon near-by establishments to provide this
facility, to sub-contract, or to introduce a concessionaire.

6. 5 *Chandlery Shop*

A shop or shops selling hardware, equipment, clothing and provisions
will be well patronised in any marina, but the larger the number of
berths the better stocked the shop can be and the more attractive it
will become. A small shop carrying a limited range of goods in a
small marina will not yield a return proportional to the large, well
stocked, shop in a larger marina.

The fundamental concept of a marina complex is not only to provide
berths for as many boats as possible, but to take advantage of such
a community to provide, profitably, the whole of the customers needs.

The chandlery shop may be self-contained and therefore suitable for
a tenant or concessionaire, but there are practical advantages to be
gained from integration with the repair and refitting activity. If the
two are separate entities, there will be some conflict between the shop
and the repair department as to which may sell equipment that has to
be installed. Also, there will be the problem of duplicated stockholding,
and both these problems can be obviated by integration.

Physically, the integrated shop may be combined with the works
stores which will help in reducing the combined stockholding, reduce
the number of staff required and quite often reduce the cost of buildings,
stock control and administration.

It is important that the overhead costs of a shop are kept to a
minimum as gross profit margins average no more than 25% in this
country, a fair amount of capital can be tied up in stock and the shop
needs to be operational for seven days a week during the yachting season.

6.6 Bunkering

Perhaps the most dubious asset in any marina is its re-fuelling installation. At one time the oil companies in more than one country were positively generous in their attitude to the emergent pleasure boat industry. Sadly, the position is very different today.

The demand for fuel at the marina is seasonal and mainly at weekends. Diesel fuel forms a much higher proportion of throughput than at the roadside filling station and turn-round is very much slower. As a result, the time and cost devoted to bunkering cannot be recouped unless the marina installation is combined with a roadside station or run on a part-time basis.

Nevertheless, the boat owner must obtain fuel and the marina must provide it unless there is an acceptable alternative source of supplies nearby. At the best, a marina bunkering installation serving pleasure craft can only break even.

One alternative, which has been tried, is the provision of a fuelling craft capable of re-filling boats at their berths. This presupposes that berth holders will order the service between week-ends and it does, in those circumstances, have the advantage of obviating the movement of boats to the bunkering point.

In the case of a marina with wide piers, of course, it is possible to re-fuel from a small mobile road tanker but whatever method is adopted, or allowed by the authorities, it is unlikely that bunkering facilities will contribute directly to profits.

6.7 New and Used Boat Sales

Quite a different picture, fortunately, is presented by the boat sales organisation which requires little in the way of additional premises.

The production of boats is continuing to move away from the riparian boatyard to the inland factory; the waterside property, at one time essential to the boat-builder, has now taken on a different role which has been greatly clarified by the marina concept.

There is no better or more effective showroom for boats than the marina. It has its own nucleus of customers, it has space for display ashore and afloat, it has demonstration facilities, it has service facilities, and it has an atmosphere conducive to selling.

In the United Kingdom, due to a long standing unreality of price structures stemming from the small, part-time boat producer, there have been inadequate margins in boat prices. But this is changing rapidly and boat manufacturers are now realising that home sales must be made at the waterside by organisations capable of stocking, showing, demonstrating and servicing their products.

With realistic price margins, the marina can undertake the sale of new boats and can offer an unrivalled service to go with them. The same organisation can provide a brokerage service which is complementary to new boat sales.

This is another aspect of marina trading which can be let to a concessionaire, but which is also readily assimilated into the marina complex and benefits from integration.

7 Marina '72

So far in this paper I have endeavoured to define the objectives and the constituent parts of the marina, and I have suggested that, whilst the elements are, to some extent, divisible there is good reason to consider them as complementary.

I believe that larger units are commercially more viable than smaller units, assuming that existing and potential demand is encouraging. It is impossible to state the size below which no marina is viable because even a few marina berths, if they can be established at minimal cost, could be of benefit to an existing boatyard, caravan park, or hotel.

However, the serious developer is likely to wish to consider something more substantial, and initially to create a marina for several hundred boats.

Finding the right site, where capital costs are proportionate to the return, and where the demand will justify the operation, is the fundamental problem. If we assume, however, that a site is available, we can project some typical figures.

It is unlikely that any estuarial foreshore with a sheltered anchorage will be completely undeveloped, but for the purpose of this exercise we will assume such a site to be available and to be in the vicinity of a public road where electricity, water supply and main drainage services are installed. The site is assumed tidal, and the foreshore made up of silt over soft clay with a harder clay stratum beneath.

The approaches to the site from the sea are assumed to be unobstructed with a minimum water depth of 2·5-3·0 m (8-10 ft), with the land shelving from the adjacent road level to the foreshore. We shall need about 14 hectares (35 acres) in all, of which 8 hectares (20 acres) may be foreshore and 6 hectares (15 acres) consolidated but unsurfaced ground.

Acquisition of the site will involve purchase of the freehold above high water level and a long term lease of the foreshore and land below low water extending to the depth we require.

It will be necessary to dredge the basin and make up the hard standing. If the sub-soil is suitable it may be possible to avoid bulkheading between the two but as we require car parking space as near to the water as possible and as we need to make the optimum use of our site it may be desirable to construct a sheet-piled retaining wall. With the type of soil we are likely to find, however, this bulkheading will probably be a necessity.

It is unlikely that we can use dredged material to make up the hard-standing area and we must assume that material removed by dredging is to be disposed of. Our initial capital costs will be considerably influenced by the availability of a suitable disposal area, and the type of plant to be used will be conditional upon whether we can pump ashore or whether we have to take dredged material to sea. In this example, we will assume that a suitable dumping area is available within 16 km (10 miles) and that we are dredging by bucket or grab rather than with cutter suction plant.

A typical cost figure for capital works sufficient to establish pontoon berths for 500 boats in a dredged basin, to make up a sufficient area for car parking and essential buildings, with retaining wall, toilet block, administrative offices and provision of services would be as follows:-

	£
Purchase of freehold land	100,000
Retaining wall	80,000
Infilling, roads and surfacing	50,000
Dredging	250,000
Pontoons and services	95,000
Offices and toilet block	10,000
	£585,000

Assuming that all berths are let from year to year at a rental of £26 per metre (£8 per ft), inclusive of direct services, but excluding the supply of electrical current and telephone charges, the maximum annual revenue will be £140,000, but we will assume £120,000 to cater for occasional vacancies. To provide the administrative structure and to defray annual outgoings inclusive of maintenance dredging and depreciation, but excluding interest on capital, an annual expenditure of £44,000 must be envisaged.

The return on capital investment will therefore be £76,000 or in the region of 13%.

Whilst this represents adequate cover on the basis of permanent capital employed, it would not provide sufficient cash, after taxation, to repay the whole of the capital if borrowed for a substantially shorter term than, say, 20 years.

Nevertheless, there is scope in these figures for a substantial loan to be serviced and repaid if the whole of the capital is not available. Inflationary effects on revenue will tend to outstrip similar effects on expenses so that progressive loan repayments will serve to increase the cash flow and profits year by year.

Whether Marina '72 is funded wholly be permanent capital, by loan capital or whether we raise money by pre-paid long term leases, by debentures, or a mixture of several methods, the prime importance of these figures is to establish the approximate profitability of the project in relation to its capital requirement. This will also establish a basis for the outright sale of berths if our objective is a short-term capital gain.

In view of the earlier references to indirect services, these should now be assessed in terms of additional capital requirements and return.

The installation of a mobile hoist and dock to provide haul-out services and to make use of hard standing for winter storage at Marina '72 will involve an additional investment of approximately £7,000 for the dock and £15,000 for the hoist.

Annual expenses, including depreciation, will amount to £6,000 a year; revenue, assuming no more than 1,000 operations in a 12-month period, should be approximately £10,000. Storage of 250 boats ashore should produce a rental income from the car parking area of £10,000.

Taking these two items together, therefore, we can expect a revenue of £20,000, a profit of £14,000 and a return on the increased capital of approximately 15%.

To provide repair and refitting facilities, we can assume an expenditure of £50,000 for suitable premises and plant, and a similar amount for working capital.

We can expect a minimum turnover of £150,000 yielding £26,250 or $17\frac{1}{2}\%$ after allowing for depreciation.

With capital increased to £707,000 our overall return will now be in the order of $16\frac{1}{2}\%$.

The chandlery shop will not make a significant contribution to direct profits, but indirectly it will have the effect of stimulating orders for the repair yard, and it will be of the greatest importance in retaining customers' goodwill.

Building costs should be some £15,000 and the average stockholding £20,000 with a turnover of not less than £80,000 per annum. A profit of £4,000 after allowing for all running costs, should represent a minimum contribution from this outlet without counting any indirect benefits.

The overall capital requirement is now £742,000 with the return virtually unchanged at a little over 16%.

If we are to establish a bunkering station, we shall probably be involved in a minimum capital outlay of £8,000 yielding virtually no profit. This will have the effect of reducing our overall return to rather less than 16% and clearly we shall need to explore alternatives.

Nevertheless, it is right to include this facility to obtain a realistic assessment of all the factors, even if the contribution is only in the sphere of goodwill.

Finally, by no means the least significant facility is the new and used boat sales department.

Allowing for additional offices costing £5,000 and an average investment of £10,000 in stock boats, this department should earn not less than £20,000 in profits.

The projected capital requirements and profits of Marina '72 may therefore be summarized:-

	Capital	*Annual Profits*	*% on Capital Employed*
	£	£	
Berthing and direct services	585,000	76,000	12.9
Haul-out and storage	22,000	14,000	63.6
Repairs and refitting	100,000	26,250	26.25
Chandlery shop	35,000	4,000	11.4
Bunkering station	8,000	-	-
Boat sales	15,000	20,000	133.3
	£765,000	£140,250	18.33% overall

Although the return on capital is shown above in relation to each activity, it must not be assumed that the figures can be taken in isolation. They are intended to show how one activity can be exploited as an addition to existing assets, as for instance, the usage of car parking space for boat storage.

It is assumed, also, that integration of each succeeding part of the commercial development with other elements provides for more economical use of assets, of labour and of management.

Fundamental to a situation capable of development on these lines is the need or potential demand for such a marina, but given these conditions the projection should hold good in general terms.

We must not assume, of course, that we can build a 500 boat marina where nothing of this kind has existed before and expect to achieve instant profitability of the order cited. Physical growth will have to be phased, but the more we can construct in the way of berths and buildings, provided they can be put to profitable use, the better.

Marina '72 has been projected here as a fairly typical cost exercise relating to the boating industry.

A development company, concerned with obtaining a short term capital profit, might wish to sell individual berths freehold or on long lease.

A marina holding company might elect to let the whole or the various elements of the marina to one or more operating companies. An existing boatyard might be interested only in the additional volume of work and sales arising from the marina and might find it desirable to form a separate marina company, largely financed by debentures securing the use of berths. A combination of financing methods may be brought to bear, such as permanent and loan capital allied to pre-paid short period leases.

We cannot here decide on a particular method of financing a project of this nature, but we can be sure that there will be no investment in a concern which fails to project adequate profitability.

Inland Marinas

B. S. Folley

Harleyford Marina (Thames) Ltd.

1 Introduction

In this paper, I have endeavoured, whilst being objective, to touch upon as many aspects as possible of inland marinas, drawing upon an experience acquired over the past fifteen years.

As is well known, the marine business in this country, and particularly the marine service complex, is mainly first generation. As a consequence, very little has been written on the subject. It is a topic, however, that at the present time is attracting a tremendous amount of public interest and is no doubt provoking a good deal of discussion and argument within the Department of the Environment.

We have often been told that 'leisure time' is likely to become a social problem within the next decade due to raised standards of living, shorter working weeks, longer annual holidays and ever-increasing incomes. Let us consider then who are the potential customers for the products of the marine manufacturing industry who are likely to require the services provided by an inland marina. This word, which originated in the United States, is widely used but seldom fully understood – the Oxford dictionary does not even list it! I would simply like to apply my understanding of its meaning – 'A marine service station comprising moorings, sales and service facilities, chandlery, provision store, fuelling and valeting service, with bar and dining room facilities available on or adjacent to the site'.

One could say that the least adventurous of the boating public are the potential customers for inland marinas. I do not consider this to be altogether true. People have to start boating somewhere and there is nowhere better to learn about boat safety and rudimentary boat handling than on sheltered inland waters. But, in my view, by far the most important reason for the keen interest in boating is that we all now live in an affluent society in which the middle income group has grown rapidly in numbers. Although people now have their colour television set, a second car, two holidays a year, they are still suffocated by the routine of their everyday lives. They still fight to board the same

Figure 1 Harleyford Marina, R. Thames

Figure 2 Bank mooring at Harleyford, R. Thames

commuter train five mornings each week, or breathe the exhaust fumes
from a million other motorists for three hours every day. They need
an escape. They need a release even from the pressures of the urban
areas in which most of them live. They need a week-end retreat!
They can no longer buy a country cottage, either because they are
unavailable or because the prices are beyond their reach. Therefore,
the obvious choice is WATER. A boat, even a modest little £1,000
cabin cruiser has romance about it. Also, and very important, it is
an activity in which the whole family may join. Thus, the modern
inland marina complex (such as Figure 1) can fulfill a very special
need in our society. At the same time it will ensure that the maximum
amount of water space, and the land around it, are left uncluttered and
free of a ribbon development of moorings, some of which may not be as
attractive as that shown in Figure 2. Despite the fact that there is
relatively little movement in and out of an inland marina basin, it must
be good planning to preserve the natural beauties of the inland cruising
waters that are available, for those who do wish to move their craft on
occasions.

Now, I would like to touch on the last problem and probably the biggest
that faces the would-be developers of any marina complex, whether
coastal or inland finance for such a project. The return on investment
on 'pure' coastal marina projects I will not discuss, but imagine the
problems facing the developers of inland sites, where the capital costs
are very nearly as high and mooring fees are generally abysmally low.

What can we do about this state of affairs? All I think we can hope
to do is to build into every scheme another commercial aspect, such as
flats or week-end cottages, or even a hotel, in order to help support
the very slow generation of cash flow that one obtains in a marina, and
to ensure that the 'overall' return on the capital invested is at a
sufficiently high and acceptable level. I know that this suggestion
contains all kinds of difficulties, mainly because local authorities tend
to be conservative, or because the local 'preservation' lobby for the
retention of the status quo is so vociferous, or because the site is in
the green belt, or for many other multitudinous reasons. However, we
must try and look at the problem realistically from all sides and accept
the fact that, unless there is sufficient profit in a scheme, then it will
not attract private or institutional support, and high quality inland
marine complexes will not be constructed at a rate in keeping with the
demand. It is estimated that at the moment, about 3% of the population
go cruising or boating, using about 700,000 pleasure craft. It has been
reported that the industry estimates that in 20 years time this will have
risen to 20%, needing about 5,000,000 craft! Where are the proportion
using inland waterways going to be moored, stored and serviced?
Very obviously, there is a big national problem. The spaces of 'open'
water in this country must be preserved for people so that they may
actively cruise in their boats. Therefore, more marine complexes
will be needed, and at an unprecedented rate of development over the
next two decades.

2 Location

Naturally the first criterion is that the site chosen should have un-
limited access to a navigable river or canal system, preferably with an
eventual outlet to the sea, or access to a sufficiently large cruising
area of open inland water consisting of lakes and/or rivers.

Having accepted that, there are really only two other factors. How
near is the site to intensive population centres and how good is the
road access? The former is not nearly as important as the latter.
Good road access is the most important consideration when looking at
a possible site. One can discount, almost completely, public transport
services, with the possible exception of air transport. People who use
boats on inland waters rarely, in my experience, use public transport
of any kind for travelling to and from their boat. The season, as one
goes further north, tends to become substantially shorter; therefore,
it would seem wise to confine marina development to within easy striking distance of the main population centres, thus enabling customers to
derive the maximum benefit and obtain the maximum utilisation from
their craft. Apart from the shorter season, these arguments currently
seem sensible because of the comparatively undeveloped state of the
business in the north of England and in Scotland, compared with the
southern half of the country. I am convinced that in the south, with the
possible exception of the extreme south-west, it does not really matter
if a development is a long way from main population centres, providing
it is a composite development and to the highest possible standards.
People will travel a long way over adequate roads if the service they
receive is of a good standard and the environment is sufficiently
attractive.

3 Demand

This is something extremely difficult to assess. We can look at the
statistics mentioned earlier, check with all the authorities controlling
inland waterways how many craft are registered or licensed, and then
take this as a percentage of the total. Whatever the percentage may be,
it is certainly more likely in future years to be a reducing, rather
than increasing figure, due to the fairly intensive usage of all inland
waters at the present time. The fact is that, when these waterways
become crowded to saturation, only the coastal waters will be left,
and, fortunately, here there is almost limitless space for cruising
and marine development although not always in such calm and congenial
conditions.

At the moment, all the inland marinas that belong to the National
Yacht Harbour Association would appear to provide approximately
2,500 berths. If we multiply this figure by four to account for all the
other mooring spaces that are not represented in this membership,

then we see that this is 1·4% of the 700, 000 pleasure craft in use at the
present time. If one accepts this as a straight statistic, then in 1992
a further 70, 000 moorings will have to be provided on inland waters.
But will the water area available be able to accommodate this number
of craft? The actual number of moorings provided by every small and
large boating establishment is, I suspect, an almost impossible figure
to assess, without carrying out a very expensive survey. One thing is
certain. Boating is here to stay, year by year it is becoming more
popular. People are being forced off the roads on to the water. It is a
tremendous growth industry, part of one of the biggest growth
industries – 'leisure'. Assessing demand in a particular area is
guestimate, based on experience allied with intuition and some cold,
hard facts taken from local market research.

4 Planning

When all the donkey work has been done and the site selected, the
first step is to engage an architect who has had some experience in
this field. This may be extremely difficult as there must be very few
sites that are at the moment fully developed, which have been designed
from scratch. Therefore, it is probably much more sensible to
approach a consultant who has had considerable experience in this field
and who probably has a wider knowledge of the business and the problems
associated with it, than any other single person. Perhaps the consultant will be as difficult to find as the architect!

Assuming that a consultant has been engaged, he will be able to
recommend a suitable architect and between them an acceptable draft
scheme will evolve, which can then be taken to the local planning and
river authority for first consultations and reaction. To many of us
within the industry, this may appear to be taking a sledge hammer to
crack a nut, as many of the establishments that we see today, both
coastal and inland, have grown up over many years in a most haphazard
way. However, in these days it is vital to have an overall scheme for
a site, with estimated completion dates for the various phases of
development, if for no other reason than the most important of all, how
much is going to be earned from entering into such a project? A consultant who has had practical experience within this specialised field
will save a developer his substantial fee many times over when the
costing stage is reached, due to his expert knowledge of the engineering
and design problems involved in inland marina development and of the
constructional materials available on the market and their practical
application. In my experience, it is much better, once a site has been
decided upon, to draw up a draft overall scheme and discuss this with
the local planning authority before even an outline planning application
is made. This will inevitably save a lot of frustration and expense in
the long term.

5 Detailed Design and Layout

I have already said that a marina scheme will hardly stand alone as a viable proposition, the only possible exception being a scheme funded from the profit of a large company which may be seeking diversified investment in another field in order to establish a capital asset. It is my belief that this is the only reason for aiming at something other than a composite development, as the generation of cash flow is slow and the percentage return on investment quite small.

Having made this point, the detailed design should incorporate the following basic services – moorings, repair/service facilities, craneage, fuel, sales area, fresh water, chemical closet disposal points, garbage disposal, flush toilet and shower blocks, and adequate car parking spaces, averaging perhaps 1.5 per berth.

Ideally, the mooring spaces should be situated off the main stream, if on the river, and in the most sheltered area of the site, if on a lake side. Very careful thought should be given to the size of the access and the shape of the basin as thoughtless planning here can escalate the investment by many thousands of pounds.

Once this has been decided upon, one should consider the site of the boatlift in relation to the repair and service building and the hard-standing area for winter storage and outside summer maintenance. Remember, every time a boat is moved a foot further than necessary, it costs the operator money. This inevitably reflects in the charge made to the customer and ultimately affects the whole industry. Repair and maintenance costs when coming out of an individual's pocket are scrutinised very carefully, perhaps unlike those which a company may pay. Therefore, the flow pattern of 'work' is terribly important.

The fuelling facility should be located where it is easy to get alongside, where it can be seen, and where it can be serviced by one of the existing staff without a lot of extra cost. Again, it should be noted that there is little or no profit in selling fuel in an inland marina. It is a necessary evil as part of the service. Therefore, it is sensible to ensure that the fuelling wharf operation influences the operating overheads to the minimum extent and that the investment in fuelling site 'works' is kept relatively low.

The car park for customers should be located right outside the showroom, or at least the access road to it should run alongside. If there is a showroom full of goods for sale, it is desirable that everyone should be able to see them. The boat owner's car park should be as near as possible to the entrances of the various mooring pontoons, for today people just do not want to walk a yard further than is necessary! In any event, an adequate number of hand luggage trolleys should be provided so that owners do not have to stagger down to their boat mooring positions under mountains of luggage, perhaps having to make several journeys.

The works reception office should be adjacent to the workshops, so that the owners can only obtain access to their boats when they are being worked upon, at the express invitation of the works manager or foreman and accompanied by him. The workshop in a marina complex can contribute handsomely to the profits, but it certainly will not if a lot of 'down-time' is added to the overheads, because an owner is standing idly chatting with staff working on his boat, who would normally be charged out at £2 to £3 per hour.

If I may quote a little story from a fitter within our own organisation — he was working on a boat afloat with the owner standing watching. The owner said "would you like some tea?" "Thank you very much" the fitter replied, as he indicated the stop-watch attached to the board containing his worksheets "but the time lost will be included in your account!" A rather suprised owner then left the boat somewhat hurriedly, leaving the fitter to get on with his work.

One could continue in this vein for several more pages, but I hope that the points I have made amply demonstrate the necessity for meticulous care, right to the final set of drawings, to make absolutely sure that the layout is as workable and as economical to construct as possible. An extra set of drawings is far less expensive than making alterations during construction. I speak from experience!

6 Aesthetic Considerations

This aspect of development is causing my own particular company more and more concern, and is undoubtedly affecting others in this industry. We have just lost a planning application on a site which in our view was ideally suited for development as an inland marina (Figure 3). There were four main reasons given for the refusal and I will not detail them here. Suffice it to say, rather sadly, that the County Planning Authority in their wisdom, imputed that such a development would have a detrimental effect on the visual amenities of the area and detract from the residential properties situated on land of high land-scape value overlooking the site, and, in addition, detract also from the residential area adjacent to the proposed yacht basin.

One could say that this is a matter of opinion, and is the reason why we have democratically elected county planning committees to give informed views on matters of this kind, and to control development in the best interests of the community. It is my firm belief that these grounds for refusal are unreasonable, are stock amunition from the phraseology locker of many local authorities and are hardly ever applicable to proposals embracing inland mooring facilities.

In days before the creation of leisure facilities had even started to become a problem, probably before the Ship and Boatbuilders National Federation was even born, people flocked in their thousands to look at boats, large and small, wherever they were. The public at large, I

Figure 3 Proposed Gossmore Marina, R. Thames

suspect, still feels the same way about boats. They create just as
much interest as they ever did. Of course, aesthetic values are of
interest and the landscaping of a marina development is one of the most
important considerations on an inland waterway. Developers must
create an acceptable and attractive environment around the yacht basin,
otherwise some owners will actually use their boats in search of something more attractive to look at, instead of just enjoying their week-end
retreat in idyllic surroundings. No, these grounds for refusal are no
longer applicable. An inland yacht basin, properly planned, well
landscaped and imaginatively laid out, looks far more attractive and
pleasing to the eye than almost any other use the site in question may
be earmarked for, including open space.

As far as the residential property next door is concerned, in these
hard commercial days and with the leisure explosion already upon us, I
suspect that most property owners would appreciate very much the
prospect of having first class boating facilities on their doorstep, even
if they did not use them. The fact that these facilities are available
must enhance their property and will certainly secure the future use of
the area for all time, which may be preferable to leaving it open to con-
jecture. The visual effect of any development is probably one of the
most important planning considerations, but with boats you are already
half-way there!

7 Period of Construction

This is a very big subject and a very difficult one. It certainly is
not possible to go into it at length here. However, I consider that,
basically, two alternative courses are open.

Firstly, if the developer has all the capital readily available, then it
must be right to buy the best expertise in the business, employ the
necessary contractors and complete the development as quickly as
possible in order that the maximum return on investment may be
forthcoming with the minimum of delay. Some typical costings for this
manner of approach are shown in the Appendix.

Secondly, if capital is a problem and the developer wishes to make
it available over a longer period of time, then it could be well worthwhile to employ direct labour for the construction and spread the work
over say six years. Meanwhile, the labour can also be made available
to give some service to the customer during this construction period.
In the end, this will in all probability not cost more in terms of capital.
However, owing to inflation, the money ultimately expended will buy
substantially less than it would if it had all been spent at the beginning.
There is the added advantage that any trading profit made in this period
will help to reduce the balance of any borrowed monies. This second
method may well suit a large company, with substantial profits, who
wished to diversify and create a sizeable capital asset with a reasonable
cash flow over a period of several years.

Before deciding which course of action to adopt I would strongly advise any developer to seek proper accountancy advice.

8 Operation

Let us consider the hypothetical site of some 4 hectares (10 acres) and 250 berths budgeted for in the Appendix. A manager would be required from the inception, with probably an office girl in the second year. Between them they would be responsible for letting the moorings and all office administration. The rest of the labour force is listed in the accounts, where the ideal situation of selling 100% of the labour is assumed. In practice this will never happen, because the fluctuations in demand will make it impossible to achieve this degree of labour utilisation. Therefore, it is fair to predict that all maintenance can be undertaken by resident staff during a 20% or so lost time period. For the purpose of the attached fictitious financial exercise the maintenance of the grounds has been excluded and this would probably be most effectively dealt with by the employment of part-time labour.

9 Conclusions

There are undoubtedly many different aspects affecting the design, construction, commissioning and running of an inland marina which it has not been possible to deal with in this paper.

The principal message I have tried to convey is that the industry and local authorities will have to do some radical re-thinking on the very special considerations that a marina application provokes if we are to see any growth in the number of inland marinas during the next ten years or so. The accountancy outline in the Appendix suggests that any commercial entrepreneur who is prepared to invest his money in a marina project, without a composite development, should indeed be welcomed and clasped to the environmental bosom most warmly.

Appendix

Outline Accounts for a Typical Inland Marina Development (area – 4 hectares (10 acres); number of craft – 250)

Production

		Cost	Sales (100% Efficiency)
1st year	2 men	3437	8640
2nd year	4 men	6873	17280
3rd year	6 men	10310	25920

Moorings 250 @ £130 per annum = 32500

1st year	–
2nd year (50%)	16250
3rd year (75%)	24375
4th year (100%)	32500

Summary

	YEAR 2	YEAR 3	YEAR 4
Labour Sales	8640	17280	25920
Moorings	16250	24375	32500
	24890	41655	58420

Overheads

	YEAR 1	YEAR 2	YEAR 3	YEAR 4
Manager	2250	2250	2250	2250
Office Girl	–	950	950	950
Wages	1000	3437	6873	10310
Advertising	–	1000	1000	1000
Stationery	–	300	350	500
Postage	–	100	150	200
Telephone	–	400	500	500
Audit and Legal	–	500	500	450
Workshop Expenses	–	400	350	600
Heat and Light	–	750	500	750
Rates	–	1500	750	1500
Insurance	–	450	1500	450
Sundries	500	1000	450	1000
Motor Car – Tractor	–	2000	1000	–
Depreciation	–	–	666	666
	3750	15037	17289	21126
Loss	3750	–	–	–
Financing 10%	375	–	–	–
Profit	–	9853	24366	37294
C/Fwd	£4125 (loss)	£9853	£24366	£37294

		TOTAL	YEAR 1	YEAR 2	YEAR 3
4 hectares (10 acres) @ £6250 per hectare		25000	11112	833	5555
	Financing 10%	2500	1112	833	556
Inland Waterway – Construct Entrance – 30 m (100 ft) @ £133 per metre (Dredging – Sheeting – Landscaping)		4000	4000		
	Financing 10%	400	400		
Basin – Dredging to approximately 3 m (10 ft) – 1·8 hectares (4½ acres). Removing 60,000 m³ (78,000 yd³) of material @ £0.50 per metre³		30000	30000		
	Financing 10%	3000	3000		
Stabilising, Piling & Landscaping to 3 m (10 ft) width 573 m (1750 ft) @ £50 per metre**		28650	28650		
	Financing 10%	2865	2865		
250 moorings @ £400 per mooring; Including Fresh Water Points (1 point per 6 berths) Electricity – Basin Lighting – Provision of Dock – Car Park for 375 cars – Landscaping Whole Area		100000	44445	33333	22222
	Financing 10%	10000	4445	3333	2222
Repairs, Service and Sales Building – 550 m² (6000 ft²) @ £54.5 per metre²		30000	20000	10000	
	Financing 10%	3000	2000	1000	
Boat Lift (2nd year)		8000		8000	
	Financing 10%	800		800	
Plant and Machinery (Second-hand)		5000		5000	
	Financing 10%	500		500	
		£253715	£152028	£71132	£30555

	YEAR 1		YEAR 2		YEAR 3
Nett Trading Loss YEAR 1	4125	Nett Income YEAR 2	9853	Nett Income YEAR 3	24366
			61279		6189
C/Fwd	156153 (loss)	Loss B/F	156153	Loss B/F	233047
		Financing 10%	15615	Financing 10%	23305
		C/Fwd	£233047		£262541
Percentage Yield on Capital Employed	2.7133% (loss)		4.0564%		8.4926%

NOTES:

No taxation has been taken into account.

Financing has been taken as 10%, although it is hoped that much more favourable terms could be negotiated.

All professional charges and architects fees, relating to the instigation and development of this project, have been ignored.

** Assuming rectangular shape.

Year 5 and *Year 6* taken exactly as *Year 4*

Balance C/Fwd	262541
Nett Profit *Year 4*	37294
	225247
Financing 10%	22525
	£247772

Percentage Yield on Capital Employed   13.08%

Nett Profit *Year 5*	37294
	210478
Financing 10%	21048
	£231526

Percentage Yield on Capital Employed   13.87%

Nett Profit *Year 6*	37294
	194232
Financing 10%	19423
	£213655

Percentage Yield on Capital Employed   14.86%

Discussion

(Session 5)

INTRODUCTION

Mr. H. J. F. Radford

I am a chartered accountant and the financial director of the Poole Harbour Yacht Club Marina, which is not to be confused with the Poole Harbour Marina about which the Minister spoke yesterday.

I am sorry that Mr. Sessions is unable to be with us.* I commend you to read-and read again-his most excellent and lucid paper. It is not my intention to precis his paper, which I am sure most of you will follow with ease, but only to highlight those point which I feel require extra emphasis.

At the outset, though, I must say that there are certain views expressed in the paper with which I disagree. In particular, I would not like it to be thought that the profitability of marinas is as great as he has projected in his illustration Marina '72 (Sect. 7).

On the question of definition—what, indeed is a marina? From Mr. Bertlin's paper we will be aware that marinas can have a wide range of shapes and sizes. The south coast is the area with which I am most familiar, and here they vary from a converted floating bridge in Southampton, to the monument to King Canute now being built just to the east of Hove. I am, therefore, in full agreement with Mr. Sessions when he assures us that the one thing of which we can be certain is that no two marinas are alike.

In looking at the development of marinas, the developer must endeavour to make maximum use of the land and water area available. He must undertake a scientific study of the available space, and endeavour to so design the berth layout to obtain the maximum amount of berth footage.

At this Symposium, there has been a lot of broad generalisation on the question of numbers of craft. Mr. Hockley, in his paper, for example, states that the projected capacity of the River Hamble has been assessed at 3,000 craft. This figure is arbitrary, particularly so when considering the varying length of craft. A marina for 250 craft, in which each vessel is 7·5 m (25 ft) long, is an entirely different proposition from a marina for the same number of craft when each vessel is 18 m (60 ft) long.

In studying the berth layout for our marina, we found that there would be a higher density of occupation, or a greater overall length of berthage, with the smaller length craft. The reason, of course, is that smaller craft are narrower in the beam and need a smaller turning circle, for access to the berth.

---

* Unfortunately, Mr. D. H. Sessions was taken ill just before the Symposium and was unable to introduce his paper. Mr. H. J. F. Radford very kindly agreed to take his place.

Where it is practicable—and assuming that the engineers advising on design say that the overall design permits this situation—it is obviously sensible to provide only sufficient depth of water needed for each type of craft. For example, a motor cruiser draws, on average, 0·75-0·9 m (2·5-3 ft). In view of the high costs of dredging, there is no point whatever, in normal circumstances, in providing 2·5 m (8 ft) of water at the berth of such a vessel.

Another important question to consider at the design stage is maintenance dredging. It is difficult to dredge when the pontoons are in place and the boats are at their berths; and it is very expensive to move craft to carry out maintenance dredging. Therefore, a margin of overdredging at the construction stage may well be desirable.

But the very first thing which a developer must do is to get his concept clear. He must study his market, and that market varies considerably in alternative locations. In Poole Harbour, for example, of the type of craft that would be expected to use the marina the ratio of motor cruisers to sailing craft is 3 : 1. In the River Hamble, the reverse is true. There the ratio of sail to motor could well be 2 : 1; and clearly, this aspect must be investigated thoroughly at the commencement. Furthermore, the developer must be quite clear about the facilities which he is proposing to provide so that the overall design can be correctly drawn at the outset.

It has been stated (Mr. Hockley's paper, p. 16) that the ideal situation occurs when the marina is an extension of a boatyard. I do not entirely agree with this concept. I do not say that it is undesirable that a marina should be an extension of a boatyard, but I do not think it right to give undue emphasis to this aspect. I believe that marinas can be built—and can be built economically and successfully—in areas away from boatyards.

Concerning the other services to which Mr. Sessions has referred, this aspect has been spelled out excellently and requires no amplification whatever.

With regard to costs, any formula which is put forward is, inevitably arbitrary. However, from a little experience, my view is that a developer of a marina should endeavour to achieve a 20% return on his capital investment, in terms of gross revenue, if the project is to be anything like viable. It is, of course, unwise to generalise, but for the purpose of this illustration I am assuming that operating costs, including maintenance dredging and depreciation, amount to up to one half of gross annual revenue.

I will try to illustrate this simply. We will assume that we have a site which we consider capable of providing facilities for 300 craft, and have been advised that this is so. The average length of the craft is (say) 10 metres. Because the marina will be built in three years' time, (allowing adequate time for planning etc.) a reasonable berthing rate may, at that time, be £30 per metre (£9 per foot) per annum. These are of course purely hypothetical figures. The average charge per berth, on this basis, would be £300 per annum for each of the 300 boats, so that the estimated annual gross revenue from letting berths would be £90,000. That figure must be discounted a little, because it is unlikely that there will be maximum usage of the marina for each of the 52 weeks of the year. Therefore, I suggest that—should the site be very good—an estimated sum of £10,000 should be deducted to represent wastage, unoccupied berths etc., and the actual gross income would then become £80,000. If a 20% gross return is to be achieved on the investment, the maximum capital sum to be invested in this project if it is to operate economically is £400,000. If it is impossible to develop the marina for £400,000, in all probability it is not viable and my advice would be to endeavour to find another site, unless of course there are other factors which affect and radically improve overall viability.

I would like to return to Mr. Sessions paper in connection with his illustration of Marina '72. The illustration in the paper is not, in my view, Marina '72 but Marina '68. Marina '68 was talked about in a yacht club, probably in 1962. Planning application was put in in 1963, it was turned down in 1965, an appeal was submitted in 1966, and the Marina was eventually built in 1968.

The formula illustrated may well have applied in 1968, but I doubt very much—in this part of the country—that the same formula would apply nowadays, largely because of the substantial increase in the cost of both land and civil engineering.

Mr. Sessions has illustrated a situation in which the estimated annual gross income is £140,000. Thus the overall berthing length available in Marina '72 would be about 4,700 m (15,500 ft), based on an annual rental of £30 per metre (£9 per foot). This means that it will be necessary to develop about 5·2 hectares (13 acres) of water.

Mr. Sessions then says that the planners in Hampshire insist on two car parking spaces per boat, and 500 boats means 1000 car parking spaces. In addition, in all probability a measure of landscaping may have to be provided. According to Mr. Bertlin's paper, it is reasonable to allow parking space of 300 cars per hectare (120 per acre). If provision is required for 1000 cars, the area required is approximately 3·4 hectares (8½ acres); and therefore, without facility buildings or landscaping, on the marina site, the development already comprises 9 hectares (21½ acres). I very much doubt that that area of waterside frontage in a suitable location can be acquired in the South of England for as little as £100,000. It just is not on in this locality, although of course it may be possible in less densely populated areas.

The title of this paper is 'Economics of the Marina'. One aspect upon which Mr. Sessions did not touch in his paper is the economics of

the marina from the point of view of the user and this is very important.
Yesterday, Admiral Gick made the point—with which I agree—that is it
unrealistic to compare the £40 per annum swinging mooring with the
facilities offered within a marina. It is difficult to quantify the benefits
offered by the modern marina, but supply and demand seem to indicate
that the annual rate now being charged on the South Coast of £26 to
£30 per metre (£8 to £9 per foot) is an economic rate, both as regard
the user and the marina owner.

Mr. B. S. Folley

Firstly, I wish to touch on the question of planning approval for inland marinas. The general reaction to marina proposals by most local
authorities—because of the policies laid down by the Government—has
very effectively contained the growth of essential yachting services
which I believe today's yachtsman and boat owner have every right to
expect.

After all, it is entirely a recreational activity and, by its very nature,
has to be confined to suitable waterside sites in mostly rural surroundings.

I would now like to refer to customer services that need to be made
available within a typical inland marina complex, and, in my opinion,
the inland waterways user is a very different person from the coastal
sailor and has different requirements.

There are two basic types of inland marina—the urban and the rural.

In the former case, there is usually the advantage of a shopping
precinct within easy walking distance which precludes the necessity
of providing these services within the curtilage of the yacht basin.

The facilities that need to be provided in a rural marina with a
minimum of 250 craft are as follows:

(1) General Store:

> From the customer's point of view it is an essential facility.
> From the developer's viewpoint, it is a non-profit-making—but, I
> hasten to add, not loss-making—service of convenience.

> Within the right environment, the inland waterway user wishes
> to forget about the clatter on the roads and the suffocation of in-
> tensive shipping precincts. He wishes to wander around a well-
> stocked shop a short distance from his mooring, passing the time
> of day with the staff, whom he probably knows well, talking about
> his boat's leaky stern tube and so on.

(2) Chandlery:

> Again, this is a complementary service expected by almost
> every boat owner in a large marina. From the operator's point of

view it is surprising what nick-nacks owners will buy for their craft when they go in to purchase an essential item.

If attractively laid out, well stocked and attentively staffed, this service can contribute substantially to the overall profits.

Both the chandlery and the shop must remain open for long hours—seven days a week during the busy season—in order to satisfy customers and catch the maximum trade which the berth-holders generate.

(3) *Laundry:*

Families often live aboard their boats at the moorings for days and sometimes weeks on end, especially during the school holidays. This inevitably creates a demand for a laundry facility, such as a launderette.

Whilst this service is not yet generally accepted as standard, I believe that it will fast become so.

From the operator's point of view, I do not think there is much attraction in operating one launderette. Therefore, it would probably be more sensible to sublet this facility to an established multiple operator for a modest rent.

This method of providing such a facility would ensure a reasonably quick capital recovery on the premises housing the launderette, and at a guaranteed rate. It would also take the administrative burden away from the marina staff, and, quite possibly, provide the customer with a better service.

(4) *Electricity:*

The availability of 240 volts A.C. for customer consumpton is, at the moment, a luxury that few inland marinas provide. My experience is that it is a facility which is not missed by the majority of clients when it is not available.

Most craft on inland waterways are not equipped with domestic-type appliances, and, therefore, have no need of it. Also, few boats are used during the winter months, when the demand for portable 240-volt heaters etc., would be at its peak.

The only other need for electricity is that required for power tools for owner maintenance. If the developer has no maintenance staff or facilities on site, then it is reasonable to have to cater for this demand.

However, if a comprehensive service is provided on site, the developer would certainly not want to see empty workshops, costing many thousands of pounds, unused while owners carried out major and minor maintenance on their craft.

Nevertheless, it is probably felt by all connected with the industry that the provision of mains electricity is an important service, as it will influence boat builders to provide mains-powered appliances, thereby encouraging a greater number of people towards the water. This will help the industry to grow stronger in the face of the stiff competition elsewhere in the leisure field.

(5) *Telephones:*

It is a nice little gimmick to be able to welcome one's friends aboard one's boat where a telephone is displayed casually upon the cocktail cabinet. It is no doubt a service which many budding tycoons would welcome. It is convenient to have the telephone close at hand.

However, is it really needed? The object of having a boat is to remove oneself as far as possible from the stresses of everyday life to prevent that early, premature coronary thrombosis. Would anyone in this hall really welcome the persistent ringing of a telephone at the very moment when he is settling down to a quiet siesta after lunch any more than its noise would be welcomed when at home? I suspect not.

Anyway, if we had to communicate with anybody, it would be far better for us to have to walk up the quay to read the message board after we have taken our siesta.

I feel that most berth-holders would prefer to use the customer service telephone in the shore building complex—or club, if there is one. The walk would probably give them a thirst, which is good for business.

(6) *Fresh Water:*

Fresh water is absolutely essential for drinking purposes, for bunkering and washing down. If every berth does not have its individual supply, then one tap with a sufficiently long hose should be shared by four or six boats, depending on the disposition of the berths.

Here I would issue a word of caution to the marina operator. If water is sold to him by a water board at a metred rate he should keep a careful eye on the cost. Boat owners, in my experience, are notorious for leaving taps running, and 200 to 300 have the capacity for using many thousands of litres of water a year, which can prove extremely expensive.

(7) *Sanitary Arrangements:*

It is my opinion that no solids of any kind should be discharged into confined water and certainly the Thames Conservancy have strict bylaws concerning toilets.

Every marina complex should have its own incinerator for disposing of refuse. This may be a sophisticated unit, contained under cover in a small yard, or it may be a pit up in the woods. Whatever it is, it will be in constant use. Collection by the local authority's refuse wagon once per week will simply not keep up with the demand during busy periods.

The only other method in common use is to contract with a waste disposal firm which, literally, takes the problem right out of the operator's hands. If this method is used, it creates aesthetic problems because a suitably screened storage area is necessary to hide the ugly—and very often smelly—containers.

While dustbins have been—and still are—in use in their thousands, I believe that the disposable large plastic bags, held in stategically placed stands, are more hygienic and less unsightly than corrugated iron tins.

An effective and well-run garbage collection service also helps to fight the possible pollution of the area. Nothing looks worse, when looking over the edge of the mooring basin, than to see plastic bags and rubbish floating in the water. If the operator strives to keep the area neat and tidy, the customer will respond to his example.

Various river and canal authorities have their own regulations concerning pollution, but it would be helpful were national standards to be adopted in dealing with a subject foremost in everyone's mind.

There are a number of other facilities, such as fire prevention, which time does not permit me to dwell upon here.

With the exception of the launderette, it is generally better to keep all the above facilities within the complete control of the developer and operator rather than to sub-let them.

I will end by dealing briefly with the administration of the yacht basin in relation to the berths. I strongly recommend to operators that no berth-holders are accepted or allowed to occupy space unless they have a term of contract with the company. Of necessity, this is a two-sided document which should enable the company to control the client and ensure that the client knows precisely what are his rights and obligations.

Furthermore, if the contract is for a 12-month period, I believe that the major proportion of the fee should be payable in advance so that the benefit of summer occupation and utilisation is correctly related and in proportion to the fee.

This will stop people enjoying the summer for half the fee and then moving away in the autumn, which they often do.

It is also far easier to relate the second, small half of the fee to the winter storage rates which the operator may wish to charge other customers who only bring their boats in for that period.

The letting of berths annually is an administrative burden. It is obviously best, therefore, that all bookings expire on the same date. April 1st in each year is probably the most convenient time. Furthermore, I believe that immense frustration can be caused when prospective clients book moorings and are then dilatory with their correspondence.

The operator can easily find himself, at the beginning of the season, with a dozen or so customers who have not paid their fee, nor completed the documentation. Therefore, I think it not unreasonable to ask for a small, non-refundable deposit of £10 or £15 when the initial reservation is made so that the operator is at least compensated for opening a file, the time taken to show a customer the available berths, and all the subsequent necessary correspondence should the booking not be confirmed.

CONTRIBUTIONS

Commander A. J. Dent (Managing Director, Lymington Yacht Haven Ltd.)

By profession, I am a seaman and a chartered electrical engineer. I am not a civil engineer, an architect, a contractor or an accountant. Perhaps, for these reasons and through a series of accidents, I have found myself building a marina.

The marina in question is shown in Fig. A, and I have just learned from Mr. Radford that it is uneconomic.

The figures given by Mr. Sessions in his paper (p. 337) relating to the economics of the harbour alone—and it is a harbour alone that we are building—are just about borne out by my personal experience.

We expect to see a net profit before tax of just over 13%. We reckon that, with 300 berths occupied, we are viable. With 350 berths occupied, we are profitable. With 450 berths occupied, we shall be all right and, if we are ever allowed to develop the site to its capacity of 750 craft, dependent upon both road and river access, we shall be in clover.

We have taken ten years to reach the stage whereby we are now contructing the marina. This delay is not, in any way, due to the Hampshire County Council Planning Department. In fact I would like to pay

---

* A general description of Lymington Yacht Haven is given on pp. 486-491.

Figure A Lymington Yacht Haven

a personal, and very strongly felt, tribute to the individual planning officials. I have found them most constructive. Their advice has been excellent, and their assistance in piloting variations of schemes through the innumerable public authorities has been quite invaluable.

Nevertheless, it was with some scepticism that I heard yesterday of the possible trend of the Government's intended support for marinas. Let me tell you that the current—and I stress 'current' and not 'tide', because tides ebb and flow—runs strongly in the other direction.

At a cost of £40, 000 we have had to install, to the highest possible standard, an entirely new surface water drainage system, for the benefit of the local authorities concerned.

In Fig. 14 (p. 236), the dredger 'Challenger' can be seen broadening the Lymington River at the behest of British Rail—in my view, as a seaman, to a quite unnecessary extent. An over-wide channel can be seen leading into the marina. What is not shown is a wide strip of dredging outside the area which has had to be provided for the Harbour Commissioners, perhaps so that they can lay additional moorings.

All these extra costs, including the afforestation which we are required to perform in an area so far denuded of trees, will run into the better part of six figures. Therefore, do not count on financial support from local government, whether directly or indirectly.

The question of the density of craft in the marina proved difficult to resolve. Evidently, a most important factor is beam. I, therefore, asked our contractors to arrange for it to be possible to vary the position of the fingers along the main walkways. This has been done and we are not now committed to a constant width between fingers. The locking device provided has, I understand, been patented.

With regard to the depth of dredging, we have heard much about the economy of dredging shallow. We have dredged deep all over the area to an average of 2·6 m (8·5 ft), and probably deeper, although we are only paying to the specified depth.

When dredging in tidal waters, what is saved by shallow dredging is lost by the limitation on the working of the dredger. Accordingly we have dredged deep and, as parts of the marina silt, the areas concerned can be allocated to craft of shallow draft.

Our geographical situation is right behind a mudbank, as Fig. 14 (p. 236) shows. The river put that mud bank there, and I have no doubt that it will maintain it. It forms a very nice natural breakwater. We are surrounded by sedge, and I think that it will be quite a good, simple harbour.

On the question of finance, we could not achieve the mystic 20%. If 20% cannot be achieved, no finance house will look at it. Therefore, we went to the contractors and said, 'Please, will you provide us with

bridging finance?' This they did. They designed the harbour, they are
building it, they have given us a guarantee of their workmanship, they
have provided the bridging finance, and we expect to repay them by the
sale of unsecured loan stock, the details of which I cannot go into without breaking the law because we are a private company.

So far in four months we have obtained one-quarter of the total
capital cost that we need and we have three years in which to repay the
loan.

We did not use consulting engineers in the ordinary sense, but relied
upon the design of the contractor. By mutual consent we brought in
the consulting engineers, Dobbie & Partners, to supervise the contract
and to act as referees.

Mr. A. C. Ball (Director, Beaulieu River (Management) Ltd.)

Some details concerning the planning, design and operation of the
Bucklers Hard Yacht Harbour may be of interest.*

The concept of the Bucklers Hard Yacht Harbour grew from the
Beaulieu Estate Conservation Plan commissioned by Lord Montagu in
1966 and prepared by planning consultant Elizabeth Chesterton in association with architects Messrs. Leonard Manasseh and Partners of
London. This report covered the conservation and recreational facilities of the whole of the 3200 hectare (8000 acre) Beaulieu Estate and
more particularly the Motor Museum, Beaulieu Village and Bucklers
Hard.

Originally, the harbour was designed for some 40 boats at the foot of
Bucklers Hard village, but initial feasibility studies, and the increasing
pressure of demand for moorings in the Beaulieu River, led to an amend-
ment of proposals, and after consultation with the County and Local
Authorities, the present site at the foot of Dungehill Wood was selected
for the following reasons:

(a) *Amenity.* It was possible to site a Yacht Harbour for 76 berths
within existing mudland, up-river but close to the facilities of
Bucklers Hard, yet sufficiently far from the village not to detract from its essential character, or from the character or
visual appearance of the River generally. Fig. B shows the
site before construction of the marina.

(b) *Separation of Tourist and Yachting Facilities at Bucklers Hard*
Bucklers Hard now has an annual visitor attendance of some
250, 000, although no additional attractions with the exception
of a small Maritime Museum in the village have been introduced. Conflict between the interests of tourists, and river

---

* A general description of this marina is given on pp. 478-481

Figure B Site of Bucklers Hard Yacht Harbour before development

yachtsmen, had grown appreciably over the last decade. By
constructing a new access roadway to the Yacht Harbour
through Dungehill Wood, together with separate car parking
facilities for yachtsmen, this conflicting interest was eliminated.

(c) *Ease of Construction.* The existence of a low-lying 7·3 hectare
(18 acre) field surrounded by an existing dyke just up-river
from the site enabled the use of economic cutter-suction dredging for the formation of the yacht basin (Fig. C).

(d) *Space Availability.* There was sufficient room to amalgamate
the Yacht Harbour and boat repair facilities, provide car parks,
and minimise dredged areas adjacent to the deep water channel.
The siting of the new boatyard immediately adjacent to the
Yacht Harbour has enabled the previous boatyard site, just
down-river of Bucklers Hard village in a site of supreme amenity importance, to be re-landscaped for tourist use.

Once the site had been selected, trial borings over the proposed area
were completed by Soil Investigations Limited. Valuable data were
supplied by Southampton University on maximum tidal variations, speed
of flow and estimation of future siltation. As a result of these tests the
original shape of the harbour was altered from a triangular basin with
the up-stream limit of dredge running perpendicular to the main river

Figure C The pier and Renner dock under construction at Bucklers Hard Yacht Harbour, with cutter-suction dredger operating nearby

channel, to closely follow the existing contour of the river over a widen-
ed area of dredge. Although principally this alteration was to reduce
siltation, it has resulted in a more natural appearance for the harbour
(Fig. D). Average tidal rate of flow is 2 knots, and siltation since completion of the harbour in October 1971 has been negligible.

The various advantages of a dock and/or slipway were carefully considered. The most convenient site for a slip lay over an area of soft
silt, which would have added considerably to construction costs (estimated at £12, 000). The provision of a concrete pier on driven RSJ
piles incorporating a dock (Fig. C) was slightly higher in initial capital cost, but provided an efficient and easy method of recovery and
launching boats both for the yacht harbour and the Beaulieu River.
The existing river moorings (260) justified the provision of a 26 t
Renner hoist and the boat repair shed was specifically designed to
accommodate this machine to reduce covered space to a minimum.
The effect of this facility has been to increase mooring rental values
throughout the River, and reduce labour requirements in the Yard itself.

Various alternative means of financing were considered, but as adequate alternative security was available a fixed-interest loan was
arranged through Hambros Bank for the total funds required. In a time
of rapid inflation this method has considerable advantages over deben-
ture sales securing the use of berths over long periods at fixed rents.

Site considerations, and not least the planning consent, restricted
the size of the Yacht Harbour to 76 berths. The initial feasibility
study indicated that in order to achieve an estimated return on capital
employed of not less that 20% for the yacht harbour and repair yard
combined, it was necessary to design for the top end of the market,
with forecast rents of £32 per metre (£10 per ft) overall length within
six months of the opening date.

At an early date it was also decided to reduce diversification of the
River Management Company, by letting the Boat Repair Yard and the
Yacht Brokerage on lease and concession arrangement respectively,
subject to short review periods. The Management Company provide
full facilities apart from the Renner Hoist, which is hired direct by the
yard tenant.

The Yacht Harbour is operated as a section of the main Beaulieu
River Management Company. Day to day administration is run by the
Harbourmaster and a staff of four, on a shift system divided between
river and harbour work. Policy discretion is exercised by Lord
Montagu through his managing agents Strutt & Parker.

Careful attention has been paid to important points of detail some
of which have already been mentioned in the Symposium.

For example, rope safety loops have been provided at water level

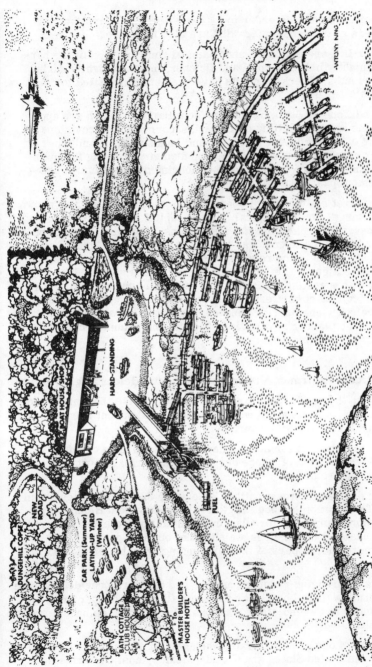

Figure D Layout of Bucklers Hard Yacht Harbour

at the end of each berth in order to increase child safety on the marina. Barriers at the end of gangwalks are also to be created

Securicor Ltd. are employed under annual contract to visit the harbour twice nightly between April and October, and once nightly during the winter months. Check-in points have been carefully sited to maximise this service.

The 'Conditions of Berthing' in the Yacht Harbour, which are applied under the terms of letting of all berths, carry strict provisions on the frapping of halliards, use of radios and loud speakers, and other possible sources of disruption of peace and quiet. By siting the main dinghy landing point downstream of the mooring pontoons, much pedestrian movement past berths is avoided.

After the first six months of operation the Yacht Harbour has shown a return on target for the magical '20% on capital cost' so often quoted by developers and financial institutions. However it should be remembered that no site cost was included in the figures, and no account has been taken of the related benefits to other River moorings which will have a general effect of increasing rental values. It is anticipated that operating costs in a full year will approximate to 9% of the gross capital cost. Certainly, even given an exceptional site and comparatively few engineering hazards, marinas often still fall a long way short of the planner's, valuation officer's and taxman's conception of 'a licence to print money'.

Mr. H. McGruer (Chairman, McGruer and Co. Ltd., Helensburgh, Scotland)

In Scotland, the prices paid for land are nothing like those in the South of England. But, unfortunately, we do not have a catchment area for marina clients which is so favourable.

In our investigations for marina development, we have carefully looked into the question of where best to site a marina and who the potential clients would be.

We have decided to site it on the Clyde some 32 km (20 miles) from Glasgow. The location is about 2½ km (1½ miles) from Helensburgh which is a dormitory town for Glasgow, with all the facilities required by marina users. Nevertheless, we shall not obtain a great deal of benefit from the developers of the surrounding area, but, in fact, we will benefit them.

There is no dredging required, and the bed contours provide adequate depth for shallow draft boats near the sea wall, whilst deeper draft boats can moor at the end of the pontoons. However, we do have a breakwater problem.

We also have one great natural advantage. I have sailed from marinas in the United States and Canada, Mexico, most countries in

Europe, Australia and Japan, and, at the risk of being considered blatantly nationalistic, I give you my biased opinion that the best cruising waters in the world are off the West Coast of Scotland!

Mr. N. A. Stead (Director, Gratispool Co. Ltd., Glasgow):

Mr. Sessions, in Sect. 2 (p. 325) of his paper, asks the question, 'What are the considerations which prompt people to go into the marina business?' I would suggest that an individual who has made his fortune elsewhere in industry and, not wishing to retire yet, may like to invest in a farm, dog breeding or some sort of self-supporting country estate. Alternatively, he might find that the development of a marina, with his own waterside home, allows him to have the security of money invested in land, sufficient income to support his property and himself in a manner which prevents him from stagnating, and also gives him the opportunity of doing something for the community.

But, I am of the opinion that, with very very few exceptions, the return on an investment in a marina development would require the investor to be motivated by public spirit rather more than a need for making himself rich. A marina development can give an investor relative security of investment in real-estate, sufficient income to live on comfortably, and an excuse to enjoy boating before tax.

In Sect. 6. 3 (p. 331), Mr. Sessions refers to covered storage which is infinitely more desirable from the customer's point of view and also, I venture to suggest, from the planner's and the neighbourhood's point of view, since boats on the hard standing, with tarpaulins all over them and people working, with pieces of timber lying everywhere, is rarely a very tidy sight.

However, the two things that kill it are, (a) rates and (b) planning departments. Perhaps the former could be overcome by having a special rating, as in the case of agricultural buildings. The planning department, on the other hand, should ask themselves again whether, in fact, some rather less expensive buildings would be as unattractive to the environment as the alternative guddle of boats which I have just mentioned. By cheaper buildings I refer to such things as the 'Gourock air houses', marquees and similar constructions.

In Sect. 7 (p. 334), Mr. Sessions comments that it is impossible to state the size below which no marina is viable. I would like to suggest that if one is employing labour around the clock, seven days per week, then there are basic wages which must be covered by a minimum number of berths. I am assuming, of course, that at any point there is a maximum amount the boat owner will pay for mooring facilities.

Mrs. M. Hadfield (Economic Associates Ltd., London)

I am an economist working on the proposal for a marina at Hastings, which will be an urban marina.

I am concerned—particularly in the case of urban marinas—that the wider aspects should be fully examined and assessed. I feel that this is where the economist has a role.

It is important to consider the impact upon the local population. There will be benefits, but there may also be a price to pay. One must try to predict the economic activity which will be generated. In the case of a resort, what will be the effect upon tourists?

That there is a demand for somewhere to keep boats is indisputable. But how much can people be charged for marina berths? Mr. Sessions has quoted, for Marina '72, a figure of £26 per metre (£8 per foot), but by my reckoning that may not allow for a viable marina. It is possible to go higher? Is the demand so great that there is no limit to what people will pay?

Although I feel sure that there is an upper limit, I am uncertain as to what the figure is. If the marina can only operate at a loss, is it fair to have land development in order to subsidise the marina? I consider that this is inevitable.

To return to the analogy of motor cars, did Mr. Ford intend people to keep the cars which he sold in garages? I think not, and I consider that marinas will be designed more and more for larger boats. Smaller boats will be kept either on land or in specially provided spaces, but not in the marina itself.

I suggest that marinas are part of the whole leisure scene. Is it possible that the answer to future requirements will be that marinas should be designed as part of an integrated leisure complex?

A few years back, people felt that they could keep their cars for free anywhere on the road, and that that was their inalienable right. This feeling applies equally to the sea. The sea is there; therefore, their boats can be left upon it free of charge. However, the sea is not free but is very expensive.

One of the reasons why the sea is becoming expensive in the same way in which I have applied the analogy of cars is that so many people want to use it. In future, people will have to pay, and will have to pay a great deal. I expect that they will want to do so.

Mr. M. E. Burton-Brown (Ormrod & Partners, Chartered Architects, Liverpool)

Many of the marinas at which we have looked seem to have been built for people who rent berths on a long-term basis. Surely one advantage which a marina can offer is to the holidaying yachtsman who wishes to call in and stop overnight while touring.

What provision of berths for such yachtsmen can be made in marinas? What traffic arrangements could be made to enable such a yachtsman to know what berths are available for people like him?

Mr. J. McNulty (Wicormarine Ltd., Portchester, Hants)

A note that has been struck frequently during these proceedings is that a great deal of consideration must be given to the boat owner who cannot afford the costs that many marina developments will expose him to. Similarly, marina owners and operators are well aware of the need to provide service as economically as possible both in terms of investment and operational efficiency.

It has been shown that the numbers of craft requiring permanent berthing facilities in the Solent will increase by 13,000 over the next decade or so and it is clear that the recreational space in such places as Chichester and Langstone Harbours or the Hamble River cannot be given over to the mooring of yachts on piles or buoys in order to provide cheap facilities. It follows that more and more boat owners are going to be forced into yacht harbours that they may not be able to afford unless developers and operators make a great effort to provide cheap facilities.

It is implied, if not actually stated, that small craft in marinas lie at their berths throughout the year and, to a large extent this is true. However, it is very obvious that a considerable number of boats are laid up ashore during the winter months for repair and maintenance or just for storage. This number is going to increase as the boat market expands and will pose increasing problems for the handling of them both in terms of space available and the costs of handling.

By far the largest number of these craft are under 10 t displacement and the few exceeding this weight tend to concentrate in the marinas and yards where expense is of less concern to the owner. It is very important therefore that the smaller craft are serviced as economically and efficiently as possible in the area of boat handling ashore. The factors mostly affecting this are the capital investment in equipment and the amount of time and labour involved in doing the job. The reduction of both factors will ameliorate costs within certain limits.

Mr. Bertlin and others have mentioned the capital cost of providing car parking space which, in itself, is non-productive. Mr. Sessions in his paper shows that this space can be put to very profitable use and that there is a very real need for winter storage space. The figures given by Mr. Sessions make it quite clear that hauling out and storing can be the most profitable part of marina operations in relation to capital employed (excluding the cost of land) and for this reason, as well as the demand for hauling out and laying up, it should be a major activity for all marinas and yards.

With yards handling anything between 100 and 1000 boat movements a year the traditional and Heath Robinson methods must go by the board and be replaced by more sophisticated mechanical/hydraulic systems. These systems need to be examined in relation to the number of movements; the size of the boats and the available space to lay them up. The Renner or Travel-Lift type of mobile hoist is quick and labour saving, and, according to size, capable of lifting up to 40 t, and is well suited to marinas handling large numbers of yachts exceeding 10 t displacement where capital and space considerations are not critical. It is less well suited for boats under this weight due to its cost and bulk. The mobile hoists cost about £1000 per ton of lifting capacity and require docks to suit their size, very large sheds and often expensive ground preparation.

As the great majority of boats are less than 10 t displacement a system particularly well suited for these is the low loader articulated tuning fork, such as the Seahorse operating from a slipway (Fig. E). The Seahorse system costs about £300 per ton of lifting capacity, is very quick and capable of handling all types of craft including catamarans. It permits excellent use of space, can operate within existing sheds and does not require expensive ground preparation. Because of its low capital cost it can well serve as an alternative system in those marinas that find it necessary to use a big mobile hoist, and can reach its capital recovery point very quickly with only a small number of movements.

Figure E　'Seahorse' transporter

A third system of boat handling is the drop-mast swing-lift fork truck which allows the forks to be lowered well below ground level to pick up a boat and can then lift them to stack the boats 2 or even 3 high. This is excellent for small motor cruisers up to 3 t displacement where mooring or berthing facilities are limited and storage space ashore is critical. The obvious need here is for a perpendicular wall not more than about 3 m (10 ft) from ground level to the bottom of the keel. The swing-lift principle allows the load to be rotated 90° so that it can be carried for and aft in the direction of the truck's motion. The cost of this system is relatively expensive, about £3000 per ton of lifting capacity, but this is offset by the saving on storage space and providing berths. Such a situation might be found in an urban waterside development such as London or Birmingham where there are many canal cruisers.

Some marina developments, such as Brighton, are of a special enough nature and large enough to justify investing in tailor-made equipment where the capital cost can be recovered in the exceptional number of handling movements undertaken, or be offset by development of extremely valuable land.

My company, Wicormarine Ltd., is primarily interested in providing low cost investment and operations through the Seahorse and fork truck systems for marinas and yards handling—for the most part, boats under 10 t displacement. It is in this area that costs are more meaningful to boat owners and yard operators alike, and the vast numbers of new owners with very limited budgets who are going to be obliged to take up marina berths will be looking to developers and operators to provide them with the inexpensive services they need.

Boat-handling ashore provides a very considerable income to yards and should be seen as a welcome and profitable activity. This can only be achieved by efficient mechanical handling such as the Renner, Travel-Lift, Seahorse or fork truck. It should be possible to haul out a boat, transport it 200-300 metres (yards) and block it off within 20-45 minutes according to size at a cost not exceeding £1 per ton displacement, which recovers all labour charges, overheads and depreciation on capital. Many boatyards, for one reason or another, do not know what their boat handling methods are costing and a prime requirement is to evaluate this important area of operations. If costs exceed £1 per ton, a careful study needs to be made and the right mechanical system considered.

Mr. S. L. Wright (Principal Water Quality Officer, Hampsire River
Authority)

It seems to me that whenever I get involved in a discussion about a proposed marina, someone will inevitably say 'Of course it will cause pollution' and then add 'but in any case the water is too polluted to sail on'.

If boats—or, I suspect, more probably other peoples boats—equal pollution, then obviously marinas will cause serious pollution. In my opinion, however, pollution can only occur when matter is discharged in sufficient quantity harmfully and significantly to alter the composition of the receiving water or in some other way demonstrably to cause harm.

If my definition of pollution is accepted, it follows that the mere presence of a pollutant, be it a boat or a constituent of sewage, is not automatically evidence of pollution and therefore that marinas do not necessarily cause pollution. It also follows that pollution is not automatically related to the composition of effluents, and, therefore, that it is possible in some circumstances to discharge untreated effluent without causing pollution.

The discharge of largely untreated sewage to a body of water such as the Solent is not, therefore, automatically evidence of pollution. In fact, to the best of my knowledge, extensive studies of the Solent have so far failed to produce any scientifically sound evidence of pollution.

It is, of course, possible for discharges from marinas to cause pollution. For example, I would expect uncontrolled discharges from boats and shore facilities to pollute the land-locked anchorage shown in Fig. 1 (p. 340) of Mr. Folley's paper and I consider that similar discharges might pollute a coastal marina which is entered through lock gates.

I think, however, that it is unlikely that matter will be discharged from small boats in sufficient quantity harmfully to affect the composition of a navigable tidal channel. The effect on tidal channels of discharges from shore facilities will depend on the volume and composition of the effluents, i.e. on the size of the establishment and the extent to which the effluent is purified, the size of the channel and the site of the outfall. Each case must therefore be considered individually on its merits.

Sewage from boats inevitably contains large, easily identified and aesthetically revolting sewage solids which float on the surface of the water and become stranded on beaches. These solids have a detrimental effect on amenities and are an extremely bad advertisement for marinas. There is also a risk that amenities will be damaged by litter, including the apocryphal gin bottle, which is thrown overboard, and that further damage may be caused by litter from the shore facilities and oils which may be spilled when boats are being refuelled. Marinas are therefore liable to cause pollution which is generally ecologically harmless, but extremely obvious and aesthetically disgusting.

In non-tidal waters, river authorities can take action against anyone caught throwing litter into a stream. They can also control discharges from boats, and, therefore, consent is required in respect of all trade and sewage effluents which are discharged to streams. I would therefore expect that the marina described by Mr. Folley is subject to control by the Thames Conservancy and I would be interested to know what steps they have taken to control discharges from the boats and shore facilities.

In tidal waters neither litter nor discharges from boats are within the jurisdiction of river authorities and in some cases the authorities consent is not required in respect of discharges from shore establishments. River authorities, however, do have control over new and altered discharges of trade and sewage effluents which are made to the tidal waters which are named in the Schedule to the Clean Rivers (Estuaries and Tidal Waters) Act, 1960.

In the areas to which this Act applies—and in Hampshire this is the Solent, and all the tributary estuaries—the discharger must obtain the prior consent of the river authority in respect of all discharges which have been created or altered since 1960 and I can only suggest that anyone who has failed to comply with the law should get in touch with the appropriate river authority with a view to regularising the position.

The general public are extremely, almost morbidly, concerned about pollution and in my experience they will rapidly and often permanently blame a new installation for conditions which might be due to other discharges or even to natural phenomena.

I, therefore, strongly advise marina operators to consult the appropriate river authority at an early stage, to comply rigorously with the conditions imposed by that authority and above all to practice good housekeeping to prevent nuisance being caused by litter, sewage solids, and possibly oil.

Mr. A. Rushby (Principal Engineer, City Engineer's Department, Plymouth)

My main interest is sewage disposal and I know that I speak for my colleagues in this field when I say that we have for years been trying to convey to the public the true facts concerning pollution.

The discharge of crude sewage into tidal waters by means of a properly designed outfall, does not necessarily constitute a health hazard. But such design is not always practicable or economic, and it is the aesthetic aspect which causes most concern and public opinion is quite sensitive on this point.

My own authority is spending between two and three million pounds over the next five to ten years in dispensing with our crude sewage outfalls to estuary and river. Our citizens would not react favourably to an application to develop a marina for luxury yachts if crude sewage is allowed to be spilled from them in restricted waters.

It is true that 300 boats in a marina is insignificant compared with the effluent from a town and that the health hazard is negligible, but it is the aesthetic aspect which offends most people. In this respect, we must remember, that sewage tends to float nearer the surface in salt water than in fresh.

I cannot overstress to developers that all schemes for marinas should include a suitable means of dealing with sewage. To put it even more strongly, within the next two years, sewage authorities will be incorporated in the new regional water authorities, and these bodies will be charged, amongst other things, with the statutory responsibility of preserving the environment. Therefore, I suggest that if developers do not make adequate design facilities for the disposal of crude sewage from yachts in marinas, then applications will be turned down by the planning officer. We are happy that he takes the criticism for rejecting these schemes, and we are glad to let him continue to do so, but it will be the regional water authority which will be objecting and which will be using him as their spokesman.

I would like to give this advice to the boat-building industry. The old method of having a toilet unit with a pump at the side discharging directly into the water, must be cut out of the catalogues. Arrange for some system of storage to be incorporated directly in series with the waste pipe. Use this as a selling factor and draw the client's attention to the fact that it has been done purposely. It costs more, but the client will have the assurance that with this facility on board he will be able to call in at any marina.

I suggest that the minimum storage capacity should be three days' use. The current use of water which is ultimately converted into foul drainage is, for house dwellers, about 230 litres (50 gal) per head per day. My experience of caravan dwelling suggests that the applicable figure could be 68 litres (15 gal) per day for a family of four. A private pleasure craft is in a somewhat similar category, which suggests that a three-day storage capacity would be easily catered for.

To marina developers, I would urge that you should, at a very early stage of your proposals, have a discussion with the relevant sewage or planning authority in order to ascertain what is required. It costs nothing and a great deal of money can be saved by obtaining this advice at the outset.

In your own interest, do not accept clients with yachts which do not have suitable disposal facilities. It will give your industry a bad name.

Mr. T. E. Robinson (Senior Fire Prevention Officer, Hampshire Fire
Service)

After reading the useful papers prepared for the Symposium, I was disappointed to find only three lines (in Mr. Bertlin's paper, (p. 208) devoted to fire precautions. That seems a not very adequate treatment of a fairly important aspect, although I may be biased.

However, any failure to pay proper regard to the measures necessary could well result in the loss, in about an hour, of months—more probably, years—of work and planning, to say nothing of the financial loss incurred. And, of course, people do get killed.

Mr. Bertlin has stated that extinguishers and hydrants need to be provided. This is true, but their use merely proves that a fire has already started somewhere in the marina. Other factors, such as the safety of marinas and their users, the prevention of outbreaks of fire— not to mention the features necessary to assist the fire brigade, should they be called upon in a hurry—must be taken into consideration.

I will deal briefly with the legal requirements. Any shop and office— and the term shop includes restaurant—associated with a marina is required, by law, to have adequate means of escape in case of fire, adequate fire-fighting equipment and, if large enough to warrant one, a fire alarm system.

Any workshop which is used for the repair of boats, or any factory, is required to have similar arrangements under the terms of the Factories Act. The local fire authority is the appropriate official body for approving the arrangements, and I am always endeavouring to suggest to people that early discussion between architects and fire prevention officers is good and sound practice.

So often I am faced with a plan which, to all intents and purposes, is a fait accompli. It grieves me to say to the architect, 'I am sorry, sir, but you will have to make a hole in this wall or provide a door at that point' when I know that it will upset his plan terribly. It is even worse when the building is finished!

On 1st June 1972 the first category of premises designated under the Fire Precautions Act, 1971—namely, hotels and boarding houses— will be required to obtain a certificate as to the adequacy of their fire precautionary arrangements from the local fire authority.

I have looked around the exhibition outside, and I noticed a number of planned marina developments with hotels and similar types of accommodation. Each will be required by law to have emergency lighting, provision for staff training in the procedure to be used in case of fire, exit signs in addition to the usual fire alarm and fire extinguishing apparatus, and adequate means of escape which includes the provision of fire doors and similar means of stopping the spread of fire. It is of no value to provide two ways out if one fire can prevent the use of both ways.

This latest Act is applicable to all sorts and conditions of buildings— premises used for entertainment, swimming pools, sports centres, blocks of flats—any type of premises not at present adequately covered by other laws concerning fire. That includes most, if not all, marina buildings.

The final legal matter to which I want to refer is the need to obtain from the petroleum officer of the local district council a licence for the storage of petrol where this is dispensed. This applies to petrol dispensed either to cars or to boats with petrol engines.

On the question of facilities to assist the fire brigade, the first consideration must be adequate access. Roads provided for delivery
lorries, fuel tankers and so on are usually adequate for fire engines,
but it is important that adequate roads or hard standing are provided
as close as possible to moored boats as well as to the buildings.

Ideally, we should be able to get within 45-60 m (150-200 ft). If we
cannot, there is a delay while firemen have to run out hose to get to
the boat, (which is always the one at the far end of the jetty!) Apart
from the delay involved, this means that the fireman is already on his
knees when he arrives, and is hardly in a fit state to carry out his work.

The provision of water for fire fighting is important. The immediate
reaction is, 'But marinas have lots of water!' It must be where we
can get at it and use it. Mr. Bertlin mentioned hydrants, which are
important. We want at least a 75 mm (3 in.) main, preferably 100 mm
(4 in.) and, if we have no hydrant, we want our fire engines to be able
to get to the water on which the boats are sitting. It is of no value on
arrival to be told, 'The water is over there' when it is a 100 m
(300 ft) or so away. We carry a few lengths of suction hose and we
need to get our machines right up to the water. This is an important
point for your consideration.

With regard to mooring, if boats are moored side-by-side, the
difficulty will arise, should fire occur, that the people on the outside
may be unable to get across the boats moored on the inside. I suppose
they can jump overboard, but it is far better, from the fire aspect, if
they are moored end-on. Their proximity, one to another, will increase
the fire hazard.

I do not want to cast too much gloom upon the gathering, so I have
not mentioned anything about fires in this country. However, in
America—where things are always done in a big way—there was recently a fire at the Essex Marina in Norfolk, New York, which destroyed
83 boats. In Miami, Florida, another marina fire occurred, causing 25
vessels to be written off.

As the number of boat owners and users increases, regrettably,
but inevitably, the number of fires in this country will increase. May I
suggest to boat owners, marina developers, engineers and architects
that early and serious consideration should be given to the matter of
fire prevention.

I would like to say, on behalf of all my colleagues in the fire services
in this country, that we are only too pleased to give help and advice at
any time, and stress that it is free.

Finally, it may be of some interest if I outline the arrangements
which the Hampshire Fire Service has made for dealing with possible
fires in the Hamble River:

(1) On receipt of a call, attendance is made to the River from a

Station on each side of the River. A list of boat owners is
maintained and contact is made with the nearest available boat
owner so that, if required, firemen can go aboard a borrowed
craft to get to a fire in mid-stream.

(2) A flat bottomed dory was kindly donated to the Fire Service
and this has been refurbished and provided with an outboard
motor and is kept at the premises of Fairey Marine Ltd. The
personnel from Hamble Fire Station can and do if necessary
man this craft and this has a certain limited fire fighting
capacity including a portable pump on board.

(3) The Harbour Master's launch, the Hampshire Rose, has also
been adapted and fitted with certain fire fighting equipment
so that it can when necessary make a preliminary attack on
a fire within the Hamble area.

These measures have been essentially taken with a view to dealing
with boats which are not moored to the bank. Where moored craft or
marinas are involved the problem so far as access is concerned is
somewhat simplified and the normal fire fighting attendance of at
least two fire engines would be made on receipt of a call. No other
special measures have as yet been taken concerning marina fires in
this particular area, although the development of risks within the area
is always kept under review and where a risk justifies because of life
hazard or fire hazard then the pre-determined attendance of fire
appliances and men can be and is up-graded.

Mr. C. H. Crowther (Member of Severn River Authority)

I must agree with earlier speakers that something will have to be
done about sewage discharge from boats. There is no doubt that when
the regional water authorities come into being they will take a very
strong line on this point.

The Severn River Authority has just passed a bye-law on pollution.
If the agriculturalist, industrialist, and other dischargers have to comply with certain standards, then why should the boating fraternity get
away with it?

In the planning of inland marinas we must not forget that there are
problems involving the utilisation of land and the rights of fishermen.
Farming land near a river is often of high quality and there may be objections to its change of use by the Ministry of Agriculture. Fishing
is a major sport and the development of inland waterways for pleasure
boating must recognise the fishery interests. To illustrate, the Severn
River Authority alone issues about 140, 000 fishing licences in a year.

The R. Avon passes within 30 miles of the large conurbation of
Birmingham and the Black Country, where there are about 5 or 6
million inhabitants.

The lower reaches of the river are navigable and the upper reaches
are being renovated by a trust. Evesham is located about half-way
along the river, and is a natural boating centre with access to canals
leading to Worcester and Birmingham. Since the R. Avon joins the
Severn at Tewkesbury and the latter is navigable to Gloucester and
the Severn Estuary, there is too a direct connection with the open sea.

In my private capacity, I have put forward a proposal for a marina
on the outskirts of Evesham on land that I happen to own. The site
could accommodate up to 120 craft. There are existing buildings which
could be utilised, together with about 12 hectares (30 acres) of land
for further development.

Unfortunately, there are planning problems concerning the routing
of a future bypass road, but I anticipate that these can be overcome
when the planners are convinced of the urgent need for a marina in this
area.

Mr. J. R. Collett (Chief Navigation Inspector, Thames Conservancy)

I would like to make a plea for the provision of facilities for very
small craft—the sort of boat that can be trailed behind the family car
and used to explore new waterways each year. On the Thames, these
craft represent about half of the 12, 500 total on our registration list.

The need is generally for a temporary mooring, perhaps for a
fornight's duration. But I suggest that the best service which the boating industry and the various official bodies could give is the provision
of dry land facilities. Simple berthing is all that is required, with
easily used slipways.

On the question of pollution, it is of course an offence on an inland
river to discharge noxious wastes into the water.

Nowadays, the yachtsman is not willing to accept the traditional
Elsan bucket. Recirculating toilets are now being installed in boats
and are probably an ideal means of overcoming the nuisance value—if
we put it no higher than that—in the river and estuary type of marina.
The discharge can be piped to a convenient point on deck, where there
is a 38 mm $(1\frac{1}{2}$ in.) B.S.P. connection which can accept a long hose.

If pollution is to be prevented, it cannot be left to the boat owner
to do his own discharging. He must not be allowed to pump his own
tank out, or else he may simply pump the effluent over the side. It is
for the marina operator, local authority, or harbour authority to provide
the wherewithal to pump these recirculating toilets out to shore disposal sites or to a main sewerage system.

A move has been made in this direction by the National Yacht Harbour Association, and there has also been a very able study by the
Norfolk and Suffolk Boat Owners' Association. Technically, there seems

to be no difficulty in providing these services on either large or small scales.

The problem of fire hazard has long been with us on the Thames. Moored craft in close company in a marina or in a lock inevitably increases the seriousness of fire risk in view of the possibility of spread.

Last year, there were nearly 900,000 lock movements on the Thames and often these involved up to 20 boats in a lock together at one time. It is quite easy to visualise what would happen if one boat caught fire.

As long ago as the turn of the century, the Conservators produced a specification for the construction and equipment of motor launches that would minimise the risk of fires and explosions. In consultation with the interested parties—boat builders and owners, fire officers, equipment manufacturers, and so on—this specification has been revised from time to time.

In addition, the Home Office has issued a useful publication (Fire Prevention Note No. 1, 1966) for the guidance of fire officers, and this now embraces fire precautions for pleasure craft.

An intention behind all this is to ensure that craft have sufficient fire extinguishing equipment of the right type on board and in good working order, so that any outbreak can at least be contained until the yard staff or fire party can assist.

No doubt marina operators will wish to consider whether the Home Office standard or the standard of their own Association should be applied to all the craft which occupy their berthings.

(In a subsequent written contribution Mr. Collett had kindly supplied the following additional information from which Fig. G has been prepared).

Table A is a list of marinas on the non-tidal Thames (above Teddington). All are sites where mooring development is made possible by excavation of an artificial cutting or basin or by utilising an existing channel not suitable for through navigation, e.g. a mill stream. It will be appreciated that because of the width of the River in relation to the passing traffic it is not possible to construct marinas out into the stream and moorings alongside the river banks are restricted and sometimes entirely prohibited. However, in a few wide reaches of the River, the Conservators have permitted moorings head-on to the bank with the mooring craft lying alongside stages or pontoons projecting lengthways into the stream. Some of these mooring areas are styled 'Marinas' but they are not included in Table A.

It follows, therefore, that a list or map of upper Thames marinas will not by any means give a complete picture of existing mooring developments, since, at the present, only a fraction of the boat population of the River is contained in marinas in the true sense of the word.

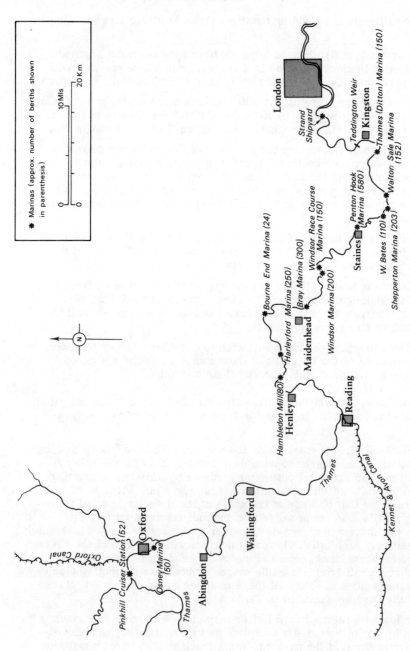

Figure F River Thames showing marinas existing or in course of development

Table A Marinas on R. Thames above Teddington Lock as at 30.11.72
(existing except where otherwise stated)

Marina	Location	Berths
Pinkhill Cruiser Station	Near Eynsham, Oxford	12 berths. Application recently made for extension to berth 40 'Caribbean' cruisers
Osney Marina	Osney Mill Stream, Oxford	40-50 berths
Hambleden Mill	Hambleden, Near Henley, Oxon.	80 berths
Harleyford Marina	Near Marlow, Bucks.	100 berths in the basin plus 150 berths in the River
Bourne End Marina	Bourne End, Bucks.	24 berths (launches under 6 m (20 ft) length)
Bray Marina	Bray near Maidenhead	274 berths, increasing to 300 in 1973 and to 320 by 1974
Windsor Marina	Windsor	198 berths
Windsor Race Course Marina	Windsor	135 berths increasing to 150 during 1973
Penton Hook Marina	Chertsey Lane, Staines	500 berths. Planning consent for additional 80 berths
W. Bates and Son Ltd.	Chertsey	110 berths
Walton Sale Marina	Walton	152 berths
Shepperton Marina	Shepperton	203 berths under construction
Thames (Ditton) Marina	Thames Ditton	150 berths

The extension of marina and other types of mooring development is now receiving very close attention from riparian planning authorities in co-operation with the Conservators to ensure that the amenities of the River are preserved and that reaches near to saturation point (as regards moorings, passing traffic and the capacity of locks at each end) are not overloaded as the result of approval of additional marinas.

In 1971, 26,764 craft of all types were registered or exempted from registration for use on the Thames with the Conservators' jurisdiction. 12,829 of these were mechanically propelled vessels, mostly up to 12 m (40 ft) in length. They are not all permanently moored above Teddington but these figures give some idea of the situation. Berkshire has by far the longest county boundary and it is understood that the County Planning Officer is considering a comprehensive survey of river moorings, possibly by aerial photography.

Mr. B. H. Rofe (Rofe, Kennard and Lapworth, Consulting Engineers,
London)

With reference to Sect. 2 (p. 343) of Mr. Folley's paper which concerns the selection of a marina site, I accept his first criterion but feel
that far more weight should be given to the possibility of dual-purpose
construction. There are a lot of places where existing or potential
holes could be utilised to advantage and the construction costs reduced
in proportion.

The strata in alluvial flood plains often consist of silts and allu-
viums overlying gravel and, in these cases, the cost of wet dredging a
hole is frequently expensive, and difficult to price, as indicated by Mr.
Sargent in his paper. In many instances, the cost is increased because
the alluvium and clays are frequently discarded as unsuitable for any
other purpose, but this is unnecessary if the site can be first dewatered
and then excavated under drained conditions. The costs of dewatering
and the subsequent use of the materials are known engineering factors
and it is therefore easier to estimate the overall cost.

With reference to Mr. Session's paper, Sect. 5. 3 (p. 329) I must join
with other speakers in emphasising the danger of pollution from an
inland marina; I accept this is less so with an estuarial marina, but
not negligible as suggested earlier by Mr. Bertlin. No planning authority
would dream of giving permission for a development of 200 houses
without proper provision for sewage disposal. It should be obvious,
therefore, that a development of 200 boats cannot be allowed to discharge crude sewage into a marina, and from thence into a waterway,
without treatment. Nowadays, most rivers and estuaries are used in
some measure for public water supply and it is the duty of the river
authorities to prevent such pollution. The danger of pollution in areas
where ground water is extracted must also be considered.

Mr. C. M. Marsh (Chartered Civil Engineer, Reading)

I would like to draw attention to plastic sheeting as a convenient
and efficient material for providing a watertight membrane in earth
banks.

In 1960, I used polythene sheeting to seal the bed of a canal in
Cheshire and, in 1962, I used Visqueen sheeting on the Lancaster Canal
where a spur motorway was being constructed under the high Lune
aqueduct approach embankment.

At York University, where it was decided to create, in 1963, an artificial lake as an amenity, P.V.C. sheeting 0·2 mm (0·008 in.) thick
was laid horizontally over the site to eliminate losses through seepage
into the pervious subsoil. An overlying bed of sand and gravel afforded
the necessary protection to the sheeting and also served to retain it
in place.

Visqueen sheeting is presently being used as a watertight seal in a riverside marina where the water is to be permanently impounded above the tidal high water level.

In fact, some type of watertight membrane could be conveniently used at sites such as mentioned by Mr. Weeks of the Thames Conservancy where there are risks of flooding due to the configuration of the ground (p. 260).

Clearly, it would be undesirable at such a site to construct subsequently a jetty with piles piercing the sheeting and destroying the watertightness of the bed. If such a structure had been envisaged at the outset, the piles would be driven before laying the sheeting which would be lapped, overlapped and sealed in situ round each pile.

Where a watertight membrane is required in the banks of a waterway or marina, the sheeting should preferably not be laid on the slope where the normal protective layer of sand and gravel would be unstable and easily eroded. If, however, for any special reason it was essential to lay the sheeting on the slope the cover would have to be concrete laid as a blanket with close-bedded slabs.

Normally, the membrane should be located vertically in the centre of a bank, either placed in a trench in an existing bank or brought up in stages as work proceeds with sand protection on both sides.

Sealing of adjacent sheets depends on the type and quality of the sheeting, using mastic or heat welding on the overlap of the sheets in accordance with the manufacturer's specification.

AUTHORS' REPLY

Mr. D. H. Sessions

I am greatly obliged to Mr. Radford for presenting my paper whilst I was otherwise engaged and I find very little in his remarks with which I am not in agreement.

Our minor areas of conflict, which Mr. Radford has so politely highlighted, are largely confined to the figures I used by way of illustration.

Whilst I had grave doubts about quoting 'typical' figures I did develop the imaginary projections from capital costs, land valuations, revenues and expenses within my current experience of building and operating marinas and from known contractual costs of dredging, piling infilling, building and equipment for 1972 completions.

I must agree that in 1973 the positions will be changed and I know
that some plant I have engaged in the past year has cost subsequent
employers almost twice as much. This, however, may have had more
to do with negotiation than with inflation!

I would not wish anyone to regard my figures as a 'formula'. Mr.
Radford, who has recently been generous enough to disclose his philo-
sophy regarding the Poole Harbour Yacht Club Marina, has clearly
arrived at a totally different target to that which is normally put in
my sights.

Viability of the marina *per se* is, in my experience, the more usually
desired target but I see no reason why marinas should not be a complementary, if dependent, part of other development. In fact, due to the
rapid consumption of 'natural' marina sites a combined development is
becoming more necessary each year. Even so one tries to design the
marina element to be self-supporting or profitable if it is at all possible.

On one aspect of Mr. Radford's comments I think we must agree to
differ. I do not subscribe to the view that marinas can be successful
'in areas away from boatyards'. We might get away with such a policy
whilst moorings of any sort are in very short supply but in a competitive situation I think it would be disastrous.

If we provide a base and port of call for boats and fail to provide
the repair, maintenance and service facilities essential to their use I
do not think we are doing our job.

Mrs. M. Hadfield is concerned with a project depending upon subsidy
from related developments or side-effect benefits.

In considering the extent to which reliance can be placed on such
subsidies we have to examine the extent and the source of funds.

A marina associated with large-scale tourist attractions in an ideal
climate may require a relatively small subsidy which is easily born
by the much greater source of revenue, in the way in which roads and
services are absorbed in a residential area.

If, however, the presence of a marina is desired as a scenic 'back
drop' in an area where the berthing demand is low, or from a low-
spending community, the attraction must be evaluated in terms of revenue from other sources.

A large seasonal growth in the sale of fish and chips from coach-
born trippers, for instance, would hardly merit subsidising a marina.
On the other hand a large and high quality tourist village for year round
occupation could well do so.

Mrs. Hadfield asks 'How high can marina rates go?'. The answer
I think, in the context of providing a marina where it is not naturally
viable, is 'not high enough'.

Mr. M. E. Burton-Brown highlights the absence of visitors' berths which is particularly evident in this country.

The reason for such scanty provision is simply that visitors' berths are uneconomic. Nearly all the demand for temporary berthing occurs in the summer and if berths are kept for this purpose they are earning no revenue in the winter.

Even if short term rates are doubled, pro rata to the annual cost, recovery will be less than from the permanent letting as visitors will not arrive or depart at the desired moment. Thus, with a six-month season, irregular occupation even during the summer and additional adminstration, a visitors berth must be charged out at about three times the equivalent annual rent.

A partial solution has been found in the use of berths temporarily vacated by annual or longer term tenants. Some marinas make a refund to the permanent berth holder and some do not.

Such an arrangement depends upon the berth holder notifying and *keeping to* his departure and return dates which can cause serious inconvenience if his itinerary is changed or if weather, illness or any other trouble intervenes. Also it demands that the visiting craft leaves on schedule, a very rare occurrence.

A further disincentive to the provision of visitors berths is that the visitor may be unknown to the marina, may steal away by night leaving his bills unpaid and may be virtually untraceable.

Where this form of visitors' accommodation is provided there is a considerable administration problem and visiting rates will still be comparatively high.

Whatever arrangements are made for visitors there remains the necessity of reserving space in advance or accepting, with good grace and prompt departure, that no berth is available.

Mr. S. L. Wright and Mr. A. Rushby are not alone in drawing attention to the problem of sewage and pollution.

This is something which has to be considered but it is really a miniscule part of the very much greater national problem we have inherited.

Sewage is not created by boats. It comes from people wherever they may be, whether on a boat or at home or at the office.

Whilst every little effort must help to solve the overall problem, the coastal marina, whether completely sewage free or contributing the maximum of which it is capable, will have very little effect on the general situation.

New legislation, clearly to be extended to coastal situations when some form of enforcement is politic, will demand holding tanks in boats.

If marinas can provide a simple pump-out installation for transfer to the public sewers, and at a covering charge paid by the boat owner, I cannot imagine that they will fail to do so.

However, in so many areas the public sewers are quite inadequate for the existing demand and often do no more than move raw sewage from one place to another.

Recently, it was suggested that the siting of a new marina might be unwise as it would collect raw sewage. The dreaded 'identifiable solids', however, were not those arising from the marina but from the local authority's outfall sited in the middle of a crowded and old-established yachting river.

If marinas are forced to establish full treatment plants due to the non-availability of public sewers they will presumably, do so. The cost will, as always, fall on the boat user and the contribution to removal of the sewage menace will probably go unnoticed.

A far greater nuisance to the small boat user is, of course, the happy-go-lucky discharge of oil, chemicals and catering refuse into sailing waters.

Boats are frequently put in danger and have been sunk through debris and, in particular, plastic bags which can block engine intakes.

Whilst a few boat users may be ignorant or careless enough to jettison this type of waste they do, for the most part, look after their own interests and, in the marina, they use the disposal facilities available.

The waste put overboard by commercial shipping and particularly ferries, however, is colossal by pleasure boat standards and again the contribution we can make is negligible in comparison.

This reply to the discussion has been written amost a year after drafting my original paper. In the period since the Symposium I have spoken to a great many new-born marina experts. Each, according to his bent, seems to think marina construction and operation is a matter for engineers, architects, developers, economists or even the boating industry.

All the Symposium papers were excellent and informative. But none of the authors would, I think, claim to have written a hand-book for the do-it-yourself marina. Nor, as most are professional men, have they told all.

The more marinas we have the better, provided they are of a reasonably high standard, well managed and continue to satisfy the customers.

I hate to think of abandoned or derelict marinas and none of us in the marina business will benefit from other people's failures.

Figure G Berthing piers at Harleyford Marina, R. Thames

Figure H Bank protection and pile-driving equipment at Harleyford Marina, R. Thames

As Mr. Radford has emphasised 'the first thing is to get the concept clear'. To this I would add 'identify your objectives and, if in any doubt, ask'.

Mr. B. S. Folley

Mrs. Hadfield asked the question: 'Is there a limit to what people will pay?' Of course there is a limit. Despite the lamentable lack of good facilities inland, I do not think that people will ever pay through the nose for a facility unacceptable in terms of its standards. If a facility is in full use, it can be assumed that, generally, the customers are satisfied.

There is not yet such a desperate shortage of moorings inland that boat-owners cannot find somewhere to put their craft, although it may sometimes be inconvenient. It is amazing the places people can find to put their boats.

Small boats should be kept on land. By this I mean dinghies, small outboard runabouts and boats of that type. Inland, they are subject to the wash of passing craft, and are frequently damaged. Trailer parks are, therefore, a very good idea.

I agree with Mr. Rofe in his advocacy of a dual-purpose type of construction. This is what we intended with the proposed Gossmore Marina (Fig. 3, p. 347). The excavated material from the marina site would have been used to restore, to the benefit of public amenity, a nearby gravel pit in the ownership of my Company. Unfortunately, our planning application has been rejected.

Some comments have been made concerning inland marina construction. We do all the design work ourselves and we have never employed a contractor. As Fig. G shows, the finished job for a marina basin of about 0·8 hectares (2 acres), with about 100 moorings, looks quite reasonable.

Fig. H shows the marina entrance under construction. 'Unibank' sheeting, which is an asbestos material, has been driven to 1 metre or so (3 ft) below the bed which is then reconstituted. In the case of a hard bed of gravel, we use 50 mm (2 in.) thick timber sheets instead of asbestos. Timber piles are driven in at intervals of 2 m (6 ft) and top and bottom walings are fitted. Each pile is anchored back with a 4·5 or 5·4 m (15 or 18 ft) long, 16 mm ($^5/_8$ in.) tie rod to a trench dug in the virgin ground, which is filled with reinforced concrete.

We have found this to be a very quick, easy, effective and inexpensive method of bank protection.

Session 6

Chairman: **Rear-Admiral P. D. Gick, O.B.E., D.S.C.**
(President National Yacht Harbour Association)

Brighton Marina: Planning and Design

H. L. Cohen

Brighton Marina Co. Ltd

D. Hodges

Louis de Soissons Partnership, Chartered Architects

and

F. L. Terrett

Lewis and Duvivier, Consulting Engineers

1 Introduction

The idea of a yacht harbour at Brighton began with a proposal by the Brighton Corporation to build a small harbour on the sea front. Lewis and Duvivier were asked in 1960 to report on the engineering aspects of the proposal and on the effect it might have on the Brighton beaches.

In 1962, Henry Cohen expanded this idea to include not only the shore development essential to the running of a yacht harbour – boatyard, chandlers shop, yacht club, and the like – but also other entertainments which would add to the attractions of Brighton as a seaside resort, together with residential development without which such a project would be unlikely, in this situation, to be viable.

Even at that time too many boats were chasing too few moorings, and cautious soundings among the townspeople and in yachting circles found an encouraging response.

The first problem was to carry out feasibility studies and surveys, and to prepare outline plans, for which finance, beyond the resources of the group of people who had joined in promoting the idea, was required. Banks are inherently conservative and what was needed was an organization with both cash and imagination. The first to help was Shell-Mex and BP; their support may have been enlightened self-interest, but without it the Brighton Marina might never have got under way.

By the Spring of 1963 an outline scheme for presentation to the
Brighton Town Council had been prepared. The site chosen was in the
vicinity of Dukes Mound about half-way along Madeira Drive. The
Town Council had a number of objections to make to this proposal and
it was suggested by the Minister that alternative sites should be
investigated. It was not until late in 1965 that the Black Rock site
was finally chosen and a revised scheme presented for approval. At
about that time, Allied Holdings Ltd. took an interest in the project
and provided the increased funding that was needed. The fact that the
City of London was actively interested at this early stage was encouraging at a time when encouragement was at a premium. The Public
Enquiry in January 1966 lasted for 9 days during which many objections
were forcefully raised.

The harbour, as envisaged at that time, could only be viable with
subsidies from land development. It is a fact of marina financing that
no-one can furnish purpose-built berthing at a reasonable charge without
an ancillary source of income. Yachtmen expect that they should be
provided with parking and servicing of cars, a sailing club, provision
stores, restaurants, hotels, flats and waterside houses with their own
private docks, hot and cold showers, on-shore sanitation, hairdressing
salons and so on. It was proposed to provide such amenities, but not
merely because they were expected.

In a section of the 'public mind' this part of the proposal appeared
to suggest something resembling the south shore at Blackpool. It was
assumed, without any reason, that bingo and not boating would be the
leading activity, a view that appeared to be held largely by people who
week-ended in Brighton, rather than the townspeople themselves. The
latter appreciated the immense contribution to the rates which the
marina would make and the need for Brighton to keep its lead over other
resorts, many of which were considering similar projects.

The Minister gave outline planning approval in September 1966 and
the Brighton Marina Bill was deposited in the House of Commons two
months later. Private bills are low in parliamentary priority and they
move slowly if the opposition is vocal enough. The Royal Assent was
not granted until April 1968, and during the proceedings in Parliament
the provisions in the Bill which would have allowed the Marina Company
to build the access roads that were needed, had been struck out. The
powers needed to build these access roads, which were going to be
needed in any case by 1980, were now to be secured by the Brighton
Corporation Bill which was lodged in November 1968.

Before the proceedings on this Bill could go ahead a Town Meeting
was required, and, unfortunately, this was held on a wet night when
only the objectors turned up. To overcome this set-back, 100
signatures were needed on a petition for a Town Poll which was held
under more favourable conditions, and produced an overwhelming vote

in favour of the Marina. The Corporation and the Company had, however, yet another set-back when the Bill was defeated on second reading in January 1969.

In March 1969, Westmoreland Properties Ltd. took over Allied Land and supported the Brighton Corporation in depositing a second access road Bill in November of that year for which a second Town Meeting and Town Poll were needed. Once again, the townspeople at Brighton voted overwhelmingly in favour of the Marina.

The Royal Assent to that Bill in July 1970 removed the last of the statutory obstacles to the scheme.

2 Selection of the Site

Three sites have been considered for the Marina – the first, at Kemp Town, about 1 km ($\frac{2}{3}$ mile) east of the Palace Pier – the second, at Ovingdean, about 3 km (2 miles) further to the east, and – finally, the chosen site, at Black Rock, about $2\frac{1}{2}$ km ($1\frac{1}{2}$ miles) east of the Palace Pier.

All three sites are at the foot of cliffs cut by the sea in the Upper Chalk, which in this area is some 250 m (800 ft) thick. At Kemp Town, the chalk in the foreshore is covered by a wide shingle beach, which has accumulated between large masonry and concrete groynes built by the Brighton Corporation. Sand overlies the chalk on the lower foreshore and sea bed beyond the ends of the groynes.

At Ovingdean and Black Rock, where the cliffs are protected by a concrete sea wall and decking (the Undercliff Walk), the chalk is exposed on the foreshore with only thin patches of sand here and there and a narrow shingle beach against the sea wall. The sea bed at these two sites is generally similar to the lower foreshore with isolated patches of sand and areas of bare or weed-covered chalk.

At Kemp Town, the sea front road (Madeira Drive) is at beach level at the foot of the cliff and would have allowed easy access to the shore for the construction of the harbour, and the associated building development. The wide shingle beach would have served as a working area and provided a ready supply of material for filling or for use as concrete aggregate. On the other hand, a great deal of the traffic approaching the site would have had to pass through the centre of Brighton and the resulting increase in congestion was considered a serious obstacle to the development.

The Ovingdean and Black Rock sites have none of these advantages, neither affording suitable access to the shore for heavy vehicles or constructional plant. At Ovingdean it was expected that the bulk of the building development would be on land inshore of the cliffs, and that cuttings into the chalk would provide sufficient filling material for the limited amount of reclamation required for building on the foreshore. The main disadvantage of this site is that it is too far from the centre of Brighton.

The main advantage of the Black Rock site is that, while it is not too far from the centre of Brighton, the new road system which will have been built by the time the Marina is due to be opened will enable traffic to avoid the centre. The main disadvantage of this site compared with the other two, apart from the access problem, is that the whole of the development has to be located seaward of the Undercliff Walk on land reclaimed from the sea, as none is available above high water mark.

3 Maritime Considerations

3.1 Physical Characteristics

The proposed Marina at Brighton is unique in that it is to be constructed on an unbroken stretch of almost straight coastline which affords no natural shelter whatsoever. It is exposed to onshore winds and waves from east-south-east, through south, to west.

During 1967, long and short wave recorders were set up at Brighton, and records of 15 minutes duration every two hours over a total period of eleven months were obtained. Waves between $1\frac{1}{2}$ and 3 m (5-10 ft) in height and from 5 to 9 second periods were recorded on forty-six days in the eleven months period – on nine occasions, extending over sixteen days, when the wind was in the south-east quarter, and thirty days with winds from the south-west quarter.

Since wave conditions are related to wind speed, a study was made of wind records for the South Coast. They showed that, over a ten-year period, for the sector east-south-east through south to west, onshore winds of Force 5 occurred on average for 3 per cent of the time, a total period of about twelve days per annum. Similarly directed winds of Force 6 and above occurred for 1 per cent of the time, that is three to four days per annum of which one day on average occurred during the summer months (April to October inclusive). For the year 1967, when the wave recordings were made, there was a higher proportion of strong winds than average.

The tidal range at Brighton is 3·15 m (10·3 ft) at mean neap tides and 5·85 m (19·2 ft) at mean springs, high water spring tides being 3·0 m (10 ft) above, and low water spring tides 2·8 m (9·2 ft) below Ordnance Datum. The extreme spring range is nearly 7 m (23 ft). Higher and lower tides than these may occasionally occur due to meteorological conditions, and it is estimated from tide records at Newhaven over a period of twenty-eight years that there is a 10 per cent chance of a level of about 4·15 m (13·6 ft) above Ordnance Datum occurring at Brighton once in any period of one hundred years.

The tidal currents at Brighton are approximately parallel to the coastline, the flood current being up-Channel with a maximum velocity of about $0 \cdot 8$ m/s ($1\frac{1}{2}$ knots) at springs and the ebb down-Channel with a maximum velocity of approximately $0 \cdot 65$ m/s ($1\frac{1}{4}$ knots) at springs. Slack water occurs at high and low tide.

3.2 Preliminary Harbour Designs: 1964 to 1968

Consideration of the data just outlined led to early decisions about the shape of the harbour and the orientation of the entrance. It is worthy of note that although many variations in the overall plan have since been considered, and a larger harbour is now being built than was originally proposed, the main features of the harbour itself are basically unchanged.

The large tidal range has precluded the use of fixed walkways or jetties for tidal moorings, and the design of the harbour has therefore to allow for mooring pontoons or floating stages which require calmer conditions than might otherwise have been acceptable. In order to achieve these conditions it was decided at an early stage to divide the harbour into two tidal basins, an outer basin with entrance from the open sea, within which waves entering would expand and dissipate their energy, and an inner mooring basin as remote as possible from the outer entrance.

Protection of the outer entrance from the prevailing south-westerly weather was considered of first importance, but, since the harbour is on a lee shore, adequate sea room must be allowed for boats entering and leaving.

Taking these various factors into account, the arrangement of the harbour as shown in Figure 1 was recommended as the best compromise. The powers granted to the Brighton Marina Company to build the works under the Brighton Marina Act 1968 were based on this harbour plan.

Economic considerations showed from the outset that it was essential, as far as reasonably possible, to limit the cost of the building of the main breakwaters if the scheme as a whole was to prove a viable proposition. A number of different types of breakwater were considered, namely:

(1) An in-situ mass concrete gravity structure.

(2) A gravity breakwater constructed of pre-cast concrete blocks.

(3) An in-situ concrete wall anchored to the chalk with tie bars.

(4) Various types of caissons or monoliths floated into position and sunk on to a prepared bed.

(5) A mass concrete buttressed design.

(6) A perforated cellular breakwater designed to reduce wave reflections and wave loadings.

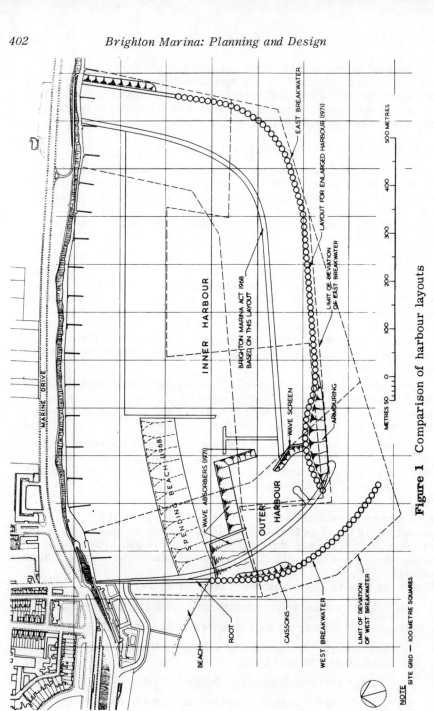

Figure 1 Comparison of harbour layouts

(Hydraulics Research Station)

Figure 2 Model for study of long waves

Examination of these various types of structure showed that proposals (1) and (5) had similar construction problems, but that (5) would require less material and be cheaper to build. Contractors who were consulted at the time tended to prefer type (2), because it would be less vulnerable during construction. Type (3) was thought to be promising, but anchorage values for the chalk were not known and neither time nor finance were available at that stage for the necessary in-situ tests to be carried out. It appeared that type (6) might show useful economies, but the design would require to be proved by model testing. All of the earlier designs and estimates for the scheme were therefore based upon breakwaters of type (5).

3.3 Investigations

Apart from the installation of wave recorders already referred to, hydrographic surveys comprising echo-soundings of the sea bed and the taking of sea bed samples were carried out at both the Ovingdean and Black Rock sites. When the decision had been made to build the Marina at Black Rock, a seismic survey was also carried out at that site and shell and auger borings were made in the cliffs, the foreshore and the sea bed.

During 1967, three hydraulic model investigations were put in hand. The first of these was a storm wave model at the Central Laboratory of Wimpey Laboratories Ltd. This was a rigid bed model built to a scale of 1/96 in a 27 m × 34 m (90ft × 110ft) indoor basin. Waves were generated by a hinged paddle driven by a variable speed electric motor with provision for varying wave period and amplitude. Tests were carried out with wave periods in the range from 5 to 20 seconds (prototype) approaching the harbour entrance from three directions, south-east, south, and south-west. Various modifications were made during this study with the aim of reducing wave reflections; the resulting standing wave pattern, particularly in the harbour entrance, and other behaviour in the model demonstrated the great importance of providing spending beaches across the northern side of the outer harbour opposite the entrance.

At the same time, a long wave model study was carried out in the starry sky basin at the Hydraulics Research Station at Wallingford. The purpose of this model was to examine the possibility of ranging in the harbour, particularly in the inner basin where movement of this kind would cause difficulty in the mooring of boats and pontoons. Although few very long waves had been recorded at Brighton, long wave activity was known to exist in the English Channel and might set up a resonance within the harbour. The model (Fig. 2) was set up with a wave generator immediately seaward of the entrance, the character-istics of the waves so generated having previously been determined from a mathematical model which had been analysed by computer at the National Physical Laboratory. It was found that there was a slight resonance at periods of 90 seconds, 180 seconds and 3 minutes, but the movements were not large. Calculation of the resulting mooring forces indicated that they would not be sufficient to break mooring lines.

A model of a perforated cellular breakwater was also constructed at the Hydraulics Research Station, Wallingford, and was tested for wave reflections and wave forces. The results of this study have been described in a paper presented in 1968. *

4 The Development of the Architectural Concept

4.1 Project Appraisal

An unfortunate delay followed the passing of the Brighton Marina Act and the granting of the initial outline planning approval of the scheme. This was due in part to a change in the control of the Marina Company, but more particularly to the fact that the Brighton Corporation Bill, which was needed to enable the Corporation to build suitable approach roads, was defeated by a narrow margin in the House of Commons.

Inevitably, doubts were cast on the future of the project, and it was not until this Bill was presented for the second time, and was seen to have a good chance of success, that the Company felt justified in making plans for the preparation of a final and comprehensive scheme.

At the beginning of 1970, David Hodges, of the Louis de Soissons Partnership, who had lately been appointed to act as architect and project manager, instructed all the consultants involved to submit all necessary information to enable him to make a first analysis of the problem for presentation to the Marina Company in June 1970.

This initial appraisal soon demonstrated the unique characteristics of the scheme and the almost limitless opportunities which it afforded. But what were the chances of success?

The first pre-requisite was the attitude of the Brighton Marina Company, and here there was no doubt that their objective was not to regard this as just another development, but to look upon it as a unique opportunity to make a contribution of real quality to twentieth century life, and to create an environment second to none.

Next to be considered was the physical effect on Brighton of this development – one of the most important in its history. In many cases a major scheme can tear the heart right out of a place, but here it seemed that what had to be done could be done without damage to the heart of Brighton – indeed the Marina might be expected to quicken its beat.

---

*Terrett, F. L., Osorio, J. D. C., and Lean, G. H. (1969), (Model Studies of a Perforated Breakwater), *Proc. 11th Conf. on Coastal Eng. (1968)*, 2, pp. 1104-1120.

Finally, there was the close co-operation which had existed between the Company and the Brighton Corporation throughout many years of struggle, and which seemed to give the promise of an atmosphere in which all things would be possible.

Here then were the ingredients of success, and the possibility of achieving it if they were used aright.

4.2 Objectives

The immediate task was to identify the objectives within the overall objective of a first class scheme. These were as follows:

(1) Yacht Harbour

One of the prime purposes of the scheme is the creation of a harbour in which the conditions and facilities for yachtsmen will equal or surpass the best in the world.

All around the world the marinas that have been built, or are being built, are designed to give better and better standards – in the services available at the mooring, in the shore facilities which the yachtsman requires, and not least in the ease and speed of access to the boat by car. The cost of harbour construction anywhere is such that it can only be supported by high charges for moorings; and these can only be obtained if the conditions are first class.

In most places such harbours are constructed within a natural inlet or at least under the protection of a headland, or by dredging out marshland to form an inlet and building up the land areas with the dredged material. These are expensive operations, but they do not compare with the enormous cost of building great breakwaters in the open sea. At Brighton, in order to cover these enormous costs, it was vital to aim for the highest standards and the top of the market.

The standard of services available at the moorings is one way in which the requisite quality can be achieved. This is largely a question of expense; it does not depend on basic planning methods. The availability and accessibility of shore facilities, however, and most important of all – the access to the boat – are fundamental elements of the plan on which the yachtsmen's judgement of this scheme will largely depend.

Ideally, the yachtsman drives his car along the quayside and parks it where his boat is moored against the quay. In a large marina such convenience cannot be provided for such numbers. Boats have to be moored at pontoons and approached for some distance on foot; cars have to be parked as close as possible to the pontoons. What had to be established was the degree of convenience which would be expected and which could physically be provided within reasonable cost limits.

A tour of American marinas on both the Atlantic and Pacific seaboards was most instructive. Nowhere in America was a pontoon to be found longer than 90 m (300 ft), nor would any yachtsman, marina

operator, or marina designer concede that a greater length than
140 m (450 ft) would be acceptable at all, since the furthest boat would
then be so divorced from car parks and shore facilities.

A successful solution to the harbour planning problem depended,
therefore, on so arranging the land reclamation and building works that
all the pontoons were of a reasonable length and easy of access.

(2) Public Amenity

The second objective was to cater for the public by way of adequate
car parking and free pedestrian movement throughout the scheme and
first class entertainment and catering facilities.

This should be a busy place, full of people. The Marina needs the
public, not just for the money which they will spend, but for the atmosphere they will create; and to bring in the public there had to be created
a first class environment, adequate car parking, and opportunities for
relaxation, entertainment and traffic-free, noise-free participation in
all the activities of the harbour.

(3) Residential Accommodation

A third objective was to provide for a large residential population.
The yachtsmen and to a large extent the public will come and go with
the seasons of the year.

The Marina needs a residential population to keep it functioning and
alive at all times, and so that the residents and hotel visitors will
provide a more or less constant clientele for the shops and restaurants.

(4) Creation of Site Values

The fourth objective was to create the site values without which the
Marina cannot be financed and built. The residential element has a
large part to play in this, but without an extensive commercial element
there was no prospect of matching capital expenditure and return.

Just as the moorings need to be of the highest quality so the flats
and houses must be so arranged that they are of the highest value, and
the commercial content must achieve its maximum potential by virtue
of its unique situation.

It had to be an important object in devising the scheme to create
the maximum length of waterfront and to ensure that no backland be
reclaimed where the buildings would lose value by being sandwiched
between the waterfront buildings and the cliff. It would be foolish to
reclaim land on this unique site at the enormous cost which this involves,
unless offering the best aspect and situation.

(5) Vehicular Access and Parking

Finally, it was necessary to hold all this together and make it work
smoothly with an internal traffic system adequate for the large numbers
of vehicles involved.

This hardly needs comment except to stress that without good traffic and parking arrangements the quality of the environment would suffer disastrously.

4.3 Co-ordinated Planning

The achievement of all these objectives on a site such as this is no ordinary architectural problem.

The diversity of the requirements of the various types of people using the Marina – yachtsmen, residents, day visitors, hotel and conference visitors, the shopping public – has to be reconciled so that no particular group suffers from any of the others. The effects of the restricted entry to the site and the conflict of vehicle, pedestrian and boat traffic have to be resolved.

The configuration and programming of the real estate development has to be dependent on the protection provided by the breakwaters, the constructional restraints imposed by building in the sea, and the mooring and navigational requirements of the harbour plan.

The delay between capital expenditure and return, far longer than usual on account of the lengthy breakwater construction, has to be minimised and the most rewarding sequence of building construction has to be reconciled with the restraints and complications already described.

Finally, the scheme, which by virtue of its very form and situation registers far more than is usual in a development of this size as a single complete entity, has to be given architectural coherence and consistency.

This is no ordinary new town or urban expansion which can be split up into sections and phased over many years, so that each new phase is developed on the basis of experience of the last and on changing patterns of demand. If it is to succeed, if it is to be financed, it has to be undertaken as one comprehensive, fully co-ordinated building operation in the shortest possible time, fully pre-planned, largely pre-fabricated and using many novel techniques. It has to be seen not as a harbour with a collection of buildings adjacent to it, but as a fully-integrated Marine City in which land and water play their part to the benefit of both.

The planning situation at the beginning of 1970 when instructions were given to start on the preparation of a final scheme was that an outline approval had been obtained for the scheme which had been prepared in 1966. The main lines of this scheme were enshrined in the Brighton Marina Act which was designed to safeguard the public interest in many ways and to limit subsequent alteration of the scheme by defining limits of deviation within which its various elements should be confined. Whereas these limits were reasonably wide, the difficulty arose that the scheme on which the Act was based proved to be incapable of adaptation so that the objectives could be achieved which the Company had by this time come to regard as essential.

4.4 The Harbour Layout

The first requirement was to enlarge the harbour to the maximum permissible within the limits of deviation since the project was one which could never be extended (Fig. 1). This enlargement, based upon the results of an additional series of model tests carried out at the Wimpey Central Laboratory in 1971, had the effect of further aggravating the most intransigent feature of the original conception, which had to do with the enormous water areas and the inordinate distances from car parks to the farthest moorings.

The scale of the scheme can perhaps best be illustrated by explaining that it extends eastward from the Black Rock Swimming Pool for a distance equal to that between Marble Arch and Hyde Park Corner, and out to sea for approximately 800 m ($\frac{1}{2}$ mile).

The most economical and simplest form of land reclamation parallel to the cliff which had up till then been adopted had to support a system of pontoons running southward from it which were up to 400 m ($\frac{1}{4}$ mile) in length.

Such an arrangement was clearly unacceptable and the first necessity was to advance the land reclamation southward to the limits of deviation, so as to reduce the water area between it and the southern breakwater to the minimum and thus to achieve a mooring and parking layout which would be a practical possibility.

The area of reclaimed land then became too large in relation to the water area so that the concept evolved of restoring the balance by letting in the water behind the southernmost strip. In this way, a land locked basin was formed which, if it were to achieve its optimum result, would have to be maintained at a more or less constant level thus overcoming in this part of the harbour the grave disadvantage of a 6 m (20 ft) tidal variation.

Accordingly, the general arrangement of land and water areas came about naturally, as a result of a study of the harbour planning problem and as a result of an attempt to increase to the maximum the potential value of the building sites.

4.5 Building Development

The preliminary decision on the real estate content of the scheme came about as a result of an assessment of the values which would have to be created if the cost of the harbour construction were to be supported.

Building development was to take place on about 18 hectares (45 acres) of former sea bed. Possible procedures were the construction of retaining walls with chalk or gravel fill, pier constructions built directly off the sea bed, or floating structures.

The main elements which it was at that time agreed should be included were as follows:

(i)   2 hotels with up to 1000 rooms.

(ii)   A conference centre to accommodate 500 delegates.

(iii) An office element sufficient for the marina administration and the administrative needs of tenants of the exhibition area.

(iv)   1000 flats and houses of various types.

(v)   A shopping and exhibition centre providing selling and exhibition space of approximately $42,000 \, m^2$ ($450,000 \, ft^2$).

(vi)   A sports and entertainment centre.

(vii) A boat store to accommodate 1275 boats.

(viii) A boatyard and workshop large enough to deal with the essential maintenance and repairs of the 3000 or so boats in the Marina.

(ix)   Yacht club, restaurants and public houses.

(x)   Parking for 6000 cars.

Before attempting to solve in any detail the intricate planning problems which the integration of so many diverse elements presents, there has to be an appraisal of the main principles to be adopted in the zoning of the scheme.

Two possibilities presented themselves which revolved around the relationship of the very large shopping, exhibition and entertainments complex with the residential and yachting environment.

The commercial element is of a size and character which require that it be supported not only by the users of the Marina, but also by Brighton residents, visitors to Brighton and a large number of people coming by car from the surrounding districts. At peak periods, therefore, it would generate a large amount of traffic on the Marina road system, and would be the meeting place for the largest concentration of people.

Should this activity be concentrated at the western end where it is nearest to the entry and exit to the site, where it will stand between the rest of Brighton and the quieter residential and yachting environment of the Marina; or should it be spread out through the very heart of the scheme where it would be a vital centre and where its facilities would be more immediately accessible to the yachtsmen?

Would the increased traffic and activity throughout the site be intolerable at peak periods or would such disadvantages be outweighed by the advantage that at other times a concentration of activity in the heart of the scheme would be a positive benefit?

The policy which has now been adopted by the Company is based on the first of these possibilities and its instructions are to plan for a fully integrated, air-conditioned commercial and entertainment complex designed to serve a public drawn from a wide area and so placed that its impact on the residential and yachting environment is not too greatly felt.

Also emerging is the very large scale of the workshop and boatyard facility which will be needed to service, repair and maintain the 3000 or so boats which the Marina is designed to accommodate. This facility has to be planned in such a way that it is near the harbour entrance, has sufficient waterfront to allow of adequate mechanical launching and retrieval of boats of all sizes, and above all does not damage the quality of the residential areas.

The residential and hotel content of the scheme occupies the largest land area. It will be built on sites with varying degrees of privacy and differing aspect. The accommodation provided will be of many types, ranging from the small pied-a-terre which the yachtsman might require to larger family flats for holiday or permanent occupation, from relatively modest homes for retired people to large flats and houses of the highest quality with private moorings at a private waterfront.

Running through these residential areas, but using different levels to maintain the required degree of separation, are the predestrian routes which bring the public into close proximity to the whole yachting scene, and which lead them on to the breakwaters and back on to the Undercliff Walk beyond the Marina to the east.

4.6 Car Parking

Finally, the distribution of the 6000 parking spaces has to be determined. These are to be allotted approximately as follows:-

Residents	1000	(on a scale of one reserved car space per unit)
Yachtsmen	2040	(on a scale of 6 car spaces per 10 moorings)
Shopping Centre	1200	
Hotels and restaurants	500	
Staff	370	
Available to visitors other than above	890	

Total 6000

The location of residents, shoppers and hotel car parks has to be decided by standards of convenience normally applied to these situations.

The general visitors' car park has to be arranged so that it can be used as flexibly as possible by yachtsmen or shoppers at periods of peak demand when casual visitors may have to be excluded.

The yachtsmen's car parks present the greatest problems. As already explained the connection between car park and mooring has to be as short and convenient as possible. At the time of writing three alternatives are being considered:

(i)   Floating car parks which would form part of the pontoon system and have the closest possible connection with the moorings, not only in horizontal distance but also vertically by remaining always at the same level as the boat.

(ii)   Fixed car park structures similarly placed but connected to the pontoons by hinged bridges or other variable means of vertical transfer.

(iii) Fixed car park structures more centrally placed and connecting with the pontoons by mechanical transport of one sort or another.

The decision between these methods will inevitably be influenced by economic factors.

The first is expensive in that the cost of the structure is attributable only to car parking. The second, although equally expensive on its own, can be more easily justified to the extent that the structure can be used to support other uses also. The third may be the most economical in that the economies of the second method are secured and, in addition, there is a saving of water area which can be used for additional moorings.

5 Breakwater Constructional Design

5.1 *Design Considerations*

The need to bring forward as far as possible the completion of the breakwaters made it necessary to undertake, simultaneously with the long range planning, the immediate task of preparing for an early start on the site.

The greatest and most urgent of the short-term problems was a final decision on the form of breakwater. Not only was it apparent that the method of breakwater construction would have a marked influence on the programme for the Marina in so far as the opening date was concerned, but there would also be a considerable influence on the layout of the land areas required for construction.

As indicated earlier in Section 3.2, preliminary estimates were based on a mass concrete buttressed design, as being the one that appeared the most economical. At this later stage, proposals for another type of design were made by Taylor Woodrow Construction Ltd., with whom the Brighton Marina Company had decided to negotiate the contract for the harbour works. This new type of design, which had been successfully employed in Denmark, involved the placing of individual circular units by means of a special crane capable of handling extremely heavy weights.

Further consideration was given to the perforated cellular form of structure, but this was rejected for economic and other reasons. A rubble-mound breakwater was also considered, but similarly rejected. Thus the design study centred on the two alternatives – mass concrete buttress or precast circular units.

Using data which had been obtained from the wave recorder installed at Brighton and the results of investigations for the Danish design at Hanstholm, Professor Lundgren of the Technical University of Denmark carried out a series of hydraulic model tests to determine the most suitable profile and level for the top of the breakwater so as to limit overtopping by storm waves and consequent disturbance in the inner harbour. These tests were made on several modifications of the Hanstholm-type breakwater and, for comparison, on the buttress-type breakwater.

Whilst this testing was in progress, Taylor Woodrow Construction undertook a thorough investigation, including model testing and computer analysis, which established the effectiveness, economy and utility of the design which they were offering as an alternative proposal.

By statistical analysis of the available wave and meteorological data it was possible to identify the worst conditions likely to occur in any given period of time. It was agreed that for overtopping considerations a 100-year storm should be considered, whilst for stability and overturning of the breakwater a 1000-year storm would be appropriate.

With the studies complete, each method of construction was considered on its merits in relation to its cost and construction time, and the conclusion was reached that the Hanstholm-type breakwater provided the greatest advantages. It was this type, therefore, which was selected, and Professor Lundgren then commenced further and more detailed hydraulic studies in his laboratory at Copenhagen.

These hydraulic studies entailed:

(i) Further examination of the hydraulic advantages of various alternative types of superstructure, including the need to ensure that overtopping would be restricted to acceptable limits.

(ii) Estimation of the horizontal forces on the structure and the overturning moments to be used in the design.

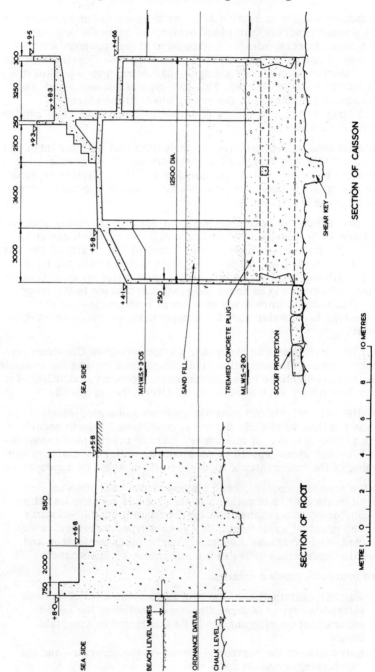

Figure 3 Breakwaters

Figure 4 Special crane for construction of breakwaters, shown here working on the construction of the new fishing harbour at Hanstholm, Denmark. Manufacturers – Sir William Arrol and Co.

(iii) Determination of the stresses likely to be encountered in the breakwater shell; this required an extensive programme of pressure cell measurements to establish the distribution of wave pressures on the breakwater.

Having established that the Hanstholm design was the one to be adopted, the Marina Company approved the purchase of the special crane which had been used in Denmark to construct the Hanstholm breakwater.

5.2 The Hanstholm-Type Breakwater

The breakwater is shown in cross section in Figure 3. Springing from a mass concrete root, it consists of a series of reinforced concrete caissons, approximately 12·5 m (41 ft) in diameter, set vertically adjacent to one another along the line of the breakwater.

A special form of joint is provided between the caissons, which carry a decking along their centre line between two heavy beams designed to carry the special crane during construction. This deck is surmounted by a superstructure which has been found to prove effective from the hydraulic point of view and, at the same time, to provide suitable access for maintenance and promenades for the public.

No major advance preparation of the sea bed will be necessary, since the crane will support each caisson with the bottom a small height above the sea bed before the tremie concrete plug which supports the weight of the caisson is placed. The height of each caisson will be determined before casting by survey of the bed level carried out in advance of construction. To stabilize the caissons in their final positions, sand filling will be pumped inside to a predetermined level to add to the weight of the tremmied concrete plug already in position.

On the seaward side of the breakwater, measures will be taken to protect the chalk foundation against scour. Additional tests on the chalk will be carried out to confirm the properties of the materials which have been used in the design.

The caissons forming the breakwater will be cast in stages in a yard built on an area of land reclaimed from the sea at the west end of the site. They will be built on soffit shutters supported on special heavy duty track and, when each is ready to be placed, will be moved on to the transporter car which runs on rails out to the turn-table at the root of the breakwater and thence out to the crane where construction is proceeding.

The crane, which is a focal point of this method of construction, is of interest by virtue of its size and is shown in Figure 4. It comprises a 600 tonne (ton) portal crane running on tracks on the top flanges of two large box girders, with these girders positioned so that they cantilever out from the last placed caisson and anchored by heavy holding down bolts to prepared foundations in the caisson previously placed.

The new caisson will be picked up from behind, travelled forward to its position and held in place above the sea bed, as described earlier.

The total weight of the crane is approximately 1200 tonne (ton) and the power for the hydraulic lifting equipment is provided by diesel-electric generators. The crane has a travelling speed of 5 m (16 ft) per minute whilst the portal crane has a speed along the box girders of 4 m (13 ft) per minute. The crane lift, which for the deepest caisson amounts to 600 tonne (ton), is provided by hydraulic jacks giving a loaded lifting speed of 3 m (10 ft) per minute through a vertical lift of 18 m (60 ft).

When the caisson has been accurately positioned, divers will clear away any material overlying the chalk foundation, the shutters which form a skirt around the base of the caisson will be lowered to the sea bed and retained in position by sandbags to form an effective seal whilst the tremmied concrete plug is placed. The tremmied concrete will be placed by equipment located on the previously constructed part of the breakwater, and the concrete will be shipped out to the point where it is being placed by trucks operating from the batching plant at the casting yard.

Provision will be made, in selected caissons on the breakwater, for measuring movement under extremely heavy wave conditions. If caisson movement is found to be excessive, then means will be taken to anchor the caissons to the sea bed, although it is considered highly unlikely that this will be necessary.

6 The Present Situation

The content of this paper will have demonstrated the varied nature of the activities which have been and are being simultaneously undertaken in the field of planning and design, ranging as they do from the broadest principles of zoning to the detailing of work already done and now in progress.

This work includes the provision of a road on land reclaimed from the sea without which there was no means of access to the site, also the formation of a path leading from the cliff top to the Undercliff Walk at the eastern end of the Marina site so that the public right of access to the Undercliff Walk would not be interrupted during construction of the Marina. These two works were completed as a preliminary works contract at a cost of approximately £250,000 during the period January to July 1971.

The harbour construction contract was started in September 1971 and is scheduled to take 5 years to complete. It involves the reclamation of a strip of land beneath the cliff to provide working space for the casting yard and for the movement of the crane and materials from the western to the eastern end of the Marina when the western breakwater is completed. The approximate cost of these works which are being undertaken by Taylor Woodrow Construction Ltd. is £7,250,000.

During this 5-year period it will be necessary to start further land reclamation and, as soon as the protection is sufficient, to start constrution of the buildings which will first be needed.

The process of deciding on the optimum construction programme is a complex one. It has to take into account the relative costs of constructional methods suitable to more or less protected conditions, the cash flow and revenue situation of the Company, the difficulties of site organization on a site which is all to be reclaimed, the effects of inflation and many other factors. Furthermore, it is not to be expected that firm and irreversible decisions on the exact balance of the many different types of accommodation will be taken quickly. The entire scheme is unlikely, therefore, to be developed rapidly to its final form.

The project is essentially one in which there is a conflict between the need to retain flexibility to meet changing or developing patterns of demand and the need, for obvious practical reasons, to pre-plan and pre-fabricate to the maximum extent.

It is on the correct balance of these two conflicting pressures and on a thoroughly effective management, both of the design process and the site organization, that the ultimate success or failure of the scheme depends.

Appendix

Chronological Summary

1960   Lewis and Duvivier requested by Brighton Corporation to report on engineering aspects of a small harbour.

1962   Mr. H. L. Cohen expanded this idea to include extensive residential and commercial development.

1963   Submission to Brighton Corporation of an outline scheme for marina development at Dukes Mound.

1965   Revised scheme for Black Rock site submitted.

1966   Public enquiry into Marina proposals. Outline planning approval granted. Brighton Marina Bill deposited in House of Commons.

1967   Wave recorders installed. Hydraulic model investigations commissioned.

1968   Royal Assent to Brighton Marina Act, but access road clauses deleted. Brighton Corporation Bill for access roads lodged.

1969   Brighton Corporation Bill defeated on a second reading. Revised road access Bill presented.

1970   Royal Assent to road access Bill. Preliminary project appraisal submitted to Marina Company by Louis de Soissons Partnership.

1971   Further series of hydraulic model studies performed at Wimpey Central Laboratory. Detailed consideration of breakwater design – model tests of Hanstholm-type structure performed by Prof. Lundgren at Copenhagen. Access road and pathway completed. Harbour contract commenced by Taylor Woodrow Construction Ltd.

French Marinas
—St. Malo to La Rochelle

Prof. A. N. Black

Faculty of Engineering and Applied Science. University of Southampton

1 Introduction

My experience of French marinas has been as a user, rather than designer or operator, but I have tried to give some information on these aspects too. Perhaps the most conspicuous developments have been on the Mediterranean, but I have no personal knwoledge of these and I am confining my attention to the coast which I know, that is the north and west coast from St. Malo to La Rochelle. In many ways, conditions there have more in common with problems in this country than have those on the Mediterranean coast. In general, I have defined a marina as a place where yachts are berthed at pontoons, but there is one exception described in the paper.

2 The Coastline and the Yachting Scene

The north and west coast of France (Fig. 1) is generally rocky and indented, with a large number of small ports, mostly well sheltered though a few are very exposed. There are a few major commercial or naval ports and fishing is very actively carried on in many places.

The tidal range is very large at St. Malo, about 13 m (43 ft) (extreme ranges are quoted throughout), and decreases westward along the north coast to $7\frac{1}{2}$ m (24 ft) at Brest. The range on the west coast is uniformly about $5\frac{1}{2}$ m (18 ft).

Over the last ten years there had been a very rapid development of yachting throughout the whole of France. At the end of September 1971 there were just over 250,000 yachts of which just over 200,000 were of less than 2 t. Of the over 2 t category 23,000 were sailing and 28,000 motor. However, the motor craft were strongly concentrated in the south. Omitting those in the Bordeaux and Marseilles areas,

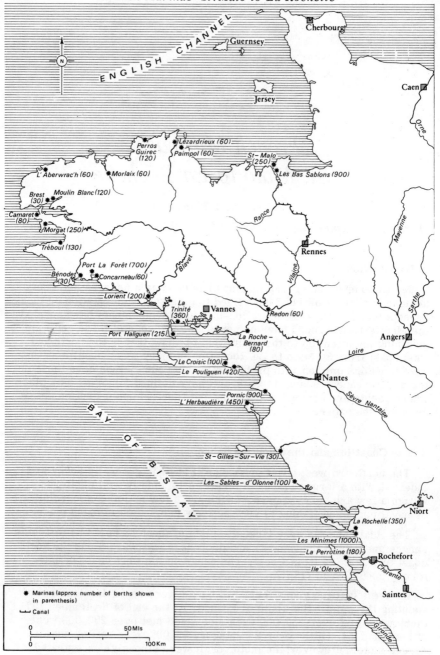

Figure 1 North-west France showing the principal yacht harbours

there were 12, 000 sailing and 8000 motor vessels. Taking the country as a whole the increase each year for the last six years, in the number over 2 t, has been almost constant at 5000 per year, and this rate is expected to continue.

3 Types of Marina Development

3.1 Range of Development

A list of marinas, existing or proposed, on this coastline is given in the Appendix. The brief details quoted are very approximate.

As is evident from this list, marinas vary in size according to the nature of the locality, from monster harbours of up to 1000 berths, to quite small provision—typically in a convenient corner of an existing harbour. It appears that a number of the latter are really a means of keeping yachtsmen in a compact body, out of the way of the other users of the harbour, such as fishermen.

In the following sections, a number of particular marina developments will be used to illustrate the various approaches which have been adopted.

3.2 Utilisation of an Existing Deep Water Area

At St. Malo, part of the existing wet dock has been adapted as a marina by the installation of pontoons. Berthing is parallel to the pontoons, but yachts lie in tiers three or four deep. This method of berthing is unusual, but it makes the maximum possible use of a restricted water plane. The inconvenience is reduced by the fact that the lock is only worked for yachts within $1\frac{1}{2}$ h of HW, so that yachts are only liable to be on the move for about 3 h each tide. The fire risk with this intensity of use must be appreciable. The range of level, between HW springs and neaps is quite large, owing to the great range of tide outside; it is about 3 m (10 ft). Capacity is normally 120, but 250 or more are accommodated at busy times.

At Le Pouliguen the yacht harbour (Fig. 2) is situated in the mouth of a river. As there is considerable water area landward the tidal streams are strong, up to 4 knots in the river. There is a bar outside the entrance, which holds up the level at LW, so that the range inside the river is less than outside. The depths at LW range up to about 1·6 m (5 ft). The upstream berths are to pontoons, yachts mooring end-on, which is the normal arrangement in France. Because of the strong tides the pontoons are very powerfully anchored by radius arms to a row of counterforts on the river bed. The downstream berths are to double-ended moorings. The shelter is complete. Capacity is about 420, on the pontoons. The cost was about £120, 000.

Figure 2 Pontoons at Le Pouliguen, showing radius-arm anchorage

At Camaret there are fewer problems and yachts berth, normally end-on, to pontoons placed inside the breakwater (Fig. 3). The harbour is not completely sheltered and there must be some discomfort in bad weather from between NE and NW, but the marina is reported to be adequately secure. Capacity is about 80.

At Brest, pontoon berths for about 30 visiting yachts are provided in the commercial harbour.

Figure 3 Pontoon berths at Camaret

3.3 Dredged Marinas

An example is L'Aberwrac'h where a trench has been dredged to
2 m (6·5 ft) below datum, wide enough to take the pontoon and the
yachts berthed, end-on, each side. The dredgings were used to create
a platform which is used as dinghy park and car park. The marina
is about 5 km (3 miles) up the river from the sea and is protected by
an existing mole, so that no extra shelter was required. Capacity is
about 60. The cost was about £100,000, but provision for dinghies was
an important part of the project.

At Le Croisic (Fig. B, p. 51), about 100 berths for small yachts have
been provided by dredging out an unwanted corner of the inner harbour.

3.4 Submersible Wall

These differ considerably in their characteristics.

At Perros Guirec the original harbour dried completely. A wall,
about 3 m (10 ft) high has been built across this harbour, with crest
level 7 m (2·3 ft) above datum, corresponding roughly to HW mean
neaps. A single dock gate (Fig. 4) is provided. At dead neaps the
water level is run down slightly to permit the gate to be opened for
about 1 h each tide; otherwise the gate is open whenever the tide covers
the wall, and indeed at springs there is more than 2 m (6·5 ft) over the

Figure 4 Dock gate and submersible wall at Perros Guirec

wall so that yachts can come and go freely. Pontoons (and some moorings) have been established in the pool (Fig. 5). Development seems to be proceeding steadily and no doubt more pontoons will be provided as demand develops. Capacity at present is 120 on pontoons. The cost was about £140,000.

Figure 5 Pontoons and submersible wall at Perros Guirec

At St. Malo, a new marina, Les Bas-Sablons, is being built outside the docks. The area has been dredged to ½ m (1·6 ft) below datum over most of the area, lower in parts. This represents a lot of work as the charts show a bottom drying 4 m (13 ft) over much of the area and a fair amount of rock. A submersible wall with crest 2 m (6·5 ft) above datum is being built, which will thus give a minimum depth of 2½ m (8 ft) inside. There will be no gates, so there will be no access unless the tide is high enough to give adequate depth over the wall, say 3½ m (11·5 ft). The restriction is not severe, since the tide only falls below this level at springs, and LW springs is conveniently at midday and midnight. Shelter will be provided by a slatted jetty covering half the length of the wall, and this, with the existing breakwater, should give good shelter. Mooring will be by double-ended moorings; presumably it would have been too difficult to locate pontoons with a tidal difference of 11 m (36 ft). Capacity is about 900. Technically, by the definition adopted, therefore, this is not a marina, but it seemed absurd to omit it. The cost is estimated at £1.4 million.

3.5 Marinas Protected by Breakwaters

Where the existing shelter is insufficient, complete new harbours, enclosed by breakwaters, have been built. An example is Pornic (Fig. 6) where the breakwaters extend from inside the former drying line into about 3 m (10 ft) of water. This is believed to be the only privately financed marina on this coast.

Figure 6 Yacht Harbour at Pornic   *(Photo: A. Perceval)*

Some dredging has been done in the drying corner to get adequate depths, but over the greater part of the harbour the existing depths were sufficient. Capacity is about 900. The cost was about £350,000.

Another example is Port Haliguen, where the development has been in two stages. The capacity in the first stage is about 350. At present the newer, western, breakwater encloses moorings only, but it is intended that full marina development will take place in due course. Again, a very limited amount of dredging was needed; the breakwaters extend to depths of about 4 m (13 ft).

At La Forêt Fouesnant, a muddy estuary has been closed off by breakwaters and dredged to provide a marina for 700. The spoil has been used to reclaim land which will be used to provide housing and other sports facilities in a fully integrated development.

4 Marina Design and Operation

Possibly because of the tax position the typical French yacht is smaller and lighter than its English counterpart, many more sailing yachts in proportion to the total have no engine, and the motor yacht, though it exists, is relatively rare. The generally lighter yachts permit the use of less heavily designed equipment, and there are some design features, such as the pontoons at Port Haliguen, which would repay study. Even in marinas provided from government funds it is common for the duties of harbour master to be officially delegated to the local club boatman.

As has been remarked, berthing is most often end-on; where parallel berthing is used yachts normally lie in tier. Consequently, the utilisation both of water plane area and pontoon footage is very much higher than is usually achieved in England. In other ways, too, the running is more economical and the upshot is that prices are considerably lower than in England. Marinas seem to be available for, and used by, a section of the yachting public in France which is less confined than in England to the very well-off. Taking a boat of 8 metres length, typical charges for full marina facilities, including supervision, are about £75 at Port Haliguen and about £150 at Pornic.

The emphasis is on encouraging active boating and discouraging house-boating. Most marinas make some provision (the planning authorisation usually requires 20% of the berths) for visitors, and the first night is usually free. The marinas in the Ports de Commerce at Lorient and Brest are specifically for visitors; the charge in the former rises after the first week to discourage long stays, while at Brest no charge is made for a stay of reasonable duration. It is note-worthy that good facilities are provided at most of the large commercial ports. La Pallice is the commercial port of La Rochelle; as provision for yachts is made elsewhere in La Rochelle (Fig. A, p. 50) it is rea-sonable that there should be nothing at La Pallice. Apart from this, it is only St. Nazaire that makes no proper provision for yachtsmen.

5 Official Attitude to Marinas

There is a climate of opinion which regards the provision of essen-tial facilities as a public responsibility; yachtsmen, who in France pay an annual licence fee, are entitled to use these. Thus it is unusual to find any charge made for the use of harbour facilities, except where use is made of a mooring, and even moorings are commonly free for a short stay; the same outlook is evidenced by the fact that yachts travel free on French canals.

Virtually all the marinas have been provided by government funds. Difficulties with the planning authorities, referred to in other papers, hardly exist in such cases. After discussion with local authorities the central government gets out its 5-year plan, and developments within this plan can go ahead subject to finance. The only problems are with inter-ministerial discussions, to ensure that all the departments affected are in agreement. The central government will provide up to 30% (usually 20%) of the basic construction cost and local authorities must find the rest, with some aid from central government in the form of loans at preferential interest rates; sometimes some private loan capital is involved. The local authorities normally aim to cover their share of the costs from receipts, but the central government share is an outright subsidy; Brittany is, of course, what we should call a development area. In the whole country the government has alloted just over £2.5 million in the VI plan (1971-75); of this £1.5 million goes to the NW area, but has to cover all kinds of yacht harbour, including dinghy facilities.

In the case of Pornic (Fig. 6), and other private schemes, no central government subsidy is paid. If the scheme is not financially viable in its own right it has to rely on integrated development with other shore enterprises, as in England. Although the Pornic scheme is part of such an integrated development, it appears that the marina is viable on its own. There are legal difficulties in allowing private enterprise to own a port. These are evaded by the device of a revocable concession, with a maximum period 50 years, usually less. There is, however, always liable to be public outcry at a private operator being permitted to operate, for private monopolistic profit, what should, in French eyes, be an essentially public utility. Some of the planning difficulties, which have appeared in England, are minimised by the preparation, by central government, of the 5-year plans. In the preparation of these plans, areas are identified in which development is desirable or to be banned on planning grounds (e.g. poor access), so that a private developer has a plan to fit in with, as is sometimes, but not always, the case in England.

If the yachting industry is to prosper there must be sufficient parking spaces, and these can only be adequately provided in the available water space by marina development. If adequate space is provided for yachts they can be kept out of the hair of other seamen. For example, since the marina was provided at Camaret, yachts have been prohibited from anchoring in other parts of the harbour, where they tended to get in the way of the fishermen. But yachtsmen are regarded as having their rights too, and at Les Sables d'Olonne, which has large yachting and fishing activities, the fishermen are not allowed to intrude into the area allocated to yachting, except out of the season, when the space is not needed for yachts.

There is very little pleasure cruising on inland waters in France; of the few hire companies operating several are British with mainly British customers, and there has been in consequence little marina development in inland waters. One has been built at Redon on the

Vilaine. This is a maritime port, accessible to coasters and masted yachts though some 32 km (20 miles) inland, but the marina development is partly based on inland cruising.

6 Summing-Up and Acknowledgements

It is fair to conclude that, in France, marina development is widespread, substantial and accelerating. The author's thanks are due to many who have helped in the preparation of this paper, and in particular to Monsieur Jean Couteaud, Ingénieur Général des Ponts et Chaussées, who provided a wealth of material which has been liberally drawn on.

Appendix*

Marina Development between St. Malo and La Rochelle

Location	Capacity	Completion	Type
St. Malo	250	1963	E
Les Bas Sablons	900	1973	SW
Paimpol	60	1969	E
Lézardrieux	60	1972/3	E
Perros Guirec	120	1969	SWG
Morlaix	60	1968	E
L'Aberwrac'h	60	1969	D
Brest	30	1967	E
Moulin Blanc	120	1968	BD
Camaret	80	1970	E
Morgat	250	1973	BD
Tréboul	130	1967	D
La Forêt	700	1973	BD
Concarneau	60	1967	D
Lorient	200	1969	DG
P. Haliguen	215	1968	B
La Trinité	360	1971	BD
Le Croisic	100	1971	D
Le Pouliguen	420	1966	E
La Roche Bernard	80	1972	D
Redon	60	1972	E
Pornic	900	1972	BD
L'Herbaudière	450	1973	D
St. Gilles	30	1967	D
Les Sables	100	1967	D
La Perrotine	180	1971	SWG
Les Minimes	1000	1971	BD
La Rochelle	350	1966	D

Symbols:

E	=	existing sheltered deep area
D	=	dredging only
SW	=	submersible wall
SWG	=	submersible wall and dock gate
B	=	breakwater with limited dredging
BD	=	breakwater with substantial dredging
DG	=	dredging and dock gate

---

*All data quoted are very approximate.

Discussion

(Session 6)

AUTHORS' INTRODUCTION

Mr. D. Hodges

In view of the wide ranging nature of the subject a triple authorship has been necessary for our paper.

Henry Cohen has been responsible for the introduction—appropriately enough, since it was in his fertile brain that this large child was conceived.

Frank Terrett has been responsible for those sections dealing with the early history of the project—the examination of alternative sites and the various engineering and hydraulic feasibility studies. This is only appropriate, since it was he who acted with Derek Head, of Overton and Partners, the architects retained by the Company, to make the first appraisals and prepare the original scheme. He has also described the engineering work that is now in progress.

I have been responsible for Sect. 4 entitled 'The Development of the Architectural Concept' and for the final Section entitled 'The Present Situation'. It is on this last aspect that I would like to elaborate.

The Brighton Marina Company, having entered into a contract for the breakwater construction, is now irrevocably committed to the completion of the outer and inner harbours in their agreed form. We are committed also to the land reclamation which either forms part of the present contract or is directly associated with it.

Beyond this commitment, there is still some freedom of choice within the limits set by the Brighton Marina Act and by the Brighton Corporation, which is the planning authority. That freedom—at least in respect of the framework of the scheme—will not last for long. In order to maintain the momentum of this scheme and to allow time for adequate planning and preparation, this framework has to be decided well in advance of the date by which the breakwater construction will have provided adequate protection for the start of the first building contract.

Six possible land reclamation layouts within the harbour have been examined, differing in principle in respect of such matters as ratio of water frontage to the area of land enclosed, cost of construction in various depths of water, the effect on the harbour layout, and many other factors.

To these six alternatives are applied three construction programmes related to fully protected, partly protected or largely unprotected conditions, each of which gives differing results in terms of construction costs, escalation over longer or shorter periods, and financing resulting in 18 cost options.

To these 18 cost options can be applied six different methods of dealing with yachtsmen's car parking and the access therefrom to the moorings, varying in terms of cost and convenience. This results theoretically in 108 possible combinations. In fact, not all six methods of parking are applicable to all six land reclamation forms. Even so, 78 are left. Many of these can no doubt be discarded quickly, but it will be seen that, whereas the scheme described in the paper remains an accepted and acceptable solution, the checking of it and comparison with possible alternatives is a very complex matter.

Added to this is the whole question of market research and the establishment of the demand and rate of absorption of the accommodation provided. Market research, as everyone will know, is, at the best of times, an imprecise affair. In this instance, it is bedevilled by two things. First, the long period over which the prediction has to be made. This is, at the very least, an eight-year programme so that there is a need for frequent updating. Secondly, there is the fact that the Brighton Marina is an entirely new concept which may generate its own unpredictable demand.

These two studies—the updated market research study and the background of possible solutions—have to be put together now, so that we can be quite sure of having the most suitable framework within which to fit the demands for accommodation of all kinds. These demands will, inevitably, conflict. It is essential to strike within them the best balance between land and water areas.

The present situation is, therefore, one in which two things are happening.

The breakwater construction programme has come through the winter on schedule and is proceeding with every prospect that it will be completed within the estimated time.

Secondly, an intense process of analysis is going on in order to check finally, during the short period now remaining, the correctness of the decisions so far taken.

Mr. F. L. Terrett

The harbour is divided into two basins as indicated in Fig. 1 (p. 402). The periphery of the inner basin will be in the form of jetties, whilst that for the outer basin is the large breakwater now under construction.

Many investigations have been undertaken for this project some of which are still continuing. One particular matter I would like to refer to is the question of what conditions are acceptable for the mooring of small vessels. It is not only a question of what wave heights are acceptable, because the phenomenon of ranging or surge is not dependent only on this factor.

There are three aspects that need to be studied:

(1) The penetration of storm waves into the mooring basin.

(2) The penetration of long wave disturbances.

(3) The generation of waves within the basin itself.

The first is referred to in Sect. 3 of the paper. A harbour entrance must be provided and it is often impracticable to prevent storm waves passing through from one direction or another. This is particularly true of a case such as Brighton, where there is no natural protection.

The storm wave models, which we built in 1967 and 1971, were used to study this problem among others, and included numerous modifications aimed at reducing wave reflections at the harbour entrance and within the outer harbour.

In the arrangement now proposed, the model tests demonstrated that the height of waves passing from the outer harbour through the inner entrance to the inner harbour should be not less than 10 per cent of the height of the waves in the open sea and, in most cases, less than 5 per cent.

It might be more meaningful if I were to convert those figures into actual wave heights. This introduces the question of the frequency of occurrence.

Using the predictions based on the record of waves which was made at Brighton in 1967, it means that waves in excess of 0·4 m (1·3 ft) should occur not more frequently than once a year on average, and, in excess of 0·5 m (1·6 ft) not more frequently than once in 100 years on average.

I would not like it to be thought that, if we were so unfortunate as to get a 0·5 m (1·6 ft) wave running into the inner basin the year after the harbour was completed, we could then feel confident that we would not get a wave of that height again for another 100 years.

That statement might perhaps be better turned around to say that there is a 1 per cent chance that we will get waves of 0·5 m (1·6 ft) in height in any one year, and that there is an approximately 50 per cent chance that we would get waves of 0·4 m (1·3 ft) in any one year.

Apart from that, the waves—once they have passed through the inner entrance—would be reduced in height as they expanded after passing the basin, and the presence of boats and pontoons would further help to dissipate the remaining energy of the waves. This applies particularly to what we call short waves, mainly in the 5 to 8 second range.

The second type of disturbance is that of ranging, which may occur if the period of long waves coincides with the natural resonances of the harbour basins. This very long wave activity occurs commonly in periods of 1 to 5 minutes, as Professor Lundgren and Mr. Stickland have mentioned, but they are of very small amplitude so that they are scarcely noticeable in the open sea. Practically speaking, it is impossible to suppress such waves, and they can penetrate the most complicated system of harbour basins.

Unfortunately, the long wave recorder at Brighton was only operating for a very short period. During that time, we recorded waves of between 45 and 180 seconds. Generally, these were not more than 0·025 m (1 in.) in height and the highest which we recorded was about 0·075 m (3 in.). This was apart from one rather extraordinary local storm surge, when we obtained a record of waves with a period of 6 to 11 minutes and up to 0·3 m (1 ft) in height. However, these were not regular waves which could set up resonance in the harbour.

The model to which Sect. 3 of the paper refers, and which is shown in Fig. 2 (p. 403), was built to study the long wave activity. Briefly, the results of the investigation showed that waves of $1\frac{1}{2}$ and 3 minute periods increased to three times their height inside the harbour. However, shorter waves were very much attenuated except close to a 90-second period, when the maximum height reached was about 50 per cent of the waves in the open sea.

Bearing in mind the very small amplitude of these waves, the consequences are really quite insignificant.

However, the movement of vessels, and the resulting forces on mooring lines depends not only upon the wave heights but on the water slopes, which are associated with waves of this kind. The model at the Hydraulics Research Station—in what is called their 'starry sky' basin—was built in order to measure these very small water slopes. From this information, mooring forces were calculated. It was concluded that the boats could be held quite easily by normal mooring systems and that this was most unlikely to constitute a serious problem at Brighton.

Lastly, there is the question of waves generated within the basin itself. If a basin the size of the inner harbour at Brighton were an open expanse of water, waves up to 0·75 m (2·3 ft) in height could probably be generated. However, the presence of jetties and pontoons would largely prevent this. Again, I do not think that this will be a problem in the case of Brighton.

The other way in which waves may be generated within the harbour is from overspill of the breakwaters. This matter was brought to the fore when the contractor submitted his proposal for the caisson type of structure. It had to be decided if what he was proposing would perform as well as—or perhaps better than—the buttress type of breakwater which had been adopted in all the preliminary schemes for the harbour.

Initially, we accepted the buttress-type breakwater as a yardstick, and comparative model tests were carried out by Professor Lundgren at Copenhagen. As he has already said, the simulation of overtopping in a model is subject to a number of limitations, to which I would like to return, and it also requires realistic wave conditions in the model.

The Danish Institute was able to produce such a pattern of waves, using a train of 250 irregular waves which had been built up mathematically by combining 100 sinusoidal components. The model was of scale 1/22 and was placed in a wave channel 0·6 m (2 ft) wide. It was subjected to repeated runs of these wave trains with wind blowing over the water equivalent to 45 knots in nature, or a Force 9 gale.

The movements of two model boats moored 60 m (20 ft) behind the breakwater were recorded, and also wave heights in that position. Later, we found that the wave height measurements were more consistent than the measurements of boat motions. Therefore, the former were accepted as the true comparison of one test with another.

For various reasons, we subsequently altered the profile of the breakwater and a further series of tests was carried out last year. By that time, the Danish Institute had been fortunate enough to obtain an actual record of a storm which had been made at one of the drilling rigs in the North Sea. This record extended over a period of about 6 hours and contained nearly 3000 waves. Since we now had a naturally occurring pattern of waves, this was used in the second series of tests.

At first, it appeared that the changed profiles resulted in a greater amount of overtopping. We then went back and repeated the tests with the natural wave train on the buttress-type breakwater which, unfortunately, also turned out to be very much worse.

From examination of the data obtained from these tests, it was decided to adopt a wave height in the prototype of approximately 0·45 m (1. 4 ft) as being acceptable for the condition estimated to occur once in a hundred years on average. This meant that there was a 1 per cent chance that we would get waves of about 0·45 m (1·4 ft) in any one year at the position at which the boats nearest the breakwater would be moored.

For a number of reasons, I believe that the results obtained from the model tests are conservative.

In the first place, the model was two-dimensional, and it was simulating waves striking square onto the breakwater and overtopping the whole length from end to end. In practice, storm waves are short-crested and will normally approach from some angle to the structure. Therefore, they will overtop only a short length at any one time. The waves generated by the overtopping water will then spread laterally within the harbour and become less in height as they travel across the basin.

Secondly, the model does not produce spray in the same way in which spray is produced in nature, and the water in the model tends to overtop in larger masses which are less scattered by the wind.

(Mr. Terrett then showed a short film of the model tests)

Prof. A. N. Black

In my paper, I have described quite briefly the yacht harbours in the north-west corner of France. I am rather inclined to compare this corner with the area of England which I know—the Solent. I warn everyone to beware of this mistake.

The Solent is the rich, warm, sunny south, whilst this area is the impoverished, windy north-west. We should compare the Solent with the Mediterranean and the Riviera, of which we have already had some good illustrations, and compare this area with the Clyde and north-west Scotland, where marina development appears to be on a very limited scale.

(Prof. Black then showed a number of slides illustrating many of the yacht harbours listed in his paper).

In the discussion during the first session, Mr. Shannon raised the question of headroom which should be provided at bridges.

On the French coast the clearance under a number of bridges is fixed by considerations other than the needs of navigation, e.g. the height of the adjacent land. Three recent bridges, where clearance for navigation was the ruling factor, have the following clearance at extreme high water:

Benodet, 30 m (100 ft); traffic includes commercial vessels up to 1500 t.

Fromentine, 24 m (80 ft); apart from yachts and fishing vessels the only traffic is the ferry to Ile d'Yeu, which does not require this height.

Oleron, 15 m (50 ft); yachts and fishing vessels only.

CONTRIBUTIONS

Mr. J. D. Mettam (Bertlin and Partners, Consulting Engineers, Redhill)

My firm is responsible for the locks providing access to the inner basin at Brighton. The high water level in this inner harbour will increase the attractiveness of the shoreward part of the development.

A lock with sector gates is worthy of serious consideration in a marina project where it is desired to limit the tidal range. This design has been adopted at Chichester Yacht Basin (Fig. 11, p. 213) and has proved very successful. Sector gates control the water levels without the need for sluicing culverts and the gates can be opened or closed with a differential head of water.

Since the Chichester project, my firm has made a study for the National Ports Council* aimed at reducing the cost of sector gates when applied to very large locks for ships—entrances of 30 m (100 ft) width or more—and I would like to explain some of our findings which are very relevant to the smaller locks as well.

Fig. A shows plan views of three types of sector gates. Type (i) is a plain radial gate with no frills. The basic principle is that water pressure on the face acts radially through the hinge position. When the gates are opened, water can only pass through the centre gap.

Type (ii) is a radial gate fitted with 'ears' at each end and it has been widely used in Sweden, America and France. The idea is that as the gate opens there is an additional flow of water around the sides into the recesses. The energy of the flow through the recesses is well dissipated, and this results in more satisfactory conditions in the lock.

Type (iii) introduces the modification used at Chichester, where the arc of the gate is just over 90 degrees. When one starts to open it there is a flow at the sides, but the ears at the centre remain in contact and there is no flow through the centre. This further improves conditions for boats in the lock.

Considering the different types of gate, it seemed to us that Types (ii) and (iii) lose much of the advantage of being radial. As soon as they are opened, there is a drop of water level near the ends of the gate, which causes differential pressures on the ears. These pressures are, of course, tangential so they produce considerable moments about the hinge face. It is only the centre part of the gate, where the water level remains fairly uniform, that the pressures are radial. Therefore, it occurred to us to consider Type (iv)—which we call the delta gate—where the face is straight.

The resultant water pressure, in the static condition when closed, on any of these gates is identical to the pressure on a straight line joining the ends of the gate so the delta gate has the same forces on it as a radial gate when it is closed. When it is opened, the differential pressures near the ends of the delta gate are more nearly radial than they are in the radial gate with ears.

---

*Bertlin and Partners (1971), Research Project on Lock Sluicing and Sector Gates—Stage 1, National Ports Council.

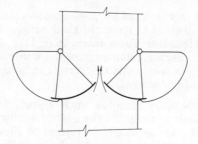

(i) PLAIN RADIAL GATES   CENTRE SLUICING

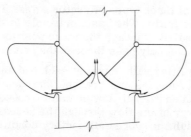

(ii) 60° RADIAL GATES WITH EARS   SIDE & CENTRE SLUICING

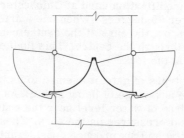

(iii) 90° RADIAL GATES WITH EARS   SIDE SLUICING

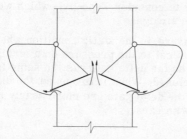

(iv) DELTA GATES   SIDE & CENTRE SLUICING

Figure A Types of sector gate

With this in mind, we went on to design, as Fig. B illustrates, a massive type of gate for an extrance 30 m (100 ft) wide and 12 m (40 ft) high. We thought that we had invented something new, and discussed with the National Ports Council who should patent it. Then I went to Chicago to see a new lock which had been built by the U.S. Army Corps of Engineers. It was of the radial type with ears. When I mentioned the delta gate they suggested a visit to the Chicago Sanitary Canal lock. I went there and discovered that, over 40 years ago, someone had built exactly this type of delta gate, which emphasises how difficult it is to think of a really new idea. But it is a pity that the prototype was not in a more salubrious location!

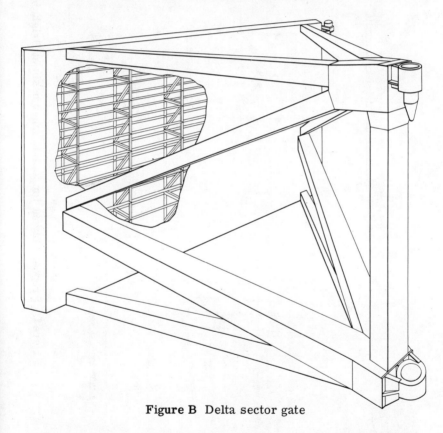

Figure B Delta sector gate

On behalf of the National Ports Council, we organised some model tests on these Type (iv) gates with the principal aim of establishing the operating forces during the extreme case of emergency closure under a large head difference. The results showed, among other things, that the gate tends to close itself which makes this type of gate very

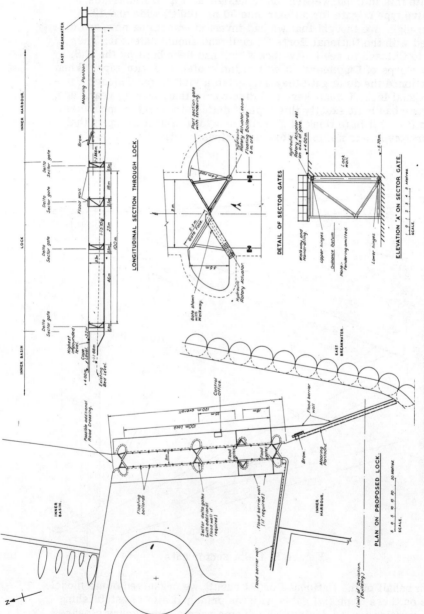

Figure C Proposed layout for lock to inner basin at Brighton Marina

suitable for use as a guard gate to be closed if the normal lock gates are damaged by, for example, a ship over-running. All that is required once closure has started is to apply a braking action of a fairly modest amount. The restraining force to control closure of a gate with prototype dimensions of 30 m (100 ft) width and 12 m (40 ft) height with a full flow through was found to be about 40 t, which is easily controlled.

Fig. C shows the proposed application of this type of gate to Brighton Marina. The lock shown would have four pairs of gates. The two outer pairs would be raised very high so as to exclude surges from exceptionally high tides.

When there were not many customers, two pairs of gates close together would be used, forming a fairly short lock; with a lot of traffic, the entire lock could be used.

Mr. F. N. Midmer (Area Engineer, Kent River Authority)

It appears that the breakwaters of the new Brighton Marina could act as a groyne intercepting the natural littoral drift of material along the coast.

Having had some experience of the type of problems which have arisen from the construction of harbours along a shingle coastline, notably Rye, I would be glad if Mr. Terrett would comment on the anticipated effect, particularly on the downdrift side of the new harbour.

Mr. T. J. C. Crocker (Trevor Crocker and Partners, Consulting Engineers, Mitcham)

Could I ask what provision will be made at the Brighton Marina for fire fighting in general and for access for fire fighting vehicles in particular?

Mr. A. W. White (Assistant Borough Engineer, Poole)

Recently, I had to give evidence at the Planning Enquiry into the Poole Harbour Marina at Baiter Point. One of the matters which caused concern was the traffic which would be generated on the highway network by the Marina.

To give evidence in this case required a number of assumptions on my part and these were as follows:

(1) The car parking provision would be 3 car spaces to each two berths.

(2) The maximum number of yachts that would be in use at any one time would not exceed 2/3 of the total provision.

(3) That each vehicle parked would make two trips per day—one inward and one outward.

(4) The maximum number of trips in the peak hour would be 1/10 of the total trips generated, the peak hour flow being the basis of design of the highway system.

These assumptions were accepted by the Inspector and the Minister. On this basis, a marina designed to accommodate 1000 yachts will generate a peak hour traffic flow as follows:—

Maximum number of vehicles = 1000 × 3/2 × 2/3 = 1000
Total number of trips per day = 1000 × 2 = 2000
Maximum number of trips in peak hour = 2000 × 1/10 = 200
Peak hour trips in both directions = 200
Inward peak hour trips = 100
Outward peak hour trips = 100

I would be interested to know what assumptions were made in the planning of the Brighton Marina concerning the vehicle trips. There has been some agreement on the numbers and ratio of car parking spaces and berths, but I have seen no mention of trips generated by the marina.

AUTHORS' REPLY

Mr. F. L. Terrett

The question has been raised as to the effect of the harbour on the movement of beach material with the natural littoral drift along the adjoining coastline. This subject was studied in some detail as part of the earlier investigations into the scheme and involved an examination of the history of the beaches for a considerable distance on either side of the harbour.

The dominant littoral drift is from west to east and, prior to the construction of the new harbour arm at Shoreham, shingle on the Brighton beaches had probably come from as far away as Selsey Bill. Since the construction of the Shoreham breakwater this source of supply has been effectively cut off and the accretion which has since occurred along the eastern part of the Brighton sea front represents a loss of material from the beaches between Brighton and Shoreham.

There are several masonry groynes along the Brighton sea front and up to about ten years ago material was accumulating between those in the Black Rock area at the rate of about 11, 500 m^3 (15, 000 yd^3) per annum. It was evident that at that time very little material was finding its way around those groynes and eastwards towards Rottingdean. The

Figure A General view (Oct. 1972) of Brighton Marina site looking west from the main batching plant showing the land reclamation, the caisson casting yard and the crane in position for placing the next caisson on the west breakwater

bays between these groynes are now almost completely filled with
shingle and, if the Brighton Marina were not being built, any further
material moving in the future into this area would travel over the
groynes to the benefit of the beaches further to the east. However, we
are fairly confident that the steps which have been taken since the construction of the Shoreham breakwater to improve the groyning system
along the main frontage at Brighton and at Hove and Shoreham have
appreciably reduced the movement of material into the Black Rock area.
In the light of these considerations it seems unlikely that the new yacht
harbour at Brighton will have significant effect on the down-drift
beaches.

A further point that should be made is that if nevertheless the
beaches to the east are found to have been adversely affected by the
harbour the Marina Company may be required to dig away any shingle
which has accumulated against the new west breakwater and deposit it
on the beaches to the east.

In order that the situation can be kept under review a survey was
made of the beaches before construction started and the Company will
make further surveys in the future if the Authorities responsible for
coast protection in the area consider that the beaches are being adversely affected and require the Company to take steps to remedy the
situation.

Mr. D. Hodges

With regard to the steps that are being taken to deal with fire hazard,
the Brighton Marina Company has appointed a very experienced fire
officer as consultant to advise the architect throughout the whole planning process. Good access for fire fighting vehicles will be assured by
virtue of the integrated treatment of land and water areas.

Also, of course, we have had discussions from time to time with the
Chief Fire Officer at Brighton and he has indicated his willingness to
co-operate with us in every possible way in the making of special arrangements to deal with this very novel situation.

The question of traffic generation is a most important aspect of the
wider planning of the Brighton Marina project.

To serve the Marina by the date it is intended that it will be in operation, it was necessary to bring forward the road programme by some
years. For that reason, it was necessary to promote a Bill in Parliament called the Brighton Corporation Roads Bill, which received the
Royal Assent in 1970.

The Corporation is now finalising the design of the road system. This
road system, clearly, has certain capacities, and, although it will be improved in small measure, it is a limiting factor which we must take into
account.

The Brighton Marina scheme has, in our view, a requirement for about 6,000 car parking spaces. The calculation that has to be done is of how those car parking spaces are to be used. The times at which these 'trips' are going to be made by a whole range of different types of user must be estimated.

We have the yachtsmen, and predictions of when they may arrive and when they may leave. We have predictions of the number of boats which may be visited at any one time. We have a large residential population, and predictions of the way in which they may use their cars and the times at which they may use them. We have proposals for a shopping centre, a conference centre, for entertainments, and sports facilities for the public; car parking spaces are allocated to all these uses.

Therefore, it can be seen that the calculations which will result in the definitive answer to the question: What are the number of trips and when will they be made?-are not easy to make. In fact, a study is now being carried out by Brighton Corporation and Ove Arup and Partners, who are acting as traffic engineers to this scheme, to try to sort out this difficult problem.

If the answer is that the mix of uses of this site and scale of them is such that, at times, these 'trips' will be of a volume which the road system cannot accept, then the only answer will be to alter that mix.

However, we have reason to believe that the mix and the number of car parking spaces, as now proposed, may well result in a traffic generation which—when it is added to the existing traffic generated by Brighton itself—will not produce a situation which is unacceptable.

Summing-up

Rear-Admiral P. D. Gick (President, National Yacht Harbour Association)

During the interesting discussion of the last two days a number of points have been raised on which I would like to make some observations.

The problem of berths for visitors is a difficult one. If a large number are to be kept vacant for casual visitors who do not materialise it could well result in a serious financial loss to the marina operator.

But it should be borne in mind that every time a yacthsman sails from a marina, he leaves an empty berth. With good organisation, and co-operation between berth-holder and marina operator, it could be established which berths will be empty and for how long. I would like to feel that in an area such as the Solent, well served by marinas, that an effective communication system will be established advising the yachtsman on the location of vacant berths.

The question of the depth of water in marinas has been raised. At Emsworth Yacht Harbour, the minimum depth varies between 1.2 m (4 ft) and 0.6 m (2 ft) and this variation has resulted in a saving of dredging costs, whilst at the same time accommodating the range of craft intended. The dredging was, however, undertaken by dragline operating from land and this might be of some significance.

Around our coasts there are a large number of little harbours which are scarcely used. We have seen how the French, by putting up a half-tide wall, have adapted quite simply a small harbour so that boats can stay afloat. There are surely plenty of opportunities in this country on these lines.

The question of planning approval has given rise to some argument. In the early days of marinas, I believe that the planners had some justification for being very chary about applications for marina development. There is no doubt that they were often confronted by schemes in the name of a marina which were just a camouflage for lucrative property development.

Relations are now, however, much better and in recent years quite a number of planners have attended our N.Y.H.A. meetings at the Boat Show and have put forward some very helpful and useful comments. Incidentally, N.Y.H.A. are now engaged in drafting a document offering guidance to planners in their consideration of applications for marinas.

I know that there are many yachtsmen who for one reason or another still do not wish to go into a marina. However, we must remember that, if they stay on swinging moorings in congested waterways such as Chichester Harbour, they are being, to put it mildly, very selfish. The majority of such people only use their boats for seven weekends or so and perhaps a fortnight during the year. All the rest of the time, their boat is getting in someone else's way.

All I ask them to do is to berth their boats in a yacht harbour when they are not using them so that the people who want to sail in estuaries and enjoy themselves can do so.

This raises the problem of the poor yachtsman who cannot afford a marina berth. Is he really all that poor? Almost all yacht owners own a car for which they have paid hundreds of pounds. Annually, they pay £50 or more for their licence and insurance, and £200 or £300 to run it; and many use their cars only for leisure. Yet, when they spend £1000 on purchasing a yacht they sometimes begrudge the £100 or so a year which is needed to look after it decently and keep it out of other people's way.

As I indicated yesterday, it is cheaper to berth a yacht in a marina in Chichester Harbour than to keep it on a swinging mooring during the summer and lay it up in one of the local yacht yards for the winter.

I think the important point is that so many people want to use the areas of sea close to the coast which are nice and sheltered that they must be, to some extent, regulated and must not be allowed to spoil other people's pleasure.

Mr. D. A. McIntyre then terminated the formal proceedings by proposing the vote of thanks to the organisers and sponsors of the Symposium.

Exhibition

A display of models, drawings, photographs and literature concerned with marinas was arranged in the foyer and surrounds of the lecture theatre. Brief particulars are given in the following pages together with a few illustrations.

Subject	Exhibitor
Heritage Coast Study	Countryside Commission
Marinas in England and Wales	University of Southampton
Marinas in the Solent	University of Southampton
The Solent as a Recreational Area	County Planning Dept., Hampshire C.C.
The Provision of Sailing Facilities	Gosport Borough Council
Woolverstone Marina, R. Orwell	K. Montgomery-Smith (Consulting Engineer), Harpenden
Royal Harwich Yacht Club	Peter Barefoot and Partners (Architects), London
St. Katherine by the Tower Yacht Basin, London	Renton, Howard Wood Associates (Architects), London
Proposed Sandwich Marina	Tucker, Joyce, Laws (Architects), Tunbridge Wells
Proposed Hastings Marina	Sir. W. Halcrow and Partners (Consulting Engineers), London
Constructional work at Brighton Marina	University of Southampton
Chichester Yacht Basin	Bertlin and Partners (Consulting Engineers), Redhill
Emsworth Yacht Harbour	Vernon Gibberd Associates (Architects), London
Proposed Langstone Marina	Bailey, Piper, Stevens Partnership (Architects), Southampton
Proposed Paulsgrove Marina	City Development Dept., Portsmouth Corporation
Camper and Nicholsons Marina, Gosport	Queen's Harbour Master, Portsmouth
The River Hamble	University of Southampton
Mercury Yacht Habour	Derek Lovejoy and Partners (Architects), Highcliffe, Hants.
Lymington Marina	K. Montgomery-Smith (Consulting Engineer), Harpenden
Model of Poole Harbour Yacht Marina	Bertlin and Partners (Consulting Engineers), Redhill

Subject	Exhibitor
Brixham Harbour	E. W. H. Gifford and Partners (Consulting Engineers), Southampton
Development of Barry Old Harbour	W. S. Atkins and Partners (Consulting Engineers), Cardiff
Proposed Pwllheli Marina	Fram Gerrard Ltd., Manchester
Proposed Conway Marina	Bradshaw Rose Hasker Associates (Architects), Liverpool
Carrickfergus Harbour, N.I.	W. J. McDowell and Asssociates (Consulting Engineers), Belfast
Coleraine Marina, N.I.	Eric Seaton (Architect), Coleraine
Canal Recreational Developments	British Waterways Board
Model of Windsor Marina	J. G. Meakes Ltd., Marlow
Proposed Marina at Evesham	A. G. Griffiths and Sons (Surveyors), Evesham
Proposed Kinnego Marina, Lough Neagh	Craigavon Development Corporation, N.I.
Princesses Pavilion Marina, W. Holland	Watersportcenter, Leimuiden, Holland
Port Grimaud, France	Sidney Kaye, Eric Firmin and Partners (Architects), London
Marina Del Rey, Los Angeles	Sidney Kaye, Eric Firmin and Partners (Architects), London
Marina Architecture	Sidney Kaye, Eric Firmin and Partners (Architects), London
Sector Gate Studies	Bertlin and Partners (Consulting Engineers), Redhill

Subject	Exhibitor
Model of Floating Breakwater	Sea Services Agency Ltd., Folkestone
Dredging Operations and Equipment	Nash Dredging Ltd., Weybridge
Pontoons	Walcon Ltd., Winchester
Pontoons	Thos. Storey (Engineers) Ltd., London
Timber for Marinas	David Roberts Ltd., Liverpool
Timber for Marinas	Millars Constructional Woods Ltd., London
Boat Hoists	Renner Ltd., Port Swanwick, Hants.
Seahorse Transporter	Wicormarine, Portchester, Hants.

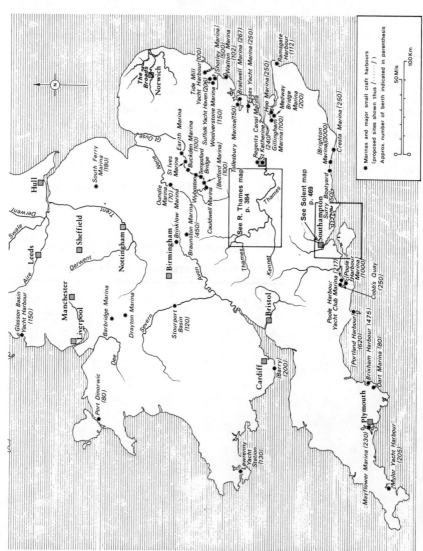

Figure 1 Map of England and Wales showing marinas (existing or proposed)

(i) Western breakwater arm

(ii) View looking east

Figure 2 Brighton Marina—initial stages of construction

(i) Oblique view

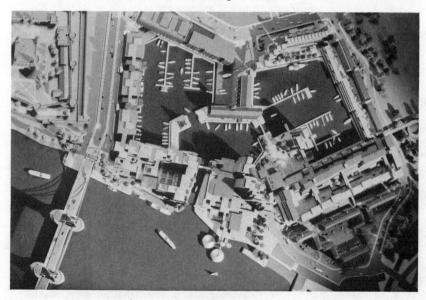

(ii) Plan

Figure 3 St. Katherine by the Tower (London) project
(Renton Howard Wood Associates)

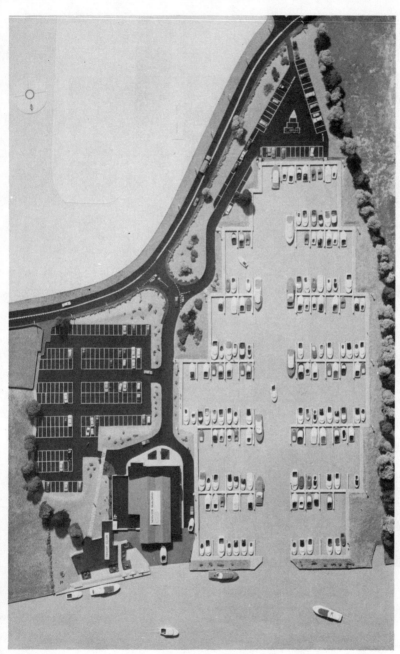

Figure 4 Windsor Marina, R. Thames

Figure 5 Yachtsmen's cabins at Emsworth Yacht Harbour *(Vernon Gibberd Associates)*

Figure 6 British Steel at a marina berth—the yacht in which Chay
Blyth in 1971 sailed around the world

Marina Tour

A number of marinas in the Solent area were visited by launch and coach on 21st April. The route of the tour is shown in Fig. 1 (overleaf). Lunch was taken at Beaulieu Abbey and Lord Montagu kindly gave a short address. In the following pages a brief description is given of the various marinas visited during the tour.

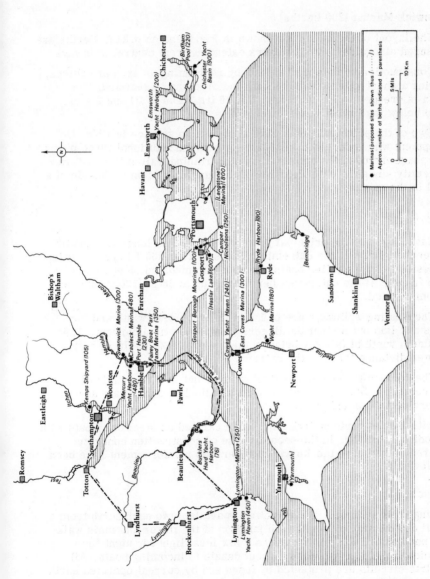

Figure 1 Map of the Solent showing marinas (existing or proposed) and route of tour

HAMBLE RIVER

Swanwick Marina (300 berths)

The layout of the marina is shown in Fig. 2 and on p. 212. Berths are arranged alongside pontoon fingers extending from central walkways.

Construction commenced in 1967 by reclaiming an area of saltings, driving a sheet-piled retaining wall and dredging to seaward. The basin is dredged to 1·5 m (5 ft), 1·8 m (6 ft), 2·1 m (7 ft) and 2·4 m (8 ft) below the lowest water level.

Two of the principal piers were brought into service in 1968. Development was undertaken in 1972 to provide an additional three piers; this phase included the construction of a training wall at the eastern extremity since the extended area of the marina lies on the inside of a bend in the estuary.

Berthing:

Each finger of the principal piers is 19 m (62 ft) long, retained by a greenheart pile at the extremity. Boats of 20 m (65 ft) can be berthed alongside or two smaller boats can be accommodated on each side of each finger. At the outermost berth, craft up to 36 m (120 ft) can be accommodated.

The floating walkways are of 1·8 m (6 ft) uniform width and the piers are laid out so that the fingers lie with the tidal current. The minimum width of fairway between the fingers is 23 m (75 ft) with a greater distance towards the extremity of the piers.

The pontoon walkways are steel framed and decked with hardwood. The central walkways are boarded longitudinally to facilitate access to service cables and pipes.

Initially, the pontoon deck units were carried on steel box floats with cathodic protection. In the second phase of construction concrete covered polystyrene blocks with non-ferrous reinforcement have been employed.

Services:

Single phase mains voltage power is available to each berth from a small distribution pillar at each junction of the finger and main walkway pontoons. Each pillar carries a low level light for night time illumination of the walkways without dazzle to incoming boats. All electric circuits are protected by fuses and by current operated earth leakage trips.

Fresh water is available to each berth and is fed to the piers by a Hill-Dickow automatic pressure pump.

(*Southern Newspapers Ltd.*)

Figure 2 Swanwick Marina

Main drainage is available close to the site but at insufficient depth for direct connection. A Tuke and Bell pumping unit was therefore installed for sewage transfer to the main sewer.

Shore Facilities:

In the design of the sheet-piled retaining wall, advantage was taken of the eastward end return to incorporate a Renner dock. With one free standing pier and the other runway on the hard standing it has been possible to employ two Renner hoists, of differing capacities, over the same dock. The Swanwick Marina is alone in this country in employing two mobile marine hoists, of 27 t and 36 t lifting capacity, respectively. Boatyard facilities are adjacent.

The amenities of the marina include a large car park (2 cars per berth), chandlery, shower room and toilet facilities. A yacht club and restaurant are planned for 1973.

In addition, there is a show area for boat sales.

Designer (Phases 1 and 2): D. H. Sessions, Marina Management Ltd., Swanwick.

Main Contractors (Phase 1): Westminster Dredging Co. Ltd.

Main Contractors (Phase 2): M. B. Dredging Ltd. and Pritchard and Peach Ltd.

Pontoons: Fabricated to the design of Marina Management Ltd. by Dibbens Structural Engineers. Flotation units by Walcon Ltd.

Berthing charge (1972): £26·3 per metre (£8 per ft) per annum.

Mercury Yacht Harbour (250 berths)*

The marina (Fig. 3 and p. 266), which was brought into operation in 1972, has been created by the excavation of an area of mudflats and saltings, and the reclamation of the adjacent low-lying areas. Badnam Creek forms the northern boundary of the harbour.

The harbour has been dredged to 2·3 m (7·5 ft) below MLWS by a 300 mm (12 in.) cutter suction dredger of 520 kW (385 hp).

The northern and southern boundaries have been excavated to slopes varying between 1 : 2 and 1 : 4 whilst the western face has been retained by an anchored sheet-pile wall which returns at the northern end beside the existing slipway. This retaining wall consists of 12 m (40 ft) long Frodingham 3N piles in high-plus steel tied back to a line of anchorages approximately 4·2 m (14 ft) long and 15 m (50 ft) behind the line of the front face.

---

* Additional information concerning this marina is given on pp. 265-267.

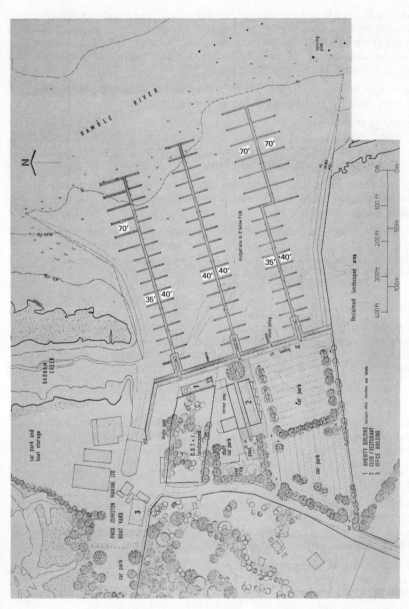

Figure 3 Layout of Mercury Yacht Harbour

Berthing:

The length, width and spacing of the various fingers and the spacing of the main pontoons were carefully decided upon after taking account of the expected market, the limitations of the fairway and the arrangement of the site. It will be seen from Fig. 3 that a variety of yacht lengths and beams is catered for.

There are three 2·5 m (8 ft) wide main pontoon walkways connected to the quay wall by access ramps of 18 m (59 ft) length.

Finger pontoons with widths of 1·2 m (4 ft) for lengths up to 12 m (40 ft) and 2 m for lengths of 21 m (70 ft) are bolted to the main pontoons, with the whole located by mooring piles spaced along the main walkways and at the ends of the longer or more vulnerable fingers.

Most of these piles are of hewn greenheart but for the north-east area, steel box piles are used because of the variable nature of the bottom of the basin.

All pontoons have a galvanised steel framework of welded or bolted construction with hardwood decking and are supported by expanded polystyrene floats which will be protected by a tough sprayed-on plastic coating.

Services:

Particular attention has been paid to the provision of the appropriate services (electricity, water) and to their location relative to each berth. Special distribution points with lighting units are located strategically with associated socket outlets placed at each berth.

Emergency service points in distinctive colours are also spaced along the main walkways.

Care has been taken to facilitate the movement of personnel and trolleys throughout the main walkways and access bridges by the elimination of loose cables, pipes, or steps.

Shore Facilities:

The Stage 1 Amenity Building provides the offices and stores, the chandlery and yacht sales office, together with the toilet and laundry facilities. The toilet arrangements have been designed to provide special accommodation for berth holders in addition to the basic facilities.

Stage 2 of the building programme will house the restaurants, bars, and club rooms, together with other special facilities. The adjacent boatyard provides repair and layout facilities whilst still maintaining production of the Knox-Johnston Marine range of K-craft.

Architects: Derek Lovejoy and Partners, Highcliffe, Hants.

Consulting Engineer: H. Denys Barron, Southampton.

Main Contractor: Nash Dredging and Reclamation Co. Ltd.

Pontoons: Thos. Storey (Engineers) Ltd.

Berthing charge (1972): £26.3 per metre (£8 per ft) per annum.

Port Hamble (230 berths)

The layout of the marina is shown in Fig. 4.

Pontoon berths provide for craft up to 36 m (120 ft). Minimum depth of water is 1·4 m (4·5 ft).

The facilities include a Travelift hoist, capacity 10·75 t and a slipway of capacity 100 t. The fuelling pontoon is shown in Fig. 5.

Berthing chage (1972): £26.3 per metre (£8 per ft) per annum.

(Southern Newspapers Ltd.)

Figure 4 Port Hamble

Fairey Boat Park (150 berths)

Dry land berthage (Fig. 6) is provided for shallow-draft boats of 6·5 m-10 m (20 ft-33 ft) length, which are suitable for being kept out of water, i.e. g.r.p. or moulded hulls.

There is sufficient concrete hard standing to park up to 150 craft together with 120 m of pontoon to accommodate boats when launched, preparing for departure or waiting to be hauled out.

Figure 5 Fuelling berth, Port Hamble

The slipway is of sufficient length to enable operation at all tides except $1\frac{1}{2}$ h either side of springs, i.e. slip extends about 9 m (30 ft) beyond the lowest tide of the year.

Boats remain on special launching trolleys or panniers which can either be hitched up to a tractor or lifted by special hydraulic lifting trolley for launching or slipping.

Owners can unload gear from their car alongside the boat before parking the car. Launching can take at little as 5 minutes from the parked position if the owner is ready.

Twin keel boats are accommodated up to 0·8 m (2·75 ft) draft on flat trailers or panniers and shaped ones for round bilge of 'V' bottom boats. Single keel boats are not yet a practical proposition for regular haul outs, due to the draft and time of securing on the trailer.

Car parking is based on 2 cars per boat on a turn out of 50% of the owners. Toilets, showers, etc. are available.

It is proposed to construct a wet marina in the creeks immediately up-river of the existing site and in the first phase this will accommodate 140 yachts of up to 2 m (6·5 ft) draft and 21 m (70 ft) length. It will include a 50 t Travelift hoist and dock to service production boats

Figure 6 Hamble River—Fairey Boat Park in foreground

from factory and marina. Dry land and wet marinas will be run under
the same management from a central control building.

Pontoons: Walcon

Boat park charges (1972): £16.4/£18 per metre (£5/£5.5 per ft)
per 6 month summer season. Winter storage-16½p per
metre (5p per ft) per week.

BEAULIEU RIVER

Bucklers Hard Yacht Harbour (76 berths)*

The yacht harbour (Fig. 7) is situated a short distance up-river
of Bucklers Hard on the west side of the estuary.

Work commenced on the construction of the harbour in April 1971
and was completed by October of that year.

Figure 7 Bucklers Hard Yacht Harbour

---

* Additional information concerning this marina is given on pp. 365-370.

Figure 8 Tour party arriving at Bucklers Hard Yacht Harbour fuelling berth

Berthing:

The use of sheet piling was avoided by dredging to the natural angle
of repose of the banks which varies from 1 : 3 on the shale shoulders
and 1 : 6 on the softer silt at the up-river end. No appreciable sub-
sidence of the banks has occurred since dredging was completed. The
depth of dredge over the whole site is 2 m (6·5 ft) below MLWS.

There are four main pontoons radiating from a spine pontoon running
parallel to the contour of the main river channel. Distances between
main pontoons are 60 m (200 ft) tapering to 40 m (130 ft) and between
fingers 11-14 m (36-46 ft), which vary in length from 10 m (33 ft) to
14 m (46 ft).

All pontoons are 2 m (6 ft) wide to enable use of service trolleys
and for lateral stability. The floats are of expanded polystyrene encased in 19 mm (¾ in.) polypropylene fibre reinforced concrete.

Services:

Electricity supply is 240 volt A.C. with 13 amp fused plugs in
Marina Management GRP boxes, which also serve as low level light
fittings. A supply of 2 kV/berth has been allowed.

An isolating transformer has been housed in the rear of the Harbourmaster's office with the main central control panel, and the circuits
include current operated earth leakage circuit breakers as an essential safety precaution.

Electricity is charged for by metered connection cables.

Diesel and petrol is available at the fuelling pontoon (Fig. 8) sited
away from the remainder of the marina. Two 910 litre (200 gal) under-
ground storage tanks are sited at the pier edge, the fuel being fed
through flexible coupling hose via booster pumps to the calibrated
autodiesel and spirit pumps on the jetty.

Shore Facilities:

There is a large boat repair shed (Fig. 9) with lockers at the rear
for storage of berth-holders outboards, sails, etc.

Recovery and launching of craft is by means of a 26 t Renner hoist
and a boat dock. The car park, constructed of concrete rubble blended
with hoggin, has an area of approximately 0·3 hectares (1¼ acres) and
accommodates 130 cars (equivalent to 1·75 cars per berth). In the winter the car park is fully utilised for boat storage and the gradients have
been designed to enable use of the Renner in this area.

A nearby cottage has been converted to a clubroom for the use of
mooring and berth-holders, their crews and friends.

Figure 9 Boat repair shed at Bucklers Hard Yacht Harbour

Bucklers Hard provides the opportunity for local shopping and the Master Builders House Hotel affords restaurant and accommodation facilities.

Contract Supervision: Strutt and Parker

Consultant: D. H. Sessions (Marina Management Ltd.)

Contractor: Walcon Ltd.

Pontoons: Floating Pontoons Ltd.

Berthing Charges (1972): Most berths are let on 5-year leases at fixed rents of between £32.8 per metre (£10 per ft) for boats up to 12 m (40 ft), and £29.5 per metre (£9 per ft) for boats of over 13·5 m (45 ft) length.

LYMINGTON RIVER

Lymington Marina (250 berths)

The Marina is situated (Fig. 10) on the west bank of the Lymington River and is opposite to the British Rail terminal for the car ferry service to Yarmouth (I. W.). The fairway is dredged on average every four years and the depth of water at the mouth at M.L.W.S. is approximately 2·4 m (8 ft).

The Marina is dredged to a depth of 2·6 m (8·5 ft) below M.L.W.S. It covers about 24 hectares (10 acres) of water and provides individual berths for 250 yachts. The shoreline frontage is formed by 270 m (900 ft) of steel sheet piling driven to a depth of 11·5 m (38 ft).

The facilities include a car park, dockmaster's office, and a comprehensively equipped toilet and shower building. The shipyard of the Berthon Boat Company adjoins the Marina and has a Renner transporter boat lift for yachts up to 14 t displacement (Fig. 11). There are also 9 slipways available, up to 27 m (90 ft) in length.

The annual berth rental for 1972 was £23 per metre (£7 per ft) total overall length of yacht.

(Mr. K. Montgomery-Smith, the consulting engineer for the project, has supplied the following additional information):

Fig. 12 shows the site before development. Constructional work was undertaken in 1968/69 in two stages.

The entire scheme includes five floating piers up to 160 m (535 ft) long. These are 2.4 m (8 ft) wide for stability alone under a 100 kg/m² (20 lb/ft²) or ½ t anywhere and a side wind force of 50 kg/m² (10 lb/ft²) on an area 3 m (10 ft) high above water level.

Piers are located by greenheart piles on each side proved by later tests to be good for a lateral force of 2 t at the top. An accidental impact force of 20 t vessel with a velocity of approach of 1 knot is allowed for with a surge in the system of 0. 6 m (2 ft).

Side arms varying from 9 m (30 ft) by 1·2 m (4 ft) up to 16·5 m (55 ft) by 1·5 m (5 ft) cantilever out from the main walkways and are connected by fully continuous joints designed to take the vertical and horizontal moments and forces and the torsion from the arms needed to stabilise these under the above loadings. It should be noted that the ½ t point load anywhere except on deck planking is roughly equivalent to 6 persons and luggage on one side or to the vertical component of the warps from a high freeboard vessel in the designed wind.

Further particulars of Lymington Marina are given in pp. 267-270.

(K. Montgomery-Smith)

Figure 10 Lymington Marina

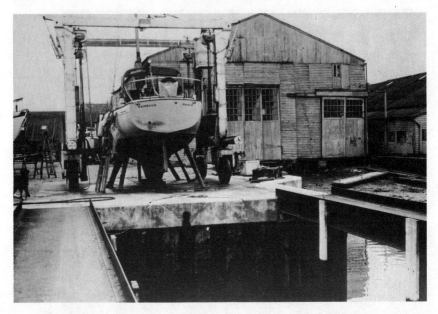

Figure 11 Boat dock and Renner hoist at Lymington Marina

Single docking is adopted which uses only about 70% of the berthage area required for tandem docking and makes a corresponding saving in the amount of dredging.

All services, water, electricity and phones, are confined to the main piers which are left permanently in position. The piles also are not required to be disturbed for maintenance work.

The side arms which are not stable alone are stabilised by torsion from the piers so that the twist does not exceed 1 in 10 in the worst position under off centre loading.

To allow access for dredger and hopper barge alongside for maintenance dredging in the most economic manner, the side arms can be removed and floated away in pairs to give the full width between the piers free of obstruction.

All the forces are taken up in a fully triangulated steel framework, hot spelter galvanised after fabrication . No essential steel members are under water. All timber except the cross cut decking has been pressure vacuum treated to preserve it.

Bridges are arranged in a new way parallel to the face of the quay to save room in the marina and are carried on self-lubricated nylon rollers on stainless steel pins at the feet and are hinged on stainless

(K. Montgomery-Smith)

Figure 12 Site of Lymington Marina prior to development

steel pins in nylon bushes at the top. Maximum slope is 1 in 5. The whole system is so steady that bicycles are ridden around it.

The tolerance for pile positions is always difficult and is better when the units are used as templates for driving. We found that not all the piles were fully stressed within the surge limits in easterly winds and some limiting guides were put in against the quay to prevent the units catching under or over the cope in passing in these conditions.

In westerlies the full surge can be allowed and the bridges are sufficiently flexible to follow.

Costs were about £1000 per berth including quay.

Later designs for marinas on the Orwell and Crouch in 3 knot currents and needing protection against debris and ice, but with only a 3 m (10 ft) approximate dredging cut, come out to about £600 per berth. Price in both cases includes for one car parking space to go with each berth.

No scrubbing of the expanded polystyrene floats has been needed at Lymington and those floats which had a trial anti-fouling are no better than the majority which did not. The swans go round and eat the weed which perhaps tastes better than that on steel tanks.

The mud is making up at Lymington at the rate of about 0·1 m (4 in.) to 0.15 m (6 in.) a year on average, as was expected, and there is a tendency for the 'horse' to reform.

Lymington Yacht Haven (450 berths)

As stated earlier (p. 365), a package contract for the design, dredging, reclamation, berth construction and bridging finance was negotiated by Westminster Dredging Co. Ltd. with the marina owners, Lymington Yacht Haven Ltd.

Because of the intensive traffic of small craft in the Lyminton River during the yachting season, it is not feasible to carry out substantial dredging works during that period of the year. It was therefore a necessary pre-requisite of any contract that the dredging should commence in September if the full marina was to become operational by spring of the following year. However, because of the late finalisation of negotiations it became a necessary part of the construction programme that 250 berths had to be made available for use by mid-May, 1972, with the balance of the works to be completed by the end of 1972. By this arrangement, sufficient working area remained available for the completion of the outstanding piling and pontoon works.

Prior to construction, the large tidal expanse of Harper's Lake was almost totally exposed at very low tides. The Lake had narrow connecting channels to the Lymington River and Oxey Lake (Fig. 14, p. 236).

Fig. 13 shows the layout of the marina. The area in use is approxi-

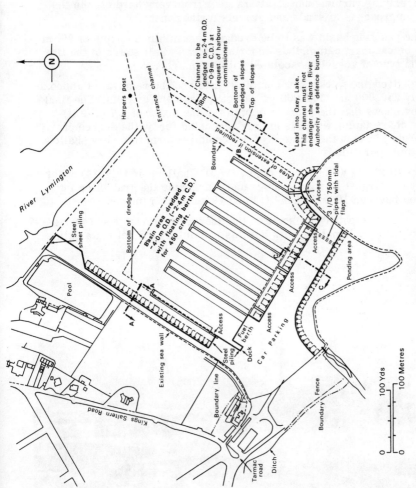

Figure 13 Layout of Lymington Yacht Haven

mately 5½ hectares (14 acres) of which 1½ hectares (4 acres) is accounted for by the yacht basin, 2½ hectares (6 acres) for car parking and shore facilities, 1 hectare (2 acres) for surface water storage and the balance remaining as a partial enclosure separating the river from the marina.

The bed of the Lake was covered with a 0·6-0·9 m (2-3 ft) depth of silt overlying various sub-strata ranging from very hard clay in the river approaches to sands and gravels further inshore.

The yachting basin was to be dredged to a minimum depth of 2·4 m (8 ft) below chart datum, thus ensuring access at all states of the tide for the type of vessels associated with the marina.

The dredging works, now complete, involved the removal of approximately 230,000 m³ (300,000 yd³) of silt, clays and gravels. The final survey shows that the average depth is in the order of 2·7 m (9 ft) below chart datum, which is mainly accounted for by the degree of accuracy to which the large dredger could perform this very shallow dredging operation.

The dredging was carried out by 'W.D.Challenger' (Fig.14) which is Europe's largest floating grab crane. Each time the grab bites into the bed between 10 and 14 m³ (13 and 18 yd³) are removed.

It was anticipated that some of the dredged material would prove suitable for reclamation work but this possibility did not materialise

Figure 14 Dredging and pump-ashore plant at Lymington Yacht Haven

since the inshore gravel deposits contained many impurities and could not be easily separated from the overlying silt layers. Also, since the dredger would not have reached the inshore gravel deposits until a late stage of the works, this could have caused further delays in the reclamation programme. All the dredge spoil was placed in self-propelled hoppers and disposed of at sea. In this connection, dredging production was curtailed since suitable vessels for transporting material to sea are of such a draft that they were unable to be loaded in the shallow depths of the marina during the time of low water. This is a common problem with marina dredging and invariably results in high unit dredging costs for such projects.

The land reclamation work to a level not less than 4 m (13 ft) above chart datum (tidal range $2\frac{1}{2}$ m(8 ft)) required the importation of approximately 76,000 m^3 (100,000 yd^3) of ballast. The major proportion of this was imported by operating the self-propelled suction dredger W. D. Merstone on Solent Banks to load 500 m^3 (650 yd^3) barges. This material was pumped ashore by the floating pumping unit Dibden Bay (Fig. 14) which has a 600 mm (24 in.) diameter delivery pipe. Production was approximately 20,000 m^3 (25,000 yd^3) per week. Initially, part of the area was reclaimed by importing gravel from land sources. This operation was to enable certain drainage works to be executed at an early stage and form control bunds for the subsequent pumped ashore material.

The civil engineering work involved the construction of protective bunds to the existing sea defence walls and slope protection to the reclaimed area (Fig. 15). The seaward facing slopes of the reclamation have been protected by means of the Intrusion Prepak system of concrete blanketing. In the area where fuelling and fitting out berths are located a steel sheet-piled quay wall has been formed. A slipway and lifting dock have been incorporated with these quay wall works.

Due to the low land levels behind the existing sea defence walls a complicated system of land and surface water drainage has had to be provided. Pipes of up to 750 mm (30 in.) diameter have been laid and two large steel piled cofferdams constructed to permit outfalls with tidal flaps to be provided. A new surface water ponding area of some 1 hectare (2 acres) has been formed to allow adequate storage of storm water from the nearby town of Lymington.

Berthing:

The flotation units providing the individual berthing layout are prefabricated with all welded steel sections and galvanised, with keruing timbered decking and the buoyancy tanks set with plastic or fibreglass covered polystyrene (Fig. 16).

A newly designed construction method has been used enabling the Haven Marina Master to move or change berthing arms to any required position on the main walkway.

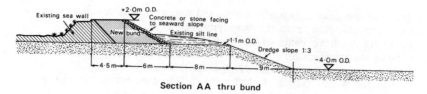

Section AA thru bund

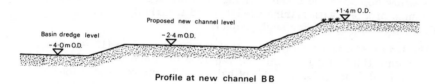

Profile at new channel BB

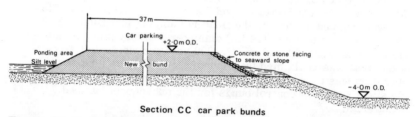

Section CC car park bunds

Figure 15 Cross-sections through bunds at Lymington Yacht Haven

Figure 16 Installing pontoons at Lymington Yacht Haven

Services:

Lighting and water facilities are available to each berth.

A fuelling berth-is being provided.

Shore Facilities:

Launching and hauling-out facilities include a 27 t hoist.

A chandlery and office block are located nearby.

During the 1972 season temporary toilets and ablutions have been provided by the use of 'Rolalong' mobile units. The permanent toilet facilities will be constructed when the site has fully consolidated.

Parking spaces for 650 cars have been provided. Access roads will be constructed to local authority specifications and finally surfaced. with tarmacadam.

The inshore facilities, when completed, will be specially landscaped with trees and shrubs and will blend with the local surroundings.

Designer/Contractor: Westminster Dredging Co. Ltd.

Consulting Engineers: C. H. Dobbie and Partners.

Architects: Imrie, Porter and Wakefield.

Pontoons: Westminster Dredging Co. Ltd.

Berthing Charges: £24. 60 per metre (£7. 50 per ft) length overall per annum; minimum £225, equivalent to 9·8 m (30 ft).

Bibliography

For the benefit of the reader who wishes to pursue the subject further a list of references is set out overleaf. No attempt has been made to include the specialist literature in harbour and coastal engineering which is very extensive, although a few such references are quoted.

Books and Reports

—— (1972), *Marinas Guide,* National Yacht Harbour Assn.
Adie, D. W. (1973), *Marinas,* Architectural Press (To be published).
—— (1969), *Small Craft Harbours,* Am. Soc. C.E. Report on Eng. Practice No. 50.
Chaney, C. A. (1961), *Marinas (Recommendations for Design, Construction and Maintenance),* 2nd Edition, Nat. Assn. of Engine and Boat Manuf., Inc.
—— (1963), *The Modern Marina (A guidebook for the Community and Private Investor Interested in Marina Development),* Nat. Assn. of Engine and Boat Manuf., Inc.
—— (1965), *Problems Arising from the Increasing Use of Yachts and Other Small Boats for Sport and Recreation,* Proc. XXIst Int. Nav. Cong. (Stockholm). Section 1, Subject 6.
—— (1973), *Arrangement of Navigable Waterways for Recreation and Preservation of Environment,* Proc. XXIIIrd Int. Nav. Cong. (Stockholm), Section 1, Subject 3 (To be published).
Countryside Commission (1969), *Coastal Recreation and Holidays,* Special Study Report Vol. 1, H.M.S.O.
Countryside Commission (1970), *The Planning of the Coastline,* H.M.S.O.
Countryside Commission (1970), *The Coastal Heritage—A Conservation Policy for Coasts of High Quality Scenery,* H.M.S.O.
—— (1972), *Recreation on Reservoirs and Rivers,* Institution of Water Engineers.
—— (1972), The Amenity Use of Water Space and the Reorganisation of the British Waterways Board, Department of the Environment, H.M.S.O.
Tanner, M. (1973), *Water Resources and Recreation,* Sports Council Study No. 3.
Addenbrooke, E. G. J. (1972), *Local Authorities and the Provision of Sailing Facilities,* Borough of Gosport.
—— (1972), *Report of the First Solent Sailing Conference* (March 1972), Hampshire County Council.
—— (1965), *River Hamble Study,* Hampshire County Council.
—— (1971), *River Hamble Policy Plan,* Hampshire County Council.
Dartington Amenity Research Trust (1973), *River Hamble,* Sports Council Study No. 5.
Dartington Amenity Research Trust (1973), *Southampton Water,* Sports Council Study No. 6.
Jefferson, J. G. and Burrows, G. S. (1968), *Chichester Harbour Study,* West Sussex County Council.
—— (1966), *Analysis on Recreational Boating in the Strait of Georgia Area,* British Columbia, Dept. of Public Works, Canada.
—— (1968), *Pleasure Boating Study—Puget Sound and Adjacent Waters,* Washington State Parks and Recreation Commission.
—— (1972), *Pollution in some British Estuaries and Coastal Waters,* 3rd Report of Royal Commission on Environmental Pollution, Cmnd. 5054, H.M.S.O.

—— (1970), *Storage of Wastes from Watercraft and Disposal at Shore Facilities,* Environmental Protection Agency, U.S. Government Printing Office.

—— (1971), *Launching Ramps for Boats,* Cement and Concrete Assn.

Duvivier, A. J. (1972), *Information and Facts Relating to the Use of Greenheart Piles in Marinas,* Millars Timber and Trading Co. Ltd.

—— (1973), *Marina Seminar 1973,* National Yacht Harbour Assn.

Papers and Articles

Beazley, E. (1963), 'Marinas', *Architectural Review,* **134,** pp. 94-108.

Dunham, J. W. (1959), 'Planning and Development of California's Marinas', *Civil Eng. (A.S.C.E.),* **29,** pp. 617-619.

Gullidge, E. J. and Urabeek, F. J. (1970), 'Planning for Pleasure Boating on Regional Basis', *Proc. Am. Soc. C.E.,* **96,** No. WW3, pp. 583-600.

Lee, C. E. (1967), 'On the Design of Small Craft Harbours', *Proc 10th Conf. on Coastal Eng. (1966),* Ch. 44, p. 713, Am. Soc. C.E.

Moissonnier, L. (June 1970), Les Ports de Plaisance en France, *Construction Aménagement,* **11,** pp. 52-75.

Pedlingham, R. S. T. and Hall, B. (July 1962), 'The Structural Use of Greenheart', *Dock and Harbour Authority,* **43.**

Raichlen, F. (1971), 'Harbours and Moored Vessels', *Proc. Symp. on the Water Environment and Human Needs (1970),* pp. 109-144, Massachusetts Inst. Tech.

Sessions, D. H. (May 1966), 'Marinas and Yacht Harbours', *The Yachtsman,* pp. 41-49.

Wand, G. D., and Cushman, M. M. (May 1967), 'Some Factors in Planning for Marinas', *Proc. Am. Soc. C.E.,* Waterways and Harbours Divn.

—— (June 1966), 'Marinas', *Yachting World,* **118,** p. 258.

Journals

Boats and Sail
Inland Waterways Assn.
Motor Boat and Yachting
Proc. Am. Soc. Civil Engineers, J. Waterways, Harbours and Coastal Eng. Divn.
Royal Yachting Association
Ship and Boat Builder
The Yachtsman
Yachting and Boating Weekly
Yachting Monthly
Yachting World

Index

When an entry in the Index constitutes the main topic of a particular paper final as well as the initial page number of that paper is quoted.